D0983399

DATE DUE

Decision making in organizations is often pictured as a coherent and rational process in which alternative interests and perspectives are considered in an orderly manner until the optimal alternative is selected. Yet, as many members of organizations have discovered from their own experience, real decision processes in organizations only seldom fit such a description.

This book brings together researchers who focus on cognitive aspects of decision processes, on the one hand, and those who study organizational aspects such as conflict, incentives, power, and ambiguity, on the other. It draws from the tradition of Herbert Simon, who studied organizational decision makers' pervasive use of heuristics of reasoning and described them as boundedly rational. These multiple perspectives may further our understanding of organizational decision making.

Organizational decision making

Cambridge Series on Judgment and Decision Making

The purpose of this series is to convey the general principles of and findings about judgment and decision making to the many academic and professional fields to which these apply. The contributions are written by authorities in the field and supervised by highly qualified editors and the Publications Board. The series will attract readers from many different disciplines, largely among academics, advanced undergraduates, graduate students, and practicing professionals.

Also in the series

Inside the Juror: The Psychology of Juror Decision Making
Edited by Reid Hastie
Psychological Perspectives on Justice: Theory and Applications
Edited by Barbara A. Mellers and Jonathan Baron
Judgment and Decision-Making Research in Accounting and Auditing
Robert Ashton and Alison Ashton

Organizational decision making

Edited by
Zur Shapira
New York University

WITHDRAWN

CAMBRIDGE
UNIVERSITY PRESS

Published by the Press Syndicate of the University of Cambridge
The Pitt Building, Trumpington Street, Cambridge CB2 1RP
40 West 20th Street, New York, NY 10011-4211, USA
10 Stamford Road, Oakleigh, Melbourne 3166, Australia

First published 1997

Printed in the United States of America

Library of Congress Cataloging-in-Publication Data
Organizational decision making / edited by Zur Shapira.
p.   cm. – Cambridge series on judgment and decision making
Includes indexes.
ISBN 0-521-48107-4 (hardback)
1. Decision making.   I. Shapira, Zur.   II. Series.
HD30.23.O744   1997
658.4'03 – dc20   96-14514
                                                              CIP

A catalog record for this book is available from the British Library.

ISBN 0-521-48107-4 Hardback

Contents

Series preface

The Society for Judgment and Decision Making first collaborated with Cambridge University Press in 1986, with the publication of *Judgment and Decision Making: An Interdisciplinary Reader*, edited by Hal R. Arkes and Kenneth R. Hammond. As the editors stated in their introduction, "Judgment and decision making are of critical importance, and the fact that it is possible to study them in a scientific, empirical manner is a new and exciting event in the recent history of science" (p. 1). The 1980s witnessed the flowering of the area of human judgment and decision making. The founding and expansion of the Society was one feature of this growth. At the same time, there has been an explosion of research and teaching in departments of psychology, economics, and schools of business, engineering, public policy, and medicine, with significant practical contributions through applied research and consulting in public and private institutions.

The Arkes and Hammond *Reader* was successful as an outline of the core ideas and approaches of the field and an illustration of the impressive range of useful applications. The Society, with Ken Hammond's encouragement, recognized the potential for a series of books to provide an educational and intellectual focus for the continued growth and dissemination of judgment and decision-making research. Each book in the series will be devoted to domains of practical or theoretical interest, offering an accessible presentation of the best new ideas and empirical approaches from the field of judgment and decision making.

The Publications Committee is pleased to offer this book, the fourth in the series. Zur Shapira has done an outstanding job as editor, bringing together a distinguished group of authors to write chapters especially for this volume. Many important decisions in commerce, government, and society occur inside large, complex organizations. In normal discourse, we often use language that implies that the entire organizational entity made the decision. However, within the organization are individuals, exercising their best judgment and using their cognitive capabilities to choose, for better or for worse. Thus, the psychology of judgment and decision lies very close to the heart of organizational decisions. At the same time, understanding decisions in organizations requires consideration of factors that we often overlook in studies of individual judgments and choices. Understanding both the similarities and differences in individual and organizational decisions can serve only to enlighten both fields. This book will help organizational researchers discover what judgment and decision making has to offer while also encouraging judgment and decision researchers to apply their theories and findings to the fertile context of real organizations.

Don N. Kleinmuntz, Former Chair
For the Publications Committee

Contributors

Margaret Cooper Brindle *Graduate School of Industrial Administration, Carnegie-Mellon University, Pittsburgh*

Colin Camerer *Division of Social Sciences, California Institute of Technology, Pasadena*

Terry Connolly *Department of Management and Policy, University of Arizona, Tucson*

Jane E. Dutton *School of Business Administration, University of Michigan, Ann Arbor*

Baruch Fischhoff *Department of Decision and Social Sciences, Carnegie-Mellon University, Pittsburgh*

Raghu Garud *Stern School of Business, New York University, New York*

Stephen Johnson *Decision Research, Eugene*

Marc Knez *Graduate School of Business, University of Chicago, Chicago*

Ken Koput *Department of Management and Policy, University of Arizona, Tucson*

Howard Kunreuther *The Wharton School, University of Pennsylvania, Philadelphia*

James G. March *Graduate School of Business, Stanford University, Stanford*

Jacqueline Meszaros *School of Business and Management, Temple University, Philadelphia*

Ellen S. O'Connor *College of Business Administration, University of Notre Dame, Notre Dame*

P. Narayan Pant *Faculty of Business Administration, National University of Singapore, Singapore*

John W. Payne *Fuqua School of Business, Duke University, Durham*

Roy Radner *Stern School of Business, New York University, New York*

Gerald Robert Salancik *Graduate School of Industrial Administration, Carnegie-Mellon University, Pittsburgh*

Zur Shapira *Stern School of Business, New York University, New York*

William H. Starbuck *Stern School of Business, New York University, New York*

Barry M. Staw *Haas School of Business, University of California, Berkeley*

James D. Westphal *J. L. Kellogg Graduate School of Management, Northwestern University, Evanston*

Edward J. Zajac *J. L. Kellogg Graduate School of Management, Northwestern University, Evanston*

Xueguang Zhou *Department of Sociology, Duke University, Durham*

Editor's preface

The topic of decision making spans many disciplines including both individual judgment and choice behavior and organizational decision making. In editing this volume I focused on potential linkages between the individual and organizational levels of analysis. My goal was to have authors describe their work, hoping to encourage cross pollination between the two domains in future research. Obviously, research that looked at the two levels of analysis has been attempted. In recent years researchers have shown renewed interest in work done at multiple levels of analysis. This volume reflects this growing trend and will contribute to more active interaction between researchers in the two traditions.

Editing this volume was a very demanding task and I would not have been able to do it without the help of several people. First and foremost is Don Kleinmuntz, who acted as series editor on behalf of the Publications Committee of the Society for Judgment and Decision Making. Don was very encouraging throughout the process and his comments on the chapters were invaluable. His insightful and prompt feedback was of great assistance. In addition, I discussed the contents of the book with Raghu Garud, Joe Lampel, Jim March, and Guje Sevon, and their advice is acknowledged. The discussions with doctoral students who took my seminar on Managerial Cognition also helped in thinking on the structure of the book. Julia Hough, our editor at Cambridge University Press, was very supportive and provided timely feedback at many points along the way. The technical assistance of Gia Pangilinan, Helen Wheeler, and Paul Dreifus was valuable. The hospitality of the Center for Rationality and Interactive Decision Theory of the Hebrew University of Jerusalem is acknowledged. Finally, the patience of my family, Gila, Romy, and Ittai, provided me with the needed support through a long journey and a demanding task.

Just as this book goes to press we heard of the untimely death of Jerry Salancik. We were saddened by the news but will long remember his friendship, collegiality, and contributions to the field.

Part I
Introduction

1   Introduction and overview

Zur Shapira

Organizational decision making can be looked at from various perspectives. This book attempts to increase our understanding of organizational decision making by bringing together researchers from two great traditions that share some common roots: behavioral decision theory and organizational decision making.

The roots of behavioral decision theory (Kahneman, 1991) include Edwards's (1954) studies of probability revision, Meehl's (1954) analysis of clinical judgment, Luce and Raiffa's (1957) description of game theory, and Simon's (1947, 1955) treatise on decision making in organizations. Over the last 40 years, research on the psychology of probability estimation and choice behavior led to the development of the heuristics and biases paradigm in the study of judgment under uncertainty (Kahneman, Slovic, & Tversky, 1982), as well as to the pursuit of prospect theory and framing in individual choice behavior (Kahneman & Tversky, 1984). Research in the behavioral decision theory tradition was carried on mainly in lab experiments and focused on the cognitive aspects of individual choice behavior. In the tradition of psychological science, the research was aimed at refuting the implications of the normative statistical decision theory's model. Over the years, behavioral decision theory produced a remarkable set of findings on individual choice behavior, albeit by neglecting the effects of social and emotional factors as well as the conflict inherent in decision making (Kahneman, 1991).

The pioneering work by Simon led to a paradigmatic development in organization theory. The Carnegie approach culminated in numerous studies that emphasized the role of information processing and decision making as the basic elements in analyzing both the process and the structural aspects of organizations. Two books from the golden period of the Carnegie school, March and Simon's *Organizations* (1958) and Cyert and March's *A Behavioral Theory of the Firm* (1963), are landmarks in the field of organization theory. In the period that followed the studies of the Carnegie school, scholars of formal theories of organizations, with the exception of March, did not treat decision making as the central focus of their framework. For example, Thompson's (1967) influential book on organization theory had many propositions related to decision making by organizations but without a focus on information processing as a unifying concept. Other research trends were pursued by various scholars on topics related to organizational decision making, such as the analysis of power (Pfeffer, 1981), escalation processes (Staw, 1981), commitment (Salancik, 1977), information processing (Connolly, 1977), and sense making (Weick, 1994), to name a few. The research agenda of March focused on alternative aspects of organizational decision making. He extended his earlier analyses in several directions. His writings suggested alternative notions of rationality (March, 1978), analysis of decisions as random processes, the most well known of which was labeled "A garbage can model of organizational choice" (Cohen, March, & Olsen, 1972). He also studied the effects of attention allocation and search on organizational decisions (March, 1988) and analyzed the role that rules, obligations, and myths play in organizational decision making (March, 1994).

The relations between the two traditions are intriguing. Simon's initial work served as an impetus for further studies in the fields of both behavioral decision theory and organizational decision making. Even though organizational processes are not the mere aggregation of individual activities, Simon treated them similarly and his approach appeared to be relevant for both levels of analysis. As March (1978) noted, "He [Simon] obscured a distinction one might make between individual and organizational decision making proposing for the most part the general ideas for both" (p. 859).

Indeed, individual and organizational decision making overlap greatly because many decisions in organizations are made by individual managers. In that sense, the reference is to decisions made in organizational contexts. Behavioral decision theory, by contrast, deals primarily with judgmental and decisional processes of individuals, but not in an organizational or any other particular context. Although the two traditions share common roots, the research agendas of behavioral decision theory and organizational decision making in the last 40 years or so reflect similarities as well as differences. These are due, in part, to some complexities and special characteristics of decision making in organizational settings.

Some characteristics of organizational decision making

There are a few characteristics that differentiate organizational decision making from individual decision making as studied in lab experiments.

First, unlike most lab studies of individual decision making, *ambiguity* is pervasive in organizations. There is often only ambiguous information, and there is ambiguity about preferences as well as about interpreting the history of decisions. In contrast, most experimental studies of individual decision making present the subject with clear information, though in the form of a probability distribution and often with monetary payoffs that direct the subject's preferences.

Second, decision making in and by organizations is embedded in a *longitudinal* context. That is, participants in organizational decision making are a part of ongoing processes. Even if they don't take on active roles in all phases of decision making, they are a part of the decision process and its consequences. Decisions in organizations are made in a sequential manner, and commitment may be more important in such processes than judgmental accuracy. These characteristics call for a history-dependent analysis of organizational decision making and highlight the role of sense making in organizational life. In contrast, most lab studies of individual decision making are conducted in artificial settings (i.e., the laboratory) that are not connected to the subjects' ongoing activities.

Third, *incentives* play an important role in organizational decision making. Incentives, penalties, and their ramifications are real and may have long-lasting effects (Shapira, 1995). These effects are intensified due to the longitudinal nature of decision making in organizational settings. Furthermore, survival is a basic aspect of life in organizations – a characteristic almost impossible to reproduce in an experimental setting. In contrast, incentives used in experimental studies of individual choice behavior are meager and do not have the potential to produce lingering effects. The argument is not that incentives eliminate judgmental biases; in fact, they may even aggravate them. The point is that incentives and penalties are very salient in organizations, and often they command managerial attention.

Fourth, many executives, especially in middle management, may make *repeated* decisions on similar issues. Consider, for example, a loan officer who reviews requests for consumer house loans. Such a manager may develop a sense of using his or her skills (which may be faulty) and a sense of having control of the situation (which may also be faulty). The beliefs of having control and using one's skills are pervasive in managerial thinking about risk taking (Shapira, 1995). In addition, several repeated decisions, such as decisions on new loans, are made by following rules rather than by using pure information processing modes (March, 1994). The idea of a "decision" in this context may take on a different meaning.

Fifth, *conflict* is pervasive in organizational decision making. Many times, power considerations and agenda setting determine decisions rather than calculations based on the decisions' parameters. Further, organizations are hierarchical systems in which people report to a superior. The nature of authority relations may have a large impact on the way decisions are made in organizations, which are basically political systems.

The goal of this book is to examine current issues in organizational decision making and bring into the arena potential contributions from behavioral decision theory to enrich the framework of analysis of organizational decision making. Another purpose is to enrich the research framework of behavioral decision theory by bringing in ideas and findings from organizational decision making. There are researchers in organization theory who question the external validity and relevance of findings from behavioral decision theory to real-life situations. However, these concerns may be exaggerated, as it is clear that managers are not immune to judgmental biases (Bazerman, 1994). It also appears that the cognitive implications of behavioral decision theory research may be highly relevant to strategic decision making (Schwenk, 1984; Zajac & Bazerman, 1991). By contrast, there are researchers in behavioral decision theory who feel that increasing the external validity of decision research will inevitably come at the expense of accuracy. However, this doesn't have to be the case. Research by Kunreuther, Hogarth, and Meszaros (1993) showed how one can employ experimental designs in studying how decisions are affected by ambiguity, a concept of major importance in organizational decision making (March, 1988; Shapira, 1993). Research that can potentially create cross-pollination between the two traditions is illustrated in Kahneman and Lovallo's (1993) study of forecasting and choice, March's (1994) analysis of decision making, Shapira's (1995) study of managerial risk taking, Staw's (1981) studies of escalation of commitment, and Starbuck and Milliken's (1988) analysis of the Challenger disaster.

Structure of the book

This book analyzes organizational decision making by taking into account the previously discussed characteristics of organizational contexts, as well as findings from behavioral decision theory that are relevant for analyzing decisions made in and by organizations.

The book comprises five different sections. In the next chapter, March lays the foundations for alternative approaches to organizational decision making. He presents four ways in which decision are made in organizations, noting the differences among rational choice, rule following, sensemaking processes, and evolutionary approaches.

The second part of the book deals with information processing and attention allocation. Starbuck and Pant analyze the informational and organizational aspects that underlie the savings and loan debacle. Kunreuther and Meszaros look at the situation in the chemical industry following the Bhopal disaster, and Dutton analyzes the importance of agendas on organizational decisions.

The third part of the book is devoted to aspects of preference processing. Salancik and Brindle analyze the importance of power and politics in organizational decision making and advance some social construction arguments. Zajac and Westphal discuss different approaches to managerial compensation, and Camerer and Knez deal with the problem of conflict in organizational decision making by proposing a game theoretical framework.

The fourth part of the book deals with decision processes in organizational settings. Staw provides a comprehensive presentation and analysis of the escalation paradigm. Fischhoff and Johnson raise the question of whether decisions in organizational settings can really be described as distributed decision processes. Garud and Shapira take a look at the alignment of risk and control in organizational decision making, devoting attention to the assumption of responsibility for failure. Zhou elaborates on the notion of rule following as a major factor in describing how decisions are made in organizational settings.

The last part of the book presents some alternative and critical approaches to the standard analysis. Connolly and Koput focus on naturalistic approaches, and O'Connor presents a narrative approach to organizational decision making. Radner provides an economist's perspective, and Payne presents a cognitive psychologist's appraisal of organizational decision making.

The different perspectives presented in this book should introduce the reader to some of the major issues of organizational decision making. By examining the similarities and differences among various conceptual, theoretical, and empirical approaches, these chapters provide multiple perspectives on the major issues underlying organizational decision making.

References

Bazerman, M. (1994). *Judgment in managerial decision making* (3rd ed.). New York: Wiley.

Cohen, M., March, J. G., & Olsen, J. (1972). A garbage can model of organizational choice. *Administrative Science Quarterly, 17*, 1–25.

Connolly, T. (1977). Information processing and decision making in organizations. In B. Staw & G. Salancik (Eds.), *New directions in organizational behavior* (pp. 205–234). Chicago: St. Clair Press.

Cyert, R., & March, G. (1963). *A behavioral theory of the firm*. Englewood Cliffs, NJ: Prentice-Hall.

Edwards, W. (1954). *The theory of decision making. Psychological Bulletin, 51*, 380–417.

Kahneman, D. (1991). Judgment and decision making: A personal view. *Psychological Science, 2*, 142–145.

Kahneman, D., & Lovallo, D. (1993). Bold forecasts and timid choices: A cognitive perspective on risk taking. *Management Science, 39*, 17–31.

Kahneman, D., Slovic, P., & Tversky, A. (1982). *Judgment under uncertainty: Heuristics and biases*. New York: Cambridge University Press.

Kahneman, D., & Tversky, A. (1984). Choices, values and frames. *American Psychologist, 39*, 341–350.

Kunreuther, H., Hogarth, R., & Meszaros, J. (1993). Insurer ambiguity and market failure. *Journal of Risk and Uncertainty, 7*, 71–87.

Luce, D., & Raiffa, H. (1957). *Games and decisions*. New York: Wiley.

March, J. (1978). The 1978 Noble prize in economics. *Science, 202*, 858–861.

March, J. (1988). *Decisions and organizations*. Oxford: Basil Blackwell.

March, J. (1994). *A primer on decision making*. New York: Free Press.

March, J., & Simon, H. (1958). *Organizations*. New York: Wiley.

Meehl, P. (1954). *Clinical vs. statistical prediction: A theoretical analysis and a review of the evidence*. Minneapolis: University of Minnesota Press.

Pfeffer, J. (1981). *Power in organizations*. Marshfield, MA: Pitman.

Salancik, G. (1977). Commitment and control of organizational behavior and belief. In B. Staw & G. Salancik (Eds.), *New directions in organizational behavior* (pp. 1–54). Chicago: St. Clair Press.

Schwenk, C. (1984). Cognitive simplification processes in strategic decision making. *Strategic Management Journal, 5*, 111–128.

Shapira, Z. (1993). Ambiguity and risk taking in organizations. *Journal of Risk and Uncertainty, 7*, 89–94.

Shapira, Z. (1995). *Risk taking: A managerial perspective*. New York: Russell Sage Foundation.

Simon, H. (1947). *Administrative behavior*. New York: Free Press.

Simon, H. (1955). A behavioral model of rational choice. *Quarterly Journal of Economics, 69*, 99–118.

Starbuck, W., & Milliken, F. (1988). Challenger: Fine tuning the odds until something breaks. *Journal of Management Studies, 25*, 319–340.

Staw, B. (1981). The escalation of commitment to a course of action. *Academy of Management Review, 6*, 577–587.

Thompson, J. (1967). *Organizations in action*. New York: McGraw-Hill.

Weick, K. (1994). *Sensemaking in organizations*. Thousand Oaks, CA: Sage.

Zajac, E., & Bazerman, M. (1991). Blind spots in industry and competitor analysis: Implications of interfirm (mis)perceptions for strategic decisions. *Academy of Management Review, 16*, 37–56.

2   Understanding how decisions happen in organizations

James G. March

A large part of contemporary research on organizational decision making is concerned with how decisions should be made. Such research seeks techniques for improving the intelligence of actions by organizational decision makers. This chapter is, on the other hand, only incidentally concerned with how decisions should be made. It focuses on how decisions actually happen in organizations and how we might think about decision processes. It is an introduction, a sketch of ideas that might be relevant to understanding decision making in organizations. The chapter is neither a substitute for nor an adequate prologue to the other contributions in this volume. At best, it sets a partial frame for considering the more elaborated versions of other chapters.

Introduction

In one of those extraordinary epigrams that become part of the folklore of a field, James Duesenberry (1960, p. 233) said that "economics [and by analogy psychology] is all about how people make choices; sociology [and by analogy anthropology and political science] is all about how they don't have any choices to make." Students of organizational decisions locate themselves happily in the midst of the distinction, trying to understand decisions as instruments of conflict and consciousness and trying to understand conflict and consciousness as embedded in social relations, rules, norms, and constraints (Allison, 1971; Hickson, 1995; March, 1981, 1988, 1994a; Pennings, 1986; Witte & Zimmerman, 1986; Zey, 1992). They focus on decision-making processes, trying simultaneously to identify the ways

This essay is based substantially on March (1994a). The research has been supported financially by the Spencer Foundations and the Stanford Graduate School of Business, and in many other ways by the Scandinavian Consortium for Organizational Research.

in which decisions unfold within them and to understand the processes as forms of social drama and locales for creating stories.

The study of how decisions happen provides a setting for a cluster of contested issues about human action (March, 1994a:viii–ix):

The first issue is whether decisions are to be viewed as *choice-based* or *rule-based*. Do decision makers pursue a logic of consequence, making choices among alternatives by evaluating their consequences in terms of prior preferences? Or do they pursue a logic of appropriateness, fulfilling identities or roles by recognizing situations and following rules that match appropriate behavior to the situations they encounter?

The second issue is whether decision making is typified more by *clarity* and *consistency* or by *ambiguity* and *inconsistency*. Are decisions occasions in which individuals and institutions achieve coherence and reduce equivocality? Or are they occasions in which inconsistency and ambiguity are exhibited, exploited, and expanded?

The third issue is whether decision making is an *instrumental* activity or an *interpretive* activity. Are decisions to be understood primarily in terms of the way they fit into a problem solving, adaptive calculus? Or are they to be understood primarily in terms of the way they fit into efforts to establish individual and social meaning?

The fourth issue is whether outcomes of decision processes are seen as primarily attributable to the actions of *autonomous actors* or to the systemic properties of an *interacting ecology*. Is it possible to describe decisions as resulting from the intentions, identities, and interests of independent actors? Or is it necessary to emphasize the ways in which individual actors, organizations, and societies fit together?

The easy (and correct) resolution of these issues is to say that decisions, decision making, and decision processes in organizations are all of these things; the largest problem is not to choose among the alternatives but to weave them together in a way that allows each to illuminate the others. This volume can be seen as an effort to contribute to that weaving and the present chapter as a modest introduction to fabric design.

Decisions as rational choices

Virtually all of modern economics and large parts of the rest of social science, as well as the applied fields that build upon them, embrace the idea that human action is the result of human choice and that human choice is intendedly rational. Rational theories picture decision making as based on four things:

> A *knowledge of alternatives*. Decision makers have a set of alternatives for action.
>
> A *knowledge of consequences*. Decision makers know the consequences of alternative actions, at least up to a probability distribution.
>
> A *consistent preference ordering*. Decision makers have consistent values by which alternative consequences of action can be compared in terms of their subjective value.

> *A decision rule.* Decision makers have rules by which they select a single alternative of action on the basis of its consequences for the preferences.

In the most elaborated form of the model, it is assumed that all alternatives, the probability distribution of consequences conditional on each alternative, and the subjective value of each possible consequence are known. A choice is assumed to be made by selecting the alternative with the highest expected value (Schoemaker, 1982). This emphasis on expected value may be moderated by attention to other features of the outcome distribution – for example, the variability (or riskiness) of the distribution (Shapira, 1995).

The durability of this structure is impressive. It is also understandable. Simple rational choice models capture some important elements of truth. Demand curves for consumer products generally have negative slopes, and employees usually are more resistant to wage cuts than to wage increases. Moreover, the core ideas are flexible. When the model seems not to fit, it is often possible to reinterpret preferences or knowledge and preserve the axioms. Finally, choice is a faith as well as a theory. It is linked to the ideologies of the Enlightenment. It is encased in habits of speech to such an extent that ideas of willful, rational choice are the standard terms of discourse for answering the generic questions: Why did it happen? Why did you do it?

Uncertainty

Students of organizational decision making share these basic ideas of anticipatory, consequential choice, but they have modified them considerably over the past 30 years, primarily through consideration of numerous limits to rationality (Cyert & March, 1992; March & Simon, 1993). Insofar as decision making can be understood as stemming from prior preferences and expectations about consequences, it is bounded by significant individual and organizational constraints on finding and implementing an optimal solution.

The earliest empirical challenges to the simple story of rational choice questioned the information assumptions of the theory. Rational actors make two guesses about the future: a guess about the future consequences of current actions and a guess about future sentiments with respect to those consequences. Classical versions of theories of rational choice assume that both guesses are improbably precise. Actual situations in which decisions are made often seem to make each of them problematic.

The first guess – about the uncertain future consequences of current action – has long attracted attention from both students of decision making and choice theorists. Even if estimates of the consequences of alternative actions are formed and action is *intendedly* rational, there are informational and computational limits on human choice. These limits on rationality stem partly from properties of individual humans as information processors. They are unable to see clearly or interpret accurately the decision situations in which they find themselves. They simplify complex situations, using heuristics and frames to cope with information (Kahneman, Slovic, & Tversky, 1982). There are limits on the number of alternatives considered and limits on the amount and accuracy of information that is available. The limits of individual human beings are modified by the organizations in which they function. In some ways, organizations are able to overcome information processing limitations, being more capable of parallel processing, of inventorying knowledge, and of mobilizing expertise (Feldman, 1989). At the same time, however, organizations introduce additional problems, problems of retention of information and communication, of coordination and conflict. As a result, virtually all modern theories of rational choice are theories of limited (or bounded) rationality (Holmstrom & Tirole, 1989; Kreps, 1990).

The core ideas of bounded rationality are elementary and by now familiar. Rather than all alternatives and all information about consequences being known, information has to be discovered through search. The key scarce resource is attention; and theories of limited rationality are, for the most part, theories of the allocation of attention (Cyert & March, 1992; March, 1988). Search is stimulated by a failure to achieve a goal and continues until it reveals an alternative that is good enough to satisfy existing evoked goals. New alternatives are sought in the neighborhood of old ones. Failure focuses search on the problem of attaining goals that have been violated; success allows search resources to move to other domains. Theories of limited rationality are also theories of slack – that is, unexploited opportunities, undiscovered economies, waste, and so on. As long as performance exceeds the goal, search for new alternatives is modest, slack accumulates, and aspirations increase. When performance falls below the goal, search is stimulated, slack is decreased, and aspirations decrease (Antonelli, 1989; Singh, 1986).

This classic system of organizational search and decision does three things to keep performance and goals close. First, it adapts goals to performance: that is, decision makers learn what they should expect. Second, it adapts performance to goals by increasing search in the face of failure and decreasing search when faced with success. And third, it adapts performance to goals by decreasing slack in response to failure and increasing slack in response to success. The result is a system that both provides resilience in the face of adversity and confounds adaptation.

In this tradition, theories of organizational choice draw rather freely from behavioral studies of individual decision making, with their emphasis on framing and human treatment of informational uncertainty (Kahneman et al., 1982; Nisbett & Ross, 1980). These efforts – in combination with concern within economic theories for the problems of incomplete information and information and transaction costs – have turned substantial parts of recent theories of choice into theories of information and attention, that is, into theories of the first guess.

Ambiguity

The second guess – about the uncertain future preferences for the consequences of current actions – has been less considered, yet poses, if anything, greater difficulties for rationality (March, 1988, chap. 13). Consider the following properties of preferences as they appear in standard theories of choice:

> Preferences are *stable*. Current action is normally assumed to be taken in terms of current preferences. The implicit assumption is that preferences will be unchanged when the future outcomes of current actions are realized.
> Preferences are *consistent* and *precise*. Inconsistencies or ambiguities in preferences are allowed only insofar as they do not affect choice (i.e., only insofar as they are made irrelevant by scarcity or the specification of trade-offs).
> Preferences are *exogenous*. Preferences, by whatever process they are imagined to be created, are assumed to be unaffected by the choices they control.

Where preferences are studied through the revelations of a series of choices, preference consistency has been notoriously difficult to establish. Possible reasons come from examination of explicit preferences. Individuals commonly find it possible to express both a preference for something and a recognition that the preference is repugnant. They are often aware of the extent to which some of their preferences conflict with others, yet they do little to resolve those inconsistencies. Many preferences are stated in forms that lack precision. Preferences change over time in such a way that predicting future preferences is often difficult. And while preferences are used to choose among actions, it is also often true at the same time that actions and experience with their consequences affect preferences, as do deliberate efforts to control them (Greber & Jackson, 1993; Mintzberg, 1994).

Such differences between preferences as they are portrayed in theories of choice and preferences as they appear in actual decision making can be interpreted as reflecting some ordinary behavioral wisdom that is not always accommodated within the theory. Human beings seem to believe that the theory of choice exaggerates the relative power of a choice based on two guesses compared with a choice that is itself a guess. They seem to recognize the extent to which preferences are constructed, or developed, through a confrontation between preferences and actions that are inconsistent with them and among conflicting preferences. Though they seek some consistency, they appear to see inconsistency as a normal and necessary aspect of the development and clarification of preferences. They sometimes do something for no better reason than that they must, or that someone else is doing it, or that they "feel" like doing it.

Human beings act as though they recognize the many ways in which talk and action are different domains and the ways in which they serve each other by their inconsistencies (Brunsson, 1989). They accept a degree of personal and social wisdom in simple hypocrisy. They also seem to recognize the political nature of argumentation more clearly and more personally than the theory of choice does. They are unwilling to gamble that God made people who are skilled at rational argumentation uniquely virtuous. They protect themselves from cleverness, in themselves as well as in others, by obscuring and managing their preferences. They construct institutions to shape preferences (March & Olsen, 1989, 1995; Wildavsky, 1987).

Risk preference

The concept of "risk preference," like other concepts of preferences in theories of rational choice, divides students of decision making into two groups. The first group, consisting of many formal theorists of choice, treats risk preference as revealed by choices and associates it with deviations from linearity in a revealed utility for money. For this group, risk has no necessary connection to any observable behavioral rules followed by decision makers. It is simply a feature of a revealed preference function. The second group, consisting of many behavioral students of choice, emphasizes the behavioral processes by which risky choices are made or avoided. This group finds many of the factors in risk taking to be rather remote from any observable preference for taking or avoiding risk (Lopes, 1994; MacCrimmon & Wehrung, 1986; March, 1994c; Shapira, 1995).

To be sure, decision makers often attend to the relationship between opportunities and dangers, and they are often concerned about the latter; but they seem to be relatively insensitive to probability estimates when thinking about taking risks. Although theories of choice tend to treat gambling as a prototypic situation of decision making under risk, decision makers distinguish between risk taking and gambling, saying that although they should take risks, they should never gamble. They react to variability more by trying actively to avoid it or to control it than by treating it as a trade-off with expected value in making a choice (March & Shapira, 1987).

Sometimes decision makers take greater risks than they do at other times, but ideas of risk, risk taking, and risk preference are all, to some extent, inventions of students of decision making. Often the taking of risk is inadvertent, as is the avoiding of risk. The factors that affect risk taking in individuals and organizations can conveniently be divided into three categories. First, decision makers form estimates of the risk involved in a decision. Those estimates are subject to the usual human biases and affect the risk actually taken. Second, decision makers seem to have different propensities to take risks under different conditions. In particular, the propensity to take risks appears to be affected significantly by the context of success and failure in which it occurs. Third, risk taking is affected (unconsciously) by the reliability of organizational actions. Unreliability translates into the taking of risks.

In estimating risk, decision makers typically attribute uncertainty about outcomes to one or more of three different sources: an inherently unpredictable world, incomplete knowledge about the world, and incomplete contracting with strategic actors. Each of these produces efforts to reduce uncertainty. For uncertainties that are thought to arise from inherently uncertain environmental processes, decision makers try to judge the likelihood of events. In general, decision makers do rather well in estimating future probabilities in situations in which they have experience. However, they use estimating heuristics that lead them astray at times. For example, events are judged to be more likely to the extent that they are representative. The most prototypical events are, however, not always the most frequent. In particular, decision makers tend to overlook important information about the base rates of events (Kahneman et al., 1982; Shapira, 1995).

Estimations of risk are systematically biased by the experiences decision makers have in organizations. Individuals are normally elevated to positions of decision-making authority by virtue of their past successes. Success makes them confident about their ability to handle future events, leading them to believe strongly in their wisdom and insight. They have difficulty in recognizing the role of luck in their achievements (Langer, 1975; Taylor & Brown, 1988). As a result, successful decision makers tend to underestimate the risk they have experienced and the risk they currently face, and intentionally risk-averse decision makers may actually be risk seeking in behavior (Kahneman & Lovallo, 1993; Keyes, 1985; March & Shapira, 1987).

For uncertainties that arise from gaps or ambiguities in their knowledge of the environment, decision makers assume that uncertainty can be removed by diligence and imagination. They try to judge and, if possible, improve the quality of information. They have a strong tendency to want their knowledge about what will happen to be couched in terms that deny doubt. They are more likely to seek to confirm their existing information than to acquire or notice disconfirming information. They prefer information about specific cases to information about general trends. They prefer vivid information to pallid information. They prefer concrete information to abstract statistics. When confronted with inconsistent information, they tend to rely on a few cues and exclude others from consideration (Shapira, 1995).

To deal with uncertainties stemming from incomplete contracting, decision makers develop intelligence systems designed to spy on the intentions of others. They pursue resources to remove dependence on others (Pfeffer

& Salancik, 1978). And they try to bind others to desired future actions rather than to predict them probabilistically.

The level of risk taking observed in organizations is affected not only by estimations of risk but also by the propensity of a risk taker to seek or avoid a particular level of expected risk. The evidence for variation among decision makers in individually stable risk-taking propensities is mixed, but it seems plausible to suspect that some such variations exist, that there may be consistent differences among people and even consistent differences among cultures or subcultures. However, the evidence also seems to indicate that, at least within a given culture, the risk-taking effects attributable to trait differences in risk propensity are relatively small compared to other effects.

Probably the best-established situational effect stems from the way decision makers distinguish between situations of success (or expected success) and situations of failure (or expected failure). Risk-taking propensity varies with the relationship between an individual's position and a target or aspiration level, and thus between contexts of success and failure (Payne, Laughhann, & Crum, 1980, 1981; Singh, 1986). When they are in the neighborhood of a target and are given a choice between two items of equal expected value, decision makers tend to choose the less risky alternative if outcomes involve gains and the more risky alternative if outcomes involve losses (Bromiley, 1991; Kahneman & Tversky, 1979).

When individuals find themselves well above the target, they tend to take greater risks – partly presumably because in that position they have little chance of failing and partly because they may be inattentive to their actions as a result of the large cushion. The risk-taking propensities of decision makers who are well below a target are more complicated, especially when their position puts them in danger of not surviving. On the one hand, as they fall further and further below their targets, they tend to take bigger and bigger risks, presumably to increase the chance of achieving their targets. On the other hand, as they come closer and closer to extinction, they tend to become rigid and immobile, repeating previous actions and avoiding risk (Staw, Sandelands, & Dutton, 1981). Since falling further from a target and falling closer to extinction are normally correlated, the effect of failure on risk taking appears to depend on whether decision makers focus attention on their hopes or their fears (Lopes, 1987; March & Shapira, 1992).

Risks may also be taken as a consequence of unreliability – breakdowns in competence, communication, coordination, trust, responsibility, or structure. Ignorance is a major source of variability in the distribution of possible outcomes from an action. As decision makers become more knowledgeable, they improve their average performance and reduce their unreliability. Similarly, social controls tend to increase reliability, thus decreasing risk taking. The mechanisms by which controls grow looser and tighter, or become more or less effective, are only marginally connected to conscious risk taking, but they affect the actual level of risk exhibited by decision makers.

Decisions as rule-based actions

A conception of decision making as resulting from consequential, preference-driven choice is not always accepted as axiomatic. In particular, it has been argued that theories of rational, anticipatory, calculated, consequential action underestimate both the pervasiveness and intelligence of an alternative decision logic – the logic of appropriateness, obligation, duty, and rules (Burns & Flam, 1987; March & Olsen, 1989; March & Simon, 1993). Much of the decision-making behavior we observe reflects the routine way in which people seek to fulfill their identities. For example, most of the time, most people in organizations follow rules even when it is not obviously in their self-interest to do so. Much of the behavior in an organization is specified by standard operating procedures, professional standards, cultural norms, and institutional structures linked to conceptions of identity.

Actual decisions in organizations, as in individuals, seem often to involve finding appropriate rules to follow. The logic of appropriateness differs from the logic of consequence. Rather than evaluating alternatives in terms of the values of their consequences, it matches situations and identities. Thus, it includes the following factors:

> *Situation.* Decision makers classify situations into distinct categories that are associated with identities or rules.
> *Identity.* Decision makers have a conception of their personal, professional, and official identities and evoke particular identities in particular situations.
> *Matching.* Decision makers do what they see as appropriate to their identity in the situation in which they find themselves.

Such identity fulfillment and rule following are not willful in the normal sense. They do not stem from the pursuit of interests and the calculation of future consequences of current choices. Rather, they come from matching a changing (and often ambiguous) set of contingent rules and identities to a changing (and often ambiguous) set of situations (Turner, 1985). The terminology is one of duties and roles rather than anticipatory, consequential choice. Choices are often made without much regard for preferences. Actions reflect images of proper behavior, and human decision makers routinely ignore their own fully conscious preferences. They act not on the basis of subjective consequences and preferences but on the basis of rules, routines, procedures, practices, identities, and roles (Anderson, 1983; Biddle, 1986; March & Simon, 1993). They follow traditions, hunches, cultural norms, and the advice or action of others.

The use of rules and standard operating procedures in routine situations is well known, but their importance is not limited to routine worlds. Behavior in ill-defined situations also often follows from identity-driven conceptions of appropriateness more than from conscious calculations of costs and benefits (Ashforth & Mael, 1989; Schlenker, 1982). Individuals follow heuristics in solving ambiguous problems, and they seek to fulfill identities in novel situations. The uncertainties of decision making are less lack of clarity about the consequences of action and decision maker preferences than they are lack of clarity about the demands of a logic of appropriateness. Decisions are derived from reasoning about the nature of an identity and a situation, reasoning that invokes cognitive processes of interpretation and social processes of forming accounts (Tetlock, 1992). The rules that match a situation and an identity may be developed through experience, learned from others, or generalized from similar situations.

Rule development

Rules evolve over time, and current rules store information generated by previous experience and analysis in a form not easily retrieved for systematic current evaluation. Seeing rules as coded information has led several recent studies of organizational decision making to focus on the ways in which rules change and develop (Schulz, 1992; Zhou, 1993) and to questions of the long-run intelligence of rule following, thus to some classical puzzles of culture, history, and population biology (March, 1994b).

Four major processes by which rules develop are commonly considered. First, rules can be seen as chosen consciously and accepted rationally by actors who calculate the expected consequences of their actions. From this perspective, rule following can be viewed as contractual, an agreement among rational parties to be bound jointly by a set of norms and conventions of behavior. Such a contractual view has led game theorists to an interest in interpreting norms and institutions as meta-game agreements among rational actors (Shepsle & Weingast, 1987).

Second, it is possible to see an organization or a society as learning from its experience, modifying its rules for action incrementally on the basis of feedback from the environment (Huber, 1991; Levitt & March, 1988). Such experiential learning is often adaptively rational. That is, it allows organizations to find good, even optimal, rules for many choices they are likely to face. However, learning from experience can produce surprises. Learning can be superstitious, and it can lead to local optima that are quite distant from the global optimum. If goals adapt rapidly to experience, outcomes that are good may be interpreted as failures and outcomes that are poor may be interpreted as successes. If technological strategies are learned quickly relative to the development of competence, an organization can easily adopt technologies that are intelligent given the existing levels of competence, but it may fail to invest in enough experience with a suboptimal technology to discover that it would become the dominant choice with additional competence. Such anomalies are frequent and important (Arthur, 1989, Levinthal & March, 1993).

Third, decision making can be seen as reflecting rules that spread through a group of organizations like fads or measles. Decision makers copy each other. Imitation is a common feature of ordinary organizational adaptation (Fligstein, 1985; March, 1991; Sevón, 1996; Westney, 1987). If we want to account for the adoption of accounting conventions, for example, we normally would look to ways in which standard accounting procedures diffuse through a population of accountants. We would observe that individual accountants rather quickly adopt those rules of good practice that are certified by professional associations and implemented by opinion leaders (DiMaggio & Powell, 1983). Like learning and selection, imitation often makes sense, but not always. The processes by which knowledge diffuses and the processes by which fads diffuse are remarkably similar.

Fourth, the population of rules can be seen as an evolving collection of invariant rules (Axelrod, 1984; Baum & Singh, 1994; Hannan & Freeman, 1989; Nelson & Winter, 1982). As with experiential learning, rules are dependent on history, but the mechanism is different. Individual rules are invariant, but the population of rules changes over time through differential survival and extension. Evolutionary arguments about the development of decision rules were originally made to justify the assumption that decision makers maximize expected utility. The argument was simple: Competition for scarce resources resulted in differential survival of decision makers, depending on whether the rules produced decisions that were, in fact, optimal. Thus, it was argued, we could assume that surviving rules (whatever their apparent character) were optimal.

Although the argument about the efficiency of historical processes in discovering optima had a certain charm to it, most close students of selection models have suggested that selection will not reliably guarantee a population of rules that is optimal at any arbitrary point in time (Carroll & Harrison, 1994; March, 1994b). In fact, the intelligence of rules is not guaranteed but depends on a fairly subtle intermeshing of rates of change, consistency, and foolishness. At the least, intelligence seems to require occasional deviation from the rules, some general consistency between adaptation rates and environmental rates of change, and a reasonable likelihood that networks of imitation are organized in a manner that allows intelligent action to be diffused somewhat more rapidly and more extensively than silliness.

Rule implementation

For most students of decision making who emphasize rules, socialization into rules and following them is ordinarily not a case of willful entering into an explicit contract. Rather, it is a set of understandings of the nature of things, of self-conceptions, and of images of proper behavior. These conceptions are often taken for granted. The implementation of taken-for-granted rules is not automatic, however. A rule basis for action ensures neither consistency nor simplicity. Rules are often ambiguous; more than one rule may apply in a particular situation; and the behavior required by the rule may be shaped through interpretation (Bardach, 1977; Pressman & Wildavsky, 1973).

As they try to understand history and self, and as they try to improve the often confusing, uncertain, and ambiguous world they live in, individuals and organizations interpret what rules and identities exist, which ones are relevant, and what different rules and identities demand in specific situations. Individuals may have a difficult time resolving conflicts among contending imperatives of appropriateness, that is, among alternative concepts of the self (Elster, 1986). They may not know what to do. Or they may know what to do but not have the capabilities to do it. They are limited by the resources and competencies they possess.

These indeterminacies lead rule-based theories of action to distinguish between a rule and its realization in a specific case. The processes of constructive interpretation, criticism, and justification through which rules and identities are translated into behavior have to be specified. Implementation of rules can be treated as simply another form of rational action in which choices are made among alternative interpretations in terms of expectations of consequences for the actor's interests. Thus, rules can be seen as interpreted in ways that favor the interpreter and as implemented in ways that favor the implementer (Downs, 1967; Tullock, 1965). In this perspective, ambiguities and conflicts are resolved by calculation, and disagreements over interpretations are results of conflicts of interest.

Although rule interpretation certainly involves various forms of self-interested calculation, it also involves a somewhat different cognitive process – an effort to match rules to situations through analogies and similar forms of recognizing similarities among situations and rules. Identities are clarified by reference to related identities; rules are clarified by reference to comparable rules; situations are clarified by reference to analogous situations. The clarifications are frequently made particularly problematic by the ambiguity of rules, an ambiguity that may itself be a natural result of policy making (Baier, March, & Sætren, 1986; Page, 1976).

Decision making and sense making

Decision making is intimately linked to sense making. The forming of preferences, identities, rules, situations, and expectations all involve making sense out of a confusing world. As a result, students of decision making are preeminently students of the ways in which individuals and organizations make sense of their pasts, their natures, and their futures (Berger & Luckmann, 1966; Fiske & Taylor, 1984; March, Sproull, & Tamuz, 1991). At the same time, decision making contributes to the sense making from which it draws. As individuals and organizations make decisions, they transform their preferences and their identities and shape the worlds they interpret. Thus, it is possible to see the construction of meaning as both an input and an output of decision making.

Sense making as an input to decision making

With the possible but limited exception of theories that emphasize temporal order, all major theories of decision making picture action as thoughtful in the sense that they assume some processes that code situations into terms meaningful to a decision maker. As a result, a description of decision making as "rational" or "rule based" is incomplete without clarifying the ways in which individual and organizational processes shape the premises of either. Theories of rational action assume that decision makers make sense of their situation by forming expectations about future consequences and preferences for those consequences. Theories of rule-based action assume that decision makers make sense of their situation by identifying situations as matching identities and rules and by interpreting the implications of those matches. Decisions are seen as predicated on these meanings that are established prior to action.

Much of the research on a behavioral theory of decision making focuses on how individuals process information in order to provide meaning in decision making (March & Sevón, 1988). Among many other things, this research has shown that individuals frequently edit and simplify situations, ignoring some information and focusing on other information. They frequently try to decompose problems into subproblems, ignoring interactions and working backward from desired outcomes to necessary preconditions. They recognize patterns in situations and apply rules of thumb that are believed to be appropriate for the particular situation. They adopt frames and paradigms that tend to emphasize aspects of a decision problem that are found in their own spatial and temporal neighborhoods. They create "magic numbers" (e.g., "profit," "cost of living") for complex phenomena, treating the numbers as equivalent to the more complex reality they represent. They interpret experience in ways that tend to conserve their prior beliefs and their own importance (Fiske & Taylor, 1984; Kuran, 1988; Nisbett & Ross, 1980).

The research similarly emphasizes the ways in which decision makers give meaning to their aspirations. Which preferences and identities are evoked and in what form? Studies of preferences suggest that information about preferences is simplified in many of the same ways other information is. Not all preferences are considered, and the processes by which some are evoked and others are not is important for decision making. Similarly, evaluation of performance relative to a particular dimension of preferences is simplified by setting targets (levels of aspiration) that define when things are acceptable and reduce attention to gradations of acceptability. Studies of identities indicate that the evocation and interpretation of a particular identity is influenced by social and experiential cues that define some identities as relevant and others as not.

Sense making as an output of decision making

A central commitment of standard conceptions of decision making is to the notion of outcome significance. Both theories of rational decision making and theories of rule-based decision making treat decision outcomes as the primary product of a decision process. Decision makers are assumed to enter the process in order to affect decision outcomes. They establish meaning prior to making decisions in order to reduce uncertainty and ambiguity. The significance of sense making lies in its effects on decision outcomes.

Studies of decision arenas, on the other hand, often seem to describe a set of processes that make little sense in such terms. Decisions often seem to be only loosely linked to the information gathered for making them. Discussions leading to decisions seem to be filled with apparently irrelevant matters, and the postdecision elaboration of justification often seems to be considerably more extensive than the exploration of reasons before a decision. These anomalous observations appear to reflect, at least in part, the extent to which meaning is not only a premise of decision making but also a result of it (March & Sevón, 1984).

Decision making shapes meanings even as it is shaped by them. A choice process provides an occasion for developing and diffusing interpretations of history and current conditions, as well as for mutual construction of theories of life. It is an occasion for defining virtue and truth, discovering or interpreting what is happening, what decision makers have been doing, and what justifies their actions. It is an occasion for distributing glory and blame for what has happened, and thus an occasion for exercising, challenging, and reaffirming friendship and trust relationships, antagonisms, and power and status relationships. Decisions and decision making play a major role in the development of the meaning and interpretations that decisions are based upon (March & Olsen, 1976).

This coevolution of meaning and decisions creates two major complications in understanding decision making. The first complication is connected to the simultaneity of the construction of meaning and the making of decisions. Most theories of choice assume some kind of consistency between actions taken and their premises. Thus, theories of rational choice assume that action will be made consistent with expectations and preferences; and theories of rule-based choice assume that action will be made consistent with a definition of the situation and the demands of identity. Almost without exception, such theories treat the premises as antecedent to the action with which they are associated and consider choice to be primarily a process of making action consistent with the premises.

Observations of decision making suggest a much more interactive relation between action and its premises (March, 1994a). Preferences and identities develop in the context of making choices. Actions come first, and premises are made consistent with them. Individuals and organizations discover their wants by making choices and experiencing the reactions of others as well as of themselves. The idea that decisions are made to reflect beliefs is paired with the idea that beliefs are formed to reflect decisions. This elementary coevolutionary feature of decision making and its premises makes their tendency to consistency both more profound and less helpful as an aid in predicting decision outcomes.

The second complication comes from the recognition that decision making may, in many ways, be better conceived as a meaning factory than as an action factory. Decision outcomes are often not as central to an understanding of decision making as might be expected. Individuals and organizations write history and construct socially acceptable story lines about links between actions and consequences, identities and behaviors. Decision making is a prime arena for developing and enjoying an interpretation of life and one's position in it. As a result, the link between the collection and display of information and its use in affecting decisions is weak (Feldman & March, 1981). Contentiousness in the discussion of alternative policies of an organization is often followed by apparent indifference about the implementation of a decision among them (Christensen, 1976).

The usual terminology in discussions of these apparent anomalies emphasizes the symbolic significance of decision participation, process, and manifest outcomes (Arnold, 1935; Edelman, 1964). For example, individuals fight for the right to participate in decision processes but then do not exercise the right. The rituals and symbols of decision making are important. The meanings involved may be as local as the ego needs of specific individuals and groups. They may be as global as confirming the central ideologies of a society or subculture.

It is hard to imagine a society committed to reason and rational justification that would not exhibit a well-elaborated and ritualized myth of choice, both to sustain social orderliness and meaning and to facilitate change. On the one hand, the processes of choice reassure those involved that a choice has been made intelligently; that it reflects planning, thinking, analysis, and the systematic use of information; and that the choice is sensitive to the concerns of relevant people – that is, that the right people are involved. At the same time, the processes of choice reassure those involved of their own significance. In particular, the symbols are used to reinforce the idea that managers (and managerial decisions) affect the performance of organizations, and do so properly.

Thus, we are led to a perspective that questions the idea, central to many modern theories of action, that life can be conceived as a sequence of choices. The alternative, well articulated in theories of literature but less familiar to theories of action, is that life is more concerned with forming interpretations than with making choices. It is a perspective in which outcomes are seen as less significant – both behaviorally and ethically – than processes. Processes give meaning to life, and meaning is the core of life. The grander forms of such a view glorify symbols, myths, and rituals as fundamental to comprehending the way decisions happen, and particularly the disconnection between decision making and decisions.

Decision-making ecologies

By emphasizing the making of decisions, theories of organizational decision making tend to focus on what is happening at a particular place (the decision-making body), in the heads of particular persons (the decision makers), and at a particular time (the time the decision is made). Such portrayals seem to underestimate the systemic properties of decision-making organizations. They tend to ignore the significance of the interactive conflict, confusion, and complexity surrounding actual decision making. The observations are familiar. Many things are happening at once, and they affect each other. Actions in one part of an organization are not coherently coupled to actions in other parts, but they shape each other. Many of the features of decision making are due less to the intentions or identities of individual actors than to the systemic properties of their interactions.

Decision making is embedded in a social context that is itself simultaneously shaped by decision making in other organizations. Premises and actions in one organization coevolve with those in other organizations. This interactive character of decision making extends over time so that the development of beliefs, rules, and expectations in one organization is intertwined with their development in others. Organizational histories, as well as interpretations of those histories, are formed through social interactions that make it difficult to understand decisions in any one organization at any one time without understanding those of other organizations and over time. Competition, cooperation, and imitation lead organizations to shape each other's decisions and decision making (Matsuyama, 1995). Since different parts of the system are connected developmentally in this way, their evolutionary path is more difficult to anticipate than in a world in which the environment can be taken as given and the primary issue is the extent and form of organizational adaptation to it.

Examining these connections and their effects requires what might be called an "ecological" vision of decision making, a vision that considers how the structure of relationships among individual units interacts with the behavior of these units to produce systemic properties not easily attributable to the individual behavior alone. Recent research on organizations has emphasized concepts of decision making that highlight such a vision. These include an emphasis on the interaction among individuals and groups with inconsistent preferences or identities rather than single decision makers; the idea that decision making is organized by time rather than causality; and the idea that the premises of decision making coevolve with the actions based on them.

Interactive inconsistencies

As numerous observers have noted, an obvious difficulty with describing organizational decision making in terms of a theory of autonomous individual choice or rule following is that organizations are not individuals but rather collections of individuals interconnected in many ways. In particular, individual identities and preferences are often mutually inconsistent, producing conflict and confusion (Coleman, 1986; March, 1981).

In standard choice theory, inconsistency among preferences is treated as a problem of assessing trade-offs, establishing marginal rates of substitution among goods. The process *within* individuals is mediated by an unspecified mechanism by which individuals are imagined to be able to make value comparisons among alternatives. The process *among* individuals is mediated by an explicit or implicit price system. In classical theories of the firm, for example, an organization is transformed into an individual by assuming that markets (particularly markets for labor, capital, and products) convert conflicting demands into prices. In this perspective, entrepreneurs are imagined to impose their goals on an organization in exchange for mutually satisfactory wages paid to workers, returns on investment paid to capital, and product characteristics paid to customers. Similarly, inconsistencies among identities or rules are treated as requiring priorities so that some take precedence over others. Organizations arrange priorities through hierarchies that both buffer rules from the consciousness of others and create orders of precedence and subordination among rules and identities.

Such processes can be treated as yielding a series of understandings by which participants divide decision making into two stages (March & Simon, 1993). At the first stage, the individuals negotiate understandings about ways of coordinating their separate behaviors. Each individual negotiates the best possible terms for agreeing to act in ways consistent with another's preferences or rules. At the second stage, individuals execute the understandings. In more sophisticated versions, of course, the understandings are designed so that the terms negotiated at the first stage are self-enforcing at the second. This two-stage vision is characteristic of much of the modern work in agency theory and applications of game theory to economic behavior (Milgrom & Roberts, 1992; Kreps, 1990), as it is of much classical administrative theory (March & Simon, 1993).

Seeing participants as having conflicting preferences and identities is also a basic feature of political visions of decision making. In political treatments, however, the emphasis is less on designing a system of understandings between principals and agents, or partners, than it is on understanding a political process that allows decisions to happen without necessarily resolving inconsistencies among the parties. The usual metaphors are those of "force" or "power," negotiation, exchange, and alliance (March, 1994a). In an exchange process, power comes either from having things that others want or from wanting things that others do not. Thus, it comes from the possession of resources and from the idiosyncrasy of desires, rules, or identities. In a preference pooling process, power comes from having resources and from having preferences near the center of society's preferences, that is, having identities that are broadly consistent with others (March & Olsen, 1989).

Picturing decisions as being based on an ecology of inconsistent preferences and identities seems to come closer to the truth in many situations than does assuming a single, consistent preference function or a collection of consistent identities and rules. Somewhat more problematic is the second feature of many of the behavioral studies of decision making under inconsistency – the tendency for the political aspects of decision making to be interminable. If it were possible to imagine a two-step process in which *first* a set of joint preferences and identities is established through side payments, formation of coalitions, and creation of a hierarchical structure of rules and identities, and *second* action is guided by those preferences and identities, we could treat the first stage as defining the constraints of action and the second stage as acting within them. Such a division has often been tempting (e.g., the distinction between policy making and administration, the distinction between "institutions" and "norms" and decision making within them), but it has rarely been satisfactory as a description of decision making. The decision processes we observe seem to be infused with strategic actions and negotiations at every level and every point (March, 1981). From this character of decision making has come the elaborate complications of what is usually called "implementation" – the relation between decisions as "made" and decisions as "realized" (Bardach, 1977).

In general, the machinations of strategic actors seem likely to produce a complicated concatenation of maneuver in which information has considerably less value than might be expected if strategic considerations were not so pervasive. That this process does not completely destroy meaning in organizational communication is a considerable testimony to the importance of trust in understanding organizational relations. In a conflict system, alliances involve understandings across time. Rarely can agreements be specified with precision. It is not a world of precise contracts but of informal, loose understandings and expectations. As a result, decision making often emphasizes trust and loyalty, in parallel with a widespread belief that these qualities are hard to find and sustain, and power comes from being thought to be trustworthy. Modern research on games of repeated interaction and iterated calculation among rational actors and on norms of enduring relationships has called into question some once standard recommendations for cleverness in bargaining and has moved trust and reputation to a central position in theories of multiactor decision making (Gibbons, 1992; Milgrom & Roberts, 1992).

Temporal orders

The ecological nature of decision making gives it an aura of disorderliness. Pierre Romelaer and I once described organizational decision processes as funny soccer games: "Consider a round, sloped, multi-goal field on which individuals play soccer. Many different people (but not everyone) can join the game (or leave it) at different times. Some people can throw balls into the game or remove them. While they are in the game, individuals try to kick whatever ball comes near them in the direction of goals they like and away from goals they wish to avoid" (March & Romelaer, 1976, p. 276).

Observations of the disorderliness in organizational decision making have led some people to argue that there is very little order to it, that is best described as random. A more common position, however, is that the ways in which organizations bring order to disorder is less hierarchical and less based on means–ends chains than is anticipated by conventional theories. There is order, but it is not conventional order. In particular, it is argued that any decision process involves a collection of individuals and groups who are simultaneously involved in other things. Understanding decisions in one arena requires an understanding of how those decisions fit into the lives of participants.

From this point of view, the loose coupling that we observe in a specific decision situation is a consequence of our theories. The apparent confusion is understandable as resulting from a shifting intermeshing of the demands on the attention and lives of the whole array of actors. It is possible to see any particular decision as the consequence of combining different moments of different lives. A more limited version of the same fundamental idea focuses on the allocation of attention. The idea is simple: Individuals attend to some things and thus do not attend to others. The attention devoted to a particular decision by a particular potential participant depends on alternative claims on attention.

Since those alternative claims are not homogeneous across participants and change over time, the attention any particular decision receives can be both unstable and remarkably independent of the properties of the decision (Kingdon, 1984). The same decision will attract much attention or little, depending on the other things that possible participants might be doing. The apparently erratic character of decision making is made somewhat more explicable by placing it in this context of multiple, changing claims on attention.

Such ideas have been generalized to deal with flows of solutions and problems, as well as with participants in what has come to be called a "garbage-can decision process" (Cohen & March, 1986; March & Olsen,

1976). In a garbage-can process, it is assumed that there are exogenous, time-dependent arrivals of choice opportunities, problems, solutions, and decision makers. Problems and solutions are attached to choices, and thus to each other, not because of their means–ends linkage but in terms of their temporal proximity. At the limit, for example, almost any solution can be associated with almost any problem – provided that they are contemporaries. The temporal pooling is, however, constrained by social and organizational structures (Levitt & Nass, 1989; March & Olsen, 1986).

Conclusion

Research on organizational decision making has influenced contemporary ideas about action throughout the social sciences. The grandest tradition of research, however, is to increase ignorance at the same time as it increases knowledge. Any consideration of the study of organizational decision making would have to conclude that it is well within that tradition. We know more than we used to know, and some of the things we know are now well encased in theoretical forms. In particular, simple ideas about rational actors and role players that were used to represent decision making 50 years ago have been elaborated and extended substantially. Ideas that emphasize limits on rationality and inconsistency in preferences and identities have become the received doctrine underlying most theories of organizational decision making.

The price of such knowledge is consciousness of other difficulties. Awareness of the instability, inconsistency, and endogeneity of preferences and identities; of the sense-making complications in acting according to either a logic of consequence or a logic of appropriateness; of the importance of decision processes for the construction of meaning; of the interactive, ecological nature of decision making; and of the potential inefficiency of history in ensuring unique optima in behavior or rules is now widely shared and some progress in dealing with such things is observable, but we are a long way from being able to deal with all of them.

References

Allison, G. T. (1971). *Essence of decision: Explaining the Cuban missile crisis.* Boston: Little, Brown.

Anderson, J. R. (1983). *The architecture of cognition.* Cambridge, MA: Harvard University Press.

Antonelli, C. (1989). A failure-induced model of research and development expenditure: Italian evidence from the early 1980s. *Journal of Economic Behavior and Organization, 12,* 159–180.

Arnold, T. (1935). *The symbols of government.* New Haven, CT: Yale University Press.

Arthur, W. B. (1989). Competing technologies, increasing returns, and lock-ins by historical events. *Economic Journal, 99,* 116–131.

Ashforth, B. E., & Mael, F. (1989). Social identity theory and the organization. *Academy of Management Review, 14,* 20–39.

Axelrod, R. M. (1984). *The evolution of cooperation.* New York: Basic Books.

Baier, V. E., March, J. G., & Sætren, H. (1986). Implementation and ambiguity. *Scandinavian Journal of Management Studies, 2,* 197–212.

Bardach, E. (1977). *The implementation game.* Cambridge, MA: MIT Press.

Baum, J., & Singh, J. (Eds.). (1994). *The evolutionary dynamics of organizations.* New York: Oxford University Press.

Berger, P. L., & Luckmann, T. (1966). *The social construction of reality: A treatise in the sociology of knowledge.* New York: Doubleday.

Biddle, B. J. (1986). Recent developments in role theory. *Annual Review of Sociology, 12,* 67–92.

Bromiley, P. (1991). Testing a causal model of corporate risk-taking and performance. *Academy of Management Journal, 34,* 37–59.

Brunsson, N. (1989). *The organization of hypocrisy.* Chichester, England: Wiley.

Burns, T. R., & Flam, H. (1987). *The shaping of social organization: Social rule system theory with applications.* London: Sage.

Carroll, G. R., & Harrison, J. R. (1994). On the historical efficiency of competition between organizational populations. *American Journal of Sociology, 100,* 720–749.

Christensen, S. (1976). Decision making and socialization. In J. G. March & J. P. Olsen, *Ambiguity and choice in organizations* (pp. 351–385). Bergen, Norway: Universitetsforlaget.

Cohen, M. D., & March, J. G. (1986). *Leadership and ambiguity: The American college president* (2nd ed.) Boston: Harvard Business School Press.

Coleman, J. S. (1986). *Individual interests and collective action.* Cambridge: Cambridge University Press.

Cyert, R. M., & March, J. G. (1986). *A behavioral theory of the firm* (2nd ed.). Oxford: Blackwell.

DiMaggio, P. J., & Powell, W. W. (1983). The iron cage revisited: Institutional isomorphism and collective rationality in organizational fields. *American Sociological Review, 48,* 147–160.

Downs, A. (1967). *Inside bureaucracy.* Boston: Little, Brown.

Duesenberry, J. (1960). Comment on "An economic analysis of fertility." In National Bureau Committee for Economic Research, *Demographic and Economic Change in Developed Countries* (pp. 231–234). Princeton, NJ: Princeton University Press.

Edelman, M. (1964). *The symbolic uses of politics.* Urbana, IL: University of Illinois Press.

Elster, J. (1986). *The multiple self.* Cambridge: Cambridge University Press.

Feldman, M. S. (1989). *Order without design: Information production and policy making.* Stanford, CA: Stanford University Press.

Feldman, M. S., & March, J. G. Information in organizations as signal and symbol. *Administrative Science Quarterly, 26,* 171–186.

Fiske, S. T., & Taylor, S. E. *Social cognition.* Reading, MA: Addison-Wesley.

Fligstein, N. J. (1985). The spread of the multidivisional form among large firms, 1919–1979. *American Sociological Review, 50,* 377–391.

Gibbons, R. (1992). *Game theory for applied economists.* Princeton, NJ: Princeton University Press.

Greber, E. R., & Jackson, J. E. (1993). Endogenous preferences and the study of institutions. *American Political Science Review, 87,* 639–656.

Hannan, M. T., & Freeman, J. (1989). *Organizational ecology.* Cambridge, MA: Harvard University Press.

Hickson, D. J. (Ed.). (1995). *Managerial decision making.* Dartmouth, NH: Aldershot.

Holmstrom, B. R., & Tirole, J. (1989). The theory of the firm. In R. Schmalensee and R. D. Willig (Eds.), *Handbook of industrial organization* (Vol. 1, pp. 61–133). New York: Elsevier.

Huber, G. P. (1991). Organizational learning: The contributing processes and the literatures. *Organization Science, 2,* 88–115.

Kahneman, D., & Lovallo, D. (1993). Timid choice and bold forecasts: A cognitive perspective on risk taking. *Management Science, 39,* 17–31.

Kahneman, D., Slovic, P., & Tversky, A. (Eds.). (1982). *Judgment under uncertainty: Heuristics and biases.* Cambridge: Cambridge University Press.

Kahneman, D., & Tversky, A. (1979). Prospect theory: An analysis of decision under risk. *Econometrica, 47,* 263–291.

Keyes, R. (1985). *Chancing it.* Boston: Little, Brown.

Kingdon, J. W. (1984). *Agendas, alternatives, and public policies.* Boston: Little, Brown.

Kreps, D. M. (1990). *A course in microeconomic theory.* Princeton, NJ: Princeton University Press.

Kuran, T. (1988). The tenacious past: Theories of personal and collective conservatism. *Journal of Economic Behavior and Organization, 10,* 143–171.

Langer, E. J. (1975). The illusion of control. *Journal of Personality and Social Psychology, 32,* 311–328.

Levinthal, D. A., & March, J. G. (1993). The myopia of learning. *Strategic Management Journal, 14,* 95–112.

Levitt, B., & March, J. G. (1988). Organizational learning. *Annual Review of Sociology, 14,* 319–340.

Levitt, B., & Nass, C. (1989). The lid on the garbage can: Institutional constraints on decision making in the technical core of college-text publishers. *Administrative Science Quarterly, 34,* 190–207.

Lopes, L. L. (1987). Between hope and fear: The psychology of risk. *Advances in Experimental Social Psychology, 20,* 255–295.

Lopes, L. L. (1994). Psychology and economics: Perspectives on risk, cooperation, and the marketplace. *Annual Review of Psychology, 45,* 197–227.

MacCrimmon, K. R., & Wehrung, D. A. (1986). *Taking risks: The management of uncertainty.* New York: Free Press.

March, J. G. (1981). Decisions in organizations and theories of choice. In A. Van de Ven and W. Joyce (Eds.), *Perspectives on organizational design and performance* (pp. 205–244). New York: Wiley.

March, J. G. (1988). *Decisions and organizations.* Oxford: Blackwell.

March, J. G. (1991). Organizational consultants and organizational research. *Journal of Applied Communications Research, 19,* 20–31.

March, J. G. (1994a). *A primer on decision making: How decisions happen.* New York: Free Press.

March, J. G. (1994b). The evolution of evolution. In J. Baum & J. Singh (Eds.), *The evolutionary dynamics of organizations* (pp. 39–49). New York: Oxford University Press.

March, J. G. (1994c). *Three lectures on efficiency and adaptiveness in organizations.* Helsinki: Svenska Handelhögskolan.

March, J. G., & Olsen, J. P. (1976). *Ambiguity and choice in organizations.* Bergen, Norway: Universitetsforlaget.

March, J. G., & Olsen, J. P. (1986). Garbage can models of decision making in organizations. In J. G. March & R. Weissinger-Baylon (Eds.), *Ambiguity and command* (pp. 11–36). Cambridge, MA: Ballinger.

March, J. G., & Olsen J. P. (1989). *Rediscovering organizations: The organizational basis of politics.* New York: Free Press.

March, J. G., & Olsen, J. P. (1995). *Democratic governance* (New York: Free Press, 1995).

March, J. G., & Romelaer, P. (1976). Position and presence in the drift of decisions. In J. G. March & J. P. Olsen. *Ambiguity and choice in organizations* (pp. 251–275). Bergen, Norway: Universitetsforlaget.

March, J. G., & Sevón, G. (1984). Gossip, information, and decision making. In J. G. March (Ed.), *Decisions and organizations* (pp. 429–442). Oxford: Blackwell.

March, J. G., & Sevón, G. (1988). Behavioral perspectives on theories of the firm. In W. F. van Raaij, G. M. van Veldhoven, & K.-E. Wärneryd (Eds.), *Handbook of economic psychology* (pp. 369–402). Dordrecht, the Netherlands: Kluwer.

March, J. G., & Shapira, Z. (1987). Managerial perspectives on risk and risk taking. *Management Science, 33,* 1404–1418.

March, J. G., & Shapira, Z. (1992). Variable risk preferences and the focus of attention. *Psychological Review, 99,* 172–183.

March, J. G., & Simon, H. A. (1993). *Organizations* (2nd ed.). Oxford: Blackwell.

March, J. G., Sproull, L. S., & Tamuz, M. (1991). Learning from samples of one or fewer. *Organization Science, 2,* 1–13.

Matsuyama, K. (1995). Complementarities and cumulative processes in models of monopolistic competition. *Journal of Economic Literature, 33,* 701–729.

Milgrom, P., & Roberts, J. (1992). *Economics, organization and management.* Englewood Cliffs, NJ: Prentice-Hall.

Mintzberg, H. (1994). *The rise and fall of strategic planning: Reconceiving roles for planning, plans, planners.* New York: Free Press.

Nelson, R. R., & Winter, S. G. (1982). *An evolutionary theory of economic change.* Cambridge, MA: Harvard University Press.

Nisbett, R., & Ross, L. (1980). *Human inference: Strategies and shortcomings of social judgment.* Englewood Cliffs, NJ: Prentice-Hall.

Page, B. I. (1976). The theory of political ambiguity. *American Political Science Review, 70,* 742–752.

Payne, J. W., Laughhann, D. J., & Crum, R. L. (1980). Translation of gambles and aspiration level effects in risky choice behavior. *Management Science, 26,* 1039–1060.

Payne, J. W., Laughhann, D. J., & Crum, R. L. (1981). Further tests of aspiration level effects in risky choice behavior. *Management Science, 27,* 953–958.

Pennings, J. M. (Ed.). (1986). *Decision making: An organizational behavior approach.* New York: M. Weiner.

Pfeffer, J., & Salancik, G. R. (1978). *The external control of organizations.* New York: Harper & Row.

Pressman, J. L., & Wildavsky, A. B. (1973). *Implementation.* Berkeley: University of California Press.

Schlenker, B. R. (1982). Translating actions into attitudes: An identity-analytic approach to the explanation of social conduct. *Advances in Experimental Social Psychology, 15,* 194–248.

Schoemaker, P. J. H. (1982). The expected utility model: Its variants, purposes, evidence and limitations. *Journal of Economic Literature, 20,* 529–563.

Schulz, M. (1992). A depletion of assets model of organizational learning. *Journal of Mathematical Sociology, 17,* 145–173.

Sevón, G. (1996). Organizational imitation in identity transformation. In B. Czarniawska & G. Sevón (Eds.), *Translating organizational change* (pp. 49–67). Berlin: De Gruyter.

Shapira, Z. (1995). *Risk taking: A managerial perspective.* New York: Russell Sage.

Shepsle, K. A., & Weingast, B. (1987). The institutional foundations of committee power. *American Political Science Review, 81,* 85–104.

Singh, J. V. (1986). Performance, slack, and risk taking in organizational decision making. *Academy of Management Journal, 29,* 562–585.

Staw, B. M., Sandelands, L. E., & Dutton, J. E. (1981). Threat-rigidity effects in organizational behavior: A multilevel analysis. *Administrative Science Quarterly, 26,* 501–524.

Taylor, S. E., & Brown, J. D. (1988). Illusion and well-being: A social psychological perspective on mental health. *Psychological Bulletin, 103,* 193–210.

Tetlock, P. E. (1992). The impact of accountability on judgment and choice: Toward a social contingency model. *Advances in Experimental Social Psychology, 25,* 331–376.

Tullock, G. (1965). *The politics of bureaucracy.* Washington, DC: Public Affairs Press.

Turner, J. C. (1985). Social categorization and the self concept: A social cognitive theory of group behavior. In E. J. Lawler (Ed.), *Advances in group processes* (Vol. 2, pp. 77–122). Greenwich, CT: JAI Press.

Westney, D. E. (1987). *Imitation and innovation: The transfer of Western organizational patterns to Meiji Japan.* Cambridge, MA: Harvard University Press.

Wildavsky, A. (1987). Choosing preferences by constructing institutions: A cultural theory of preference formation. *American Political Science Review, 81,* 3–22.

Witte, E., & Zimmermann, H.-J. (Eds.). (1986). *Empirical research on organizational decision making.* Amsterdam: Elsevier.

Zey, M. (Ed.). (1992). *Decision making.* Newbury Park, CA: Sage.

Zhou, X. (1993). The dynamics of organizational rules. *American Journal of Sociology, 98,* 1134–1166.

Part II

Information processing and attention allocation

3 Trying to help S&Ls: How organizations with good intentions jointly enacted disaster

William H. Starbuck and P. Narayan Pant

Failures of U.S. savings and loan institutions (S&Ls) in the 1980s added up to one of the largest financial disasters ever to hit the nation. The costs fell on everyone because the Federal Savings and Loan Insurance Corporation (FSLIC) insured the deposits. In 1990, the General Accounting Office estimated that the insurance losses would ultimately exceed $325 billion – over $1,000 for each resident of the United States (Barth, 1991).

Since many books and articles have appeared about this disaster, a reader might wonder what else there is to say. Improbably, this chapter argues that several explanations do not work and that analysts have slighted some important factors. Analysts have ignored or deemphasized the effects of decision processes and nearsighted analyses. Most analysts have also focused on events during the 1980s and understated the importance of long-term trends and abrupt policy changes.

The decision processes involved many organizations. Most of these were loosely coupled in that their actions only sporadically affected others, and they often acted without considering the likely impacts on others. Many organizations were also tightly coupled in that broad agreement and shared perceptions shaped most actions, and one organization's acts could sometimes profoundly affect another's future.

Because the disaster had many possible causes and involved many actors, understanding it requires a grasp of numerous details. The first section of this chapter recounts the history of the S&L industry, setting a context for events in the 1980s. The second section then assesses nine theories about what went wrong. The third section describes the disjoint interactions in decision processes. The fourth section emphasizes how long-term trends made a disaster of some size inevitable.

This manuscript benefits from the insights of Joan Dunbar, Roger L. M. Dunbar, Marshall Kaplan, Richard T. Pratt, Joseph Rebovich, Harry S. Schwartz, David Seiders, and especially Kathryn Eickhoff and Lawrence J. White.

A brief history of the S&L industry

The government confers favored status

American S&Ls originated to support home building (Strunk & Case, 1988). People wanting to build homes made deposits in S&Ls that lent funds contributed by many, and depositors could withdraw deposits only at substantial cost. Nearly all S&Ls were mutual associations owned by depositors. As White (1991, p. 61) explained, "The attitude that many thrift executives had about their business could almost be described as a 'calling': After all, they were actively involved in promoting home ownership and encouraging thrift. It was no accident that Jimmy Stewart's George Bailey ran a small savings and loan association in Frank Capra's 1946 film *It's a Wonderful Life.*"

S&Ls originally faced little competition. Commercial banks and mutual savings banks raised funds mainly by issuing notes payable on demand. They then made short-term loans, usually commercial ones. S&Ls made no commercial loans.

Many S&Ls failed in the 1930s. Since depositors could not withdraw funds on demand, S&Ls experienced no runs, but many depositors did make withdrawals (Barth, 1991). Also, S&Ls had few or no retained earnings to cover losses. States often did not require S&Ls to maintain minimum reserves of capital, and some states forced S&Ls to distribute all earnings.

Prompted by S&L failures, Congress created 12 regional Federal Home Loan Banks (FHLBs) in 1932. These were corporations owned by the S&Ls in their districts. FHLBs were supposed to keep S&Ls liquid by judiciously advancing funds. The new Federal Home Loan Bank Board (FHLBB) would supervise both FHLBs and S&Ls.

Two years later, the government created FSLIC to insure S&Ls' deposits. Congress wanted to give depositors confidence but feared that deposit insurance might enable S&Ls to compete with commercial banks. So, Congress forbade S&Ls to accept demand deposits and restricted their assets to fixed-rate mortgages on homes. These restrictions basically continued until 1980, although Congress did authorize loans for education and housing fixtures in the 1960s and added some depository options in the 1970s.

Until 1932, all S&Ls held state charters. However, Congress authorized federal charters when it set up FHLBs. By 1993, two-thirds of all S&Ls had federal charters, and these controlled 85% of all assets. Thus, federal regulators gradually became much more relevant than state regulators.

FHLBB required S&Ls to have only small amounts of equity capital. In 1934, FHLBB set the requirement at 5% of insured deposits, about 4.6% of assets, which was far below the requirement for commercial banks. In 1980, Congress opined that 5% seemed too high, so FHLBB lowered the requirement to 4% and later to 3%. The solid line in Figure 3.1 shows that

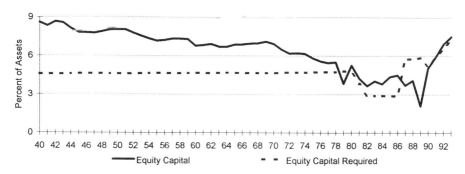

Figure 3.1. S&Ls' equity capital.

S&Ls' equity declined from 8.5% in the early 1940s to a reported low of 2.1% in 1989.

S&Ls' true net worths were even below those shown in Figure 3.1 after 1981. Instead of widely accepted accounting practices, FHLBB told S&Ls to use Regulatory Accounting Practices (RAPs) that FHLBB defined. One RAP let S&Ls with deficient equity capital report capital-to-assets ratios that averaged data from more than one year – the current year plus 1 to 4 preceding years. This was an old RAP that suddenly began causing trouble in the 1980s. Another troublesome RAP, created in 1981, allowed S&Ls to classify losses on bad mortgage loans as "goodwill" that they could amortize over 40 years. As a result, when S&Ls sold bad mortgages, their profit statements could ignore nearly all losses, and most of the losses appeared as equity capital on their balance sheets. Barth (1991, p. 50) reported that by late 1983, this "goodwill" constituted over 90% of S&Ls' reported equity capital. Also in 1981, FHLBB authorized S&Ls in financial trouble to issue Income Capital Certificates that FSLIC purchased. Although these were loans from FSLIC, a RAP said that they should appear as equity capital on S&Ls' balance sheets. By this means, FSLIC could make insolvent S&Ls appear solvent by loaning them equity capital. A former FHLBB staff member explained that "there really was no capital-to-asset requirement" in the 1980s. This was literally true for new S&Ls, which could take 20 years to satisfy FHLBB's equity capital requirement.

Favoritism extended to income taxes. Until 1951, S&Ls paid no federal taxes. When they became subject to federal taxes in 1951, they could avoid paying them by deducting from income any funds reserved for bad debts. Many S&Ls did begin paying taxes in 1962, when Congress limited this deduction to 60% of reserves for bad debts. The deduction was cut to 40% in 1979, 34% in 1982, 32% in 1984, and 8% in 1987.

In 1966, rising interest rates led Congress to put ceilings on the rates S&Ls could pay depositors. Industry representatives protested that these ceilings suppressed deposit growth. But as Figure 3.2 shows, deposit

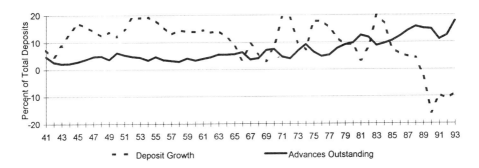

Figure 3.2. How FHLB advances varied with deposit growth.

growth began declining in 1964, 2 years before the ceilings; and by 1971, deposit growth resembled that during 1945–1963.

Next, S&Ls faced competition from money market mutual funds that offered higher interest rates, and deposit growth dipped again in 1973–1974. In response, Congress let S&Ls offer depository options closely tied to short-term interest rates. These included interest-bearing checking accounts, short-term money market certificates, and small savers' accounts. However, these options did not keep pace with interest rates available elsewhere, and deposit growth sagged again in 1978–1981.

FHLBs' stabilizers become a steady source of funds

FHLBs were to ensure the availability of enough funds for home mortgages by making "advances" whenever S&Ls faced temporary shortages (White, 1986). These advances had two important properties. First, because advances came from money borrowed by the U.S. government, the advances let S&Ls borrow as if they were only as risky as the government. Second, because the S&Ls owned the FHLBs, S&Ls could strongly influence the amounts advanced.

Figure 3.2 states FHLB advances outstanding at year end as percentages of S&Ls' total deposits and compares advances to changes in deposits. Advances did sometimes compensate for fluctuations in deposits – especially in 1966–1983, when changes in advances correlated -0.53 with changes in deposits. But over the period 1940–93, changes in advances correlated slightly positively (0.14) with changes in deposits.

Figure 3.3 shows that advances became an ever larger fraction of S&Ls' funds. A former FHLBB staff member portrayed this expansion as a policy shift: "Then when their deposits went to hell, they began to try to use advances to keep the S&Ls going." Yet, the data show no sudden changes from a policy shift. From 1947 to 1987, outstanding advances grew at a rather steady rate that exceeded the growth rate for S&Ls' assets. (Growth at a constant percentage rate generates a straight line on a logarithmic scale.)

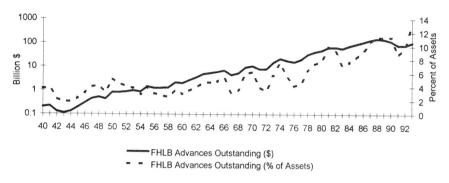

Figure 3.3. Growth in FHLB advances.

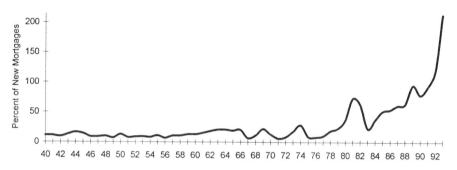

Figure 3.4. New FHLB advances.

Figure 3.4 compares new advances with new mortgage loans by S&Ls. Until 1980, advances underwrote less than a quarter of S&Ls' new mortgage loans; after 1980, they underwrote over half.

Thus, FHLBs played an amazing role in S&Ls' evolution. Although Congress set up FHLBs to provide short-term liquidity for home mortgages, FHLBs gradually became long-term sources of funds that were going into commercial mortgages, mortgage-backed securities, and nonmortgage investments. By 1993, FHLBs' new advances were more than twice S&Ls' new loans for home mortgages.

The Federal Reserve Board (FRB) shifts interest rate policies

Since the 1930s, the U.S. government has used interest rates to influence macroeconomic variables such as investment, employment, and inflation. FRB's federal funds rate influences the rates at which commercial banks lend to commerce and industry, and hence affects investment and employment.

For many years, FRB had kept the federal funds rate low and changing slowly. Then, on October 6, 1979, FRB announced policies "that should assure better control over the expansion of money and bank credit, help

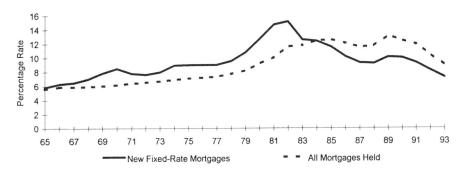

Figure 3.5. Interest rate on mortgages.

curb excesses in financial, foreign exchange and commodity markets and thereby serve to dampen inflationary forces." These policies included "less emphasis on confining short-term fluctuations in the Federal funds rate" (Document S241-6.1 of the Congressional Information Service, 1980, p. 44).

Uncontrolled, interest rates rose rapidly. Figure 3.5 shows rates for new conventional mortgages; other rates behaved similarly. The dashed line graphs S&Ls' average rates on all outstanding mortgages, which, of course, lagged the current rates.

As interest rates shot up, protests arose over FRB's policy. In mid-1982, FRB again began trying to control interest rates and dropped the federal funds rate substantially. Interest rates started to subside.

When in 1979 FRB announced its intention to let interest rates rise, it had not said that it was doing so because it was expecting a recession. It had explained that it needed to reduce inflation and that controlling the money supply was more important for that purpose than controlling interest rates. Yet, in March 1983, FRB's chairman blamed the high interest rates during 1980–1982 on the recession of 1980–1981 (Committee on the Budget, 1983). The chairman also stated firmly in 1983 that interest rates would have to remain high as long as the federal deficit remained large. During 1982–1986, interest rates dropped 33% while the federal deficit rose 73%.

When we asked former FHLBB staff members if they had forecast the interest rate rise, they said they had not seen interest rates as something to forecast. "Short rates are cyclical; they go up and down. Who would have forecast that the Fed [FRB] would do what they did?" Furthermore, they said, no one would have believed such a forecast, let alone have acted on it. "Everybody knows that forecasts have a risk about them, and every organization has an institutional bias."

Congress grants freedoms in 1980 and 1982

The Depository Institutions Deregulation and Monetary Control Act of 1980 (DIDMCA) phased out ceilings on the interest rates S&Ls could pay

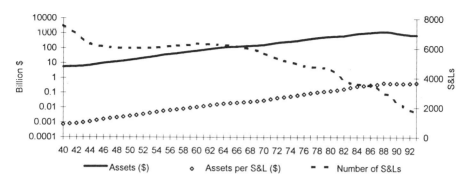

Figure 3.6. S&Ls' assets and numbers.

depositors (Brewer et al., 1980; Garcia et al., 1983). It raised the maximum deposits that FSLIC insured from $40,000 to $100,000 and let S&Ls offer Negotiated Order of Withdrawal (NOW) accounts to individuals and not-for-profit organizations. In addition, S&Ls could issue mutual capital certificates that counted toward equity capital. S&Ls could now make credit card loans, lend for personal and commercial purposes, and lend for acquisition and development of real estate. Congress told FHLBB to set S&Ls' equity capital requirement between 3% and 6%, implying that it should be lower than 5%.

In 1982, the Garn-St. Germain Act let federally chartered S&Ls offer deposit accounts that would compete with money market mutual funds. It also said S&Ls could accept demand deposits if these facilitated business relations. S&Ls gained added flexibility for commercial mortgages and consumer loans.

Even the extensive freedoms granted in 1980 and 1982 had short-term effects on S&Ls' assets and deposits. Deposit growth fluctuated but remained positive until 1989. As Figure 3.6 shows, total assets and assets per S&L rose steadily for at least 50 years until 1989, when assets turned down.

Assets per S&L increased more rapidly than total assets because the number of S&Ls kept declining. Figure 3.6 shows how the number of S&Ls declined after the early 1960s.

S&Ls back away from home mortgages

Total mortgages, the solid line in Figure 3.7, developed less linearly than assets and deposits, and they departed markedly from linearity after 1980. Lending for traditional home mortgages flattened in the early 1980s and then declined even though home ownership was booming. In 1977, S&Ls held 47.5% of all home mortgages; by 1993, they held only about 4%.

One factor in this change was mortgage securitization. Instead of holding mortgages, originators of mortgages sold them to investors as securi-

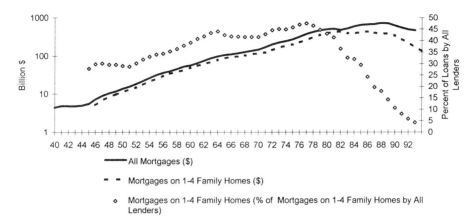

Figure 3.7. Mortgages held by S&Ls.

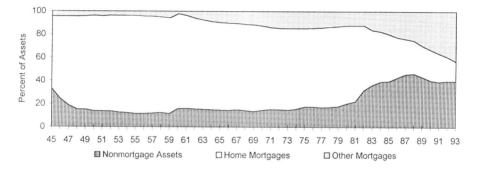

Figure 3.8. Distribution of S&Ls' assets.

ties. In 1980, 17% of the new mortgages were going into securities; by 1986, this percentage had shot up to 58% (Brumbaugh, 1988). S&Ls both sold mortgages and bought mortgage-backed securities. In many instances, a S&L sold mortgages at a discount and then bought them back as mortgage-backed securities that paid higher interest rates (Lewis, 1989).

The upper portion of Figure 3.8 shows increasing commercial mortgages and mortgages on multifamily buildings, and the lower portion shows increasing nonmortgage investments. In 1975–1979 nonmortgage assets comprised 17% of the total; from 1990 to 1993 they comprised 40%.

These investment changes likely reflect S&Ls' ownership. By 1993 only 28% of S&Ls were mutual associations; 72% were stock companies.

New tax laws take effect in 1981 and 1986

Confronting recession, the Reagan administration tried to stimulate the economy. Two tax changes in 1981 created investment opportunities for

S&Ls: The investment credit went up, and the allowable depreciation on real estate doubled. These changes made real estate partnerships more profitable, and investors created many new partnerships – which sought mortgages or other loans from S&Ls.

The new real estate partnerships were willing to pay high interest rates, and they made speculative investments. Entrepreneurs created partnerships in which investors would incur operating losses throughout the period of ownership but would receive capital gains (gains over what properties originally cost) when partnerships liquidated. Since investors could deduct the operating losses against ordinary income, the government was sharing the losses. Indeed, for most investors, the U.S. government was paying about half of the losses. Because the U.S. government taxed capital gains at only 40% of the rate on ordinary income, moderate capital gains could more than offset accumulated losses. At least, this was the plan. Most partnerships never produced gains.

These partnerships disappeared rapidly after Congress enacted tax changes in 1986 that made real estate partnerships less desirable. Capital gains lost their favored status. Maximum tax rates dropped. Depreciation periods for real estate rose again. Losses on passive activities – those in which a taxpayer plays no administrative role – could no longer offset highly taxed ordinary income. Nearly all investors in real estate partnerships had passive roles. Partnerships that might once have made after-tax profits over the long run suddenly turned into heavy financial drains with no prospect of profit. Investors lost interest in real estate partnerships, so new ventures could not attract funds and existing ventures could not find buyers for their properties. Finding themselves with unsaleable properties and the prospect of continuing annual losses, many existing partnerships declared bankruptcy. S&Ls that had lent to partnerships found themselves holding land or buildings that were very difficult to sell.

The solid line in Figure 3.9 shows the percentage of loans outstanding that S&Ls foreclosed. In the late 1970s, this rate was at or below 1%. After 1986, it exceeded 2%.

Disaster strikes

The number of S&Ls had declined for many years, and it was not unusual for 2% or even 3% to close in a year. But 6% closed in 1980 and 11% in 1981. S&Ls had regularly earned 10% to 15% on equity capital, and in 1978–1979 their profits soared to 20–24%. Then their earnings dropped to only 4% in 1980, and they lost 22–23% in 1981 and 1982. Figure 3.10 graphs these shifts.

Some 1980–1982 closures were due to insolvency. The insolvency rate, which had traditionally stayed below 0.1%, rose to 0.8% in 1980, 1.9% in 1981, and 6.6% in 1982. For public consumption, RAPs made it appear that insolvencies declined in 1983–1987. Yet the real situation was very differ-

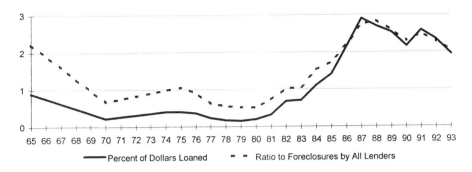

Figure 3.9. Mortgage foreclosures by S&Ls.

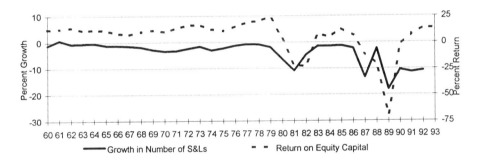

Figure 3.10. S&Ls' profits and growth.

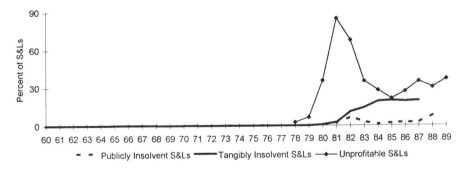

Figure 3.11. Insolvent and unprofitable S&Ls.

ent. The solid line in Figure 3.11 shows what insolvency rates would have been if S&Ls had counted only tangible assets.

Figure 3.11 also shows the public data about unprofitable S&Ls over the period 1978–1989. These data show that earlier losses spread broadly: 91% of S&Ls shared losses in 1981–1982 that equaled 43% of the equity capital of all S&Ls. Later losses were more concentrated. 40% of S&Ls shared losses in 1987–1989 that equaled 75% of the equity capital of all S&Ls. However, after 1981, the public data understate S&Ls' losses because RAPs let S&Ls amortize losses on bad mortgage loans over many years.

In May 1987, Congress's investigative unit, the General Accounting Office (GAO) (1987, pp. 6–7), declared that FSLIC had misrepresented its earnings. FSLIC had reported breaking even in 1985 and losing $3.6 billion in 1986; but GAO estimated that FSLIC had lost $1.1 billion in 1985, had lost $10.9 billion in 1986, and was $6.3 billion in debt.

Also in 1987, FSLIC estimated that "the cost of providing assistance to about 280 currently insolvent institutions may range up to $21 billion. Assistance to another 100 institutions that currently appear to have little chance of recovery could add $4 billion to [FSLIC's] losses" (GAO, 1987, p. 6). Actual events made these estimates wildly optimistic.

Congress creates new regulators and imposes new requirements

Doing something about the S&Ls was a priority of the Bush administration when it took office; and in August 1989, Congress set aside more funds for resolving insolvencies and changed the regulatory structure. It created an agency to deal with insolvent S&Ls and replaced FHLBB with two new agencies, one to regulate S&Ls and another to supervise FHLBs. Congress abolished the bankrupt FSLIC and placed S&L deposits under the agency that insures deposits in commercial banks. Congress also raised insurance premiums, set more stringent standards for equity capital, and authorized more penalties for mismanagement or criminal acts. In 1991, Congress (1) required annual examinations by federal examiners, (2) placed limits on deposits made through deposit brokers, and (3) said S&Ls with state charters must observe most limitations placed on S&Ls with federal charters.

These changes evidently affected many trends. The percentage of equity capital shot up (Figure 3.1). Deposit growth turned negative for the first time (Figure 3.2). Assets and deposits turned down, and assets per S&L flattened (Figure 3.6). S&Ls' investments in mortgages, especially home mortgages, turned down (Figure 3.7). Nonmortgage investments stopped increasing, and investments in commercial mortgages increased even more (Figure 3.8).

Summary

The S&L industry followed several long-term trends. Assets and deposits grew steadily until 1989, when they turned down. The number of S&Ls declined regularly, a trend that accelerated slightly after 1980, so the average size of an S&L increased until 1989. Other trends were less stable but persistent. Equity capital shrank as a fraction of S&Ls' assets until 1990. FHLB advances were a growing source of long-term funds until 1988. S&Ls

invested increasing amounts in mortgages until 1989; and until 1981, they invested increasing amounts in home mortgages.

The industry also faced challenges in the 1980s. FRB let interest rates rise in 1980–1982 then lowered them again. Congress let S&Ls engage in new activities, and they responded by investing in commercial mortgages and especially nonmortgage investments. New tax policies in 1981 and 1986 first encouraged and then discouraged risky real estate partnerships.

However, these short-term changes all occurred before 1989. According to the public data, long-term trends did not change much until 1989. That year, Congress passed legislation that was supposed to end the S&L disaster.

Theories about the S&L disaster

Analysts have advanced at least nine theories about this disaster, all of which blame actions by the U.S. government partly or wholly. However, some theories contradict the existing evidence, and others explain only small fractions of the losses. Each theory focuses on a few phenomena while ignoring others.

Theory 1. Government regulations forced S&Ls to make long-term loans from short-term funds, thus making them vulnerable to rising interest rates. Until 1980, regulators barred S&Ls from borrowing long-term funds or making short-term loans. S&Ls offered chiefly long-term home mortgages at fixed rates of interest, whereas their depositors could withdraw on short notice. Friend (1969) pointed out that this made S&Ls vulnerable to losing money. When interest rates go up, S&Ls might have to pay more for deposits than they would receive from mortgage loans issued earlier.

Such a rate change did occur in the early 1980s (Figure 3.5), but this interest-fluctuation theory cannot explain all the losses by S&Ls in the 1980s. Figure 3.12 graphs two key interest rates: The interest rates that S&Ls received on mortgages stayed above those S&Ls paid for borrowed funds in every year except 1981.

The rates in Figure 3.12 may explain S&Ls' losses in 1981 and 1982, but even this is questionable because the recession in 1980–1982 caused bad loans that lowered S&Ls' profits (Kane, 1985). After 1983, S&Ls' differential between interest revenue and interest cost attained new highs. Figure 3.13 shows this differential and the industry's before-tax profit. S&Ls were suffering their largest losses in 1988–1989, when the interest rate differential was setting all-time highs.

Theory 2. FRB caused S&Ls' losses by abandoning a long-standing interest rate policy that was a key basis for S&Ls' practices. The abrupt rise in interest rates in 1979–1982 is the basis for a theory voiced by former officials at FHLBB. When FRB allowed interest rates to rise freely in late 1979, S&Ls were caught holding long-term fixed-rate mortgages, while depositors discovered opportunities to invest elsewhere at higher rates.

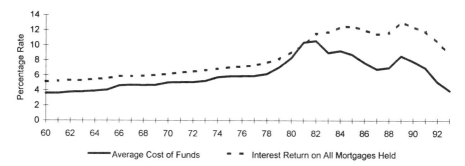

Figure 3.12. S&Ls' interest income and interest cost.

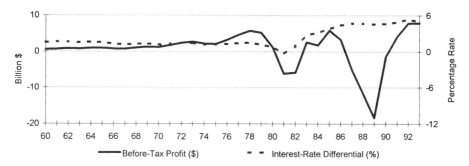

Figure 3.13. S&Ls' profit and interest-rate differential.

Nevertheless, S&Ls' industrywide profit turned negative for only 1 year, and then by only a small amount. When S&Ls issued new mortgages, they did so at higher and variable rates. At most, the interest rate differential may explain S&Ls' losses in 1981–1982, which totaled $12 billion before taxes. Although these losses affected almost all S&Ls and consumed almost half of S&Ls' equity capital, they came to less than 4% of the insurance loss paid by American taxpayers.

Theory 3. FRB's allowing interest rates to rise led S&Ls to take extreme risks. S&Ls with negative implicit equity capital supposedly take extreme risks because they have nothing to lose. Friend (1969) pointed out that rising interest rates would reduce implicit market values of S&Ls mortgage loans and thus their implicit equity capital. For example, if an S&L has loaned $100 million at an average interest rate of 6%, its interest income is $6 million. If the current interest rate is 8%, the S&L's existing loans are worth only $75 million because $75 million in new loans would yield $6 million of income. If this hypothetical transaction did occur, the S&Ls' equity capital would drop by $25 million.

In 1978, the equity capital of federally insured S&Ls averaged only 5.6% of assets, so the average S&L would have been implicitly bankrupt if the interest rate rose to 106% of the rate at which it had issued loans. However, this did not happen. In the worst year, 1981, S&Ls' current interest rate for new funds rose to only 103% of the rate at which they had issued loans.

Moreover, principles of accounting bar S&Ls from recognizing loans' market values unless they liquidate. Thus, this theory may help to explain the large insurance losses after S&Ls became insolvent, but it does not explain why S&Ls became insolvent.

Theory 4. Because the federal and state governments gave S&Ls more freedom, S&Ls pursued risky policies that caused large losses. White (1991) compared the 1985 assets of S&Ls that survived and failed in 1986–1990. On average, soon-to-fail S&Ls had more nontraditional assets and less equity capital, more were stock companies rather than mutual associations, and more held state charters rather than federal ones. White also said that rapidly growing S&Ls were more likely to hold nontraditional assets and more likely to receive funds from nontraditional sources such as large certificates of deposit.

However, White did not make multivariate analyses or control for the states in which S&Ls operated. Failure rates differed greatly among states, with Texas, California, Louisiana, Florida, and Ohio accounting for about 40% of the failures. Californians are among the heaviest users of S&Ls, but Louisianans are among the lightest. Thus, both failure rates and nontraditional investments might have reflected regional economic conditions or states' regulatory practices. White's argument about rapid growth focused on 1980–1986; he said that growth had been much higher in 1983–1984 than before or after. Although 1983–1984 had a high growth rate, similarly high rates had occurred several times before, whereas unusually slow growth distinguished 1979–1982 and 1985–1988 (Figure 3.2).

From January 1985 through September 1986, 284 S&Ls failed. GAO (1989) "judgmentally" selected 26 of these S&Ls that had caused 57% of the insurance losses and compared them with a matched sample of 26 solvent S&Ls. All the failed S&Ls had made nontraditional investments, and most had taken nontraditional deposits. Compared to 12 solvent S&Ls, 19 failed S&Ls had made loans to developers for land and construction. Compared to 5 solvent S&Ls, 21 failed S&Ls had issued "jumbo" certificates of deposit for the insurance maximum of $100,000. The jumbo deposits had often come through deposit brokers who place clients' funds at high interest rates. GAO stressed the volatility of such deposits. However, GAO merely looked at raw frequencies without weighing alternative factors. For instance, of the 19 failed S&Ls that loaned money to developers for land and construction, 11 were in the Dallas (Texas) FHLB district, and others had made such loans in Texas.

Benston and Pant did make multivariate analyses. Focusing on 1981–1985, Benston (1985) found that failing S&Ls had the same percentages of nontraditional investments and nontraditional deposits as sound ones, and that S&Ls with state charters had lower failure rates than ones with federal charters. Pant (1991) estimated that S&Ls' aggressiveness and prod-

Theory 9. The tax laws changed. An S&L trade association, the Savings & Community Bankers of America (1994, p. 2), explained: "Changes in real estate tax laws in 1986 led to a rapid and unanticipated fall in real estate values in many over-built markets, causing many borrowers to default on loans. Increasing competition from banks, nonbank financial institutions, and government-sponsored housing finance agencies decreased the profitability of residential mortgage lending and worsened the growing thrift crisis. This confluence of events led to the failure of a large number of savings institutions, eventually bankrupting the Federal Savings and Loan Insurance Corporation, at a huge cost to the taxpayer."

The dashed line in Figure 3.9 compares S&Ls' mortgage foreclosures to those by all lenders. Until 1983, S&Ls' foreclosure rate was the same as or less than that of other lenders. After 1986, S&Ls foreclosed at more than twice the rate of other lenders, whereas other lenders' post-1986 foreclosure rates were similar to their pre-1986 rates.

The 1986 tax changes may not have caused the higher foreclosure rates in the late 1980s. First, S&Ls' foreclosure rates started to move up in 1981, right after speculative real estate partnerships became more profitable and 5 years before passage of the 1986 tax law. Second, S&Ls held less than 10% of the commercial mortgages. Mortgages on apartments and commercial buildings were held mainly by commercial banks and life insurance companies, so these lenders should have had larger losses from the tax changes than S&Ls. They did not. However, the tax changes probably hit S&Ls' investments more heavily. S&Ls had less experience with commercial mortgages than commercial banks and insurance companies, so they invested less wisely. Some S&Ls followed poor practices (Table 3.1), and some were pawns of real estate opportunists. S&Ls had little equity capital (Figure 3.1), so small losses could make them insolvent.

An appraisal

The disaster likely had several causes that differed over time. Figures 3.10 and 3.11 suggest that it included at least three periods: 1980–1982, 1983–1986, and 1987–1991. A fourth period may have started in 1992, as White (1991) predicted that the 1989 legislation would cause more insolvency.

Low equity capital caused trouble through all three periods (Barth, 1991). After 1979, S&Ls' economic environments became much less stable, and S&Ls made much riskier investments. Congress or FHLBB should have required much more equity capital, since companies in construction and real estate, the domains where S&Ls were investing, had equity capital that averaged 26–28% of assets. Instead, Congress urged FHLBB to lower the capital requirement, and it did so.

FRB's abrupt shift in interest rate policy made low levels of equity capital visibly problematic in 1980–1982 because S&Ls lost money for 2 years. A more gradual policy change would have let S&Ls adapt to higher interest rates without incurring losses.

By 1983, S&Ls had raised interest rates, but then they ran into trouble of their own making. They had begun making more loans for apartment buildings and commercial buildings in the 1960s and stepped up this practice after 1980. They also made many more nonmortgage investments after 1980. Meanwhile, they were converting from mutual associations to stock companies. These changes not only made their investments riskier, they erased S&Ls' support from depositor-owners and their privileged status as the government-supported lender for home mortgages. That is, S&Ls voluntarily abandoned their distinctive competence and their grass-roots political support.

Not only did S&Ls lack experience in appraising nonmortgage loans, their regulators assumed that S&Ls took little risk and had little criminality or corruption. Federal S&L examiners overlooked problems, and FHLBB corrected problems apathetically. Thus, self-interested opportunists came as borrowers and owners.

A combination of less competence, more risk taking, more criminality, more self-interest by S&Ls' managers, and impotent regulators invited trouble. However, the effects of these factors should have built up gradually, so they do not explain why the disaster accelerated suddenly in 1987–1991. Similarly, delayed recognition of problems – due to either bureaucratic oversight or deceptive accounting standards – should have occurred gradually. The new regulatory structure authorized in 1989 probably had no effects until after the massive losses had abated.

Thus, the sudden, massive losses in 1987–1991 probably had two main causes. First, stricter regulatory standards after 1986–1987 may have forced S&Ls to acknowledge more bad debts and helped FHLBB to see the disaster's size. Second, tax changes in 1986–1990 transformed many investments into bad loans that no longer had as much concealment from RAPs.

Government agencies caused trouble both by ignoring problems or reacting too slowly and especially by overreacting or acting too quickly. The disaster might have been much smaller if FHLBB or the Reagan administration had acted more swiftly or more forcefully. FHLBB could have raised the equity capital requirement gradually as S&Ls made riskier investments. FRB could have changed its interest rate policy in stages, allowing S&Ls to adapt incrementally. Congress tended both to overreact and to take misguided actions.

Decision making by loosely coupled organizations that use distorted data

The story of this disaster resembles a play in which some actors form groups that move together but most actors seem to ignore each other. Ropes link certain actors, and every so often, an actor who feels constrained jerks a rope and unwittingly upends another. Some actors interject fragments from other plays, and some rewrite the script. Different people play each role in each scene, bringing sundry abilities and changing emphases.

Sitting in the middle of the stage is a draped object that grows more and more immense. But not only do the actors not peek under the drapery, they ignore this object entirely. One actor constantly dances around this object without acknowledging its presence, except when he tosses more drapery over it. Mainly, this actor seems to be echoing the motions and statements of others.

Despite distractions and diversions, the motions have an overall consistency, as if specific actors and specific actions and statements do not matter all that much. Everyone gradually drifts closer and closer to the large object, until finally several bump against it and dislodge its drapery. Then all the actors assail the one who has been dancing around the object, killing him as well as a few of themselves. The survivors celebrate their triumph.

The S&L industry attracted different managers at various times. Long ago, managers were proponents of home building who saw themselves as serving their communities as well as their firms' depositor-owners. As mutual associations gave way to stock companies, some owners became managers serving their own interests. By the 1960s, managers were showing less interest in home building as such and more interest in profit making. After 1982, the industry drew many opportunists from construction and real estate development, who used S&Ls to abet sales at inflated prices.

In Washington, the S&L industry supported two trade associations that did not always agree. One represented mainly large S&Ls, and in the 1980s it tended to argue that each FHLB district presented distinct issues that called for different treatment. The other, which represented diverse S&Ls, tended to argue that all S&Ls deserved similar treatment. A Washington insider told us that both trade associations exerted strong influence on Congress in the 1980s, and Congress's behavior is consistent with such influence until 1989.

Specific S&Ls also exerted strong influence. Brumbaugh (1988, p. 174) remarked:

Throughout the 1980s, for example, the industry demanded and received regulatory forbearance, primarily in the form of lower net-worth requirements, accounting forgiveness, and forestalled closure of insolvent thrifts. Each of these acts provided short-run subsidies to thrifts – insolvent and solvent. A microcosm of this behavior exists today in Texas, one of the states hardest hit by thrift insolvencies – over 40 percent of income losses for the third quarter of 1987 were in thirty-nine Texas thrifts. Powerful thrift interests successfully lobbied Congress, particularly the Texas congressman who is Speaker of the House, to make regulatory forbearance part of the scaled back FSLIC recapitalization plan [passed in 1987]. The result of the early 1980s forbearance, however, was an unintended exacerbation of thrift problems, as insolvent thrifts gambled for resurrection, fraud grew, and deflation further ravaged thrifts' portfolios.

Not only did S&Ls strongly influence Congress, they also influenced FHLBB. Presidents of the S&L-owned FHLBs met frequently with FHLBB, and FHLBB staff members told us that these presidents strongly influenced policy decisions. In an internal memorandum a senior official in the executive branch reported in 1985, "They [the senior officials in FHLBB] clearly feel impotent to close down insolvent thrifts as rapidly as they would like. They feel tightly bound by lack of FSLIC funding and also by opposition of the insolvent thrifts themselves, who are perceived to dominate the trade groups and to have much clout on Capitol Hill."

Influence flowed the other direction only rarely. FHLBB occasionally toughened its rules, although FHLBB probably never took actions that most S&Ls opposed and it seldom punished rule violations. In 1989, Congress imposed heavy costs on S&Ls.

That 1989 legislation, passed shortly after a change of administration, shows how personnel changes altered policies. The Reagan administration had taken little action because of internal debate about the disaster's size and the need to close insolvent banks promptly. One side questioned FHLBB's efficacy and advocated swifter, stronger action; the dominant side insisted that the federal budget not include larger sums for this purpose. An internal memorandum stated, "Because of deposit insurance, failure in the thrift industry is a bureaucratic decision as much as an economic fact." Thus, stronger action did not occur until the Bush administration took office.

The Reagan administration also did not act more forcefully because formal reports said S&Ls were doing rather well. Internal memoranda observed that "In 1984, FSLIC insured thrifts ended in the black" and "1985 may be one of the most prosperous years for thrifts." Of course, those ideas arose from RAP profits, which understated losses from bad loans. Only later did the administration discover that they had relied on deceptive reports.

Others were also misled by RAP reports, including FHLBB, FSLIC, and the S&Ls' trade associations. Given its optimistic appraisal of the industry's condition, the Reagan administration wanted S&Ls themselves to pay for cleaning up their industry, and the trade associations endorsed this view. Because the trade associations doubted the competence of FHLBB and FSLIC, they proposed new organizations to resolve bad loans, and the Office of Management and the Budget (OMB) refused to give FHLBB more staff to dispose of insolvent S&Ls. Within OMB, a staff member reported:

Chairman Gray [of FHLBB] stressed the point that the industry feels that FSLIC staff are incapable of solving the current problem. This has been the main reason why the industry is unwilling to capitalize the FSLIC fund.

We have talked with thrift industry trade groups and disagree with Chairman Gray. First, we believe that the distrust is not confined to FSLIC staff, but that the industry also distrusts Bank Board staff and the Board. However, we believe there is support for raising the funds needed to shore up the FSLIC fund. The industry is clearly divided on this issue. While a majority of the members favor solving the industry's problems in-house, there are a few large, powerful thrifts which do not want to bear the additional costs (they would rather see the Federal government pay for it).

Chairman Gray thanked OMB for having authorized FSLIC an additional 40 [employees], but mentioned that this was not enough to solve the problem. He contends that FSLIC needed flexibility from Federal civil service rules to hire and retain qualified personnel. Chairman Gray indicated that the FDIC [which insures commercial banks] has 2,500 employees involved in liquidations, compared to FSLIC's professional staff of only 81. He pointed out that the average salary of a FSLIC professional was $35,800, while people on Wall Street doing equivalent work earned over $100,000. Chairman Gray believes that the only people who would work for FSLIC were the ones that could not get a job on Wall Street.

The 1986 tax changes show actors ignoring their effects on others. According to a person who helped to design these tax changes, no one thought about their possible effects on S&Ls' solvency.

FRB's policy shifts in 1979 and 1982 also show actors ignoring their effects on others and show roles changing when new actors step in. The 1979 policy shift followed appointment of a new chairman. The 1982 policy shift, backing away from high interest rates, occurred even as Congress was passing the Garn-St. Germain Act to help S&Ls deal with high interest rates. If one takes FRB's public statements at face value, neither policy shift took account of potential effects on institutions for lending money, such as the regulatory structure for S&Ls. However, some of FRB's public statements lack credibility. It explained its 1979 shift differently at times; and although FRB did not say so publicly, its 1982 shift was likely intended to quiet complaints about high interest rates.

Apparently, key actors did not see connections between FRB's control of interest rates and FHLBB's equity capital requirement. FHLBB could get by with a low equity capital requirement as long as (1) S&Ls made low-risk investments, (2) S&Ls' economic environment was stable, and (3) S&Ls remained profitable. FRB's policies strongly influenced S&Ls' profits and their environment's stability. When FRB shifted policies, FHLBB needed to require more equity capital.

FHLBB was, of course, the actor who danced around the disaster while ignoring it, and in 1989 FHLBB became the scapegoat everyone assailed. But it is hard for someone sitting in the audience to see FHLBB as the villain or to interpret FHLBB's slaying as a triumph. Congress designed FHLBB to reflect influence from S&Ls themselves; and when FHLBB attempted to restrain S&Ls, Congress intervened on the side of S&Ls. The executive branch gave FHLBB far too few resources for it to act effectively. With the executive branch, Congress, and the trade associations all doubting FHLBB's competence and effectiveness, it certainly could not exercise moral leadership.

On occasion, FHLBB tried to use symbolism to show mastery of its environment. For example, amid the turmoil of 1980, Richard Marcis and Dale Riordan (1980) of FHLBB's Office of Policy and Economic Research made elaborate forecasts of the industry's balance sheets and income-and-expense statements for 8 years. One scenario assumed that interest rates would decline from their highs reached in early 1980; a second scenario envisaged interest rates remaining steady through 1988; and a third scenario postulated interest rates increasing from current levels.

Marcis and Riordan made predictions without explaining them. They did not specify why they expected interest rates to have predicted effects. They (1980, p. 5) asserted that the newly passed DIDMCA would "significantly impact S&Ls" and that S&Ls' new abilities would be "of great significance" on both the asset and liability sides of balance sheets (p. 5), but they did not describe the nature of this significance.

Yet, Marcis and Riordan described S&Ls' future in minute detail. For each scenario, they specified percentages of assets in various classes to three decimal places. They detailed assets, liabilities, income items, and expenditure items painstakingly for 9 years. It seems that they intended this detail to demonstrate their understanding of the industry's condition and developmental possibilities and to legitimize their conclusion: that S&Ls would be far down the path to total recovery by 1988.

Regulatory agencies and bank examiners in 50 states and federal examiners in 12 FHLB districts played ostensibly minor roles. But some explanations of the disaster have said that these bit players were among the true villains (Kane, 1989).

With all these changing actors and changing actions, it is amazing that long-run trends persisted. Yet, the disaster seemed to have sprung from interactions between consistent long-run trends and erratic policy shifts. The actual character of these policy shifts appears secondary. Long-run trends were constructing an increasingly unstable situation in which a large perturbation would someday trigger disaster.

How long-term trends made large perturbations disastrous

Four long-run trends framed the disaster: (1) high and increasing favoritism by Congress, (2) escalating support from and trust by regulatory agencies, (3) low and declining equity capital requirements, and (4) declining holdings of home mortgages and declining ownership by depositors. Ironically, three of these trends arose from others' efforts to help S&Ls, and S&Ls themselves helped to shape all four trends.

First, Congress showed favoritism toward S&Ls. Congress set up FHLBs in a way that let S&Ls borrow via the U.S. government, and it insisted that S&Ls should pay artificially low premiums for deposit insurance. Kane (1985) argued that the low premiums gave S&Ls an incentive to minimize equity capital.

One reason for Congress's attitude may have been S&Ls' standing as symbols of home ownership – almost as central to the American dream as motherhood and apple pie. Another reason may have been that S&Ls'

depositors and borrowers were voters. S&Ls represented respected political constituents.

S&Ls grew more influential in Congress over time. They created active
trade associations and hired effective lobbyists. The U.S. League of Savings
Associations made large political contributions, along with the National
Association of Realtors and the National Association of Home Builders.
S&Ls focused contributions on members of the House and Senate banking
committees (Kane, 1989, pp. 52–53), and they expressed strong opinions
about relevant legislation.

Second, the S&Ls had ongoing aid from regulatory agencies. FHLB advances
gradually became a significant source of funds for the industry, and indirectly for home ownership and home construction. Advances outstanding
were 13.3% of S&Ls' assets by the end of 1993, and FHLBs treated advances as support for the S&L industry rather than as funds owed to the
American public. Even after the industry's deplorable condition became
obvious, FHLBs did not reduce their advances.

In the early 1980s, FHLBB permitted S&Ls to portray losses on bad
mortgage loans as assets and allowed S&Ls in trouble to issue Income
Capital Certificates for purchase by FSLIC. Thus, insolvent S&Ls could
describe themselves as solvent and continue in business with FSLIC as a
silent partner.

FSLIC made perfunctory examinations of S&Ls. Rarely did an S&L have
reason to fear examiners' arrival. Examiners came infrequently; they lacked
competence; and when they found deficiencies, FHLBB, FSLIC, and the
S&Ls ignored their complaints. S&Ls had great discretion.

Third, S&Ls had to meet no effective capital requirements. FHLBB and Congress set very low equity capital requirements, which they relaxed when
S&Ls could not meet them.

Although S&Ls did not have to lower equity capital to the minima set by
FHLBB, S&L managers may have assumed that FHLBB knew how much
equity capital was essential. That is, some S&L managers may have
thought they were behaving prudently as long as they exceeded FHLBB's
requirements.

Favoritism, advances, RAPs, Income Capital Certificates, perfunctory
examinations, and low equity requirements proved harmful in the long
run. Low equity capital made S&Ls vulnerable to environmental changes.
Escalating FHLB advances made S&Ls less dependent on and presumably
less concerned about depositors. RAPs and Income Capital Certificates
encouraged insolvent S&Ls to speculate recklessly and thus to multiply
losses. Perfunctory examinations and nonenforcement of rules kept S&Ls
from having to show competence. Congress did not question S&Ls' ability
to use freedoms intelligently and prudently.

*Fourth, S&Ls evolved from mutual associations that invested in home mortgages
to stock companies that invested in commercial mortgages, mortgage-backed securities, and nonmortgage investments.*

Not even FHLBB challenged the wisdom of S&Ls' strategic change. Through political influence and participation in governmental decision making, S&Ls made their existence an autonomous goal. FHLBB, Congress, and the executive branch all accepted the premise that S&Ls ought to exist even if they no longer promoted home ownership. So they agreed to S&Ls' proposals for change.

But this change meant that S&Ls were politically vulnerable when the Bush administration and Congress acted in 1989. S&Ls no longer symbolized home ownership and thrift, and they no longer had widespread political support. They had become merely another financial retailer, competing with commercial banks, insurance companies, and loan companies.

Large perturbations of the 1980s caused steplike departures from long-term trends. Institutional practices had adapted to long-standing policies. Then policy shifts upset the institutional practices.

Three types of perturbations seem to have been especially important. First, many years of slowly changing interest rates shaped expectations and institutional practices. Then FRB let interest rates rise rapidly for 2 years. Second, for many years, S&Ls had faced tight restrictions on deposits, investments, and interest rates. Then Congress gave S&Ls much freedom. Third, tax policies toward real estate had been stable during the 1960s and 1970s. Then the government made changes that encouraged speculative partnerships. Five years later, it not only repealed the earlier changes but eliminated policies that had been in effect for a quarter of a century.

Decisions shared by many loosely coupled organizations

Collisions between long-run trends and short-run perturbations probably typify decision processes involving many loosely coupled organizations. Because loose coupling makes communication difficult, organizations coordinate on the basis of expectations. Nearly all organizations adhere to traditions and avoid abrupt innovations, and trends tend to persist. Even nuclei of tightly coupled organizations, such as the networks of FHLBB and FHLBs, avoid abrupt innovations because they are unsure about the limits of their discretion.

But sometimes organizations do make abrupt innovations that perturb the overall system to significant degrees. The S&L disaster suggests that these perturbations have two properties: They involve unusually large actions, and the actors fail to anticipate secondary effects of their actions. FRB's 1979 policy shift stood out because FRB departed radically from recent tradition. The tax and S&L legislation called for sudden, significant changes rather than small, incremental ones. FRB forecast effects of its 1979 policy shift on inflation and employment but did not forecast the effects on S&Ls' profits. The Reagan administration forecast effects of the 1986 tax changes on taxes paid by partners but not on S&Ls' outstanding loans.

Both abrupt actions and blindness to secondary effects are prevalent in decision processes involving many loosely coupled organizations. Involvement of many participants who hold divergent views creates a need to motivate actions. Participants must achieve agreement that there is need for action and then agree on specific actions, so they are prone to define chosen actions as final solutions rather than experimental trials. Participants with divergent views need to focus on specific symptoms that are motivating them to act, so they tend to forecast only first-order results of their actions. Indeed, such decision processes often have an emotional air – as in "the first 100 days."

Thus, there is hope for democracy. Citizens worry about cozy relations between Congress and lobbyists, about regulatory agencies being captured by the industries they supposedly regulate, and about government support flowing to special interests. These worries would be well founded if lobbyists, special interests, and industry representatives actually knew where their long-run interests lay. But the S&L disaster suggests that they lack such foresight. Indeed, this disaster suggests that strong influence may lead special interests and industry representatives to misjudge their abilities, to give away their assets, and to make more erroneous forecasts.

Washington's political climate leads participants to lie about current goals, to reconstruct past goals, to conceal actions, to generate deceptive information, and to disclose others' secrets. Since no one dares to trust those with whom they form coalitions, cooperation becomes unreliable. Since no one can depend on public reports about what is happening, actions have unstable bases. Since dependable facts do not exist, people act on the basis of theories that contradict available facts. The powerful cannot exploit power consistently. They cannot be sure who their friends really are. When they try to help friends, they often harm them inadvertently.

References

Barth, J. R. (1991). *The great savings and loan debacle.* Washington, DC: AEI Press.

Baum, J. A. C., & Oliver, C. (1992). Institutional embeddedness and the dynamics of organizational populations. *American Sociological Review, 57,* 540–559.

Benston, G. J. (1985). *An analysis of the causes of savings and loan association failures.* New York: Salomon Brothers Center for the Study of Financial Institutions, Monograph 1985-4/5.

Brewer, E., Gittings, T., Gonczy, A. M., Merris, R., Mote, L., Nichols, D., & Reichert, A. (1980). The Depository Institutions Deregulation and Monetary Control Act of 1980. *Economic Perspectives,* 4(5):3–23. (Chicago: Federal Reserve Bank of Chicago)

Brumbaugh, R. D. (1988). *Thrifts under siege: Restoring order to American banking.* Cambridge, MA: Ballinger.

Committee on the Budget. (1983). *Hearing before the Committee on the Budget, House of Representatives, Ninety-Eighth Congress, March 8, 1983.* Serial No. 98-5. Washington, DC: U.S. Government Printing Office.

Eichler, N. (1989). *The thrift debacle.* Berkeley: University of California Press.

Friend, I. (1969). *Study of the savings and loan industry.* Washington, DC: Federal Home Loan Bank Board.

Garcia, G., Baer, H., Brewer, E., Allardice, D. R., Cargill, T. F., Dobra, J., Kaufman, G. G., Gonczy, A. M. L., Laurent, R. D., & Mote, L. R. (1983). The Garn-St. Germain Depository Institutions Act of 1982. *Economic Perspectives, 7*(2), 3–31. (Chicago: Federal Reserve Bank of Chicago)

General Accounting Office. (1987). *Financial audit, Federal Savings and Loan Insurance Corporation's 1986 and 1985 financial statements.* Pub. GAO/AFMD-87-41. Washington, DC: U.S. Government Printing Office.

General Accounting Office. (1989). *Thrift failures: Costly failures resulted from regulatory violations and unsafe practices.* Pub. GAO/AFMD-89-62. Washington, DC: U.S. Government Printing Office.

Kane, E. J. (1985). *The gathering crisis in federal deposit insurance.* Cambridge, MA: MIT Press.

Kane, E. J. (1989). *The S&L insurance mess: How did it happen?* Washington, DC: Urban Institute.

Kormendi, R. C., Bernard, V. L., Pirrong, S. C., & Snyder, E. A. (1989). *Crisis resolution in the thrift industry.* Boston: Kluwer.

Lewis, M. M. (1989). *Liar's poker: Rising through the wreckage of Salomon Brothers.* New York: Norton.

Marcis, R. G., & Riordan, D. (1980). The savings and loan industry in the 1980s. *Federal Home Loan Bank Board Journal, 13*(5), 3–15.

Pant, P. N. (1991). *Strategies, environments, effectiveness: Savings and loan associations, 1978–1989.* Ph.D. dissertation, New York University.

Savings & Community Bankers of America. (1994). *1994 Sourcebook.* Washington, DC: Author.

Strunk, N., Case, F. (1988). *Where deregulation went wrong: A look at the causes behind savings and loan failures in the 1980s.* Chicago: U.S. League of Savings Institutions.

Wang, G. H. K., Sauerhaft, D., & Edwards, D. (1987). *Predicting thrift-institution examination ratings.* Washington, DC: Office of Policy and Economic Research, Federal Home Loan Bank Board (working paper).

White, L. J. (1986). The partial deregulation of banks and other depository institutions. In L. W. Weiss & M. K. Klass (Eds.), *Regulatory reform: What actually happened* (pp. 169–209). Boston: Little, Brown.

White, L. J. (1991). *The S&L debacle: Public policy lessons for bank and thrift regulation.* New York: Oxford University Press.

4 Organizational choice under ambiguity: Decision making in the chemical industry following Bhopal

Howard Kunreuther and Jacqueline Meszaros

4.1 Introduction

Organizational decision making would be a relatively simple matter if probabilities could always be estimated and objectives were clear and consistent. Under those conditions, a decision maker could systematically compare and evaluate alternative courses of action with ease. These are not the conditions in the world of modern business, however. Most important, organizational decisions today are made under clouds of ambiguity.

In this chapter we examine how managers in the chemical industry made a set of particularly difficult decisions under ambiguity. Specifically, we explore how several large chemical firms made choices related to reducing the chances of catastrophe following the December 1984 Bhopal disaster. The Bhopal explosion, in which a release of methyl isocyanate from a Union Carbide India plant killed 3,000 people and injured tens of thousands (Shrivastava, 1987; Steiner, 1991), profoundly affected the chemical industry. It led the entire industry to reassess its approach to dealing with low-probability, high-consequence (LP-HC) risks, which are at once intrinsically ambiguous and enormously frightening.

To set the stage for our analysis of ambiguity, we describe, in Section 4.2, how a decision-analytic approach deals with choices among alternatives when probabilities, outcomes, and preferences are not ambiguous. In Section 4.3 we describe types and sources of ambiguity and explore some of their effects on organizational choices. In Section 4.4 three case studies illustrate how ambiguity affected decisions by chemical firms faced with LP-HC risks. Based on these studies, we develop a conceptual framework

Partial support from NSF Grant Number CMS-9415730 and from U.S. EPA Cooperative Agreement Number CR 821947010 is gratefully acknowledged. The authors would like to thank Karen Chinander, Neil Doherty, Paul Kleindorfer, Patrick McNulty, Isadore Rosenthal, and the anonymous company participants in this study for invaluable discussion and comments.

describing how firms deal with these types of ambiguous risks in Section 4.5, then offer some concluding comments in Section 4.6.

4.2 Decision analysis and LP-HC events

Decision analysis techniques help decision makers identify the course of action that will maximize or minimize some prescribed objective (e.g., expected profits, expected utility, expected costs).[1] First, alternative courses of action are identified. For each alternative, potential outcomes are specified and the probabilities associated with each outcome are delineated. The most basic type of decision-analytic problem is one for which the probabilities of all outcomes are easily estimated, where only a single, easily quantified attribute of each outcome matters,[2] and where the individuals making the choice are risk neutral. In this case, the decision analysis will identify the alternative that maximizes expected monetary value.

To illustrate a simple, unambiguous decision-analysis problem, imagine that a large, diversified chemical firm has to decide whether to continue operating a particular business or to sell it. Suppose there is a well-specified annual probability p that this business will suffer an accident, with losses totaling L dollars. The only important consequences that are readily foreseeable are financial ones such as costs due to physical damage to the property. No one would be hurt, and the company's long-term reputation and liabilities would be unaffected by the event. If the firm keeps the business, it will earn R dollars on the investment next year with probability $1 - p$ and $R - L$ dollars with probability p. If the firm sells the business to another company, it will be paid C dollars, which can be invested in other activities yielding an annual rate of return of r percent.

For this problem, only two alternative courses of action need to be considered – selling or keeping the business. The company knows the probability of an accident. The value of each outcome is fully captured by dollar losses and gains. Since the decision makers are risk neutral, the utilities of each outcome can be evaluated in terms of monetary values. The relevant trade-offs are summarized by the decision-analysis diagram in Figure 4.1. As mentioned earlier, decision analysis would lead the firm to choose the alternative that maximizes expected monetary value (EV).[3] Let EV_s = the expected value of selling the business. Let EV_k = the expected value of keeping the business. Then

$$EV_s = rC$$
$$EV_k = p (R - L) + (1 - p) R = R - pL$$

The firm should sell the business whenever $EV_s > EV_k$. Suppose that $R = 200$, $C = 1,000$, $r = .10$, $p = .001$, and $L = 50,000$. In this case, $EV_s = 100$, and $EV_k = R - pL = 150$, so the firm will want to keep the business.

Now assume that the firm is risk averse. Utilities for risk-averse decision makers, in contrast to risk-neutral ones, do not mirror the order and scaling

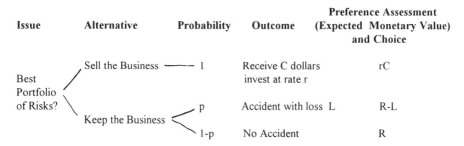

Figure 4.1. Decision analysis: Sell or keep the business? (Risk-neutral firm.)

Issue	Alternative	Probability	Outcome	Preference Assessment (Subjective Expected Utility) and Choice
Best Portfolio of Risks?	Sell the Business	1	Receive C	$U(W + rC)$
	Keep the Business	p	Accident	$U(W + R - L)$
		1-p	No Accident	$U(W + R)$

Figure 4.2. Decision analysis: Sell or keep the business? (Risk-averse firm.)

of dollar values. For example, a risk-neutral individual would consider a 10% chance of a $1,000,000 loss to be equivalent to a sure loss of $100,000. A risk-averse person would treat the uncertain event as *more* than 10 times worse than the sure loss. When such subjective risk preferences are relevant, the optimal course of action maximizes *subjective expected utility (SEU)* rather than EV. Let $U(x)$ represent the utility associated with outcome x.

Initial asset or wealth (W) positions affect the choices of risk-averse decision makers. In particular, the ratio of maximum potential loss to total wealth matters to them. Thus, firms with greater wealth will generally be willing to take more risks than firms with less wealth.[4] The elements of a decision analysis with the objective of maximizing expected utility for risk-averse firms are depicted in Figure 4.2. The firm should sell the business whenever $U(W + rC) > (1 - p) U(W + R) + p U(W + R - L)$. Using the values from the previous numerical example, the firm will want to sell the business if $U(W + 100) > .999 U(W + 200) + .001 U(W - 49,800)$.

Note that in contrast to the risk-neutral firm, a risk-averse company might prefer to sell the business rather than subjecting the firm to the large negative disutility of an accident. In other words, if a firm is sufficiently risk averse and is concerned with the impact of a possible large loss on its asset or wealth level, it may prefer a course of action that avoids this outcome even when the probability of loss is extremely small.

4.3 Types of ambiguity and their effects on organizational choices

The choice process is much more complicated when there is ambiguity about probabilities and/or outcomes. As will be described later, both of these types of ambiguity normally accompany LP-HC risks because it is difficult to estimate probabilities for rare events and to define objectives for catastrophic ones. Although a decision-analytic representation, similar to the ones depicted earlier, may be useful for structuring LP-HC decision problems, decision analysis has limited usefulness in ambiguous contexts.

4.3.1 Ambiguity about probabilities

When the distributions of probabilities associated with specific outcomes are uncertain, *probability ambiguity* is present.[5] Let us consider how probability ambiguity complicates the problem discussed earlier: the firm's decision to sell or keep a business that poses a small chance of an accident with severe consequences.

Limited past data. When there is considerable experience with a particular phenomenon, process, or technology, then it is often possible to estimate the probability *p* of a common outcome with some precision. A large sample of experiential data can often yield reliable estimates of the probabilities of various events. When a phenomenon is new or rare, only limited experiential data are available. LP-HC industrial risks are, by definition, rare and usually are related to phenomena with which there is limited past experience. Hence there is considerable ambiguity about experience-based estimates of probabilities of bad events. For example, it is hard to assess the reliability of estimates of the chances of nuclear power plant accidents for several reasons. Such accidents are rare events because there are only a few nuclear plants with any single design operating in the world, and no nuclear plant has been operating more than 30 years (Perrow, 1984). The available experience base is not adequate to yield reliable estimates of the low-probability dangers associated with these essentially new technologies.

As a supplement to experience-based estimates of accident probabilities, organizations can base probability estimates on near misses. For example, by collecting information about near-accidents from pilots and air traffic controllers, the sample of events related to potential airline accidents is considerably expanded (Hardy, 1990; March, Sproull & Tamuz, 1991). In order for these estimates to be accurate, though, managers have to interpret near-miss experiences appropriately. NASA's experience with faulty O-rings on the space shuttle Challenger shows that organizations can learn the wrong things from small samples. Several successful Challenger missions were flown with faulty O-rings. These events were interpreted by many engineers as lucky draws from a probability distribution where there was a good chance of a disaster. Other NASA managers felt that the success of these missions indicated that the O-rings would not pose a problem (Starbuck & Milliken, 1988).

Causal ambiguity. Scientific or causal models of how certain accidents, injuries, or diseases occur can sometimes be the best basis for estimating outcome probabilities. Causal ambiguity exists when it is not clear whether particular actions will produce particular outcomes (Lippman & Rumelt, 1982; Reed & DeFillipi, 1990). This can make it hard to specify outcomes, probabilities, or both. Alvin Weinberg (1972) coined the term "transcientific" to categorize hazards for which there are no causal models and insufficient data to specify potential outcomes and their probabilities. In situations where consensus among experts or scientists is the best available approximation of truth, either absence of causal models or disagreements among experts about the implications of available models and evidence yields ambiguity about probabilities.

A familiar situation where causal ambiguity operates has to do with childhood vaccinations. Hundreds of thousands of babies receive pertussis vaccines in this country every year. In a few unfortunate children, severe brain damage occurs in the days following vaccination. These instances of brain damage are so rare that statistical tests have never established whether the vaccine causes it (Rabinovich & Robbins, 1994). To date, no causal models exist suggesting that any of the components of the vaccine cause brain damage.

Some expert medical groups have responded to the available evidence by emphasizing that they "cannot conclude that the vaccine causes chronic brain damage" (Child Neurology Society, 1991), and others have declared that "there may or may not be a causal connection" (Howson & Fineberg, 1992). The subtle differences in language chosen by these groups suggest expert disagreement and ambiguity to some readers. At least one highly visible parents' group has raised questions about the quality of the research on which these experts' judgments are based and appears to believe that the vaccine does cause serious brain damage (Coulter & Fisher, 1985), further highlighting the ambiguity in the situation. Each year, millions of parents must decide whether to vaccinate their children. They must make this decision under conditions of probability ambiguity with their children's well-being at stake.

4.3.2 Ambiguity about preferences

When decision makers are uncertain about their own utility functions, *preference ambiguity* is present (March, 1988). Even if all the objectives, alternatives, probabilities, and outcomes associated with a decision situation have been identified, a decision maker will not be able to choose among alternatives if the relative preferences for different outcomes cannot be specified.

Differing objectives. Identifying a firm's preferences relative to LP-HC hazards is a complex problem. Suppose a manager seeks to make a decision that would be perceived to be socially responsible. It is likely that different constituencies – including internal stakeholders like managers from different functional areas, as well as external stakeholders like communities and customers – will have different preference functions and risk propensities. No single choice of objectives will be perceived as most responsible by all. Some individuals will advise that the action taken should minimize maximum potential harm (Rawls, 1971). This rule would lead firms to reduce the chances of catastrophic accidents but might lead them to accept a higher probability of less severe accidents if limited resources prevent them from mitigating both types. The U.S. 1990 Clean Air Act Amendments (Section 112r), which force firms to develop risk-management plans for analyzing worst-case accident scenarios, reflect this type of risk preference.

Other constituencies might prefer that a firm minimize the number of people exposed to risks or that a firm minimize the risk to highly vulnerable populations, such as small children and fetuses. Fetal protection policies, which exclude women of childbearing age from jobs that might be hazardous to fetuses, reflect this value (Murray, 1985). There is empirical evidence that other members of society want firms to eliminate certain psychologically disturbing risks (e.g., nuclear power plant risks, large airplane crashes) but are willing to accept more likely but less dreaded ones (e.g., smoking cigarettes, auto crashes) (Sandman, Weinstein, & Klotz, 1987; Slovic, 1987).

Accountability and responsibility. External forces are not the only influences on preference ambiguity in an organization. Internal forces, such as formal and informal incentives and accountability, can also affect it. As defined by Tetlock (1985), accountability is a social–psychological link between individual decision makers and the social systems to which they belong. Operationally, accountability is what links responsibility with incentives. Individuals are accountable when their performance is monitored and when they know that positive or negative rewards will follow their efforts and outcomes.

The more ambiguous the incentive system and the degree of accountability, the less sure the decision maker will be about the firm's preferences. Garud and Shapira (this volume) have conducted research suggesting that when information about the repercussions of bad outcomes is not shared in advance, employees and supervisors are more likely to disagree about who is responsible when decisions lead to bad outcomes.

The distribution of responsibilities among organizational entities can sometimes contribute to preference ambiguity as well. If it is known that a particular business unit will be held budgetarily responsible for the consequences of a particular decision, the managers in that unit will be more likely to pay attention to the associated risks. If managers are unsure about who will pay if an accident occurs (i.e., the department, plant, business unit, corporation, insurer, or reinsurer), or if they have never been forced to consider the question, they may pay too little attention to the attendant risks because they assume they will *not* be held responsible for the consequences.

Another determinant of agents' preferences is their anticipation that they will have to justify their decisions after they are made. In a set of experiments exploring for possible psychological sources of ambiguity aversion, Curley, Yates, and Abrams (1986) found that the anticipation that others would later evaluate their decisions led subjects to make ambiguity-averse decisions. Since managers know that others will later evaluate their choices, they may prefer unambiguous to ambiguous alternatives. As Casey and Scholz (1991) point out, a choice involving a precise probability is more easily justified than one involving a vague or ambiguous one. Even if managers' judgments are not scrutinized at the time their decisions are made, they may anticipate that if a bad outcome, such as an accident, occurs, they will have to justify their previous decisions both to other firm members and to outsiders (Staw, 1980).

If plant managers know that they will be held accountable for the environmental and financial effects of a chemical release, and if they know that their compensation and advancement will be affected, then they will be more likely to avoid these risks. In surveys of Israeli and American managers, Shapira (1995) found that many executives advised new managers to avoid taking risks if these managers perceived that they might have to assume full responsibility for negative outcomes.

4.3.3 Implications for organizational behavior

Ambiguity about probabilities and preferences parallel two kinds of uncertainty that Thompson (1967) long ago identified as having organizational significance: uncertainty about cause–effect relations and uncertainty about outcome preferences. Thompson hypothesized that when there is a great deal of ambiguity about cause–effect relations – which means that the organization cannot easily predict the effects of its actions on its task environment (i.e., a form of probability ambiguity) – an organization will include more technical specialists in its dominant coalition. Similarly, he posited that when there is ambiguity about which alternatives an organization ought to pursue (i.e., a form of preference ambiguity), the dominant coalition will include representatives of the knowledge areas relevant to all the dimensions of the alternatives and outcomes that might matter to the organization. Thompson's rationale for these predictions was that ambiguous conditions create opportunities for people with information to gain power. These people can either help resolve the ambiguity or help the organization to operate in spite of it.

4.4 Three case studies on decision making under ambiguity

In this section we examine three case studies of firms in the chemical industry making highly consequential decisions in the ambiguous context of LP-HC risks. All three were making choices about whether to accept, divest, or somehow mitigate LP-HC risks following the accident at Bhopal. In complex and ambiguous situations, managers often rely on heuristics, or rules of thumb, to simplify decision making. By proceeding in this way rather than using more formal benefit–cost approaches, such as decision analysis, firms avoid estimating ambiguous probabilities and clarifying ambiguous preferences. The three case studies indicate that the chemical firms used nonprobabilistic reference points in conjunction with or instead of using decision analyses to reach decisions under ambiguity. They also indicate that the firms were aware that they were avoiding the use of ambiguous information. The cases suggest a model for how firms cope with probability ambiguity and preference ambiguity when making decisions, at least with respect to LP-HC risks.

Consider the overall context in which a major multinational chemical firm makes its strategic decisions. Most firms make some potentially hazardous products and use some hazardous products during production. Like any other corporation, a chemical firm must address such issues as what existing products should be retained; what new products should be introduced; where they should be produced; where they should be sold; and what investments should be made to improve the operation of existing businesses. In the background, there are questions about how the firm should relate to its stakeholders, such as employees, customers, and environmental activists. Since the possibility of catastrophes cannot be eliminated, it is a constant backdrop to strategic decision making in this industry.

Each of the firms in the case studies faced considerable probability and preference ambiguity, making it difficult to use decision analysis to choose among alternatives. Probability ambiguity occurred for all of the reasons discussed in Section 4.3: Experts disagreed about the probability of catastrophic risks; there was limited experience with the technologies involved; complexity, specificity, and uncertainty characterized some of the technologies; and interpretations of the causes of past accidents and near misses varied, making it hard to draw lessons for safer operations. Preference ambiguity also operated. Externally, no social norm or well-established standard or regulation indicated which risks would be considered worse than others (Breyer, 1993). Stakeholder risk preferences were neither constant nor consistent. Internally, there was often uncertainty about who would be accountable or responsible and what the consequences would be if a catastrophe occurred. These internal vagaries exacerbate preference ambiguity.

4.4.1 Decision making at Chemco

Background information. Chemco is a pseudonym for a multinational Fortune 500 chemical firm. A set of 20 hour-long interviews conducted immediately after the Bhopal disaster made it clear that the disaster led Chemco to make significant changes in some of its decision-making procedures and to reevaluate certain business strategies that earlier had not been considered troublesome (Bowman & Kunreuther, 1988).

Following Bhopal, Chemco ordered a systematic reevaluation of all of its chemicals with the potential to cause a catastrophic accident. In performing this analysis, the company did not conduct formal risk assessments to estimate the probabilities of such events. Instead, Chemco developed worst-case scenarios (WCS) characterizing the effects of the worst imaginable releases of their most hazardous substances. In doing so, they sought to identify any substance that, if released under worst-case conditions, could produce an incident that resembled Bhopal.

Another set of interviews was conducted at Chemco in 1991 to determine what major strategic changes had occurred in the $6^{1}/_{2}$ years since Bhopal and the rationales used to justify them. Ten executives with line or staff responsibility for safety and environmental issues were interviewed.

Selling the surfactant business. One unexpected but important action taken by the firm as a result of Bhopal was that it sold its surfactant business. The sale of this business was not foreseen by any of the Chemco executives interviewed immediately after Bhopal. Chemco had operated this business, which used ethylene oxide (EO) in its production process, for many years. It was a profitable operation, but its value to the company was entirely self-contained; its outputs were not used in any of Chemco's other production processes.

Chemco had always known that EO was potentially explosive. Prior to Bhopal, they were comfortable using EO because their analyses indicated that their protective measures were sufficient, so that no employee was subject to significant risks from the chemical. As one Chemco executive explained, they felt there was less chance of an employee being hurt in a serious EO accident "than of [that] person being hit by lightning." Those outside the plant, farther from the EO, faced even less risk. Before Bhopal, the company did *not* focus directly on risks to the community; rather, they focused on minimizing risks to those closest to hazards as a means of minimizing risks to those farther away.

Chemco decided to sell its surfactant business in 1990. Managers in the firm agreed that the Bhopal accident was an important trigger for this action. All of those interviewed felt that the risk of transporting EO was the principal reason for this decision. No estimates of the probability of such an accident were ever made by Chemco. Rather, in the aftermath of Bhopal, the specter of a truckload of EO being released into a community was something the firm did not want to live with. As one Chemco executive noted:

Transportation risk got us out of the surfactant business. The facilities were old and needed upgrading, but the principal reason for getting out of the business was that we had to ship EO (Kunreuther & Bowman, in press).

Economic considerations such as decreased profitability of the business, capital constraints and an attractive opportunity to sell the plant, were factored into the final choice. Still, the Bhopal accident was considered an important trigger for this action. When the firm focused on WCS involving people outside the plant gates, they concluded that they were not willing to live with this risk.

The final decision to sell the surfactant business involved all the managers concerned with the risk of EO in a process of shared decision making. The managers participated in considering the consequences and in developing and evaluating alternatives. However, none of them ever considered utilizing formal risk assessment methods to evaluate the risk. Rather, they preferred to focus on WCS instead of grappling with ambiguous probability estimates.[6]

4.4.2 Decision making at Twochem

Like Chemco and other firms in the industry, Twochem initiated a review of all of its chemicals with catastrophic potential following Bhopal. Also as with Chemco, this initial review focused on credible WCS without attempting to estimate their associated probabilities. Twochem's executives indicated that they expected that, following Bhopal, any catastrophe by any chemical firm would very likely bankrupt the firm through severe liability awards, penalties, damage to reputation, and increased regulatory scrutiny. Twochem therefore chose to investigate the advisability and feasibility of reducing risk from any substance in their firm that could bankrupt them if the worst possible release occurred.

Initial screening. Twochem first screened all of their most hazardous substances – every hazard for which they felt an accident involving deaths outside plant gates was credible, even if it was extremely unlikely. The definition of *credibility* derived from safety engineering practices. A common safety engineering technique is to design against known or possible failure modes until the decision makers believe the protections are so reliable that they essentially could not fail in the event of an accident. At this point, the accident is considered "noncredible." A noncredible event thus reflects decision makers' intuitions about when probabilities have become so small that they are viewed as negligible. Twochem chose to conduct probabilistic risk assessments (PRAs) for all hazards with credible catastrophic potential.

Issue identification. Previous experience with PRAs had taught Twochem that they could not reach decisions based on the results of such analyses alone. The analyses did not indicate the relative priorities of risks because they did not incorporate the firm's safety objectives. Initially, Twochem's safety objectives were not well formulated. The managers wanted the firm to satisfy the safety concerns of its many business and societal stakeholders, but it had never resolved conflicting preferences across these groups. To resolve this preference ambiguity, the corporation's process safety director consulted past corporation studies and, based on these, developed an *analytic funnel* for prioritizing risks and risk reduction measures (Bailey & Rastogi, 1994).

The analytic funnel classified catastrophic outcomes. Hazards were sorted into three categories of potential accidents: those with low, medium, and high levels of potential off-site fatalities. Twochem first gave priority to reducing the risks from the high-consequence accidents. The company's policy was that these risks had to be mitigated immediately. Medium-consequence hazards would be addressed later, and low-consequence risks were given the lowest priority. This procedure ensured that the hazards with the most extensive worst-case damage potential were mitigated first, an objective that the company felt was consistent with expressed societal priorities following Bhopal.

The funnel procedure used by Twochem does not allow the firm to make trade-offs among high-, medium-, and low-consequence events. There are situations in which reducing a high-probability of a relatively low loss might result in more lives saved per dollar than reducing the probability of an LP-HC risk. Thus, an unresolved concern with this approach is that it may not yield the greatest social benefit, that is, the greatest overall reduction in risk.

Role of probability assessments. Twochem conducted PRAs, sometimes called *quantitative risk assessments,* to assess the mitigation risks generated by their WCS-based screening. For each major hazard, a multifunctional team of engineering, safety, and operations personnel under the direction of an engineering project manager was assigned to analyze the risk mitigation alternatives and make recommendations. These teams used PRAs to examine production configurations and mitigation alternatives.

To construct its PRAs, Twochem first identified its hazardous chemicals and then developed fault trees specifying all the ways in which those chemicals could be released. For each mitigation alternative being considered, probabilities were estimated for each failure path and the consequences of each failure were characterized and weighted by their probabilities to yield expected loss estimates.[7]

To illustrate the use of this approach, suppose the potential failure of a storage tank containing a flammable material was considered a credible event that would have severe impacts on the surrounding community. Assume that this tank has been built with several concentric walls or skins that make it hard to penetrate. Analysts would first specify all the ways in which a serious leak might occur. For example, a plane could crash into the tank or some other projectile (e.g., shrapnel from a nearby explosion) could puncture the multiple skins.

The analysts would then create a fault tree composed of all potential penetration events combined with their probabilities (e.g., the probability of a plane crash in this location; the conjunctive probability of explosions nearby coupled with the probability of shrapnel from such an explosion penetrating the tank). The damage that would result from each of these events would be evaluated and weighted by its respective probability. The sum of these products would constitute the expected losses for this tank. Assume that several tank designs were being considered for reducing the risk. The expected losses for each alternative design would be estimated and compared.

The analysis team reached a consensus on each part of the PRAs as they proceeded. In part because of this stepwise consensus, they were comfortable with their final estimates even though they recognized the inherent ambiguity of the probability estimates. The sharing of responsibility for obtaining these figures helped the relevant decision makers determine what actions needed to be taken to avoid future chemical disasters.

In sum, Twochem used a two-stage process for coping with probability ambiguity. First, a WCS was used to determine which hazardous chemical risks would get attention. Second, for these chemicals, the firm used sophisticated risk assessment procedures to estimate probabilities of different events occurring in order to determine which mitigation options would be most desirable.

4.4.3 Decision making in Threechem

Threechem also conducted a post-Bhopal WCS-based assessment of hazards with off-site catastrophic potential. Unlike Twochem, the firm chose not to use PRAs because they were uncomfortable estimating probabilities for catastrophic accidents and were not sure how they would use these figures if they were provided by risk analysts. As one manager noted:

We can't deal with probabilities. We don't know what an acceptable probability is. If it's one in 28,000 years but next year is the year, you are in big trouble.

Use of consequence analyses. Threechem conducted consequence analyses (CA), which described the outcomes of worst-case accidents for all the hazards the firm had identified as having catastrophic potential. Although probabilities were not explicitly addressed, they played an implicit role in the CAs because Threechem evaluated "credible" WCS rather than absolute worst cases.[8] To illustrate the difference between these two types of scenarios, consider the potential release of a firm's entire supply of toxic gas into a community. If experts could not envision a way that the entire tank could rupture and release all its contents at once, this scenario would be considered *noncredible*. If they could envision scenarios in which the toxic gas could be released into the community over a period of several hours, this would be a *credible* WCS.

At one site, Threechem was concerned about the potential release of a large amount of EO into a residential neighborhood that included schools. They believed that such an accident could result in a number of deaths in the community, and they considered the risk credible though extremely unlikely. They assembled a team of safety and business managers to conduct a CA for this EO hazard and hired an engineering consulting firm to assist the team.

The Threechem employees on the team were not closely involved in the analyses. They mainly deliberated over the final recommended alternatives. Interestingly, the preferences of team members reflected their functions in the organization. Three alternatives were analyzed. Everyone rejected Alternative 1, a plan to refurbish the existing plant. That plan would, in the opinion of team members, keep the firm involved with some (albeit fewer) credible bankrupting risks. The team was split in its preferences between the remaining two alternatives. Business managers preferred Alternative 2, an extensive renovation plan that met most safety concerns. Safety managers favored the third and most expensive option, complete redesign and relocation of the facility. This was the only option that met all safety concerns. This interdisciplinary team – which, like Twochem's team, included managers representing many company functions but that, unlike Twochem's, had not engaged in progressive consensus building during analysis – could not reach a consensus on the choice.

The firm had no well-defined mechanism for resolving the impass. The team turned to the CEO for guidance. He stated, informally but forcefully, that he thought the firm should "develop a world-class system so that we provide maximum protection for our own employees, the general public, and the environment." The team adopted this statement as a proxy for the firm's preferences. *Maximum protection* was not an operational term at Threechem; they had no guidelines on what was an acceptable risk. Therefore, the team deliberated and decided that the third, most expensive option – redesign and relocate – was most consistent with the CEO's statement. They adopted that plan.

4.5 A conceptual framework for choices involving LP-HC events

The ambiguity associated with LP-HC events leads organizations to approach choices somewhat differently than decision-analysis methods pre-

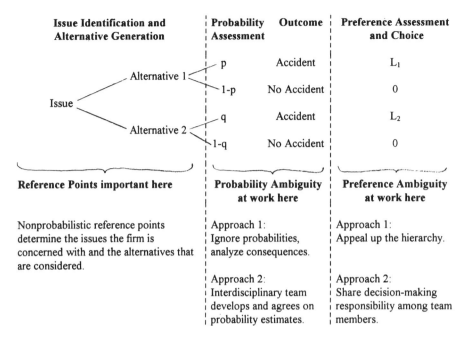

Figure 4.3. Sources and mechanisms for coping with ambiguity in the LP-HC decision making.

scribe. In this section we expand the decision-analysis framework developed in Section 4.2 to encompass the processes the firms in our case studies used to cope with LP-HC decisions under ambiguity. As depicted in Figure 4.3, the steps in the cases parallel the steps prescribed by decision analysis (Fig. 4.1 and Fig. 4.2). However, the types of information collected and the way the data are used in choosing among alternatives are different in the presence of ambiguity.

4.5.1 Issue identification and alternative generation

Before considering alternative courses of action, a firm must consider moving from its current position. It must acknowledge that an issue must be addressed; otherwise, it will not consider changes. A large literature in organizational theory emphasizes the tendency of firms to *use the status quo* as a *reference point* and resist change (Cyert & March 1963; Samuelson & Zeckhauser, 1988). Miller and Friesen (1980, p. 591) contend:

The one theme that stands out in the literature is that organizations tend to demonstrate great sluggishness in adapting to their environments. Organizations often resist change even when their environments threaten them with extinction.

An organization's interest in change is sometimes triggered by an external event that raises a new, highly salient reference point for the firm to focus on. *Ruin or survivability reference points* have been found to be particularly salient. Libby and Fishburn (1977), reviewing several studies of managers making decisions with potentially ruinous downside risks, found that the best model for predicting individuals' decisions was one in which the potential for a ruinous loss is used as an absolute constraint: Any project for which a WCS included insolvency of the firm was removed from consideration. A set of interviews exploring managers' attitudes toward risk reported in March and Shapira (1992) found a similar threshhold-triggered unwillingness to take risks with any potential to jeopardize the survival of the firm.

In the cases we have examined, the consequences of the Bhopal disaster acted as a ruin-related reference point that displaced the status quo as the motivating reference point for the firms. The firms indicated their belief that societal attitudes following Bhopal had shifted so that any firm having an accident with significant off-site consequences would not survive. They therefore focused on the need to avoid worst cases that resembled Bhopal. This forced them to move away from their status quo positions.

The most elaborate example of using a Bhopal-based reference point to identify issues was the analytic funnel used by Twochem. In designing that device, Twochem made it explicit that catastrophes with off-site potential would have to be mitigated due to their similarity to Bhopal. Less elaborate but similar processes were used by the other two firms. By defining the issue-generation process in terms of a nonprobabilistic reference point, the firms avoided ambiguous probabilities at this initial stage of decision making.

Once a firm accepts an issue, it identifies potential courses of action. Nonprobabilistic reference points were also used to determine which hazards would receive attention. By using nonprobabilistic WCS as reference points, the firms avoided working with ambiguous estimates at this stage as well. It is worth noting, however, that the firms did not escape probabilities entirely because probabilities were implicit in the firms' worst-case *credible* scenarios.

4.5.2 Probability assessment

Figure 4.3 also outlines the two approaches firms took to dealing with the analysis of probabilities in this ambiguous context. Firms that chose Approach 1 avoided explicit estimates of probability entirely by focusing only on consequences. They were not willing to estimate probabilities that would necessarily be ambiguous. Those that chose Approach 2 employed past experience, scientific models, and interdisciplinary teams of experts to quantify relevant probabilities. In Chemco and Twochem, interdisciplinary teams conducted the analyses. The teams included all relevant technical specialties, ensuring that the best available information and judgment would be incorporated into the final estimates. Also, the analysis process was designed so that these teams built consensus at each stage of the estimation process. This design gave the decision makers confidence that the team had developed the most reliable probability estimates possible, though ambiguity was unavoidable. Hence, the design of the analysis process was important to the eventual usefulness of the final products.

4.5.3 Preference assessment and choice

At the choice stage of the decision, as reflected in Figure 4.3, preference ambiguity operates. The outcomes that mattered to the firms in our cases included potential immediate damage and losses to the organization itself, health and safety effects on the surrounding region, and long-range consequences to the firm and its constituents. Having estimated these, though, the firms still faced preference ambiguity, that is, uncertainty about which sets of outcomes would be preferable to which others.

Threechem suffered preference ambiguity arising from internal conflicts: Managers with different functional responsibilities had different preferences. They dealt with this problem by appealing to executives higher up in the hierarchy. This meant that they adopted the preference order expressed by the CEO, the least hierarchically vulnerable individual (Approach 1). Chemco and Twochem had to grapple with preference ambiguity arising from external sources – from conflicting stakeholder preferences. They dealt with this issue by using shared decision making. Responsibility for the final choice was diffused among everyone involved in the process (Approach 2). Thus, the way these organizations managed responsibility and accountability affected their ability to reach decisions under preference ambiguity.

4.6 Conclusions

The three case studies illustrate mechanisms that allow firms to cope with probability and outcome ambiguity when making major decisions. Nonprobabilistic reference points and responsibility-managing mechanisms were important in all three cases.

4.6.1 Nonprobabilistic analyses: The roles of reference points

For all three firms, the Bhopal explosion led to new reference points for catastrophic risks. First, the firms' ruin or survivability reference points shifted, causing them to worry that they might be living with some low-probability risks that could ruin them. The new reference point led to new hazard-mitigation priorities in all three firms.

Second, the types of risky phenomena the firms monitored to ensure safety changed. Prior to Bhopal, the firms had focused on reducing hazards to workers, presuming that the safety measures for the employees would also provide the greatest protection for those outside plant gates.

After Bhopal, all of these firms measured the catastrophic potential of their chemicals in terms of their possible impact on surrounding communities.

Finally, the firms used WCS in various ways as reference points for identifying hazards that needed attention or for choosing among mitigation alternatives. Chemco generated WCS and compared them with the accident at Bhopal to identify those that could have serious financial repercussions for the firm. Twochem used the analytic funnel to ensure that the firm first mitigated the risks with the greatest potential to ruin it (which corresponded to the greatest off-site damage). Threechem rejected mitigation alternatives that did not pass the survivability test. These devices related closely to the survivability or ruin reference points; the firms were anxious not to live with any risks involving the chance that the firm would be ruined.

4.6.2 Coping with ambiguity: Managing responsibility for decisions

With regard to probability ambiguity, Threechem's managers knew that any estimates of the likelihood of a catastrophic accident would be fraught with ambiguity. Hence they were unwilling to estimate probabilities in their evaluations of their LP-HC risks. They relied instead on WCS-based consequence analyses. Since their definition of *worst case* included the credibility criterion, they were, in fact, implicitly considering probabilities.

Chemco and Twochem, on the other hand, used probabilistic risk analyses to determine which mitigation alternatives should be adopted. They involved managers from all relevant functions, with all forms of relevant technical expertise, in these choices. This built confidence that the estimates were the best ones that *could* be developed. This inclusive process allowed the participants to accept the results of the analyses while still recognizing their inherent limitations.

In addition to the previously discussed methods for dealing with probability ambiguity, the firms had to cope with preference ambiguity. Chemco and Twochem were concerned about preference ambiguity arising from conflicts among external stakeholder goals and objectives. They coped with these differences by developing priorities that they thought reflected overall societal preferences, as explicated in public debates over Bhopal.

The principal source of preference ambiguity for Threechem was different. It was due to conflicting objectives among functional departments within the firm. Threechem resolved the problem by adopting the preferences of the highest-ranking corporate executive with a stake in the decision as a proxy for the firm's preferences.

The firms in these three cases frequently expressed frustration and dissatisfaction with the need to make weighty decisions under ambiguity for LP-HC risks. Better techniques for drawing probability estimates from low-frequency data, more consensus about societal risk preferences, better ex ante understanding of the consequences of future accidents, and arrangements to mitigate the effects of accidents if they occur would all help these firms feel more comfortable when making such decisions. In the meantime, the ambiguity-coping mechanisms that have evolved have several traits in common. They put survivability first, focus on the effects of accidents outside plant gates, encompass diverse technical experts to develop the best estimates under ambiguity, and diffuse decision-making responsibility and accountability for the final choice.

Notes

1   For a systematic overview of decision analysis, see Raiffa (1968) and Keeney (1982).
2   For most real-world problems, multiple objectives or attributes, including hard-to-quantify and incommensurable attributes, matter to the decision maker. Corporate objectives, for example, often include minimizing health and safety hazards, minimizing environmental impacts, and minimizing costs. In these situations, multiattribute utility assessment procedures can be used. For more detail on alternative ways of structuring these problems, eliciting the relevant utilities, and combining them into a single outcome measure, see Keeney and Raiffa (1976).
3   The expected value of any course of action is the value of each outcome multiplied by its probability summed over all outcomes.
4   An exception to this general rule occurs when maximum losses exceed total firm wealth. Firms should be willing to invest in risk prevention or care up to the point where the value of the care (i.e., the reduction in expected loss) exceeds the cost of the investment (Landes & Posner, 1987; Shavell, 1987). Since a firm cannot be held liable for losses that exceed its assets, there is no incentive to prevent against these losses.
5   The concept of *ambiguity* was initially introduced formally into the literature by the economist Frank Knight (1921) when he distinguished between risk and uncertainty. Knight defined a random variable as risky if the probabilities of the outcomes were known. He defined it as uncertain if the probabilities were not known (i.e., if the distribution of the probabilities was uncertain). Daniel Ellsberg (1961) used the term *ambiguity* much as Knight used *uncertainty*. To Ellsberg, ambiguity was a state between ignorance and knowledge of a probability distribution. This is the definition we are using here. For a comprehensive review of work on probability ambiguity, see Camerer and Weber (1992).
6   For more details on this case, see Kunreuther and Bowman (in press).
7   For a more detailed discussion of the use of probabilistic or quantitative risk assessments, see Morgan and Henrion (1990). Graham and Rhomberg (1996) provide an overview of the scientific basis of risk assessment and the capabilities and limitations of risk analysis. The elements of a PRA are also described in detail in Rasmussen (1981).
8   Threechem used the term *credible* the same way Twochem used it.

References

Bailey, E., & Rastogi, A. (1994). *The decision funnel approach for preventing major process accidents*. Public policy department working paper, the Wharton School, University of Pennsylvania, Philadelphia.

Bowman, E., & Kunreuther, H. (1988). Post-Bhopal behaviour at a chemical company. *Journal of Management Studies*, 25(4), 387–401.

Breyer, S. (1993). *Breaking the vicious circle: Toward effective risk regulation.* Cambridge, MA: Harvard University Press.

Camerer, C., & Weber, M. (1992). Recent developments in modeling preferences: Uncertainty and ambiguity. *Journal of Risk and Uncertainty, 5,* 325–370.

Casey, J. T., & Scholz, J. T. (1991). Boundary effects of vague risk information on taxpayer decisions. *Organizational Behavior and Human Decision Processes, 50,* 360–394.

Child Neurology Society, Ad Hoc Committee. (1991). Pertussis immunization and the central nervous system. *Annals of Neurology, 29*(4), 458–460.

Coulter, H. L., & Fisher, B. L. (1985). *DPT: A shot in the dark.* New York: Warner Books.

Curley, S., Yates, J. F., & Abrams, R. A. (1986). Psychological sources of ambiguity avoidance. *Organizational Behavior and Human Decision Processes, 38,* 230–256.

Cyert, R., & March, J. (1963). *A behavioral theory of the firm.* Englewood Cliffs, NJ: Prentice-Hall.

Ellsberg, D. (1961). Risk, ambiguity, and the Savage axioms. *Quarterly Journal of Economics, 75,* 643–699.

Graham, J., & Rhomberg, L. (1996). How risks are identified and assessed. *Annals of the American Academy of Political and Social Science, 545,* 15–24.

Hardy, R. (1990). *CALLBACK; NASA's aviation safety reporting system.* Washington, DC: Smithsonian Institution Press.

Howson, C. P., & Fineberg, H. F. (1992). Adverse effects following pertussis and rubella vaccines: Summary of report of the Institute of Medicine. *Journal of the American Medical Association, 267*(3), 392–396.

Keeney, R. (1982). Decision analysis: An overview. *Operations Research, 30,* 803–838.

Keeney, R., & Raiffa, H. (1976). *Decisions with multiple objectives: Preferences and value tradeoffs.* New York: Wiley.

Knight, F. H. (1921). *Risk, uncertainty, and profit.* Boston: Houghton Mifflin.

Kunreuther, H., & Bowman, E. (in press). A dynamic model of organizational decision making: Chemco revisited six years after Bhopal. *Organization Science.*

Landes, W. M., & Posner, R. A. (1987). *The economic structure of tort law.* Cambridge, MA: Harvard University Press.

Libby, R., & Fishburn, P. C. (1977). Behavioral models of risk taking in business decisions: A survey and evaluation. *Journal of Accounting Research,* Autumn, 272–292.

Lippman, S. A., & Rumelt, R. P. (1982). Uncertain imitability: An analysis of inter-firm differences in efficiency under competition. *Bell Journal of Economics, 13,* 418–438.

March, J. G. (1988). *Decisions and organizations.* Oxford: Basil Blackwell.

March, J. G., & Shapira, Z. (1992). Variable risk preferences and the focus of attention. *Psychological Review, 99*(1), 172–183.

March, J. G., Sproull, L. S., & Tamuz, M. (1991). Learning from samples of one or fewer. *Organization Science, 2*(1), 1–13.

Miller, D., & Friesen, P. H. (1980). Momentum and revolution in organizational adaptation. *Academy of Management Journal, 23,* 591–614.

Morgan, G., & Henrion, M. (1990). *Uncertainty: A guide to dealing with uncertainty in quantitative risk and policy analysis.* Cambridge: Cambridge University Press.

Murray, T. (1985). Who do fetal-protection polices really protect? *Technology Review, 88,* 12–13, 20.

Perrow, C. (1984). *Normal accidents.* New York: Basic Books.

Rabinovich, R., & Robbins, A. (1994). Editorial: Pertussis vaccines: A progress report. *Journal of the American Medical Association, 271*(1), 68–69.

Raiffa, H. (1968). *Decision analysis: Introductory lectures on choices under uncertainty.* Reading, MA: Addison-Wesley.

Rasmussen, N. (1981). The application of probabilistic risk assessment techniques to energy technologies. In T. Glickman & M. Gough (Eds.), *Readings in risk* (pp. 195–206). Washington, DC: Resources for the Future.

Rawls, J. (1971). *A theory of justice.* Cambridge, MA: Harvard University Press.

Reed, R., & DeFillipi, R. J. (1990). Causal ambiguity, barriers to imitation, and sustainable competitive advantage. *Academy of Management Review, 15,* 88–102.

Samuelson, W., & Zeckhauser, R. (1988). Status quo bias in decision making. *Journal of Risk and Uncertainty, 1,* 7–59.

Sandman, P. M., Weinstein, N. D., & Klotz, M. E. (1987). Public response to risk from geological radon. *Journal of Communication, 37*(3), 43–108.

Shapira, Z. (1995). *Risk taking: A managerial perspective.* New York: Russell Sage Foundation.

Shavell, S. (1987). *The economic analysis of accident law.* Cambridge, MA: Harvard University Press.

Shrivastava, P. (1987). *Bhopal: Anatomy of a crisis.* Cambridge, MA: Ballinger.

Slovic, P. (1987). Perception of risk. *Science, 236,* 280–285.

Starbuck, W. H., & Milliken, F. J. (1988). Challenger: Fine-tuning the odds until something breaks. *Journal of Management Studies, 25*(4), 319–340.

Staw, B. M. (1980). Rationality and justification in organizational life. In B. M. Staw & L. L. Cummings (Eds.), *Research in organizational behavior* (Vol. 9, pp. 191–233). Greenwich, CT: JAI Press.

Steiner, J. F. (1991). *Industry, society and change: A casebook.* New York: McGraw-Hill.

Tetlock, P. (1985). Accountability: The neglected social context of judgment and choice. In *Research in organizational behavior* (Vol. 7, pp. 297–332). Greenwich, CT: JAI Press.

Thompson, J. D. (1967). *Organizations in action.* New York: McGraw-Hill.

Weinberg, A. (1972). Science and trans-science. *Minerva, 10,* 209–222.

5 Strategic agenda building in organizations

Jane E. Dutton

Some issues get attention in organizations and others do not. For example, in some organizations, in some industries, issues of sustainable development and the natural environment dominate the organization's strategic agenda. In other organizations, in the same or different industries, issues of the natural environment have never been broached or thought about by organizational members. I could make the same comparisons between organizations, looking at very different kinds of issues: regulatory issues, human resource issues, competitor issues, and issues of new technology. Why is this so? What is the process by which issues reach an organization's strategic agenda? Why does strategic agenda building matter for understanding the process of decision making in organizations?

The goal of this chapter is to address these questions by elaborating four different perspectives on agenda-building processes, all of which are implicitly or explicitly in currency within organizational studies. Perspective 1 looks at agenda building as the product of top management's perceptions. Perspective 2 emphasizes that middle managers are active agents in the construction of strategic issues for the organization. Perspective 3 depicts agenda building as the activation of organizational routines. Finally, perspective 4 portrays agenda building as an intraorganizational ecological process. I describe each perspective and extract important insights that each perspective provides for thinking about strategic agenda-building processes. I conclude the chapter with a discussion of what an agenda-building perspective adds to the way organizational scholars and practitioners think about decision making.

The author wishes to thank Gelaye Debebe, David Obstfeld, Zur Shapira, Janet Weiss, and Mayer Zald for useful comments on earlier drafts of this manuscript.

Laying the definitional groundwork

Social scientists other than organizational scholars have become attuned to the significance of agendas as meaningful structures for explaining patterns of organized action. Political scientists assert that governmental organizations have agendas, and that understanding these agendas is critical for understanding patterns of policy-related action (e.g., Cobb & Elder, 1972; Kingdon, 1984; Walker, 1977). Communication scholars see agenda setting as a means by which the mass media affect the allocation of public attention and, ultimately, policy choices (e.g., Rogers & Dearing, 1988). In a very different realm, sociologists concerned with the domain of social problem theory and social movements acknowledge and describe societal-level agendas that determine patterns of public attention (e.g., Hilgartner & Bosk, 1988; Schneider, 1985; Zald, 1993). In contrast, organizational scholars have barely considered the idea that organizations have agendas, and that their content and the process by which they are created matter for organizational action. Although some researchers consider individual managerial agenda-building processes and patterns (e.g., Bowman & Bussard, 1991; Kotter, 1982), with few exceptions there has been limited consideration of the process and substance of organizational agendas, or what Pondy and Huff (1983) called the *issue portfolio.* I see this conceptual gap as an opportunity. By seizing this opportunity and describing different views of agenda building in organizations, I try to develop a way of understanding how structures, processes, and individuals interact in context to create the set of issues that consume collective attention in organizations.

Defining the strategic agenda

I begin with definitions. At any point in time, an organization has a strategic issue agenda. By *strategic issue agenda* I am referring to the set of issues that is demanding top-level decision makers' attention. I assume that attention is a limited and scarce resource (March & Shapira, 1982). It involves the investment of an organization's information processing capacity to an issue (Dutton, 1988b). In organizations, members know that attention has been allocated through both informal and formal means. Informal means include the naming of an issue, the existence of issue-focused conversations, and the collection of issue-related information (Dutton, 1988b). More formal means involve the declaration of the organization's top priorities by powerful individuals, the formation of a task force or some social group that is organized around the issue, the creation of a role or position dedicated to the issue, or the identification and incorporation of the issue into some formal issue processing system (e.g., an environmental scanning, strategic issue management, or strategic planning system). Researchers who have traced issue resolution processes in organizations suggest that issues proceed through a sequence of attention allocation in organizations that is similar to what Downs (1972) has identified as the cycle of attention allocation for issues in the public domain (Dutton, 1988a).

This focus on strategic agendas as opposed to broader, more inclusive organizational agendas or more limited departmental agendas is intended to narrow the domain of issues and players that compete in the market for issues in organizations that I consider for this analysis. There are two ways that I narrow the focus by talking about strategic agendas. First, a focus on *strategic issues* or events, developments, or trends that are perceived by top managers to have the potential to affect organizational performance (Ansoff, 1980) is intentionally narrow. It restricts our focus to strategic agendas in which issues are the mostly likely to have the strongest relationship to patterns of organizational action. This assertion, of course, assumes that there are meaningful differences across issues in the degree to which they are likely to connect to organizational action. For example, it would assume that, on average, an issue that affects the way a private firm competes and whether or not such competitive tactics work is more strategic (and more likely to predict organizational action) than issues that affect the way this firm determines its dress codes or allocates retirement pay to employees. Although these latter issues are relevant and important to everyday organizational functioning, the allocation of attention to them is less likely to engage and direct patterns of organization-level activity.

A second way that a focus on strategic agendas narrows the focus of this chapter is by restricting attentional resources to top management's attention. In this way, the chapter is consistent with a strategic choice perspective. Although frequently associated with Child (1972), this perspective asserts that the actions (and, in this case, attentional allocations) of top managers matter in explaining patterns of organizational action.

Differences in strategic agendas across organizations

A *strategic agenda*[1] refers to the set of issues that is receiving the attentional investment of decision makers at any point in time. As has been argued in the case of decisions (March, 1981), attentional resources are distributed across a set of strategic issues. The form and content of this issue set vary across organizations. In some organizations the issue set is very large, and decision makers allocate attention to a large number of strategic issues at any one point in time. Organizations with larger agendas have a greater carrying capacity. The idea of *carrying capacity* comes from the social problem theorists Hilgartner and Bosk (1988), who suggest that different social arenas have different carrying capacities that "limit the number of social problems that [they] can entertain during a given period" (p. 70). The concept that agendas vary in size is very similar. It emphasizes the capacity limits constraining the set of strategic issues that can be active or consuming attention at any point in time. Agenda size can vary, depending on the institutionalized mechanisms that enhance an organization's information processing ability, the number of top managers, and the amount of time that decision makers have to think about strategic issues.

Organizations' strategic agendas also vary in the variety or range of issues that are considered at any point in time. In some organizations the range of issues on the agenda is quite narrow, whereas in others it is quite large. In one study of the agendas of the top management teams of 77 hospitals, researchers found that variety of issues on the agenda was strongly positively correlated with agenda size (Houghton, Zeithaml, & Bateman, 1994). Finally, strategic agendas vary in turnover rate. For some organizations, issues move into and out of decision makers' attentional fields very quickly, whereas in others, issues move very slowly onto and off of the strategic agenda (Dutton & Duncan, 1987b, p. 104). All three agenda characteristics – size, variety, and turnover – contribute to our understanding of the processes and consequences of strategic agenda building.

The importance of strategic agenda building[2]

The heart of this chapter is a description of four different models of the agenda-building process. However, the motivation to describe this process rests on an understanding of the importance of the process more generally. We can appreciate the importance of agenda building from at least four vantage points. The four lenses come from considering the significance of agenda building from the organizational and individual-level units of analysis and by applying both instrumental and symbolic logics. Instrumental focus highlights the concrete and substantive outcomes associated with agenda building. Symbolic logic focuses on agenda building and the creation of meaning for individuals and for organizations. An organizational lens highlights what agenda building does to promote organizational effectiveness and survival. In contrast, an individual lens portrays agenda building as significant to individual outcomes. Each lens contributes a way of understanding why organizational scholars should care to understand strategic agenda building (and agenda building more generally).

Organizational-instrumental

The basic argument from this vantage point is that agenda building matters because an issue's entry to the agenda is the first step in the initiation of issue-related action. Where the taking of issue-related action is viewed as an indication that a decision has been made, then agenda building creates the momentum and sets parameters for the set of strategic decisions that are made in an organization. Agenda building is an important mechanism by which issues emanating from the organization's internal and external environments activate and direct top management's attention, beginning the process of decision making. By organizing and activating the decision-making process, agenda building, when viewed through this lens, is an important mechanism of organizational adaptation to environmental (internally or externally induced) change. For example, a study of how the Port Authority of New York and New Jersey dealt with the issue of homelessness showed how a set of decisions was activated by top management's recognition that this issue was urgent and important over time. However, an agenda-building perspective on this issue emphasizes that one cannot understand the allocation of attention to homelessness in isolation from the other set of issues that confronted the Port Authority (Dutton & Dukerich, 1991).

Organizational-symbolic

The set of issues that consume top management's attention in an organization help organizational members and outside stakeholders interpret what is important and what counts in the organization. Thus, an organization's strategic agenda is one representation of the core beliefs and values of the organization and its leaders. The language used to describe issues and the actions that accompany an issue's placement on the strategic agenda (e.g., the creation of a task force or committee) are both symbolic and carry meaning for members inside and outside the organization (Gioia, Thomas, Clark, & Chittipeddi, 1994). For example, when the issue of homelessness made the Port Authority's strategic agenda, this action carried meaning to all organizational members. For organizational insiders, it signaled a commitment to the organization's ethical and altruistic identity (Dutton & Dukerich, 1991). For outside stakeholders, it affirmed and built aspects of the organization's reputation (Dutton & Dukerich, 1991).

Individual-instrumental

Successful agenda placement of an issue that generates positive tangible or intangible rewards for the organization can be a substantive act with career consequences. Orchestrating the right issues to the agenda at the right time can signal a managers' competence in reading the environment, discerning what is important, and caring enough to promote the issue to top management. At the same time, promoting the wrong issue (e.g., an issue that brings reputational risk to the organization or turns out to be relatively unimportant) can deplete a manager's reputational capital in an organization. Thus, for better or for worse (literally), agenda building – its process and its outcomes – creates substantive career outcomes for individuals.

Individual-symbolic

Finally, solo acts of agenda building like selling an issue or participating in an issue coalition are acts that communicate meaning to participants and to others who observe these actions. Issues have language and valences attached to them that often generalize to the individuals who promote them (Nelson, 1984). As a result, individuals are sometimes unwilling to sell certain issues (e.g., the women's issue) because of their possibly stigmatizing effects (Ashford, Rothbard, Piderit, & Dutton, 1995). Thus, agenda-building processes are subject to individuals' concerns and reactions to the meaning implied by their affiliation with an issue before, during, and after it has been on the strategic agenda. Agenda building is significant because it is a process by which individual managers acquire and build their own sense of who they are and what they stand for.

These four justifications for agenda building are a platform for proposing what agenda building looks like in organizations. The remainder of the chapter is dedicated to describing the process of agenda building, accepting the multiple bases for its importance.

Four perspectives

There are at least four different depictions of what agenda building looks like in organizations: (1) agenda building as top decision makers' perceptions; (2) agenda building as active issue construction by mobilized managers; (3) agenda building as routine; and (4) agenda building as an intra-organizational ecological process. All four perspectives assume that agenda building can be affected, directly or indirectly, by the actions of managers (although each perspective allows for this possibility to varying degrees).[3] We develop and describe each depiction with an appreciative eye, asking: What does such a portrayal of agenda building add to our understanding of this vital process?

Agenda building as top management's perceptions

Most depictions of how issues receive attention in organizations focus on what goes on inside the heads of top decision makers. These perspectives on agenda building assume that issues will reach the strategic agenda if top decision makers see them as important, legitimate, and feasible to resolve. Thus, agenda placement is preceded by a specified set of perceptions. This agenda-building perspective relies on believing in cerebral rationality or the existence of "a cognitive process that can be decomposed into a sequence of simple, programmed steps" (Langley, Mintzberg, Pitcher, Posada, & Saint-Macary, 1995). Researchers who study processes of problem formulation (e.g., Cowan, 1990; Lyles, 1981; Lyles & Mitroff, 1980; Moreland & Levine, 1992; Smith, 1994; Volkema, 1986) and issue diagnosis or interpretation (Dutton, Fahey, & Narayanan, 1983; Milliken, 1990; Nutt, 1979; Thomas, Clark, & Gioia, 1993; Thomas & McDaniel, 1990; Thomas, Shankster, & Mathieu, 1994) typify this agenda-building perspective. Both sets of researchers assume that the strategic issues that absorb attention are ones that are perceived in such a way that individuals feel compelled to invest time in understanding and/or doing something about them. Most accounts assume that efforts devoted to understanding an issue begin with issue identification (Mintzberg, Raisinghini, & Theoret, 1976). *Identification* refers to the detection and recognition that some kind of issue (development, event, or trend) exists. Identification of an issue is commonly assumed to be related to the number, congruence, and vividness of issue-related symptoms. Some researchers assume that the symptoms indicate the existence of a type of gap between a desired and an actual state (e.g., customer orders drop below projected levels or a performance gap exists; Downs, 1967). Others argue that the symptoms are important for indicating the existence of tensions or contradictions between competing interests and values (Nutt & Backoff, 1993). The symptoms affect the levels of arousal that decision makers experience, as the existence of a gap or tension activates feelings of anxiety and/or uncertainty (Moreland & Levine, 1992). Assuming that the symptoms exceed some threshold or triggering point, indicating that decision makers sense the issue exists, descriptive and normative accounts argue that decision makers attempt to understand or diagnose the issue. Issue interpretation or diagnosis is important in separating issues that are agenda worthy from those that are not.

There are two different accounts of the process of strategic issue diagnosis. Some assume that issues acquire meaning by being classified into categories (e.g., this is a "political issue" or this is a "regulatory issue"). Categorization accounts of issue diagnosis assume that managers spend relatively little effort or cognitive resources in understanding issues. The process is automatic and relatively unreflective (Dutton, 1993a). In this account, managers rely on well-used categories built from their personal or organizational experience that allow them to impose meaning by classifying an issue as a member of a particular class of issues. Once classified this way, the issue takes on the attributes shared by other issues in that category. Thus, issues that are classified as opportunities are characterized by an expectation of gain, a sense of the positive, and a feeling of control (Jackson & Dutton, 1988). In this version of agenda building, issues will reach the agenda when top managers can classify them into categories that indicate they are important and worthy of attentional investment. Decision makers' experience and expertise are more important in this version of issue diagnosis because they determine the range and type of issue categories in use. These categories, in turn, determine whether or not an issue will be understood and perceived as important by decision makers (Day & Lord, 1992), that is, whether or not it makes the strategic agenda.

A different account of issue diagnosis portrays it as a more complex and effortful activity. In this depiction, the process is intentional and conscious, involving a much greater degree of information search and analysis than implied by the automatic diagnosis model (Dutton, 1993a, p. 342). In this portrayal, individuals weigh issue attributes and form judgments that determine whether or not an issue is likely to make the strategic agenda. Rochefort and Cobb (1994) describe this process as involving definitions of an issue's causality, severity, incidence, novelty, and a variety of other attributes that determine the likelihood of an issue's agenda placement. Another model of issue diagnosis portrays assessments of an issue's urgency and feasibility as key to predicting whether or not an issue will make the strategic agenda (Dutton & Duncan, 1987a). Some empirical work supports the importance of these assessments in predicting outcomes such as the allocation of time and money to an issue (e.g., Dutton, Stumpf, & Wagner, 1990), issue-related commitments (e.g., Ginsberg & Venkatraman, 1992), and the extent of organizational product and service change (Thomas et al., 1993). Other research provides limited support for the relationship between these issue interpretations and issue-related action (e.g., Penner, 1993).

When considered as a set, the studies that focus on problem formulation and issue diagnosis as central to agenda building contribute two key ideas to our understanding of this process. One implication is that agenda building is importantly shaped by the subjective interpretations of issues by decision makers. As discussed earlier, issues are ambiguous and unbounded clusters of data. Through the perceptual process, managers come to see, organize, bound, and understand a data cluster as an issue. Although issues vary in the kinds of information available for interpreting their meaning, no issue is inherently important, feasible, or legitimate. Rather, these judgments depend on how a decision maker or set of decision makers sees an issue. How an issue is perceived is affected by characteristics of the issue, of the perceiver, and of the context.

Second, this perspective emphasizes that the way issues are interpreted depends on decision makers' personal and organizational frames of reference (Shrivastava & Schneider, 1984). Thus, whether or not an issue will make the strategic agenda in an organization is predictably related to the organizational context and the local context of the issue perceiver, which shape the available information about an issue and motivate managers to interpret issues in particular ways. Whether it is an organization's competitive posture (Ginsberg & Venkatraman, 1992), the information processing structure of the top management team (Thomas & McDaniel, 1990), or the organization's performance history (Milliken & Lant, 1991), empirical evidence suggests that context shapes issue interpretations. In one study on the relative effects of different levels of context on issue interpretations, Thomas et al. (1994) found that characteristics of the top management team (e.g., its information processing capacity, its level of political activity, and its strength of identity) predicted the degree to which the issue was seen as political and strategic. In addition, this perspective reminds us that the way decision makers interpret issues (e.g., in an active or an automatic mode) is context sensitive (Dutton, 1993a). Accordingly, what issues reach the agenda and how they are framed are context dependent.

Agenda building as active issue construction by mobilized managers

Whereas the first perspective focused on what goes on in the minds of top management, the issue construction perspective is that persons outside the top management group are the movers and shapers of the strategic agenda. This perspective takes seriously the political and social nature of the agenda-building process. It puts middle managers at center stage in attracting and directing top management's attention to some issues and helps to explain top management's issue ignorance or neglect.

There are at least two versions of agenda building as the active direction of attention by middle managers. One version focuses on individual managers' efforts to claim top management's attention. We will call this version *issue selling* (Dutton & Ashford, 1993). Issue selling is very similar in form to what political scientists identify as the behaviors of policy entrepreneurs (Kingdon, 1984) (although in policy research many of these individuals are outside the organizations they are trying to influence) or the actions taken by those whom innovation researchers call *champions* (e.g., Burgelman, 1983; Chakrabardi, 1974; Howell & Higgins, 1990; Schon, 1963). In all cases, the intentional actions of individuals are consequential for building or dissolving exposure to and interest in particular strategic issues (Dutton, 1988a). The other version, which focuses on the collective and coordinated processes of a group of individuals designed to claim the attention of top management we shall call *coalition mobilizing*. This process is similar to what sociologists call *resource mobilization* processes, in which groups in organizations try to affect the priorities, policies, and actions outside of conventional political channels (Zald & Berger, 1978).

Whether one describes agenda building as issue selling or coalition mobilizing, this perspective makes five assumptions that are important for how we understand agenda building from this point of view. First, it assumes that individuals are motivated to direct and shape the attention of top management toward some issues and not others. In our own studies of issue selling in a hospital (Ashford, Dutton, & O'Neill, 1996), telecommunications (Dutton, Ashford, Wierba, O'Neill, & Hayes, 1994), and diversified conglomerate (Dutton, 1988b), we found ample support for this assumption. Middle managers talk easily and willingly about the intentional efforts they exert to have top management recognize certain issues and view them in a particular way.

Second, given that issue selling or coalition mobilizing is initiated by one set of individuals and directed toward shaping the thoughts, feelings, and understandings of others (in this case, top management), the process involves social influence. Because it is a social influence process, we assume that whether such actions are initiated (e.g., managers engage in issue selling or coalition mobilizing) and the form such processes take depend upon characteristics of the target (top management), characteristics of the seller or coalition members, characteristics of the issue, and characteristics of the context (and their interactions). For example, in one study of middle managers' issue selling, top management's perceived willingness to listen was the key target characteristic that managers considered when choosing whether or not to sell an issue (Dutton et al., 1994). This field-based study and other simulation-based research (Burgelman & Mittman, 1994) illustrate that managers attend to the risk of their own reputational or image damage in assessing whether or not to initiate agenda building. A focus on the idea of image risk makes it clear that attempts to sell issues to top management involve costs. Managers are aware of and assess the costs and benefits of initiating issue selling, and these assessments also affect the form or the process of issue selling that is used.

A third assumption of the issue construction perspective is that issues are not prepackaged. They are not inherently bound and limited. Strategic issues in particular are ambiguous and contested. Consistent with a social constructionist perspective, the meaning of issues is actively made and formed in a social context through processes of social interaction (Berger & Luckmann, 1967, Dutton et al., 1983). The ambiguity of strategic issues allows different groups (including top management) to have a say in how issues are constructed, building the interest in the issue and commitment to taking action. Schneider (1994) documents this interpretation process in the issue of "1992" as it was seen by managers in both a Danish and a Spanish bank. Fox-Wolfgramm, Boal, and Hunt (1994) describe the changes in meaning by two banks in their understanding of the significance of the Community Reinvestment Act over the 1984–90 time period. In a different context, in a study of the processing of 12 strategic issues over a 5-year period, the meaning of 11 of the 12 issues changed substantially over the study period (Dutton, 1988a). All three studies illustrate the fluidity of issue meaning over time.

Fourth, the ambiguity of strategic issues implies that language and issue labels are important for drawing attention to or away from an issue. Political scientists document and explain the significance of language as a way to influence politics and policy (Edelman, 1964). Clever policy entrepreneurs (Kingdon, 1984) know how to label policy issues in particular ways to create or dissolve support for an issue. In an organizational context, intentional and unintentional usage of language to frame an issue mobilizes different groups of managers to invest in the issue. These framings, in turn, reflect different understandings of an issue and result in different patterns of attention allocation. As Rochefort and Cobb (1994) argue, "language can be the vehicle for employing symbols that lend legitimacy to one definition [of an issue] and undermine the legitimacy of another" (p. 9). For example, Mylonadis (1991) describes the evolution of different labels that were used to refer to the issue of waste prevention in ECoTEC and its relationship to agenda prominence. In a study of the Port Authority of New York and New Jersey (PA), Dutton and Dukerich (1991) document the changing labels used for the issue of homeless persons present in PA facilities, and the link between changes in the issue's framing and where the issue stood on the PA's strategic agenda. As these examples illustrate, an issue construction perspective on agenda building expects the meaning of issues to change over time. It also suggests that modifications in language and meaning applied to issues result in changed patterns of attention allocation.

Fifth, an issue construction perspective recognizes the importance of timing. Effective issue sellers or players who are trying to affect the strategic issue agenda understand and sense that there are moments (what Kingdon calls *policy windows*) when top management is pressed for action or external events occur that translate into an openness to new agenda items. For example, the availability of new data or the pressure resulting from a crisis can make a condition compelling (Kingdon, 1984), forcing top management to be more open to issues. The press for action, top management succession, or the availability of an action to couple with an issue are all favorable conditions for issue inclusion on the strategic agenda. Astute issue sponsors and mobilized managers sense this and use timing effectively to increase their success at agenda building.

Agenda building as routine

A view of agenda building as routine stands in stark contrast to the mobilized manager depiction. By *routine* I mean the patterns of behavior that are engaged in by more than one person oriented to a common stimulus (Feldman, 1989). Routines capture an organization's method of doing things or a type of organizational performance (Winter, 1990). Elsewhere I have talked about organizational routines constraining the process of agenda building (Dutton & Penner, 1993). Here I argue that strategic agenda building can be described as a set of routines. Consistent with this view, attention allocation to some issues and not others comes from the existence and application of rules that are embedded in formal procedures, policies, or organizational norms, not from the intentional behaviors of motivated managers. Thus, internal and external demands are sorted and directed by routines that determine whether or not these demands draw attention. March and Olsen (1989) remind us that "routines are independent of the individual actors who execute them and are capable of surviving considerable turnover in individuals." (p. 22). The existence and use of these routines contributes to reliable organizational action, which, according to several organizational scholars, contributes to an organization's long-term viability (e.g., Hannan & Freeman, 1984).

In this view of agenda building, the motivated actions of individual managers or a collective group of individuals are activated and directed by the existence of and application of rules. These rules determine when attentional resources for an organization are applied or removed from an issue, what kinds of issue frames are readily available, who gets attached or connected to what issue, and whether or not action is taken on the issue. Organizations have a "repertoire of procedures, and they use rules to select among them" (March & Olsen, 1989, p. 21). According to Zhou (this volume), these rules are "a way to manage conflict, manage uncertainty, and represent the retention of learned experience" (p. 7). They also imbue the process and outcomes of agenda building with legitimacy. For example, in Capital Corporation, the rules followed as part of the formal strategic issue management system granted the process a sense of appropriateness and rationality that managers valued. When describing the process pertaining to a particular issue, these managers talked about their belief that if an issue became part of the strategic issue management process, "things would get better" or "the crazy politics would be lessened" (Dutton, 1988a, p. 233).

Several kinds of rules or clusters of procedures are important to agenda-building processes. First, there are the rules that specify *how* and *when* strategic issues can be raised in public, local, and organizational arenas. Often budgeting and planning cycles determine when there are open windows for issue recognition and discussion. For example, one study of the processing of 12 strategic issues over 5 years at Capital Corporation documented the routine communication pattern that was part of the issue-processing sequence. The routine had three parts: (1) a task group report made to the Policy and Executive Committee (PEC); (2) a formal written response to the task group from the PEC; and (3) monitoring of the task group's compliance using quarterly monitoring reports (Dutton, 1988a). Across all 5 years and all 12 issues studied, there were 21 cases in which this sequence was confirmed and 5 cases in which it was disconfirmed (actions occurred out of order or one of the activity elements was missing; Dutton, 1988a, p. 233). The structure and process of meeting rules also determine how and when new issues can be raised or old issues discussed. This is why some organizational scholars argue that a significant source of power and control is accorded to those who control the design of meeting agendas (Pfeffer, 1982).

Second, there are rules for *how* strategic issues will be *framed*. For example, organizations often use issue management or environmental scanning systems that institutionalize a narrow set of categories for framing the dominant meaning and recording the urgency of issues. For example, many organizations apply a simple classification system of "threats" and "opportunities" for categorizing and framing the issues deemed potentially significant for organizational performance. If an agenda issue is deemed a threat, it is likely to evoke one set of organizational responses; if it is considered an opportunity, it triggers another response set (Dutton & Jackson, 1987).

March (1994) argues that the most important rules for agenda building are those applied to demands or events that answer the questions "What kind of issue is this?" and "Who should be dealing with this?" March's argument is that the logic of appropriateness is applied in organizations and determines, in part, whose attention and how much attention are invested in an issue or set of issues. An example from the Port Authority and its struggle with homeless persons illustrates this assertion. In the 1970s and early 1980s, the Port Authority was viewed by insiders as the builder and guardian of public transportation resources. From this organizational identity standpoint, members saw the issue of homeless persons inhabiting the buildings as one of security and as appropriately handled by the organization's police staff. When applying the logic of appropriateness, decision makers did not see the issue as one worthy of major attention. However, as different aspects of the organization's identity became salient, applications of the logic of appropriateness revealed a new construction of this issue. Faced with "bashing" in the press for its treatment of homeless persons, Port Authority managers increasingly saw the organization as the region's (i.e., New York and New Jersey) representative, symbolizing the region's health or demise. From this vantage point, the issue of homeless persons using the facilities came to be viewed as an issue of regional vitality and therefore better handled by the organization's top management (Dutton & Dukerich, 1991).

When viewed in this light, agenda building is a process that evolves from the application of rules based on the logic of appropriateness. This logic certifies what kind of organization this is – issues of organizational identity that capture the central, enduring, and distinctive characteristics of the organization (Albert & Whetten, 1985) and are closely connected to an organization's competence (Fiol, 1991). Issues of identity work through the logic of appropriateness to determine what issues draw and what issues repel attention. For example, in a case study of one public library's reaction over time to the issue of homeless individuals using library facilities, the logic of appropriateness figured prominently. For the librarians in this context, the "public servant" aspects of their professional and organizational identities helped them to see the issue as an appropriate one, drawing their attention and concern about the issue. At the same time, the aspects of their identity that saw the library and their positions as professional and technically expert drew attention away from the issue. The contradictory beliefs embedded in these hybrid identities (Albert & Whetten, 1985) led to a sense of ambivalence and inaction with respect to the issue (Pratt & Dutton, 1993). The logic of appropriateness implies that rules and routines encode organizational and, by implication, individual identities. Application of these rules determines an issue's eligibility for inclusion in or exclusion from the strategic agenda. This logic implies that an organization's strategic agenda will contain primarily identity-consistent issues. This may be why some authors argue that it takes earthquakes (Rheger, Mullane, Gustafson, & DeMarie, 1994) or significant stressors (Huff, Huff, & Thomas, 1992) to induce strategic change. Where strategic change requires meaningful change in the set of issues that command top management's attention, such changes may require fundamental changes in organizational identity and its embedded set of rules that derive from the logic of appropriateness.

Agenda building as intraorganizational ecological process

This last perspective on agenda building can be viewed as a combination of the previous three, with a few important complications. A view of agenda building as an intraorganizational ecological process uses evolutionary thinking as a metaphor to conceptualize a key strategic process (Van de Ven, 1992). By taking this view of agenda building, I try to build on what Weick (1979) has done in his application of natural selection ideas to theories of organizing. From this viewpoint, the allocation of attention is a dynamic process that proceeds through the continuous processes of variation, selection, and retention. It implies that agenda building is a nondeterministic process subject to the changing conditions that affect variation, selection, and retention. By looking at agenda building this way, the model resembles applications of evolutionary ideas to explain other intraorganizational processes (e.g., Burgelman, 1990, 1994; Burgelman & Mittman, 1994; Miner, 1994; Singh, 1990).

We can see the usefulness of this perspective in understanding strategic agenda building by considering the processes of variation, selection, and retention as described in the answers to three questions: (1) How is variation in the pool of possible strategic issues created? (2) What kinds of selection mechanisms exist, and how do they select out some issues and not others? and (3) How are these new issues retained or passed on in subsequent time periods?

Variation in strategic issues. There are many mechanisms by which the variation in the pool of strategic issues is created. Issue variation is created by individual initiatives, by institutionalized routines, and by changes in the organization's environmental context that generate, bracket, and frame issues that may or may not end up on the strategic agenda.

Burgelman (1983) has studied the managerial initiatives that make up what he calls *autonomous processes* in organizational change. He argues that the major driver of these autonomous initiatives is the career opportunity structure of managers, which encourages them to propose initiatives (or issues) in some cases while holding back in others. Sue Ashford and I have argued that the social psychology of putting forth issues is more complex than Burgelman asserts (Dutton & Ashford, 1993). We argue that the move to speak out publicly on an issue and to try to get others to see it as important is personally and organizationally consequential. Managers pay attention to contextual cues beyond the career opportunity structure in deciding whether or not to try to sell an issue to top management. However, we agree with Burgelman's assertion that the initiatives of middle managers are a critical source of variation in the pool of strategic issues that could become part of the strategic agenda. As Miner (1994) argues, champions and entrepreneurs, like issue sellers, are "explicit, providing a conscious engine of variation within some organizations" (p. 78). The actions of these individuals are the centerpiece of the active issue construction perspective on agenda building.

Beyond the initiatives or actions of mobilized individuals who bring issues to the fore, routines or clusters of routines inject variation into the issue pool. As described in the third perspective on agenda building, there are multiple ways that routines introduce information, select participants, and activate action that are the seed corn for issues. Routines such as environmental scanning, issues management, and strategic planning systems represent complex and dedicated issue generators. Other formal systems such as performance evaluation practices systematically uncover discrepancies between desired and actual behaviors, prompting the consideration of issues. Simpler procedures or routines such as using meeting protocols, which ask if there are issues that should be considered, reliance on suggestion boxes, or the rewarding of new ideas represent additional means by which variation is created in the set of issues that "bubble around in an organization." The bubbling metaphor matches Kingdon's (1984) characterization of what happens in congressional agenda building. He talks about the process as one of natural selection, where there are proposals that bubble around like "primeval soup" before some subset of proposals get selected. Organizational routines are important contributors to the issues that make up this primeval soup.

Changes in the organization's internal and external environments also inject variety into the issue pool. A common assumption in organizational theory is that changes in the organization's environment somehow relate to change in an organization (e.g., Meyer, 1982; Milliken, 1990, Tushman & Romanelli, 1985). Changes in an organization's environment introduce new information and pose requirements (i.e., technological, political, competitive) that become the raw material for strategic issues (Cowan, 1986; Huber & Daft, 1987). Changes in the organization's environment help to make managers more aware of discrepancies and conditions that can be constructed as possible strategic issues. For example, Rogers (1993) provides an in-depth description of four banks' responses to major environmental changes occurring in the banking industry, such as increased competition, a decline in corporate loans, and the rise of mutual and money market funds. Each of these environmental trends creates new information patterns and changes the bases for political support and interests. In some banks, these environmental changes drew attention and spawned new strategic issues for the firms to consider; in other banks, there was no addition to the set of issues given consideration.

Selection of strategic issues. Some subset of the pool of potential strategic issues in an organization is selected out and becomes the strategic issue agenda. We know if this selection process has happened by whether or not some new issue begins to consume attention in an organization. There are at least four factors that contribute to this selection process: active decision premises, shared identity beliefs and values, selling norms, and characteristics of the external environment.

In the works of Weick (1979), selection gets lodged in decision premises that are used in organizations (e.g., accept issues that involve stakeholder A and reject those that concern stakeholder B). Most often these premises reside in individual managers (ties to this individual's values, experience, and expertise). Individual decision makers who are in more powerful positions can apply their own decision premises and command the attention of others. As McKelvey (1994) argues, "Most selection is done by superiors – inside, I repeat, inside organizations" (p. 322). At other times, selection by decision premises occurs through the operation of institutionalized scanning and monitoring systems that execute decision premises by considering some issues relevant and important while deeming others unimportant or illegitimate.

The organization's belief system and values also contribute to the selection process. An organization's cultural context sets parameters on how issues will be understood (e.g., is the issue important? Is it urgent?), the degree to which managers see the issues as feasible to act upon, and how legitimate it is assumed to be. Consistent with assertions developed in our description of agenda building as top management perception, we assume that issues that are perceived as important, legitimate, and feasible will have a greater probability of making it onto the strategic agenda. For example, Dutton and Penner (1993) develop a set of arguments for how organizational identity beliefs shape the strategic agenda through their effect on the way issues are perceived and the set of routines that operate in agenda-building episodes. A variety of empirical studies (e.g., Meyer, 1982; Milliken, 1990; Thomas et al., 1994) suggest that organizational beliefs systematically affect how ambiguous issues are interpreted, and these interpretations affect an issue's survival or death in the market for issues in an organization. For example, if an issue is framed in such a way that it conflicts with valued aspects of the organization's identity, decision makers are more likely to see the issue as important and worthy of attentional investment. This is one explanation for why, in Meyer's (1982) study of hospitals' reactions to an unexpected doctors' strike, some hospitals ignored the issue by defining it as an aberration, whereas others defined it in a way that made the issue a legitimate and central agenda item. This idea resonates with work done on social movements that points to the importance of belief systems in determining levels of consensus and commitment to mobilizing about an issue. For example, Snow and Benford (1988), in their study of the peace movement, point to the importance of an issue's relevance to control beliefs held by organizational members in determining levels of motivation around an issue. Where an issue is seen by members as tied to important values and beliefs, that issue is likely to be favored for selection. Thus, an organization's beliefs and values determine how issues are interpreted, which increases or decreases an issue's selection and retention in the market for issues that exists in an organization.

Norms for issue selling also act as a selection device by setting parameters for what is viewed as normative or not in the process of selling and legitimating an issue. Organizations develop expected patterns for raising issues. Violation of or conformity to these standards affects an issue's success in commanding top managers' attention as well as managers' willingness to sell an issue to top management. For example, in one study of middle managers' issue-selling behaviors in a firm in the telecommunications industry undergoing rapid change, we uncovered a clear recipe or accepted pattern for issue selling: Bring up an issue to your boss first, back up claims with quantified data, and bundle the identification of an issue, with the proposal of a solution (Dutton et al., 1996). Norms for acceptable individual selling or collective coalition mobilizing set constraints on what issues are likely to be considered and treated as legitimate, keeping some issues off an organization's strategic agenda. Thus culture plays a selection role through both an interpretive and a motivational pathway.

An organization's external context is also a factor in issue selection. The external environment creates demands (e.g., deadlines, events that force accountability, changes in market demand) that affect the substance and timing of what issues command top management attention. For example, in Burgelman's (1994) elaborate account of Intel's exit from the dynamic random access memory (DRAM) business, he shows how the external context affected the strength of selection processes occurring internally. His research indicates that external market changes can translate into differing levels of support for different businesses, which in turn affect the initiatives and autonomous activities of middle-level managers. Thus, the external context affects the selection of issues by determining what issue sellers have currency in the market and how much support there is likely to be for the issues that are proposed.

In our research on middle managers' issue selling in a telecommunications firm, we have found a similar connection between external context changes and internal dynamics (Dutton et al., 1996). Basically, greater perceived environmental uncertainty helped middle managers to perceive the internal context as more favorable for issue selling. We found that middle managers considered environment-driven change (e.g., downsizing and total quality initiatives induced by major changes in the competitive context) as opening windows of opportunity for selling issues. This finding resembles Kingdon's (1984) idea that there are times when policy entrepreneurs can affect the selection and placement of an issue on the docket. Similarly, middle managers sense that changes in the external environment create safe times and places in which it is legitimate and wise to propose issues as possible agenda items.

Besides creating a sense of safety and support for potential issue sellers, the external context contributes to the selection of strategic issues for the agenda via a very different route. The broader environmental or institutional context helps to legitimate or delegitimate the framing of particular strategic issues. Framing, in turn, can ease or make more difficult the allocation of attention to an issue inside the organization. For example, Weiss (1989) described the use of a "paperwork reduction" definition in government and the effects of this broader frame on the legitimacy of federal agencies' claims that they could burden citizens with information collection opportunities. Another example from the Port Authority's struggle with the issue of homeless persons frequenting its facilities illustrates this process. As described in Dutton and Dukerich (1991), empirical evidence supporting this issue as a Port Authority problem had existed for years before the issue was selected and entered the organization's strategic agenda. The heightened sense of homelessness as a national issue, and as a symbol of the demise of the New York City region, contributed to the selection of homelessness as an issue inside the Port Authority. With the publishing of Ann Marie Rousseau's *Shopping Bag Ladies* and Ellen Baxter and Kim Hopper's book *Private Lives, Public Spaces*, public attention was directed to homelessness as a national issue (Stern, 1984). Correspondingly, the rise in national attention made it much easier for Port Authority facility managers to make the case internally that homelessness was a strategic issue (Dutton & Dukerich, 1991). "Legitimated societal issues outside the organization provide valuable 'hooks' that issue sponsors can use to 'hang' organizational issues which they wish others to recognize and support" (Dutton, 1993b, p. 215). Thus, the external context helps to select strategic issues internally by providing foundations for issue legitimation.

Retention of strategic issues. The process by which issues are retained on the agenda and persevere across time is more difficult to describe than the previous two processes. At one level, retention occurs when an agenda item is institutionalized into an organizational unit's practices or goals. In this case, the issue then comes up when the unit's performance is evaluated or budgets are formed. When the practice is invoked, the issue is incorporated anew into organizational action. At another level, retention is indicated by the perseverance of a particular agenda structure over time. Consistent with the evolutionary mechanism, it is assumed that organizations reproduce themselves over time through the inheritance and transmission of certain routines or clusters of routines. We assume that the structure of an organization's agenda, as a complex routine, is fairly stable over time (e.g., the agenda's capacity, variety, and turnover stay stable over time), contributing to the stability of organizational actions over time. The stability of an organization's agenda structure helps to replicate the organization over time and, as discussed earlier, can create problems of inertia and nonresponsiveness when the environment changes.

Contrasts in the agenda-building perspectives

The four perspectives on agenda building provide a rich portrait of a critical process that occurs in organizations. The four perspectives vary in several important ways. First, they differ in the level of emphasis placed on the role of individual agency in creating an organization's strategic agenda. The top management perception and active construction perspectives accord significance to the role of individuals (their interpretations and motivations) in understanding what issues make the strategic agenda. In contrast, the agenda building as routine and ecological perspectives place far less weight on individuals' motivated actions in directing and explaining an organization's strategic agenda.

The perspectives also differ in terms of what aspects of the context matter in determining the strategic agenda. The first two perspectives highlight the local context of actors involved in the noticing, communicating, and considering strategic issues. The second two perspectives add layers of context (organizational and broader institutional) as important in shaping the content and process of agenda building. The ecological perspective highlights the important role of the broader institutional context in shaping language and support, which can be used inside the organization to rally and direct attention to issues. Together, all four perspectives suggest that nested levels of context contribute probabilistically to the creation of an organization's strategic agenda over time. These levels of context determine the types of information, interests, and rules that are activated over time, shaping the organizational pattern of attention to issues. This pattern of issues, in turn, sets the stage for patterns of committed action. Together all four approaches contrast with a more reactive view of agenda building that says that issues are driven by conditions in the external context.

A third contrast across the four perspectives is in the degree to which each provides continuity and stability in the process and substance of agenda-building episodes over time. The first two perspectives are relatively silent regarding the role of history and precedent in creating pattern and stability in an organization's strategic agenda. In contrast, the second two perspectives see the past as pivotal (via routines and via selection mechanisms) for explaining current and future agenda content. All four perspectives acknowledge that new episodes of agenda building are affected by the content and form of the old strategic agenda. The old agenda sets capacity constraints on the amount of uncommitted attention that can be devoted to an issue. Thus, the incrementalism often observed in strategic decision making (Quinn, 1980) is created, in part, by the similarity of the set of issues over time that make it onto an organization's strategic agenda.

Although the perspectives vary, as a set they pose an important set of questions and answers for how we think about organizational decision making. I will close the chapter with three questions that an agenda-building analysis both asks and begins to answer for students of organizational decision making.

Question 1: Are beginnings or endings more important in organizational decision making?

Researchers who study organization decision making typically focus on commitments, choices, and resource allocations as key to identifying the relevant process that explains these outcomes. For example, Eisenhardt's (1989) study of fast decision making in high-velocity environments; Hickson, Butler, Cray, Mallory, and Wilson's (1986) study of 150 decisions across a wide range of contexts; and Mintzberg et al.'s (1976) investigation of the process involved in 25 varied strategic decisions firms all begin with an ending – a choice point – and study the process leading up to that endpoint or act of commitment or investment. These researchers, I would argue, treat endings as more important in defining what aspects of the process matter. In contrast, a focus on agenda-building processes points to the importance of beginnings in explaining and defining what, when, and why commitments occur. Agenda-building researchers suggest that commitments and choices are tied importantly to the initial allocation of attention to some issue and the way that issue is defined. The action is a function of how issues become issues. As Kingdon (1990) puts it, "We're talking here not about how issues get decided nor about how decisions are implemented and what impacts they have, but rather how issues come to be issues in the first place" (p. 1).

Question 2: Who are the relevant actors in organizational decision making?

Many treatments of organizational decision making assume that top managers make the big decisions. They study the thoughts and behaviors of top management as the major players to explain organizational choices. This approach is consistent with a strategic choice perspective (Child, 1972) and with an elitist view of who participates in strategic-level decisions. An agenda-building perspective opens up the set of participants who are involved in shaping the choices that are activated and who participates in building commitments to action. The agenda-building view assumes a wide range of potential participants, and the activation of various rules creates choices patterns (Cohen, March, & Olsen, 1972). As illustrated by the first two perspectives, the motivated actions of interested individuals are important drivers in determining attention allocation to issues in organizations. Some agenda-building perspectives describe the value that individuals place on getting issues on the agenda (or keeping them off) and the set of behaviors that are used toward this end. Thus, by analyzing agenda-building processes, researchers and theorists consider a wider range of interested and consequential participants in the organizational decision-making process.

Question 3: Why and when does interpretation matter in decision making?

Traditional models of decision making assume that if interpretation or the social creation of meaning matters, it matters in the articulation and choice between decision alternatives. Thus, the interpretation of alternatives affects what commitments are made in organizational decisions. Interpretations are much more central in the agenda-building perspective. Issues are not prepackaged. They are ambiguous, contested, and subject to deliberate and automatic constructions that imbue an issue with meaning. An agenda-building perspective treats the activation of choice through the imposition of meaning on issues as problematic and worthy of considerable conceptual and empirical scrutiny. As such, it considers the allocation of scarce attentional resources as critical and consequential, and it highlights the language used to capture and communicate meaning.

This chapter celebrates the insight that develops from considering agenda-building perspectives in organizations. From a practical point of view, it implies that meaningful differences in agenda-building capabilities exist across organizations. Consistent with this point of view, agenda-building processes are an important means by which organizations renew themselves by improving their alignment with internal and external demands (Huff et al., 1992). Strategic management researchers might call agenda building a type of dynamic capability – a capability that builds competitive advantage over time (Teece, Pisano, & Sheun, 1994). In some organizations, the content of the strategic agenda may mirror consequential issues that the organization would be better off responding to in some way. In other organizations, there may be total disconnection between what is on the strategic agenda and the issues of concern in the internal and external environments. The former type of organization may be more resilient or a better learner than the second. One could consider what is it about the way issues are perceived, how members are mobilized to construct issues, the bureaucratic routines that exist, or the way the ecology of issues works in the organization that produces this adaptive advantage.

Rather than attributing the adaptive advantage to the wisdom of decision making, it attributes adaptive advantage to the wisdom embedded in the agenda-building process. This chapter invites researchers and practitioners to better understand the logic of such wisdom. Unlocking the wisdom in agenda building helps to unlock the wisdom of organizational decision making. Agenda building is the prelude and the pattern setter for organizational decisions. It is the process by which meaning, interest, and rules are developed that set the parameters for subsequent choice.

Notes

1 In previous writing (Dutton & Duncan, 1987b) we have called this the strategic issue array. We think the structure is more appropriately labeled the strategic agenda.
2 Portions of this section are taken from J. E. Dutton and S. J. Ashford (1993), Selling issues to top management, *Academy of Management Review, 18,* 397–428.
3 By focusing on agenda-building views that feature managerial choice, I deliberately ignore views of agenda building that assume that agenda items are created by forces outside of the organization or from previous decisions that need follow-up. Thanks to J. Weiss for this clarification.

References

Albert, S., & Whetten, D. (1985). Organizational identity. In L. L. Cummings & B. Staw (Eds.), *Research in Organizational Behavior* (pp. 263–295). Greenwich, CT: JAI Press.

Ansoff, H. L. (1980). Strategic issue management. *Strategic Management Journal, 1,* 131–148.

Ashford, S. J., O'Neill, R., & Dutton, J. (1994). *Moves from the middle: Profiles of successful and unsuccessful issue selling.* Working paper, University of Michigan.

Ashford, S. J., Rothbart, N., Piderit, S., & Dutton, J. (1995). *Out on a limb: The role of context and impression management in issue selling.* Paper presented at the National Academy of Management meetings, August 10–12, Vancouver, British Columbia.

Berger, P. L., & Luckmann, T. (1967). *The social construction of reality.* Garden City, NY: Anchor Books.

Bowman, E. H., & Bussard, D. T. (1991). Managerial agenda setting: An exploratory study. In P. Shrivastava, A. Huff, & J. Dutton (Eds.), *Advances in strategic management* (pp. 61–93). Greenwich, CT: JAI Press.

Burgelman, R. A. (1983). A process model of internal corporate venturing in a diversified firm. *Administrative Science Quarterly, 28,* 223–244.

Burgelman, R. A. (1990). Strategy-making and organizational ecology: A conceptual integration. In J. V. Singh (Ed.), *Organizational evolution: New directions* (pp. 164–181). Newbury Park, CA: Sage.

Burgelman, R. A. (1994). Fading memories: A process study of strategic business exit in dynamic environments. *Administrative Science Quarterly, 39,* 24–56.

Burgelman, R. A., & Mittman, B. S. (1994). An intraorganizational ecological perspective on managerial risk behavior, performance and survival: Individual, organizational and environmental effects. In J. A. C. Baum & J. V. Singh (Eds.), *Evolutionary dynamics in organizations* (pp. 53–75). New York: Oxford University Press.

Chakrabardi, A. K. (1974). The role of champion in product innovation. *California Management Review, 17,* 58–62.

Child, J. (1972). Organization structure, environment and performance – The role of strategic choice. *Sociology, 6,* 1–22.

Cobb, R., & Elder, C. D. (1972). *Participation in American politics: The dynamics of agenda building.* Boston: Allyn & Bacon.

Cohen, M. D., March, J. G., & Olsen, J. P. (1972). A garbage can model of organizational choice. *Administrative Science Quarterly, 17,* 1–24.

Cowan, D. A. (1986). Developing a process model of problem recognition. *Academy of Management Review, 11,* 763–776.

Daft, R., & Weick, K. (1984). Toward a model of organizations as interpretation systems. *Academy of Management Review, 17,* 1–24.

Day, D. V., & Lord, R. G. (1992). Expertise and problem categorization: The role of expert processing in organizational sense-making. *Journal of Management Studies, 29,* 35–47.

Downs, A. (1972). Attention cycle: Up and down with ecology – the issue. *The Public Interest, 28,* 38–50.

Dutton, J. E. (1988a). Perspectives on strategic issue processing: Insights from a case study. In P. Shrivastava & R. Lamb (Eds.), *Advances in strategic management* (pp. 223–244). Greenwich, CT: JAI Press.

Dutton, J. E. (1988b). Understanding strategic agenda building and its implications for managing change. In L. R. Pondy, R. J. Boland, & H. Thomas (Eds.), *Managing ambiguity and change* (pp. 127–144). Chichester, England: Wiley.

Dutton, J. E. (1993a). Interpretations on automatic: A different view of strategic issue diagnosis. *Journal of Management Studies, 30,* 329–357.

Dutton, J. E. (1993b). The making of organizational opportunities: An interpretive pathway to organizational change. In B. M. Staw & L. L. Cummings (Eds.), *Research in organizational behavior* (Vol. 15, pp. 195–226). Greenwich, CT: JAI Press.

Dutton, J. E., & Ashford, S. J. (1993). Selling issues to top management. *Academy of Management Review, 18,* 397–428.

Dutton, J. E., Ashford, S. J., Wierba, E., O'Neill, R., & Hayes, E. (1996). Reading the wind: How middle managers assess the context for issue selling to top management. *Strategic Management Journal* (in press).

Dutton, J. E., & Dukerich, J. (1991). Keeping an eye on the mirror: The role of image and identity in organizational adaptation. *Academy of Management Journal, 34,* 517–554.

Dutton, J. E., & Duncan, R. B. (1987a). The creation of momentum for change through the process of strategic issue diagnosis. *Strategic Management Journal, 12,* 76–90.

Dutton, J. E., & Duncan, R. B. (1987b). The influence of strategic planning on strategic change. *Strategic Management Journal, 8,* 103–116.

Dutton, J. E., Fahey, L., & Narayanan, V. K. (1983). Toward understanding strategic issue diagnosis. *Strategic Management Journal, 12,* 307–323.

Dutton, J. E., & Jackson, S. (1987). Categorizing strategic issues: Links to organizational action. *Academy of Management Review, 12,* 76–90.

Dutton, J. E., & Penner, W. J. (1993). The importance of organizational identity for strategic agenda building. In J. Hendry & G. Johnson with J. Newton (Eds.), *Strategic thinking: Leadership and the management of change* (pp. 89–113). Chichester, England: Wiley.

Dutton, J. E., Stumpf, S., & Wagner, D. (1990). Diagnosing strategic issues and managerial investment of resources. In P. Shrivastava & R. Lamb (Eds.), *Advances in strategic management* (pp. 143–167). Greenwich, CT: JAI Press.

Edelman, M. (1964). *The symbolic uses of politics.* Urbana: University of Illinois Press.

Eisenhardt, K. (1989). Making fast strategic decisions in high-velocity environments. *Academy of Management Journal, 32,* 543–576.

Feldman, M. (1989). *Understanding organizational routines: Stability and change.* Working paper, University of Michigan.

Fiol, C. M. (1991). Managing culture as a competitive resource: An identity-based view of sustainable competitive advantage. *Journal of Management, 17,* 191–211.

Fox-Wolfgramm, S. J., Boal, K. B., & Hunt, J. G. (1994). *A dynamic, configurational study of strategic issue processing and adaptation.* Working paper, San Francisco State University.

Ginsberg, A., & Venkatraman, N. (1992). Investing in new information technology: The role of competitive posture and issue diagnosis. *Strategic Management Journal, 13,* 37–53.

Gioia, D. A., Thomas, J. B., Clark, S. M., & Chittipeddi, K. (1994). Symbolism and strategic change in academia. *Organization Science, 5,* 363–383.

Hannan, M., & Freeman, J. (1984). Structural inertia and organizational change. *American Sociological Review, 49,* 149–164.

Hickson, D., Butler, R., Cray, D., Mallory, G., & Wilson, D. (1986). *Top decisions: Strategic decision making in organizations.* San Francisco: Jossey-Bass.

Hilgartner, S., & Bosk, C. L. (1988). The rise and fall of social problems: A public arenas model. *American Journal of Sociology, 94,* 53–78.

Houghton, S. M., Zeithaml, C. P., & Bateman, T. S. (1994). *Cognition and strategic issues in top management teams.* Working paper, University of North Carolina at Chapel Hill.

Howell, J. M., & Higgins, C. A. (1990). Champions of technological innovation. *Administrative Science Quarterly, 35,* 317–341.

Huber, G. P., & Daft, R. L. (1987). The information environments of organizations. In F. M. Joblin, L. L. Putnam, K. H. Roberts, & L. W. Porter (Eds.), *Handbook of organizational communication* (pp. 130–164). Newbury Park, CA: Sage.

Huff, A. S., & Pondy, L. R. (1983). *Issue management by school superintendents. Final Report to the National Institute of Education, Part 1.* Working paper. Champaign, University of Illinois.

Huff, J. O., Huff, A. S., & Thomas, H. (1992). Strategic renewal and the interaction of cumulative stress and inertia. *Strategic Management Journal, 13,* 55–75.

Jackson, S. J., & Dutton, J. E. (1988). Discerning threats and opportunities. *Administrative Science Quarterly, 33,* 370–387.

Kingdon, J. W. (1984). *Agendas, alternatives and public policies.* Boston: Little, Brown.

Kingdon, J. W. (1990). *How do issues act on public policy agendas?* Paper presented at the American Sociological Association meetings, August 11–15, Washington, DC.

Kotter, J. P. (1982). *The general managers.* New York: Free Press.

Langley, A., Mintzberg, H., Pitcher, P., Posada, E., & Saint-Macary, J. (1995). Opening up decision-making: The view from the black stool. *Organization Science, 6,* 260–279.

Lyles, M. A. (1981). Formulating strategic problems: Empirical analysis and problem development. *Strategic Management Journal, 2,* 61–75.

Lyles, M. A., & Mitroff, I. I. (1980). Organizational problem formulation: An empirical study. *Administrative Science Quarterly, 25,* 109–119.

March, J. G. (1981). Decision making perspectives. In A. H. Van de Ven & W. H. Joyce (Eds.), *Perspectives in organization design and behavior* (pp. 205–244). New York: Wiley-Interscience.

March, J. G. (1994). *A primer on decision making: How decisions happen.* New York: Free Press.

March, J. G., & Olsen, J. P. (1989). *Rediscovering institutions: The organizational basis of politics.* New York: Free Press.

March, J. G., & Shapira, Z. (1982). Behavioral decision theory and organizational decision theory. In G. R. Ungson & D. N. Braunstein (Eds.), *Decision making: An interdisciplinary inquiry* (pp. 92–115). Boston: Kent.

McKelvey, B. (1994). Evolution and organizational science. In J. A. C. Baum & J. V. Singh (Eds.), *Evolutionary dynamics of organizations* (pp. 314–326). New York: Oxford University Press.

Meyer, A. D. (1982). Adapting to environmental jolts. *Administrative Science Quarterly, 27,* 525–537.

Milliken, F. J. (1990). Perceiving and interpreting environmental change: An examination of college administrators' interpretations of changing demographics. *Academy of Management Journal, 33,* 42–63.

Milliken, F. J., & Lant, T. K. (1991). The impact of an organization's recent performance history on strategic persistence and change: The role of managerial interpretations. In P. Shrivastava, A. Huff, & J. Dutton (Eds.), *Advances in strategic management* (Vol. 7, pp. 129–156). Greenwich, CT: JAI Press.

Miner, A. S. (1994). Seeking adaptive advantage: Evolutionary theory and managerial action. In J. A. C. Baum & J. V. Singh (Eds.), *Evolutionary dynamics in organizations* (pp. 76–89). New York: Oxford University Press.

Mintzberg, H., Raisinghini, D., & Theoret, A. (1976). The structure of unstructured decision processes. *Administrative Science Quarterly, 21,* 246–275.

Moreland, R. L., & Levine, J. M. (1992). Problem identification by groups. In S. Worschel, W. Wood, & J. A. Simpson (Eds.), *Group process and productivity* (pp. 17–47). Newbury Park, CA: Sage.

Mylonadis, Y. (1991). *Environmental concerns as a source of organizational learning.* Paper presented at the International Strategic Management Society Conference, October 23–26, Toronto.

Nelson, B. (1984). *Making an issue of child abuse.* Chicago: University of Chicago Press.

Nutt, P. C. (1979). Calling in and calling off the dogs: Managerial diagnosis in public service organizations. *Academy of Management Review, 4,* 203–214.

Nutt, P. C., & Backoff, R. W. (1993). Strategic issues as tensions. *Journal of Management Inquiry, 2,* 28–42.

Penner, W. J. (1993). *Organizational responses to environmental conservation issues: Local contexts and issue interpretations.* Ph.D. dissertation, University of Michigan, Ann Arbor.

Pfeffer, J. (1982). *Organizations and organization theory.* Boston: Pitman.

Pratt, M., & Dutton, J. (1993). *Owning up or opting out: The role of interpretation and emotion in creating issue ownership.* Paper presented at the National Academy of Management meetings, August 6–11, Atlanta.

Quinn, J. B. (1980). *Strategies for change.* Homewood, IL: Irwin.

Rheger, R. K., Mullane, J. V., Gustafson, L. T., & DeMarie, S. M. (1994). Creating earthquakes to change organizational mindsets. *The Academy of Management Executive, 8,* 31–41.

Rochefort, D. A., & Cobb, R. W. (1994). Problem definition: An emerging perspective. In D. A. Rochefort & R. W. Cobb, *The politics of problem definition* (pp. 56–98). Lawrence: University of Kansas Press.

Rogers, D. (1993). *The future of American banking: Managing for change.* New York: McGraw Hill.

Rogers, E. M., & Dearing, J. W. (1988). Agenda-setting research: Where has it been, where is it going? In J. A. Anderson (Ed.), *Communication yearbook* (pp. 555–594). Newbury Park, CA: Sage.

Schneider, J. W. (1985). Social problems theory: The constructionist perspective. *Annual Review of Sociology, 11,* 209–229.

Schneider, S. C. (1994). Interpreting strategic issues: Making sense of "1992." In C. Stubbart, J. Meindl, & J. Porac (Eds.), *Advances in managerial cognition and organizational information processing* (Vol. 5, pp. 253–274). Greenwich, CT: JAI Press.

Schon, D. A. (1963). Champions for radical new inventions. *Harvard Business Review, 40,* 2, 77–86.

Shrivastava, P., & Schneider, S. C. (1984). Organizational frames of reference. *Human Relations, 37,* 795–809.

Singh, J. Ed. (1990). *Organizational evolution: New directions.* Newbury Park, CA: Sage.

Smith, G. F. (1994). Classifying managerial problems: An empirical study of definitional content, *Journal of Management Studies, 32,* 679–706.

Snow, D. A., & Benford, R. D. (1988). Ideology, frame resonance and participant mobilization. *International Social Movement Research, 1,* 197–217.

Stern, M. J. (1984). The emergence of homelessness as a public problem. *Social Science Review, 58,* 291–301.

Teece, D. J., Pisano, G., & Sheun, A. (1994). Dynamic capability and strategic management. Working paper, Harvard Business School.

Thomas, J. B., Clark, S. M., & Gioia, D. A. (1993). Strategic sensemaking and organizational performance: Linkages among scanning, interpretation, action and outcomes, *Academy of Management Journal, 36,* 239–270.

Thomas, J. B., & McDaniel, R. R. (1990). Interpreting strategic issues: Effects of strategy and the information processing structure of top management teams. *Academy of Management Journal, 33,* 286–306.

Thomas, J. B., Shankster, L. J., & Mathieu, J. E. (1994). Antecedents to organizational issue interpretation: The role of single-level, cross-level and content cues. *Academy of Management Journal, 37,* 1252–1284.

Tushman, M., & Romanelli, E. (1985). Organizational evolution: Interactions between external and emergent processes and strategic choice. In L. L. Cum-

Strategic agenda building 107

mings & B. M. Staw (Eds.), *Research in organizational behavior* (Vol. 7, pp. 171–222). Greenwich, CT: JAI Press.

Van de Ven, A. H. (1992). Suggestions for studying strategy process: A research note. *Strategic Management Journal, 13,* 169–188.

Volkema, R. J. (1986). Problem formulation as a purposive activity. *Strategic Management Journal, 7,* 267–279.

Walker, J. L. (1977). Setting the agenda in the U.S. Senate: A theory of problem selection. *British Journal of Political Science, 7,* 423–445.

Weick, K. (1979). *The social psychology of organizing.* Reading, MA: Addison-Wesley.

Weiss, J. (1989). The powers of problem definition: The case of government paperwork. *Policy Sciences, 22,* 97–121.

Winter, S. G. (1990). Survival, selection and inheritance in evolutionary theories of organization. In J. V. Singh (Ed.), *Organizational evolution: New directions* (pp. 269–298). Newbury Park, CA: Sage.

Zald, M. N. (1993). *Catching the eye of the public: Events and social movements on the public agenda.* Working paper, University of Michigan.

Zald, M. N., & Berger, M. N. (1978). Social movements in organizations: Coup d'état insurgency and mass movements. *American Journal of Sociology, 83,* 823–861.

Part III
Preference processing

6 The social ideologies of power in organizational decisions

Gerald Robert Salancik
and Margaret Cooper Brindle

There are two kinds of power: the clean and the dirty. The dirty kind is what people usually mean when they talk about politics. It is the power with a bad reputation. It is visible. It engenders outrage. It is the power you see when clashing interests subside, with one party always being disappointed. Dirty power is the kind that gets reported in the newspapers, like the flap reported about the U.S. Commerce Department's veto of a recommendation that Westinghouse receive the Baldridge Award in 1992. Unknown to Westinghouse or the judging panel recommending the company, the Commerce Department conducts its own investigation to determine the suitability of an applicant. In this case, the concern might have been national attention being drawn to the government's handling of nuclear waste (Fuchsberg, 1992).

Here we will not focus on this familiar form of power, since others have done so, and well (e.g., Ferris, Russ, & Fandt, 1990; Pfeffer, 1981). Instead, we will examine the other kind: the clean form of power. This form of power doesn't have a familiar name, although it had been called *institutional power* in earlier work (Salancik & Pfeffer, 1977). It is the invisible form of power. Here we will argue that this form of power underlies much of the stability observed in the decision making of organizations. It is the reason the powerful retain their positions and the reason discriminations of the past continue becoming discriminations in the present. This argument is not new. Recently, Warren Boeker (1989) explored it in 53 Santa Clara and San Jose, California, semiconductor firms, and confirmed that organizations hold on to their past, barring declines or the loss of their creators.

In this chapter, we will try to describe where the cleaner form of power comes from and how it relates to organizational decision making and functioning. We will try to describe its importance in making organizations work and its importance in deciding their demise.

Because the institutions we live within are less visible, people in organizations are typically blind to the role of institutions in shaping organizational dependencies and decision making. This is not always their fault. There is something intrinsically deceptive about institutional forms of power that leads even the brightest to ignore how it shapes their decisions. As faculty, we select students into our doctoral programs for their performance on the quantitative section of the admission test. Two years later, when the students take qualifying exams, we lament our disappointment that they don't seem to understand the bigger picture or the subtle lifelike nature of organizations. It hardly occurs to us that the things we selected for and the things we gave them to read were the things we were reading on their exams.

Bright young accountants and financial analysts seem to go endlessly to their superiors with bright young ideas for improving their firms' procedures or serving their customers better. The bosses often don't have the background to understand, and more often can't even conceive that an idea so important wouldn't have crossed their desks or minds before. So they reject the ideas, and keep things as they were and as they understand them. It is not that they are mean to the young or unopen to the new ideas. It is that they are trapped by their own knowledge of the world. They lack the experience of the young in the same way the young lack their experience. It is also that they are trapped by their positions; they are empowered to make decisions, and it never occurs to them that they can't and that the unempowered might make them more effectively.

So what is power? This question is both easy and difficult to address. Defining power is easy. Power is potency, the ability to have an effect. Social power is the ability to have an effect on other people, on strangers or colleagues, friends or relatives. Organizational power is the ability to have an effect on collective, organized entities and those who participate in them. Collective entities are organizations, groups, and their relationships with individuals or other collective entities.

Although power is easy to define, understanding it is more difficult. One difficulty is the definition. It is too broad. It covers too many of the things that happen in the world. Such breadth prevents us from creating a theory of power to cover all of its relevant cases. We, individuals and organizations, both have many influences and many potencies. If I step on a man's foot in a subway, I will have an effect. The man will move his foot, say "Excuse me," or in turn step on my foot, depending on his inclinations and breeding. However he acts, I will have affected him. I will have caused him to behave in some manner. But this, and many other ways we affect each other, is not what we normally think to study when we study power.

To understand power, we need to restrict the meaning of power in ways that will be helpful for a theory of power that is relevant to organizations. Here we restrict ourselves in two ways. We restrict our interest in power to the potencies of parties when they intend or seek certain effects on other parties with whom they are interdependent. Social power, in this sense, is social in two ways. We are interested in power as it affects others, and we are interested in the power that comes from our social relations with others. So the study of power we will discuss here is the study of how people or organizations are affected by, and affect, others upon whom or which they depend.

The dependence model of power

A fairly well developed theory of power based on resource dependence has been around for some 15 years, since the publication of "Who Gets Power and How They Hold On to It" (Salancik & Pfeffer, 1977) and *The external control of organizations* (Pfeffer & Salancik, 1978). Since then, many studies have either accepted the main tenets of their view or tested and examined implications of the theory. Still others, like Burt (1992), have extended the view to a network level. Yet, some important implications of this point of view have gone unexamined, such as the ideological foundations of dependencies and the relationships between interdependent agents. For this reason, the most important factor in the theory – resources – has been viewed within unrealistic and unnecessarily restricted limits.

The ABCs of organizational power

The resource dependence theory of power restricts itself to considering power that arises through a social relationship. It asserts that one party, B, has power over another, A, to the extent that the other, A, is dependent upon the first, B. It also asserts that A is dependent upon B to the extent that A desires something and lacks the capability for fulfilling the desire personally. To the extent that B is believed to have such ability and is free and able to use that ability in the service of A's interests, A will depend upon B. These are minimal and necessary conditions. If they are not present, dependency is also not present, and hence, power as we mean it is not present in the relationship between the two parties.

The extent of a dependency is further affected by the context within which the parties construct their relationship. This context is defined by three elements: alternatives for A, alternatives for B, and a third party who regulates all parties in the situation. This context is illustrated in Figure 6.1, which depicts a dependency relationship between A and B. Most important to the context is the existence of alternatives for satisfying A's purposes or desires. These are other agents who may play the same role as B and are referred to as *B-primes* (B'). They are potential parties with whom A may establish a relation similar to the one with B. B also may have alternatives, other agents who can play the same role as A, such that B's resources may well serve their interests as well as A's. These alternatives for B are hence identified simply as *A-primes*. The more alternatives B has, the greater is B's discretion; the more alternatives A has, the less dependent A is on

Figure 6.1. ABCs of power.

the particular B with whom a relationship is established for satisfying A's desires. The resource dependence view asserts that B always has discretion. The reason is that one party B may serve is B, and that all resource providers are free to use their resources for their own interests rather than those of others.

The third element of this context is a third agency, C, that regulates the relationship between A and B. We use the word *agency* rather than *agent* because a regulator may be a person or an organization or an ideology. This regulatory agency may be an actor, such as a state, or an institution, such as a norm. It takes many forms, and its presence may be felt to a greater or lesser extent and attended to more or less often. The regulatory agent does not formally belong to the relationship between A and B, but is part of the context that regulates how they behave toward one another and to other elements of the context, such as the presence of alternatives for either. Laws passed by a state to limit contractors to particular groups, for instance, are regulations that increase one group's dependency on another, much as licensing physicians controls the dependency of patients on a select few. Such laws do this not by directly influencing client and contractor relations but by controlling the number of alternatives available.

But regulatory agents need not be states or even actors. Organizations and their rules, ideologies, mythologies, and systems of authority and supervision are also regulators. Policies that mandate who reports to whom in an organization, or who may evaluate whom, explicitly determine dependencies among its personnel. Even less commonly considered constructors of dependency relations are the beliefs, assumptions, and definitions that parties have about one another and about themselves. A woman who believes her proper place is with a man also places herself in a more dependent role than do other women who believe otherwise.

Besides creating dependencies, regulations can help manage dependent relationships satisfactorily by getting those with power to do as we wish.

An employee who believes the pap of Total Quality Management will be much easier to control by others who depend on his or her activities. An executive who believes that status and self-esteem come from making excessive salaries is also more controllable, as agency theory recognizes. The most important source of a regulator's power in constructing dependency relationships is the acceptance of its mandates by the parties themselves. This is the major difference between the power of a regulatory agent and the power of parties in a resource dependence relationship.

Together, these elements (see Figure 6.1) define the kinds of relationships we intend when we speak about power dependence.

One can describe the same two parties as having the roles of either A or B in dependency relationships. In most organizational and social relationships, such is usually the case. Thus, one can speak of John as being dependent on Mary and of Mary being dependent on John. In the first dependency relation, John is the role of A, and his dependency defines Mary's power; in the second relation, John is in the role of B, and Mary's dependency defines his power. Because parties play these dual roles in their relations with others, one can also discuss and study the relative power of parties. We did so in an earlier analysis of the relative power of Department of Defense contractors and the U.S. government (Salancik, 1979). A colleague has provided a much more extensive and thoughtful discussion of relationships between department store buyers and their suppliers (Buchanan, 1992). Interdependent relations can thus be symmetric or asymmetric, with the power of one being greater than the power of the other.

Our knowledge of pairwise dependency relationships can be used to analyze the distribution of power for an entire network of actors within a field of interorganizational relations or the distribution of power among subunits or persons within a single organization. Pfeffer and Salancik's *The External Control of Organizations* (1978) makes general use of this view of resource dependence to great effect, and writers like Dan Brass (1992) and David Krackhardt (1990) have examined some power implications for newspapers and banks. Others have studied journal networks (Johnson & Podsakoff, 1994) and the relative power of publications in organizational studies (Salancik, 1986).

Yet, these larger-scale systems cannot be adequately understood without first understanding the dynamics of power and politics in the most fundamental dependency relationship between two agents in the roles of A and B. And so, this detailed level will be the starting point for our analysis here of the cleaner forms of power. Later we will show that even the institutional aspects of power and politics can be made more understandable by appreciating the details of dependency relationships. Institutional power is the most pervasive form of power as it operates in most organizational settings; it is one of the cleaner forms of power, and those subject to it often do not recognize their subjugation as political.

Ideological and institutional foundations of power

A serious, perhaps the most serious, mistaken impression reflected in many references to resource dependence is that the elements of interdependent relationships – the desires of A, the capabilities of B, the presence of alternatives, and so on – are fixed and given in any situation. This is not how we view it. The truth is that every key element of interdependent relations between two parties is subject to, and part of, the politics of their relationship. Every element is open to creation, manipulation, fabrication, definition, and most important, social construction. Every element is mutable and subject to social negotiation and redefinition. At the institutional and organizational level of analysis, such politics are continually going on to provide for the management of dependencies and the satisfaction of particular parties' interests. In the view we present of power in organizational decision making, nothing in the situation will be taken as a given, or taken for granted, even if it appears to be taken for granted to the actors involved.

Consider a young manager we knew who was charged with organizing data for scheduling a $10 million production system. The person who did this task before was a young female secretary to the plant manager. She filled her role by pulling together a mass of data on costs, labor, supplies, and sales orders and their delivery dates, which she kept on a set of disks in her desk. The secretary was leaving for another firm, and when the young manager "took over," he discovered that there was no documentation on the disks' contents or the procedures for compiling them into the appropriate reports. As the secretary's "superior," he brashly demanded that she spend the evening documenting the materials. This obvious if vain regulatory attempt got him nowhere in managing his dependency, for the woman deflected his order by saying, "Ah, I'd love to help you. But at the moment, I have to get this report out for Bill." Bill was the plant manager and the young man's supervisor. Similar exchanges went on for weeks, until the young manager had to report to Bill that he didn't think the secretary was being very helpful. Bill said, "I don't see why you say that; she helps me a lot. Maybe this job is too big for you." The secretary clearly understood her dependencies and options; the young manager clearly did not.

Resources as social constructions

Resources are often taken to be substantial material things and events, and this leads many readers and writers away from the ideologies underlying them. Here we correct this view by emphasizing how a resource is a socially constructed object that depends for its very meaning on the ideological beliefs that function in a dependency relationship. Among these beliefs are A's desires and needs, A's beliefs about his or her own capabilities and about B's capabilities for fulfilling those needs or desires, beliefs about B's control over those capabilities, and B's beliefs about his or her discretion regarding the use of his or her capabilities. And finally, there are the beliefs of both about the alternatives available to each. All such beliefs, moreover, are open to influence and social control.

By implication, a resource is not defined and has no meaning outside of the role it plays in the interdependency between the two parties, A and B. If B has a capability that is believed to be serviceable to A's desire, then that capability is a resource. Otherwise, it is not. A valuable resource is simply a capability of B that is believed to be serviceable for fulfilling the desires of many others. Thus, if a professor's ability to put a high grade on a student's paper were not something desired by many (students, their parents, their future employers), the ability would have little meaning and grades would not be resources.

But resources are socially constructed in a more important way as well. The capabilities that underlie them are frequently generated through a social process or through social institutions. Thus, the ability of the professor to put grades on students' papers is not an astonishing physical or mental ability of the professor. Rather, it is a capability that is available to many, perhaps all humans who can form the appropriate letters or numbers used to represent the grades. To make it scarce, a set of institutions evolved, or perhaps were created intentionally, to underlie the relationship between the student and the professor. These institutions and their supporting ideologies uniquely ascribe meaning to the professor's scribbling and deny it to all others. Such institutions thus socially construct the dependency of the student upon the professor for a grade, and such institutions exemplify one of the cleaner forms of power.

Although particular institutions will favor some interests over others, over time other institutions may evolve to maintain a balance of power between conflicting interests. In today's universities, students have considerably more power than they used to, partly because of universities' need to charge very high tuition to make up for losses of other funding. Reflecting students' greater power are new, socially constructed dependencies and resources associated with the rather novel practice of students "grading" professors. Introduced in the venue of quality improvements, student evaluations rapidly became institutionalized. University administrators, tenure review committees, and colleagues all began demanding good or above-average course evaluations from new faculty hires and for promotion. And with this social construction, internalized as pride and self-esteem, faculty, particularly the untenured, depend on their students to provide the coveted resource in written evaluations. Although subject to the same fabrication and manipulation as student grades, from both student and faculty, the rules regulating the practice practically ensure that faculty will work hard and charmingly to earn brownie points from their classes. When these grades are published for the community's consumption, moreover, the students can exercise a great deal of power over their teachers, especially since anonymity protects them from reprisal and accountability.

Like student grades, faculty grades gain their resource dependence quality from the institutional activities organized around them. Whereas students' clamor for effective teaching in the 1970s fell on deaf ears, the raised eyebrows of hiring and promotion committees in the 1990s succeeded. And although faculty grades may or may not have achieved greater teaching effectiveness, they have done well in forcing organizations to organize many new activities around these new resources.

Social construction of interests and needs

It should be obvious from the example of the professor and the student that dependency relationships are partly socially constructed because desires can be socially constructed, with the constructions even being made independent of the professor or the student. The student comes to the situation with a set of ready-made beliefs about grades, probably most of which did not originate with him. In former interactions, parents may have praised the student needlessly about how wonderful and smart he was to get an "A" instead of a "C." Or the student may himself have mistakenly come to the conclusion on his own that the only way he could gauge his self-worth and competence was to be told by teachers that he was an "A" rather than a "C." Believing thus, the student thus comes to the professor, paper in hand, ready to be dependent.

But desires, and the things they point to or mean for us, are socially constructed in a more important way as well. We live in interdependent worlds, and the things we desire are usually sought to enable us to participate in those worlds. Grades would have little meaning to the student or the parent if other activities of some importance to both were not organized around them. Thus, the social construction of grades is sustained, and perhaps controlled, by the employing organizations that ask each potential college graduate being hired. "What was your grade point average?" Grades would also have little meaning if universities themselves did not reproduce their own beliefs in the meaning of grades by asking for "official transcripts" rather than the student's less valued self-report.

Such socially constructed resources play important roles in shaping organizational decision making. Business schools since the late 1980s provide a good example of a newly created external resource with profound effects on their internal activities. Before 1986, business schools vied with one another for public attention, applicants, and talented personnel with reputations that were largely constructed from the opinions of their own faculty, or former faculty who abandoned the ranks to become deans and department heads. And because faculty members ranked each other, one can expect that the basis for the rankings was closely aligned with the interests of the faculty, as well as of the schools where they worked. Faculty had power because of their important role in conducting the activities that gained a reputation for a school. However, in 1986, a new source of business school rankings took root and eventually took over. In 1986, *Business Week* published its first ranking of the top 20 business schools in America. Unlike previous rankings, these were derived from the opinions of recent graduates and the job interviewers who recruited them. The rankings are unstable because of their statistical properties, but the important effect of this instability is that the top schools bounce around in the ranks from year to year. Such shifts, in turn, cause the schools to become nervous about their standing in the community and rankle their students. This fear brings with it pledges of reform and improvement, all of which leads to new activities and programs and appeasement in the next issue of *Business Week*, which loudly proclaims the deans turnabout wizards. Faculty complain increasingly about their heavier workloads, or the considerable time and money going into student lunchrooms and glossy publications. In short, by taking the ranking game away from faculty, the business schools have become responsive to a resource created and controlled by this magazine and, to some extent, more controlled by both the business community and the students who aspire to it.

The role of power in organizational decision making

Power, as a topic of research or conversation, would be of little interest if it lacked important consequences for us or for the world of organizations. Here we present a model of how power affects organizations and show what it implies about an organization's adaptation to its environment. As said before, this adaptation must of necessity be suboptimal (Salancik & Pfeffer, 1977), and can account well for the common downfalls of even the largest and most resourceful organizations, like IBM, Xerox, and GM. It would be laughable, if it were not so sad, to know that organizations of such girth fall so gracelessly, despite the extraordinary access to resources and talent they command.

The story of organizations failing is a familiar one. Most observers readily recognize the problem in other organizations, if not their own. James J. Cramer, the money manager and financial columnist, noted in 1988 that IBM would surely fall to Intel and Microsoft, as it surely did in 1993. He wrote of the computer revolution as "a revolution that will finally take its toll with the unraveling of I.B.M." (Stewart, 1993). Consider Louis Salvatore's observations about Empire Blue Cross, one of the larger Blue Cross plans and one of the most troubled in recent years, with losses of $250 million between 1991 and 1993. Salvatore is a managing partner with Arthur Andersen, a consulting firm hired by the New York State Insurance Department to assess why Empire's financial performance was so dismal in the 1980s and early 1990s. Their answer was that Empire's management failed to position the company to compete in New York, even though it was the largest medical insurer in the state. Not unlike managements of other large firms, Empire's was "slow to appreciate the accelerating pace of change in the insurance market and even slower to respond" to the changes (Salvatore, 1993).

We emphasize, however, that these failings are less often the result of boardroom power plays as they are often described by many amusing journalists and writers. Rather, the power plays being described are more typically the result of wrenching power from the failing dominant players after the ill effects of their mistakes are discovered and understood by other, less powerful stakeholders in the organization. The failings of organizations that arise from power effects in organizations are the by-products, the residue if you will, of ordinary people trying hard to do a good job within the limits of their ordinary minds, making ordinary and carefully considered decisions.

Reproducing the power structure

Uncertainty and disagreements are at the heart of the use of power in organizations (Salancik & Pfeffer, 1974). Power serves to resolve disagreements, as each party is faced with a choice to uphold a view held dearly and chance losing support from those who hold opposing views. An easily provable theorem is that such direct conflicts will necessarily end in ways that favor the powerful. The proof follows from the expectation that people, when given an opportunity to decide, will choose what they depend on for their own interests. By implication, when opinions are in contest among individuals who depend on one another, all parties will be forced to choose between the value of one of the contested positions or the persons who hold them. Since the individuals who set the debate will have strongly held views and are unable to accept alternative views, those parties who are indifferent to the contested positions will end up deciding the issue, and will do so by supporting the combatant upon whom they most depend.

When push comes to shove and the choices are real, the opinion that survives will be the opinion that is usually in the true interests of all parties involved. I first described this outcome by reference to a situation my brother described from Vietnam (retold in Pfeffer, 1981). He told me of an injured corporal who needed some lifesaving medical supply at the same time a lieutenant needed the same supply. There was only enough for one man, however, and the decision was in the hands of the medical officer on duty at the time. This is a classic problem of scarcity, and all kinds of criteria and arguments could be generated to rationalize who would get the medicine. Rather than risk his own death, the corporal quickly picked up his M-16 rifle, loaded it, and pointed it at the medical officer, saying, "Well, doc, its your choice. Me or you." Students are usually horrified when we tell this story, especially how it ends: with the lieutenant dying and the corporal spending a scant 2 years in Leavenworth. They are even more horrified when we reveal that every actor in the situation made a sensible self-interested decision. The corporal certainly did, since Army rules nearly guaranteed that his lower rank would bar him from getting the medicine he needed. But the medical officer also took the decision appropriate for his own interests. Certainly, he would rather dispense his scarce supplies to anyone rather than offer up his own life. That the corporal engineered the situation is irrelevant. The corporal made use of his capabilities as a combat soldier and created a dependency between himself and the medical officer.

When students hear this story, they raise many issues about how the medical officer and the corporal should have chosen. They should have "gone by the rules" is one suggestion. Mindful of their own stations, they propose that rank should decide. Or they offer criteria for establishing relative merit. Soon they are arguing about the best rules and how to choose among them. But they rarely get the important point: All rules and the institutions underlying them favor particular interests. The rules about military rank and its privileges, for instance, favor people of rank and were written by them.

Even if dependencies were not engineered to effect a particular decision, they will affect how social and organizational contests of opinion are resolved. Consider a situation facing a bright economist who worked for a well-respected consulting firm in Washington, D.C. He sat on a committee charged with recommending a new hire for the firm. The committee did all the preliminary work of setting criteria for applicants, gathering applications, interviewing applicants, and, after weeks of interviewing the selected ones, settled on three candidates who met their requirements (basically, a Ph.D. in economics from a major university and quantitative skills). Two candidates were strongly advocated by two members of the committee, one a junior of the other. The debate between these two got intense, and the other committee members were rather indifferent between the favorites. Yet, they had to make a choice, because only one candidate could be recommended to the senior manager of the firm who would actually select the hire. So the committee met to come to a final decision. Prior to the showdown, the junior member went to his other junior colleagues on the committee and persuaded them that his favored candidate was really the "better choice." His friends agreed and even offered him some pointers for arguing the case to the full committee. Because they held the majority on the committee, he went to the meeting well prepared, spoke brilliantly about the talents of his favorite, and smiled proudly as other committee members nodded. Little wonder, then, that when the vote was called, this young man was completely at a loss upon learning that only one of his colleagues supported his position.

Such situations are quite common. And although the details may vary, the principles that lead to their resolve are also common. Ultimately, contests of opinion are unresolvable. Each contestant understands the value of his or her own position very well and fails to understand the opposing position equally well. The contestants thus are unable to resolve their differences, so this must be done by other parties, who may well be indifferent to the positions but still need to make a choice. Sometimes the party resolving the conflict is someone with more authority than the contestants; sometimes it is a peer, as in this case. Regardless, the third party is put in a situation where a choice has to be made, not on the basis of the merits of the alternatives but on the basis of the value of each contestant to his or her own interests. Since the third party may be more dependent on one disputant than on another, the choice will usually favor the more powerful contestant. Moreover, the more difficult it is to distinguish alternatives on the basis of current ideologies and information, the more important dependencies become in determining the resolution of contests of opinion in organizations.

Such is the case here. The two applicants for the job meet the criteria of interest to the organization and most of the committee. A random choice would be wise. But decision makers typically don't think that flipping a coin makes sense, or they think any selection is under their control (Langer, 1977; Shapira, 1995), so they invent new criteria to make finer and finer distinctions between choices, often unaware of the criteria influencing them. The criteria they select are likely to be increasingly particularistic, and of interest to some parties to the contest but not others. When it comes time to make a choice, everyone involved in the situation will select positions according to their interests, which include their dependencies on others in the situation. If you extend this logic to the multitude of conflicting opinions that make up the day of any large organization, it should be obvious that decisions will be taken that reflect the dominant dependencies of the organization, that is, the power structure.

The president of the University of Pittsburgh, Dennis O'Connor, resigned his post in 1995 because the groups he needed for support chose less on the merits of his position than on the merits of their dependencies. Four years earlier, he had joined the university under a hail of accolades. He began by doing everything right. He wisely forged good and open relationships with faculty and students. He worked hard to correct the shameful financial problems of his predecessor. His innovative programs addressed current issues important to the students and faculty and to the board of directors. Success seemed assured until he innovated by allowing health benefits for same-sex couples. It was a popular issue on campus. Faculty and students approved. The business community didn't like it, but O'Connor didn't know about their reactions because they were relatively invisible as constituents. But the board of trustees did know; their main constituents came from the business community. And eventually this did O'Connor in, as such second-order, less visible dependencies often will. And consequently, the decisions of organizations reflect these less visible dependencies even though CEO's and other recognized decision makers may ignore them.

Dearborn and Simon revisited

Dependencies are only part of the story. More often than not, decision makers agree on the merits of the choices they debate. The search committee for the Washington economic analysis firm was quite sure that a successful job candidate should have a Ph.D. in economics and be familiar with the latest analytic and computational techniques. That these were the right criteria was never questioned. Quite possibly they were, but the fact that no one on the committee questioned them or considered any other criteria is the important fact. The decision was largely already made because of it. We might wonder why obviously talented and intelligent decision makers view certain things as valuable and necessary for their organizations. In general, what they consider to be an acceptable premise to work from, and what they consider to be matters for debate and evaluation, are critical for the decisions taken.

To a great extent, it is inevitable that organizations will re-create their current reality. The reason is quite simply that people can only know what they know and can only do what they know how to do. Managers necessarily develop views about what is best for an organization, or for solving its problems, based on their available knowledge, expertise, and well-developed skills in solving problems. With rare exceptions, persons can only solve problems using the ways they know and can only know well what they have experienced. When the knowledge and ideas of individuals clash, as they will when persons with different knowledge are brought into an organization, or when the organizational experiences of individuals specialize their knowledge, the disagreements will be resolved through argument and politics, and ultimately in ways that replicate the current power structure. As Dearborn and Simon (1962) showed so elegantly, accountants speak and think accounting and marketers speak and think marketing. Such limits nearly guarantee that decision makers will take decisions that reflect and reproduce their minds.

Agreement is the power structure in disguise. When disagreements on important organizational matters are easily resolved, this signals that the parties share considerably each other's knowledge and ideas. If so, it is likely that the knowledge is institutionalized, either through ideologies or through structural features of the organization and the residue of past contests of opinion. The current distribution of power reproduces itself for lack of any serious contention.

The politics of normal choice

Although power is still not the first thought in people's mind when they make decisions in organizations, enough has been said on the topic by management scholars that many managers at least think about how their plans lace through the politics of a firm. But the politics we mostly consider so openly are the politics of normal choices faced by organizational actors. The word *normal* is not used to contrast it with *abnormal* but rather to emphasize its typicality to our standard image of a choice situation and to contrast it with situations we don't normally see as choices. By *normal choice*, we mean a situation in which a decision maker faces more than one alternative. Each alternative is available for selection, and the decision maker has some discretion in choosing one of the alternatives. When several parties have an interest in the outcomes of such choices, their interests by definition disagree, and typical visible political activities will be undertaken to resolve the disagreement and implement a particular selection.

Some of the "tactics of influence" commonly used in such disputes include argument, assembling experts, coalition formation, and bargaining. These are the occasions when dirty politics can be seen among players. The young manager at the economics firm, for instance, tried to form a coalition. The effectiveness of these tactics, however, depends on whether decision alternatives are visible and contested. When they are, the arguments of experts can be summoned and stapled into four-color velum brochures, coalitions can be mustered on both sides, and bargains can be hammered out during the final hours of heated conflict.

But many selections in organizations never take place in open confrontations. Many never involve visible alternatives. Many selections are made merely because alternatives are inconceivable, or without considering other options as feasible or meaningful. They are made under constraints set in motion long ago in the history of the organization. When this is the situation, the visible politics of normal choice are irrelevant and the cleaner forms of power are usually at work. In contrast to normal choices, such selections come from either decisionless choices or choiceless decisions. Although we are purposefully being playful with this choice of words, we mean by *choices* selections among alternatives and by *decisions* choices selected by taking deliberative action.

Power and decisionless choice

A decisionless choice is a situation in which a decision maker faces more than one choice but is not free to choose any but one particular alternative. The decision maker has little or no discretion. Decisionless choices are common in social psychological experiments where the experimenter uses knowledge of the social demands of the situation that will cause the subjects to make the choice desired for the experiment. Even though the experimenter says "Now, it's your choice," it usually is not, and most or all subjects select as expected. Another form of decisionless choice arises when the weight of value is so slanted to a particular outcome that it is a "no-brainer" and most actors make the same choice. Some situations depend on maldistributed information to ensure selections; others prime overwhelming ideologies to support particular selections.

Standard and not so subtle implementations of decisionless choice use coercion. A favorite demonstration used to emphasize the point to students in a classroom has the professor take out a pistol, load it in front of the students, and, when finished, untie one shoe, remove the stocking, point the gun at a student's head, and simply say, "You have two choices. You may choose to clean out the dirt between my toes, or you may provide an opportunity to your colleagues to witness firsthand the sight of a human being's head being blown away from a 45-caliber bullet passing through it. How do you choose?"

More subtle, common reasons for decisionless choices are commitment processes related to decision makers' previous choices or organizational prior choices in the form of ordinary "policies" and "precedents." A common form of these politics is the invocation of role obligations and expectations (also see the chapters by March and Zhou in this volume). Role definitions, and the politics that surround them, offer powerful and somewhat invisible social controls, as the social psychology of commitment demonstrates (Kiesler, 1971; Salancik, 1977, 1982). When a lover says to a partner, "I thought you loved me," choice alternatives are usually being manded through the question. When a supervisor reminds a subordinate about the desire to "get ahead," the subordinate's understanding of how to behave is usually being affected, possibly to conform to the images of the supervisor.

Another common way organizations make decisionless choices is through the use of authority. Organizations distribute authority by giving the right to take certain actions to some employees while forbidding it to others. Thus, as we saw, faculty are authorized to give grades; other staff are not. Authorization for important actions, like signing checks and making promotions, is usually reserved for the ideologically correct and thus may participate in the normal politics of organizations. But with an employee who thinks like a bureaucrat, the ability to say 'I can't do that" or "this is not allowed" renders many choices without decision. The institutions underlying these pronouncements often remain invisible and unquestioned.

Whatever the mechanisms, they are powerful ways of controlling decisions in organizations. In other work, we illustrated how ideology and role definition changed a fundamental institution – the definition of death – with the introduction of brain death criteria (Brindle & Salancik, 1994). The process of introducing and crystallizing the new definition of brain death relied heavily on role obligations and expectations. Introduced in 1968 by a group of physicians associated with organ transplantation, brain death criteria were touted as a means of solving the difficult problem associated with patients whose vital functions continued on ventilator support while their brains ceased functioning. The brain death criteria were first introduced into the medical literature by aligning them with the dominant ideology of the Hippocratic oath: "to relieve the burden on patients, their families, the hospitals and on those in need of hospital beds already occupied by these comatose patients" (Beecher et al., 1968). But the particularistic interests of surgeons were also noted: "The obsolete criteria for the definition of death can lead to controversy in obtaining organs for transplant" (Beecher et al., 1968).

Aligned with important ideologies, the idea was accepted with little contest from lawyers, the clergy, or the public and was never voted upon by any official public or professional body. To become part of the everyday decision making of thousands of hospitals, however, required more than ideology. Brain death quickly progressed to becoming institutionalized through a mechanism we labeled *procedurizing*.

Procedurizing reduces difficult and potentially conflicting decisions to a set of small, inert tasks that generate a decision without anyone's having to take one. One example is the rendering of nearly overwhelming moral actions into small, unquestioned tasks. For example, the firing of massively destructive nuclear missiles is transformed through procedurizing into a script of unlocking boxes and pushing innocuous buttons. In the case of brain death, the difficult task of declaring a breathing human dead was similarly procedurized for the thousands of physicians and medical personnel who had to implement it (Brindle & Salancik, 1994). They followed small, repetitive procedures and carefully outlined steps that were, each in itself, legitimate. Forms were filled out meticulously to record the sequence of tests and checkpoints. Occupied with such tasks, personnel became oriented to the process while complying unquestioningly with its otherwise potentially questionable purpose. In short order, a rather radical idea became policy in all U.S. hospitals, usually written into standard binders of protocols.

One could, of course, rationalize massively moral actions by using equally massively moral principles, such as "freedom for the human race" or, as in the case of bombing Hiroshima, "to save 5 million lives." But the limit of rationalizing through values and principles is that one may be unable to find suitably convinced persons when needed, or that they may waver in their faith when the time comes. Procedurizing removes moral deliberation from the choices taken and provides the cover of ordinary routines for effecting them in organizations. This is not unlike March's point (in this volume) about decision making through "rule following." And although decisions that later become routines may have been taken with deliberation by some members of an organization initially, the point is that procedurizing removes choice from those who subsequently reproduce the choices. In such ways, the power reflected in setting up the procedures is institutionalized and exercised thereafter, as Zucker (1977) illustrated with her study of persistence of the autokinetic effect.

Power and choiceless decision

A choiceless decision is a situation in which selections among alternatives are being made by the decision maker, but none of the alternatives are considered to be part of the choice. That is, only one alternative is seen as available, or others are not seen as part of the choice. Yet, these situations are decision because alternatives from some real set are being selected, and the consequences of those selections will be experienced by the organization or the individual. The courses of action taken through these kinds of decisions are what many would consider taken-for-granted practice. People walk through doorways to enter a room, even though perfectly good windows could serve the same function. People answer phones in the middle of other conversations simply because the phone rings and that's what is done with a ringing phone.

Organizations that make many choiceless decisions are probably in a rut and at a disadvantage in dealing with future overt demands from constituents. IBM's intelligent stewards, for instance, simply believed that mainframes would always be used by business; auto makers in the 1970s couldn't fathom that American drivers would want anything but the large, snazzy cars they knew how to make.

The politics of choiceless decision making are not well articulated. Most choiceless decisions are the residue of history and the institutionalization of past choices.

An important effect of choiceless decision making on power is that actors either believe they have no alternative ways to satisfy their interests (B-primes in Figure 6.1) or no alternative ways to define their interests (X in Figure 6.1). The two are related. If you define your interests in a unique and particularistic manner, you invariably limit yourself to being very dependent on a small set of potential suppliers. Love is the prototypical example. Someone who seeks companionship when enjoying a movie has far more options than someone who can't enjoy a movie without sitting side by side with a best friend.

Choiceless decision making is similar in effect to bounded rationality issues in the behavioral decision literature. However, that literature often concerns questions about the search for alternatives. Here we emphasize that alternatives are not just unavailable, but inconceivable even when available. A lover can't imagine going out on the town alone. When organizations can't conceive of alternatives, however, it is not because of obsessions as much as the institutionalized residue of past political activities, with their effects on the distribution of authority and knowledge throughout an organization.

In organizations, strongly held beliefs about what needs to be done and how are equally limiting. A former student, Margaret, learned this when she was a system manager with a "holding" bank that submerged 13 other banks acquired in five states. Used to being independent, and with numerous idiosyncratic computer systems to prove it, the acquired banks protested loudly when Margaret suggested converting their systems to make them compatible with those of the flagship bank. She prepared careful charts illustrating to the banks and her boss how everyone would save weeks in time and $1 million by not having to customize each new financial or cash management product introduced by the holding bank. The satellite banks agreed with her figures, but when it came time to do the conversion, employee after employee informed her that it couldn't be done because "we don't work that way around here." This was not mere resistance to change, however. The satellites actually could not conceive how the changes Margaret suggested would do the job she wanted done without changing the fundamental way they had been doing business for years.

The inability to conceive of doing things differently is the most common way that managers and organizations take choiceless decisions. Sometimes this is due to lack of training, as it was for Margaret's banks. But more often than not, the persons making a decision simply don't have the necessary knowledge to determine, if an alternative is sensible, yet they are the only ones authorized to make the decision. This situation usually comes about when young managers propose to their superiors a major and potentially important innovation. One young systems analyst we knew was perplexed by just this issue. He was a computer whiz and had created a computer program to track and report on the firm's data base system as it was used. His solution had some generalizability, so he created a prototype application that he introduced at a software development conference, to the applause of all. The people he met there are agreed that it was a valuable new tool and wanted to know how they could get hold of it for their own businesses. Elated, he went back to his office and worked up a business plan and the numbers for his boss. Aware that there were no other products on the market, he estimated $5 million plus in service contracts. Yet when he presented the plan, his boss simply dismissed it because it was "too sophisticated for their clients." The conversation ended in frustration for the analyst, who later learned that his boss didn't understand what he was proposing.

Whether ideas get labeled "uppity" or "brilliant" largely depends on the ability of people to understand them. For many young, bright engineers or computer whizzes, this often is taken to mean that they need to present their ideas better. So they translate this lack of others' understanding into even more sophisticated reports and analyses. In truth, that's not what they need to do. The real problem is not with the presentation but with the persons to whom they are presenting. Although it is impolite to say so, some people are stupid about some things. But mostly they are simply ignorant, or lack the cultural or professional experience necessary for understanding, or lack the basic knowledge to understand the information being presented to them.

Consider a common conflict in organizations: between the management information system (MIS) department and a unit it serves. In this case, the conflict was between the MIS group and two brilliant process engineers in a large manufacturing firm. The firm was installing a new control system. The system selected would have major long-term effects on managing the production work of the firm in a competitive environment demanding flexibility and quick responsiveness to customer needs. The two bright engineers were unimpressed with the computer selected for the task by the firm's MIS department. So they did their own evaluation of alternatives, talked with computer scientists at a local university, gathered performance data and purchasing information, and ended with a recommendation they believed would meet the needs of the firm's production system. Their boss agreed and pursued the matter with the head of MIS, who asked his own assistants to re-research the issues and compare the initial recommendation with the production plans. A meeting was called to decide, and the sparks flew. The engineers' best arguments were how their computer fit their department's needs and its superior performance. The MIS experts conceded all points, then gave their best arguments regarding costly delays in making changes at this point and innumerable horror stories about system-wide failures from using incompatible computers and different suppliers for computer needs. The two lead managers sat by, admiring their underlings' presentations. Data flew like missiles through the air. It was, as they say, "a good meeting." But in the end, the two engineers were disappointed. The resolution of the conflict landed on the desk of a corporate executive, who said little more than "Well I'm going to have to go with MIS on this one."

A common problem and its common resolution. The fault here is not with the managers or the agency problems associated with them, but with the misalignment between the distribution of knowledge in an organization and distribution of authority for evaluating that knowledge and putting it into service. The authority for a decision rests with MIS personnel, who know much about computers and data systems but little or nothing of production. The underlings and their managers live in different worlds, so they can't come to terms. The senior executive who ends up making the decision knows even less about any of the technical issues. But he knows who is in charge, who is authorized to make certain decisions, and who is legitimated as the expert on such decisions. Some agency theory might lead us to think that these kinds of problems are a matter of constructing the right incentives for various parties. But actions require more than motivation; they require capability as well, and there are many situations actors are asked to decide upon about which they know nothing and cannot understand simply because it is outside their experience.

Such misalignments of personal knowledge and institutional legitimacy are common. It is to be expected that young, newly trained, talented individuals will bring their newly trained ideas into an organization. It is also expected that their more senior colleagues have not had the same opportunities to acquire these new ideas. Yet the latter, and not the former, are empowered to make choices, and this puts them and the organization in a bind. They may want to make the right choice, but lacking the requisite experience to understand if they have done so, they may simply avoid the choice and defer to the institutionalized alternatives. Choices, then, don't get made but rather fall back on the institutions of the past – institutions that are themselves the residue of the past politics of the organization.

Conclusions

We began this chapter by asserting that two forms of power characterize organizations: dirty and clean. Why two forms? The dirty forms are visible, and the stuff of "power plays," gossip, and snickering. Those who have power often don't have to do much to use it, but when they do, they are encouraged to use the politics of manipulation and coercion to achieve their ends. More often, the politics we see come from those who lack power. They are encouraged to form coalitions, create deceptions, or simply ingratiate themselves to get what they want.

Organizational theorists acknowledge that these forms of power exist in organizations, and the methods of political and social influence they encourage are worth understanding. These theorists teach it in their classes as if the wisdom of social control could be passed on through lectures and exercises on "tactics of influence" and other such dubious formulas. Or they lecture about how these forms of power affect decisions in organizations and distort the rational decision processes. From there, they may continue on about ways of limiting such distortions or how to manage them better, depending on their own ideologies. Yet what they miss, and what their students don't get a chance to understand, is how much of the decision making of the organizations is already set by the structure of power and the institutions it has created.

To appreciate these constraints on decisions, we need to concern ourselves more with the cleaner forms of power. They account for much of the stability and regularity that can be observed in the way organizations go about their business. They are the taken-for-granted beliefs that decide whether a change in the market really exists. They are the presumptions of purpose and possibility that determine whether innovations were decreed useful or foolish. They frame the criteria for decisions and decide what is meaningful information to consider. They are the rules and policies that shape the roles and definitions everyone in the organization works from, determining who has the right to make decisions or approve those of others. And they shape the dependencies that determine whose opinions will weigh more in contested decisions – dependencies that will shape the behavior of decision makers and make salient what information will be attended to.

These more subtle forms of power affect decision makers in ways they are not typically aware of because they are unmeasurable and shrouded by the formal structure in an organizational chart. And like the more visible forms of power, the taken-for-granted forms are products of dependencies and resources socially constructed during the organizations' long history of previous decisions and activities. Hidden or ignored, they are less subject to negotiation or revision. Usually outsiders change them after an organization has failed, when they bring in new personnel, with new presumptions and different knowledge that begin another cycle of institutionalization.

Although they are typically not part of the curriculum on management and decision making, these cleaner forms of power can also be the subject of lectures to students, much like the more visible forms. Anthropologists and historians have no trouble talking about the assumptions that underlie the structure of societies. Organizational theorists and lecturers should be no less capable. We do think it is possible to understand institutions and their origins. We, you and us, are, after all, not only influenced by the institutions that control us, but we also contribute to their creation. It is harder to appreciate their effects on decisions because these cleaner forms of power are less visible, but it is not impossible.

But it will take a different mindset than that exhibited by those who present overhead slides on the sources of power, with bullets to reward expert, coercive, and referent power. It will require exercises that have students form the criteria by which they make optimizing decisions, and then have them redo the optimization with a new set of criteria, and let them know that the real decisions are in the criteria they choose to accept. It will also require finer attention to dependencies than we now give, or that many disposed CEOs give – such as Christopher Steffen, who lost his top job at Kodak after only 11 weeks because he ignored the institutionalized dependencies between the president and the board of directors. To understand how the structure and institutions of power affect organizational decision making, one must invest time in its diagnosis, discovering where the dependencies lie, and how the resources and desires that determine them came to be that way. One has to understand the social constructions of power and dependence.

That is, we don't need better information or better decision models for processing the choices. We need a better understanding of the context in which decisions are created and framed and defined and resolved rather than chosen.

References

Beecher, H., et al. (1968). A definition of irreversible coma. Special communication: Report of the Ad Hoc Committee of the Harvard Medical School to examine the definition of death. *Journal of the American Medical Association, 205,* 337–341.

Boeker, W. (1989). The development and institutionalization of subunit power in organizations. *Administrative Science Quarterly, 35,* 388–410.

Brass, D. J. (1992). Power in organizations: A social network perspective. In G. Moore & J. A. White (Eds.), *Research in politics and society* (pp. 295–323). Greenwich, CT: JAI Press.

Brindle, M., & Salancik, G. R. (1994). *The social construction of an institution: Brain death and organ transplantation.* Proceedings of The Social Construction of Markets and Industry Conference, the University of Illinois at Urbana–Champaign, Chicago, April 15–17.

Buchanan, L. (1992). Vertical trade relationships: The role of dependence and symmetry in attaining organizational goals. *Journal of Marketing Research, 29,* 65–75.

Burt, R. S. (1992). *Structural holes: The social structure of competition.* Cambridge, MA: Harvard University Press.

Dearborn, D. C., & Simon, H. A. (1958). Selective perception: The identifications of executives. *Sociometry, 21,* 140–144.

Ferris, G. R., Russ, G. S., & Fandt, P. M. (1990). Politics in organizations. In R. A. Giacalone & P. Rosenfeld (Eds.), *Impression management in the organization.* Hillsdale, NJ: Erlbaum.

Fuchsberg, G. (1992). Westinghouse case stirs questions over Baldridge Award. *Wall Street Journal,* October 14, p. 19.

Johnson, J. L., & Podsakoff, P. M. (1994). Journal influence in the field of management: An analysis using Salancik's index in a dependency network. *Academy of Management Journal, 37,* 1392–1407.

Kiesler, C. A. (1971). *The psychology of commitment: Experiments linking behavior to belief.* New York: Academic Press.

Krackhardt, D. (1990). Assessing the political landscape: Structure, cognition and power in organizations. *Administrative Science Quarterly, 35,* 342–369.

Langer, E. J. (1977). The illusion of control. *Journal of Personality and Social Psychology, 32,* 311–328.

Pfeffer, J. (1981). *Power in organizations.* Mansfield, MA: Pittman.

Pfeffer, J., & Salancik, G. R. (1978). *The external control of organizations: A resource dependence perspective.* New York: Harper & Row.

Salancik, G. R. (1977). Commitment and the control of organizational behavior and belief. In B. M. Staw & G. R. Salancik (Eds.), *New directions in organizational behavior* (pp. 1–54). Chicago: St. Clair Press.

Salancik, G. R. (1979). Interorganizational dependence and responsiveness to affirmative action: The case of women and defense contractors. *Academy of Management Journal, 22,* 375–394.

Salancik, G. R. (1982). Attitude–behavior relationships as social logics. In M. P. Zanna, E. T. Higgins, C. P. Herman (Eds.), *Consistency in social behavior: Volume 2, The Ontario Symposium* (pp. 51–74). Hillsdale, NJ: Erlbaum.

Salancik, G. R. (1986). An index of subgroup influence in dependency networks. *Administrative Science Quarterly, 31,* 194–211.

Salancik, G., & Pfeffer, J. (1974). The bases and use of power in organizational decision making: The case of a university. *Administrative Science Quarterly, 19,* 453–473.

Salancik, G. R., & Pfeffer, J. (1977). Who gets power and how they hold on to it: A strategic contingency model of power. *Organizational Dynamics, 5,* 2–21.

Salvatore, L. P. (1993). Troubles at Empire Blue Cross reflect a failure of management. *New York Times,* "Editorials/Letters," July 15, p. A14.

Shapira, Z. (1995). *Risk taking: A managerial perspective.* New York: Russell Sage Foundation.

Stewart, J. (1993). Whales and sharks: The unexpected fates of I.B.M. and A.T.&T. may offer a lesson to the Clinton Justice Department. *The New Yorker,* February 15, pp. 37–43.

Zucker, L. (1977). The role of institutionalization in cultural persistence. *American Sociological Review, 42,* 726–743.

7 Managerial incentives in organizations: Economic, political, and symbolic perspectives

Edward J. Zajac and James D. Westphal

Introduction

It may be only a slight exaggeration to suggest that the topic of incentives in organizations – particularly managerial incentives – has received more sustained attention from a more diverse set of scholars, consultants, and business reporters than any other topic relevant to the functioning of organizations. For example, some economists have gone so far as to maintain that "incentives are the essence of economics" (Lazear, 1987), and interest in this topic has recently spawned a substantial literature drawing from agency theory (Beatty & Zajac, 1994; Jensen & Murphy, 1990a, 1990b; Lewellen, Loderer, & Martin, 1987; Murphy, 1985). Similarly, the topic of incentives and motivation has long been a central area of research for psychologists and micro-organization behavior researchers (Kerr, 1975; Tosi, House, & Dunnette, 1972). Sociologists, organization theorists, and strategic management researchers have also devoted considerable effort to the study of managerial incentives in organizations (Finkelstein & Hambrick, 1988; Kerr & Bettis, 1987; Westphal & Zajac, 1994; Zajac, 1990). Finally, the popular business press has persistently tracked, publicized, and, most recently, critiqued the compensation of top managers (*Business Week*, 1992; Crystal, 1991; *Time*, 1993).

Given these circumstances, we must be clear regarding the objective of this chapter. We do not intend to provide a comprehensive review of research on managerial incentives.[1] On the contrary, the discussion to follow reflects our biases, prior writings, and research preferences. Our objective is to explain what appears to be a fundamental paradox: namely, that the massive amount of attention devoted to the topic of managerial incentives

Both authors contributed equally to the chapter. The helpful comments of Zur Shapira and Don Kleinmuntz are gratefully acknowledged.

in organizations has not led to any corresponding growing consensus. Indeed, the opposite seems to be true. Greater research and discussion from more researchers and commentators have produced more vigorous disagreement and debate regarding the use of managerial incentives in organizations.

For example, the popular business press has tended to portray executive compensation as "excessive" (Crystal, 1991; *Time,* 1993) or even "out of control" (*Business Week,* 1992), and has generally supported legislative initiatives aimed at reform (*Time,* 1993). Interestingly, a central target of this criticism is long-term incentive compensation, which has become an increasingly significant component of executive pay (Jarrell, 1993). Once viewed by most observers as connoting managerial value and devotion to shareholder interests (e.g., Crystal, 1984), long-term incentive plans have recently been negatively portrayed as insidious devices that serve only to enrich top management at the expense of shareholders (*Business Week,* 1992; Crystal, 1991).

Such trenchant criticism has helped create widespread skepticism among corporate stakeholders regarding the motivation for managerial incentives (Jensen & Murphy, 1990a) while bolstering legislative efforts to curtail their use (*Time,* 1993). Jensen and Murphy (1990b, pp. 254–255), who advocate the increased use of long-term incentives, go so far as to claim that the threat of "media criticism and ridicule" following large long-term incentive payouts effectively deters companies from using long-term incentives in designing CEO compensation contracts. Moreover, they suggest that this "implicit regulation" encourages suboptimal compensation contracts and a weak pay–performance relation. The inability of empirical studies to consistently demonstrate a significant relationship between CEO pay and firm performance (Jensen & Murphy, 1990a; Kerr & Bettis, 1987) has led some researchers to explore more behaviorally oriented explanations for the board's apparent failure to fulfill its nominal function. These studies typically focus on the social, political, and/or psychological aspects of the CEO–board relationship, including how the CEOs' relative power over board members may influence cash compensation, such as salary and bonus (Finkelstein & Hambrick, 1989; Hill & Phan, 1991).

Note the parallels between the debate in the popular press and the debate in the academic literature between researchers taking economic and behavioral perspectives (e.g., Beatty & Zajac, 1994; Finkelstein & Hambrick, 1989; Jensen & Murphy, 1990a; Tosi & Gomez-Mejia, 1989; Zajac, 1990). Economics-based research, relying primarily on agency theory (Jensen & Meckling, 1976), emphasizes how contingent compensation contracts for managers, that is, contracts linking pay to firm performance, can align the interests of CEOs and shareholders and lead to optimal risk sharing. The board of directors is responsible for fashioning contingent contracts and functions more generally to monitor executive behavior (Fama & Jensen, 1983). Most behavioral research on incentives, by contrast, tends to focus on the overtly political aspects of top management compensation, emphasizing how powerful CEOs are able to pressure boards into giving the CEO higher levels of cash compensation. In other words, the academic debate surrounding CEO compensation can be characterized in terms of the tension between the economic efficiency of an ideally constructed compensation contract (as agency theorists seek to devise) and the presumed political reality of entrenched executives and weak boards.

Given our preferences for studying the phenomenon of managerial incentives, rather than showing how a single discipline addresses the question of incentives, our approach is inclusive, drawing from economic and political perspectives. This is not to say, however, that we do not have a particular point of view. In fact, as will be shown, this chapter argues for the need to consider a third perspective: namely, the possibility that managerial incentive compensation debates – and the use of incentives themselves – are driven largely by symbolic considerations (Westphal & Zajac, 1994; Zajac & Westphal, 1995). A symbolic management perspective would, for example, ask a question rarely posed in the top management compensation debates: Why should anyone care whether CEOs in large U.S. corporations are grossly overpaid or "worth every nickel they get" (Murphy, 1986)? From a substantive standpoint, even if an individual in a large corporation is overpaid, that individual's (over)compensation would likely amount to a trivially small proportion of the organization's total yearly expenses and would thus be only a minor source of inefficiency.[2]

Thus, it is not surprising that the CEO compensation debate is rarely couched in terms of whether an organization's financial performance has been substantively damaged through overpaying its CEO. Rather, the basis for the debate is more symbolic, and the implicit question is whether CEO compensation is justifiable in the eyes of organizational stakeholders (Zajac & Westphal, 1995). This can be seen in recent attempts to objectify the issue of CEO compensation justification, expressed either in dollar terms (e.g., the recent U.S. political decision to question the corporate tax deductibility of executive salaries above $1 million) or in correlational terms (e.g., the relation between CEO compensation and firm performance or the multiplier between entry-level compensation and CEO compensation). This focus on measurement, however, implicitly deemphasizes perhaps the most salient features of a justification problem: namely, that such a problem is socially defined, inherently subjective, and potentially subject to manipulation. Accordingly, this chapter suggests that the domain of managerial incentives may represent a justification problem for organizations, and that by taking a symbolic management perspective, one can gain greater understanding of the social definition and possible manipulation of the phenomenon.

Thus, the symbolic management perspective developed in this chapter differs markedly from more traditional economic and behavioral perspectives on managerial incentives and organizational decision making. Both economic and political theories view managerial incentives as a substantively meaningful vehicle for translating interests into organizational action. Whereas in the economic model interests are unified at the organizational level, in the political model interests are factious and competing (March, 1962). From the symbolic perspective, by contrast, the preferences that inform incentive structure, whether unified or divergent, are defined by broader, macro-social forces (Friedland & Alford, 1991). Indeed, in the symbolic model, the very purpose of managerial incentives is to articulate social values. To the extent that incentives articulate divergent social values that are represented by competing interests within the organization, a political perspective on managerial incentives and organizational decision making can be incorporated within the symbolic model (DiMaggio, 1988; Zajac & Westphal, 1995).

The economic perspective on managerial incentives, however, is not easily reconciled with the symbolic approach. Whereas distinctive competencies and strategic imperatives vary across organizations, variation in incentive structure is limited by social construction processes and by the need to articulate social values in a clear, consistent manner. Accordingly, from the symbolic perspective, incentive structures are either decoupled from substantive organizational decision making (Meyer & Rowan, 1977) or encourage suboptimal decision making (from the standpoint of organizational efficiency; see DiMaggio & Powell, 1983).

The chapter is organized as follows: It begins with a rather brief review of the economic literature on managerial incentives, followed by a similarly brief review of the behavioral research that emphasizes the political aspects of incentives. It then introduces in greater detail the symbolic management perspective on managerial incentives. The chapter concludes with a discussion of how a cross-level perspective that considers individual, sociopolitical, and social-structural factors can integrate currently fragmented perspectives and begin to resolve long-standing debates surrounding the use of managerial incentives in organizations.

Economic perspectives on incentives

Perhaps the most influential economic perspective on managerial incentives is derived from agency theory (Jensen & Meckling, 1976; Ross, 1973). This theory examines the problems – and partial contractual solutions – that exist when a principal delegates decision-making responsibility to an agent who is paid a fee but whose own objectives may conflict with those of the principal. Not surprisingly, this theoretical perspective is seen as having considerable potential for the analysis of executive compensation contracts (Fama, 1980; Lewellen et al., 1987). In fact, much of the growth in executive compensation research in the economics literature can be traced to the continued development of the economic theory of agency as a framework for analyzing the relationship between principals (e.g., shareholders–board of directors) and agents (top managers). Not surprisingly, this approach is seen as having considerable potential for the analysis of executive compensation contracts (Fama, 1980; Lewellen et al., 1987).

However, the agency literature relevant for studying executive compensation has developed into what Jensen (1983, pp. 334–335) has referred to as two "almost entirely separate" agency literatures: a normative principal–agent literature that emphasizes formal modeling approaches to designing the optimal principal–agent contract (see Levinthal, 1988, for a review of this literature) and a positive (i.e., descriptive) agency literature that seeks to explain the observed existence of certain contractual structures (e.g., Jensen and Murphy's 1990a exhaustive empirical study on the CEO pay-for-performance relationship).

These distinct paths of development have led to some disagreements among agency researchers. Indeed, with respect to the topic of executive compensation, one could argue that agency theory is at a crossroads. More specifically, whereas normative agency theorists continue to seek to formally derive optimal incentive contracts (see Harris & Raviv, 1979; Holmstrom, 1979, 1982; Ross, 1973) prominent empirical agency researchers have begun to question the usefulness of agency models in actual executive compensation contracts. For example, Jensen and Murphy (1990a, p. 246), after searching in vain for evidence of a pay-for-performance relationship for CEOs in large corporations, concluded that normative models of incentive contracts, such as Holmstrom's (1979), are largely "irrelevant to most compensation contracts."

This empirical work on the relationship between CEO compensation and organizational performance in large corporations (see Benston, 1985; Coughlin & Schmidt, 1985; Jensen & Murphy, 1990a, 1990b; Murphy, 1985) is similar to the earlier work of economists such as Masson (1971) and Lewellen and Huntsman (1970), which was spurred by the growth of managerialist theory in the 1960s. Like agency theory, managerialist theory addresses the issue of conflict between owners and managers, but without the explicit emphasis on contracting solutions that agency researchers have typically studied. Thus, much of the empirical agency-based literature on executive compensation resembles that of the traditional managerialist school (exceptions include Beatty & Zajac, 1994; Larcker, 1983; and Lewellen et al., 1987). In fact, Jensen and Murphy's (1990a) widely cited study can be viewed as yet another descriptive managerialist study that searches (with little success) for evidence of a strong "CEO-pay-for-firm-performance" relationship among CEOs of large corporations. This unsuccessful search often leads to calls for greater regulation or reform of executive compensation practices, invariably with an implicit or explicit recommendation for an increase in the pay-for-performance component of compensation contracts (Jensen & Murphy, 1990a).[3]

It is interesting to note that in the last decade, the agency literature has gone from conjecturing that efficient managerial labor markets provide an "*ex post* settling up" for shirking managers that minimizes agency problems (Fama, 1980), to formally modeling that such markets do so only under certain restrictive conditions (Holmstrom, 1982), to finding empirical evidence that they do (summarized in Jensen & Zimmerman, 1985), to believing that such markets are largely corrupted and barely functioning (e.g., Jensen & Murphy, 1990a)! Regardless of one's beliefs regarding the relative efficiency of the managerial labor market, it is noteworthy that the empirical basis for the calls for regulation or reform are grounded almost exclusively in positive agency research that correlates firm performance with executive compensation – with little success.

Beatty and Zajac (1994) suggest, however, that such studies neglect potentially important organizational factors that might explain – without reference to political behavior – the variation in observed compensation contracts. Specifically, they note that whereas the positive agency literature highlights the value of placing greater amounts of managerial compensation and managerial wealth at risk by tying them closer to firm performance (e.g., Jensen & Murphy, 1990b), the normative agency literature stresses the need to consider the potential *disadvantages* of forcing managers to bear "excessive" compensation risk (Harris & Raviv, 1979; Holmstrom, 1979, 1987; Shavell, 1979; Stiglitz, 1987).

Thus, although Jensen and Meckling (1976) originally defined the magnitude of the agency problem in terms of the degree of separation between owner and manager interests, subsequent clarifications suggest that linking a manager's compensation too closely to firm wealth might lead to risk-avoiding behavior on the part of the agent (the point where a linkage becomes "too close" remains unclear, however). This argument, as summarized in Holmstrom (1987), stresses the fact that although contingent compensation may seem to have desirable incentive/motivational properties relative to noncontingent forms of compensation, it also has undesirable risk-bearing properties. Such a compensation contract would cause a manager to bear risk that could be more efficiently borne by diversified stockholders (the underlying assumption is that the manager, unlike the owners, has already invested most of his or her nondiversifiable and nontradable human capital in the firm; in this way, the agent can be treated as risk averse and the principal as risk neutral). It follows that agents would be reluctant to bear this risk of firm performance, or, stated differently, that it is difficult and costly for the principal to have the agent bear this risk (this argument for managerial risk aversion does not require owners to be fully risk neutral, but only for managers to be more risk averse than owners).

Interestingly, whereas there is a substantial body of research that seeks to find strong correlations between managerial compensation and firm performance, there is little corresponding empirical research on the question of managerial incentives and risk aversion. Organizational research has also generally placed greater emphasis on the importance – from an incentive and control standpoint – of imposing strong pay-for-performance linkages rather than on the possible disadvantages of imposing risk bearing in managerial compensation contracts. The lack of debate in the recent organizational literature on this issue is somewhat surprising, given that the organization behavior literature on compensation has historically recognized that different forms of compensation, such as pay-for-performance, vary in their attractiveness to individuals and, therefore, vary in their appropriateness as incentive-motivational tools (Lawler, 1971; Mahoney, 1979).

Recently, however, Beatty and Zajac (1994) have examined the question of risk aversion in a large study of firms undertaking an initial public offering. They suggest that there is a need to (1) recognize explicitly the potential costs, rather than just the benefits, of using incentives and (2) start to identify the organizational and individual contingencies that could affect the consideration of the incentive cost–benefit trade-off. They focus on one such organizational contingency – firm risk – that may increase the riskiness of incentive compensation contracts and therefore may make managers particularly reluctant to accept such contracts. They find evidence consistent with their argument that more risky firms face great difficulties (and thus greater costs) when using incentive compensation contracts, given the risk aversion of top managers, and, as a result, are less likely to emphasize incentive compensation. They also find that firms generally respond to this problem of inadequate incentive compensation by structuring boards of directors to provide greater levels of monitoring. Their findings suggest that incentives, monitoring, and risk bearing are important factors shaping the structure of firms' executive compensation contracts, ownership, and boards of directors.

Zajac and Westphal (1994) found similar results using longitudinal data over 5 years from a sample of over 400 of the largest U.S. corporations. They developed and tested a contingency cost–benefit perspective on governance decisions as resource allocation decisions, proposing how and why the observed levels of managerial incentives and monitoring may vary across organizations and across time. They also proposed that there may be salience threshold levels for managers, or, stated differently, that there may be considerable diminishing "behavioral returns" to increases in incentive compensation. Their findings suggest that the contingent relationships proposed by Beatty and Zajac (1994) may be more logarithmic than linear.

In summary, agency theory and the literature that has developed from it have brought at least two significant issues to the study of managerial incentives. First, the normative literature has highlighted the potential importance of managerial risk aversion as affecting the choice of an optimal incentive arrangement. Second, the positive literature has focused attention on the need to establish ways to improve the managerial pay-for-performance relationship.

Political-perspectives on incentives

*Political dynamics in the CEO–board relationship
and the form of managerial incentives*

Ironically, agency theory essentially provides a theoretical transition from managerialist to political perspectives on management compensation. Whereas managerialist perspectives presume a tension between shareholder and management interests, the interests of managerial elites (i.e., corporate officers and directors) are assumed to be relatively homogeneous. Agency theory, however, moves the border between management and shareholder interests inside the organization by assuming that corporate directors represent shareholder interests rather than the interests of top management, thus providing a basis for political behavior (see, Finkelstein & Hambrick, 1989). Although agency theory assumes that shareholder interests dominate, its premise of conflicting interests within the organization, together with growing empirical evidence that incentive contracts frequently do not reflect shareholder interests, has spurred behavioral researchers to consider more directly the political determinants of executive compensation contracts.[4]

Political perspectives on executive compensation have developed together with a larger empirical literature on how structural and demographic indicators of relative power in CEO–board relationships can impact corporate policy outcomes. Drawing on important case-based studies of board behavior (e.g., Alderfer, 1986; Mace, 1971; Vance, 1983), as well as theory and research on political processes in organizations (Pfeffer, 1981a), this research has examined specific bases of power by which top managers can influence board decision making.

Perhaps the most widely studied source of CEO power is formal board structure. For instance, considerable research has examined whether the ratio of inside to outside directors diminishes board effectiveness in protecting shareholder interests. Given that insiders are "beholden to CEOs for their jobs" (Fredrickson, Hambrick, & Baumrin, 1988, p. 262; Pfeffer, 1981a), they are expected to defer to the CEO's preferences regarding compensation and other governance arrangements. Indeed, there is some qualitative evidence that inside directors are reluctant to challenge the CEO's preferences in board and committee meetings (e.g., Alderfer, 1986, p. 44). However, as Pettigrew (1992) notes, the overall evidence is mixed.

One explanation for a weak relationship between formal board structure and CEO compensation is that additional, more informal political processes serve to compromise the nominal independence of outside directors. Although a variety of influence processes could be involved, thus far researchers have focused primarily on the role of board cooptation. Specifically, based on qualitative evidence that top managers usually identify new director candidates (Mace, 1971), and evidence from the organizational literature that control over appointments and promotions is an important source of power (Perrow, 1972; Pfeffer, 1981a), it is argued that CEOs "co-opt" the board by appointing "sympathetic" new directors during their tenure (Finkelstein & Hambrick, 1989; Frederickson et al., 1988; Wade, O'Reilly, & Chandratat, 1990). Consistent with this argument, Finkelstein and Hambrick (1989) found a relationship between the CEO's tenure and the level of CEO compensation. Similarly, Hill and Phan (1991) showed that the correlation between CEO pay and firm performance declined with increases in CEO tenure, suggesting that the incentive effect of CEO compensation declines as CEOs coopt the board with supporters.

However, although these findings are consistent with the cooptation hypothesis, they are also consistent with a human capital perspective, whereby long-tenured CEOs are rewarded for their accumulated firm-specific knowledge and expertise. Moreover, as Finkelstein and Hambrick (1989, p. 124) note, the effect of CEO tenure may also derive from distinct political processes, such as the emergence of a "personal mystique or patriarchy" over time or the creation of image dependencies as CEOs "[work] to link their personas with their companies in the public eye" (Walsh & Seward, 1990, p. 432). However, using a more precise measure of cooptation introduced by Wade et al. (1990) in their study of golden parachute adoption, Westphal and Zajac (1994) found that the portion of the board composed of outside directors appointed after the CEO was negatively related to the use of performance-contingent CEO compensation after controlling for CEO tenure.

Although this study provides stronger evidence for cooptation, it does not reveal exactly why outsiders appointed after the CEO behave more like insiders than truly independent board members. This reflects a general ambivalence in the governance literature regarding the specific mechanism(s) driving cooptation. In other words, although cooptation is most frequently described as the appointment of "sympathetic" individuals to the board (e.g., Finkelstein & Hambrick, 1989, p. 124; Wade et al., 1990, p. 592), the theoretical basis of this sympathy is unclear. According to Wade et al. (1990), cooptation relies on norms of reciprocity between CEOs and new appointees, so that the latter feel obligated to return the favor of appointment by supporting the CEO. However, Fredrickson et al. (1988) and others (e.g., Mace, 1971; Patton & Baker, 1987) attribute new director loyalty to social ties (e.g., friendship) between CEOs and their appointees, whereas O'Reilly et al. (1988) suggest that CEOs might exploit social comparison processes in determining their compensation by appointing highly paid executives to the board. Thus, additional research evidence is clearly needed to verify these and other specific mechanisms of cooptation and to adjudicate between them.

As an initial step in this direction, a recent study of new director selection and CEO compensation by Westphal and Zajac (1995a) found strong evidence that demographic similarity between CEOs and new directors can provide a basis for cooptation. Specifically, the results suggested that relatively powerful CEOs (as indicated by relative CEO–board tenure, board leadership structure, and other indicators) were better able to appoint demographically similar new directors, and that increased CEO–board similarity largely mediates the effect of relative power on the use of performance-contingent CEO compensation. Thus, to the extent that similarity in functional background, age, and other demographic characteristics indicates similarity in underlying attitudes and beliefs relevant to strategic decision making, the "sympathy" of new appointees regarding relatively high or risk-free CEO compensation may derive from trust in the CEO's decision making rather than from perceived social obligations. In effect, it appears that demographic similarity reduces the perceived need to minimize shirking behavior and otherwise control CEO decision making with incentive compensation.

More generally, this study and others (e.g., O'Reilly et al., 1988; Wade et al., 1990) suggest the value of enriching political models of CEO compensation with related behavioral perspectives, including relevant theory and research from cognitive and social psychology. Such models provide a more detailed theoretical explanation of how CEOs wield power over their boards. For instance, Westphal and Zajac's (1995a) model of board cooptation predicts CEO–new director demographic similarity and the consequences for compensation arrangements by incorporating social psychological research on hiring and performance evaluation into a CEO–board power framework. Moreover, the use of demographic variables to examine social psychological processes underlying executive incentive practices indicates the potential for organizational demography (O'Reilly, Caldwell, & Barnett, 1989; Pfeffer, 1983) and upper-echelon paradigms (Hambrick & Mason, 1984) to advance research on executive compensation (Zajac and Westphal, 1996, also take a similar approach in extending research on executive succession. Specifically, they show how social psychological and sociopolitical factors can create divergent preferences between the incumbent CEO and the existing board regarding the desired characteristics of new CEOs – with each preferring a new CEO whose characteristics resemble their own – and how relative CEO–board power can predict whose preferences are realized.

The role of director networks in the political model

Political and social psychological perspectives can also illuminate relatively distal causes of compensation practices. O'Reilly et al. (1988) argued that social comparison processes lead compensation committee members to use their own compensation, and that of similar other CEOs, as a benchmark in determining the focal CEO's compensation. The findings were supportive, suggesting that compensation practices may originate with the practices of other companies rather than with organization-specific factors such as firm performance.

In a more recent study, Westphal and Zajac (1995b) investigated the spread of specific changes in board structure and compensation contracts across organizations. They suggest that CEO-directors (i.e., outside directors who are themselves CEOs of other large corporations) may play a more complex role in corporate governance than was previously assumed in the literature. Specifically, they propose that CEO-directors may typically support fellow CEOs by impeding increased board control over management, but that CEO-directors may also incite this change *if they have experienced it in their own corporations.* Drawing from social exchange theory (Ekeh, 1974), they developed the argument that these CEO-directors may experience a reversal in their perceived basis for social exchange with top managers from one of deference and support to one of independence and control.

Using longitudinal data from a large sample of companies over a recent 10-year period, Westphal and Zajac (1995b) first observed a negative relationship between the proportion of the board composed of CEO-directors and the likelihood of changes in board structure. This suggests that, consistent with a social exchange model emphasizing generalized norms of reciprocity, CEO-directors perceive a generalized obligation to support other CEOs. In this system of social interaction among status equals, sufficient trust exists such that CEO-directors believe their support for CEOs will be reciprocated indirectly from someone and somewhere else in the future. This finding is also consistent with social psychological research showing that group solidarity or mutual identification can generate cooperative behavior (Dawes, 1991).

However, their subsequent findings suggest that when CEO-directors have experienced increased board independence in their home corporations, they spur – rather than resist – such change for those firms on whose boards they sit. This result is consistent with the notion that when generalized exchange partners are no longer of equal status and prestige, such inequality may "force a rupture" in the system of exchange (Lévi-Strauss, 1969, p. 266). Thus, it appears that social solidarity among corporate leaders can provide a context for generalized retaliation or defection as well as cooperation (see Axelrod, 1984; Gouldner, 1960).

One can also treat the director network as endogenously determined and consider how powerful corporate actors may influence the structure of the director network through the director selection process. Specifically, given that corporate leaders' prior experiences influence their relative allegiance to shareholder interests versus management interests in designing executive incentive arrangements, powerful top managers may seek to perpetuate incentive compensation practices favored by managers by selecting for the board director candidates with experience in supporting managerial preferences and excluding individuals with experience on active boards. Conversely, powerful boards can mobilize support for performance-contingent managerial compensation by selecting candidates who have participated in such change elsewhere and excluding individuals with experience on passive boards.

In fact, we have also found that directors who participate in increased compensation contingency subsequently tend to gain directorships at companies characterized by high board control and lose appointments at companies characterized by low board control. Moreover, there is also some evidence that directors who participate in decreased compensation contingency tend to gain (lose) appointments at low (high) board control companies. This finding suggests a dynamic selection process wherein director ties across similarly active or passive boards (as indicated by incentive practices) are maximized, and ties between dissimilar boards (i.e., active and passive) are minimized, leading to a "segmented" director network. Overall, these findings demonstrate how changes (or lack thereof) in managerial incentive practices are affected by political dynamics in CEO–board relationships, and how reward structures more generally reflect macropolitical conflict between managerial and shareholder interests (Useem, 1993).

Directions for future research on political determinants of managerial incentives

Although archival research on the political processes affecting CEO compensation has burgeoned in recent years, as the previous discussion suggests, it has generally not been adequately complemented by survey and qualitative research examining these processes in greater detail. Pettigrew (1992, p. 171) notes a similar shortcoming in the larger literature on boards of directors: "great inferential leaps are made from input variables such as board composition to output variables such as board performance with no direct evidence on the processes and mechanisms that presumably link the inputs to the outputs." Such field research would seem especially valuable in confirming the microbehavioral, social psychological mechanisms by which power is thought to be exercised. For instance, survey research could examine whether CEO-directors enjoying risk-free compensation feel obligated to meet the preferences of fellow CEOs in designing compensation contracts, whereas CEO-directors subjected to increased compensation contingency feel motivated to increase compensation risk elsewhere.

Survey research could also be used to test the various mechanisms of board cooptation thought to lessen the use of CEO incentives. For example, researchers could examine whether directors appointed after the CEO do, in fact, feel personally obligated to back the CEO's preferences regarding compensation arrangements (see Alderfer, 1986; Wade et al., 1990). Such research could also assess whether CEO–board demographic similarity enhances directors' trust in the CEO's decision making, thus reducing the perceived need to align CEO compensation with firm performance (see Westphal & Zajac, 1995a), and whether directors with friendship ties to the CEO acknowledge a certain allegiance or loyalty to him or her (see Fredrickson et al., 1988; Patton & Baker, 1987).

Similarly, as also noted by Pettigrew (1992, p. 171), field research is needed to enhance our understanding of the behavioral dynamics supporting suboptimal compensation practices. Such research may help to explain inconsistent findings regarding the effect of board composition on CEO compensation. In other words, what are the actual behavioral processes by which the ratio of inside to outside directors can affect board decision making with respect to incentive arrangements? One possibility is that board composition influences discussion norms in board and committee meetings (see Lorsch & MacIver, 1989). For instance, where insiders comprise a relatively large proportion of the board, they might enforce informal, interpersonal sanctions against challenging the CEO's position or preferences. The proportion of the board comprised of CEO-directors or outsiders with friendship ties to the CEO could have similar effects on board dynamics, and because compensation committees include only outsiders, the mediating effect of board norms or informal sanctions on incentive practices may be especially strong for these variables (O'Reilly et al., 1988). Thus, formal board structure and informal sources of cooptation may have both individual-level and group-level effects on CEO compensation contracts.

Alternatively, field research on the behavioral dynamics of CEO–board relationships might reveal that social ties provide a basis for more efficient board monitoring. Relatedly, to the extent that demographic similarity enhances social integration and facilitates efficient communication (O'Reilly et al., 1989; Zenger & Lawrence, 1989), similarity could also promote effective board monitoring activity. Thus, it is possible that CEO–board demographic similarity and social ties reduce the *actual* need for CEO incentive alignment. Research evidence regarding whether and when these dimensions of board social structure enhance or diminish board control would contribute significantly to normative models of CEO incentive compensation, as well as the literature on board composition and director selection.

Finally, survey and qualitative research could investigate whether informal, political influence processes in CEO–board relationships affect compensation practices. Although several studies have examined the relationship between structural power (whether formal or social in nature) and CEO incentive arrangements, researchers have not considered how CEOs use other sources of power, such as expert power (Finkelstein, 1992; French & Raven, 1959), in seeking to influence board decision making. For instance, CEOs enjoying relatively little structural power over their boards might instead leverage their superior firm-specific expertise, or the presumption of such expertise, by engaging in informal politicking behavior vis-à-vis powerful board members (see Eisenhardt & Zbaracki, 1992;

Pfeffer, 1981a, 1992; Porter, Allen, & Angle, 1981). Such tactics may enhance board support for the CEO's strategic initiatives and bolster confidence in his or her decision-making capability, thus potentially reducing the perceived need for high incentive alignment (Westphal, 1995).

In summary, whereas the majority of prior research taking a political perspective on CEO compensation contracts has examined the direct relationship between structural CEO–board power and the size or form of CEO compensation, further inquiry is needed on the role of microbehavioral mechanisms in mediating or offsetting these relationships. In addition, however, this stream of research can be usefully complemented by greater attention to *macro*structural processes underlying CEO compensation contracts. In the following section, we discuss recent studies attempting to bridge the micro and macro perspectives on CEO compensation and suggest fruitful avenues for future research in this area.

The symbolic management of incentive compensation

Whereas researchers interested in incentive compensation tend to focus on the economic or motivational significance of aligning pay more closely with performance, incentive practices have also acquired considerable *social* significance in recent years. As institutional investors and other corporate stakeholders seek greater CEO accountability and board responsibility, external criticism regarding the size and form of CEO compensation contracts has increased dramatically (e.g., Crystal, 1991; *Business Week*, 1992). Consequently, although top managers may prefer to avoid incentive arrangements that increase their financial risk, they should also seek to design *formal* compensation contracts that demonstrate their accountability to increasingly vigilant external stakeholders.

In recent research on the adoption and use of long-term incentive plans (LTIPs) among large Fortune and Forbes 500 corporations, Westphal and Zajac (1994) considered how institutional and symbolic management processes might resolve these apparently competing interests. Prior research has given only limited consideration to the implications of symbolic and institutional perspectives for executive compensation issues (DiMaggio & Powell, 1983; March, 1984). This omission in the literature is surprising, because increased institutional pressures for equitable CEO compensation contracts would seem likely to encourage symbolic action by entrenched top managers.

Accordingly, in this study Westphal and Zajac examined the potential for symbolic use of LTIPs. Although very little behavioral research has examined the antecedents and consequences of LTIPs, a number of studies in the financial economics literature have investigated the consequences of their adoption. In particular, several event studies have demonstrated a favorable stock market reaction to the announced adoption of executive incentive plans (Gaver, Gaver, & Battistel, 1992; Kumar & Sopariwala, 1992; Larcker, 1983; Tehranian, Travlos, & Waegelein, 1987).

Although these studies implicitly assume that adopted LTIPs ameliorate the agency problem between CEOs and shareholders in a substantive way, newly adopted LTIPs do not require a particular amount of incentive compensation, so boards can announce a new LTIP and subsequently make no grants under the plan. Consequently, LTIPs provide a vehicle for symbolic action in which actual compensation arrangements are decoupled from formal policies (Edelman, 1992; Meyer & Rowan, 1977; Pfeffer, 1981b). In fact, preliminary descriptive results indicated that a significant proportion of adopting firms did not subsequently make grants under the plan.

Specific hypotheses addressed the possible political and institutional forces driving this decoupling of substance and symbolism in incentive compensation. The first set of multivariate results showed that relative CEO power over the board, measured three different ways, was positively associated with the likelihood of LTIP adoption but negatively related to the likelihood and extent of LTIP use. Thus, it appears that relatively powerful CEOs seek to enhance their reputation among external stakeholders by formally adopting mechanisms of incentive alignment (see Elsbach & Sutton, 1992; March 1984) while avoiding compensation risk in their actual contracts.

A second set of findings provided evidence for institutionalization in the diffusion of LTIPs. In particular, later adopters were also less likely to make grants under newly adopted plans, suggesting a growing separation of substance and symbolism over time. This result is consistent with an institutionalization process (Baron, Dobbin, & Jennings, 1986; Tolbert & Zucker, 1983) wherein LTIPs are increasingly adopted to address institutional demands rather than technical needs. More specifically, it appears that whereas early adopters seek to reduce agency costs by aligning CEO compensation with shareholder returns, later adopters incorporate LTIPs into their formal compensation arrangements to enhance the external legitimacy of their compensation contracts. Moreover, this finding is also consistent with speculation in the managerial and academic literature that executive compensation policies are often driven more by faddism (see DiMaggio & Powell, 1983; Hirsch, 1972) than by specific economic or strategic goals (Crystal, 1991; Finkelstein & Hambrick, 1988, p. 547).

In order to investigate further the role of symbolic management in CEO incentive compensation, Zajac and Westphal (1995) also examined verbal justifications for new LTIPs in proxy statements. These justifications can be viewed as "motive statements" (Dewey, 1922) designed to preempt cynical interpretations of long-term incentives (e.g., as "tacked-on" compensation [Crystal, 1991]) by linking new plans with valued stakeholder objectives (Elsbach & Sutton, 1992). To this end, boards invoke credible rationales or "institutional logics" (Friedland & Alford, 1991) to enhance the legitimacy of new LTIPs (Meyer & Rowan, 1977; Pfeffer, 1981b).

Content analyses of LTIP justifications revealed two dominant rationales: an agency theory logic and a strategic human resource (HR) logic. The HR logic emphasizes the need to attract and retain scarce leadership talent by providing competitive compensation arrangements that raise the upper bound of total compensation levels (see Milkovich & Newman, 1984; Pfeffer, 1994; Wright, McMahan, & McWilliams, 1994). In contrast, the agency logic stresses the need to control management actions or decision making by aligning their compensation with shareholder performance (Beatty & Zajac, 1994; Jensen & Meckling, 1976). The following sample justifications illustrate agency and strategic HR logics, respectively:

Alcoa's Board of Directors has decided to place an increasing share of management's overall compensation at risk rather than in fixed salaries. The new approach to compensation was recommended by the Board's compensation committee, which is composed solely of outside directors. The board believes that granting stock options, performance shares and [bonuses] will create a more appropriate relationship between compensation and the financial performance of the company in order to increase key employees' personal financial identification with interests of the Company's stockholders. (Aluminum Company of America, 1988).

The Board believes that adoption of the Plan will enhance the Company's ability to attract and retain individuals of exceptional managerial talent upon whom, in large measure, the sustained progress, growth and profitability of the Company depends. . . . (AT&T, annual report, 1985)

The first set of results indicated that later adopters were more likely to use an agency justification, and less likely to use a strategic HR justification for new LTIPs. Thus, it appears that the legitimate, socially constructed purpose for executive incentive compensation has changed over time (Friedland & Alford, 1991). Although incentives used to be considered a mechanism for attracting and retaining scarce human resources, they are increasingly viewed as a means of imposing compensation risk on recalcitrant agents. In other words, the notion of protecting shareholder interests through incentive alignment may have acquired institutional or symbolic value over time as a rationale for long-term incentive compensation (Davis & Thompson, 1994). More generally, this finding reminds us that assumptions underlying theory and prescription on executive incentives are bound by the changing social context (Friedland & Alford, 1991; Scott, 1987).

Additional findings concerned relationships between CEO–board demographic similarity and the use of different justifications. Specifically, it was found that higher levels of demographic similarity increased the likelihood of strategic HR justifications and reduced the likelihood of agency justifications for new LTIPs. As noted previously, to the extent that demographic similarity enhances directors' trust in the CEO's strategic decision making (Kanter, 1977), the perceived need to control the CEO's behavior (i.e., reduce "agency costs") through incentive alignment is reduced where similarity is high. Conversely, where similarity is low, diminished communication and reduced social integration should augment the perceived need for control through incentive mechanisms (Westphal & Zajac, 1995a). Thus, it appears that rationales for incentive compensation vary with the perceived threat of shirking by top managers and the availability of alternative, more social control mechanisms (Ouchi, 1980). More generally, in combination with the apparent effect of institutional factors on justification content, these results suggest that both micro and macro elements of the board's structural context can influence the professed motives for introducing CEO incentives.

Finally, a third set of findings addressed the role of political factors in determining justification content. In particular, the results showed that relatively high CEO power (measured three different ways) increased the likelihood of strategic HR justifications for new LTIPs, whereas relatively high board power increased the likelihood of using an agency justification. In effect, whereas powerful boards prefer accounts that advertise their control over management, powerful CEOs favor justifications that reflect romanticized conceptions of corporate leaders (Finkelstein & Hambrick, 1988; Meindl, Ehrlich, & Dukerich, 1985) in order to emphasize their value to the firm and rationalize their power over the board. More generally, it appears that interest-based factors, as well as more structural or contextual factors, can influence the stated purpose of CEO incentives.

In summary, Zajac and Westphal (1995) provide further evidence for the role of symbolic management in CEO incentive compensation practices. According to Meyer and Rowan (1977, p. 50), "The incorporation of institutionalized elements provides an account of activities that protects the organization from having its conduct questioned." In this case, boards incorporate institutionally legitimate logics to bolster the legitimacy of new formal structures (i.e., LTIPs) with external stakeholders. This interpretation is also consistent with a symbolic management perspective (see Pfeffer, 1981b, p. 1), wherein organizational participants exercise power not only "on the level of substantive action" (e.g., to determine the form of executive compensation contracts), but also "on the expressive or symbolic level" to ensure the commitment and support of organizational stakeholders.

Expanding the scope of compensation research

Overall, whereas research has focused almost exclusively on defining the relationship between specific aspects of board structure and the level or performance sensitivity of management compensation, researchers are beginning to broaden the scope of inquiry into managerial compensation practices. This chapter has outlined recent empirical research addressing the role of macrostructural factors in determining the form of managerial compensation contracts, as well as recent theory and research describing how microbehavioral processes and managerial preferences affect compensation decisions.

Much more research is clearly needed, however, to fully develop this expanded model. For instance, in order to describe adequately the effect of board processes and institutional demands on compensation decisions, we must develop a better understanding of how these micro- and macro-factors relate to each other. Specifically, how do stakeholder demands for greater board control affect CEO–director interaction, and conversely, how do top managers and corporate directors socially construct those expectations? It seems likely that socially constructed board responsibilities will be quite different when powerful shareholders or their representatives sit on the board, thus participating in the social construction process. Indeed, it can be argued that symbolic changes in compensation arrangements, as described previously, result from biased social construction mediated by powerful top managers (see Goffman, 1971; Zajac & Westphal, 1995), whereas substantive changes reflect the participation of independent directors in the construction process. Thus, further research is needed regarding the emergence of "compensation ideologies" among corporate leaders (see Hirsch, 1986).

Furthermore, researchers should investigate how incentive arrangements, in turn, affect microbehavioral processes and institutional demands. March (1984) has suggested that pay-for-performance plans encourage political behavior and impression management tactics by top managers toward board members. Moreover, it seems plausible that widespread symbolic or substantive adoption of specific incentive practices may eventually change institutional demands regarding executive incentive arrangements. To the extent that the issue of CEO compensation serves as a scapegoat for more fundamental organizational problems, boards may ritualistically change incentive arrangements during periods of poor shareholder performance, so that different incentive arrangements (or new logics for existing arrangements) may acquire normative status after they become widely diffused. Accordingly, change in incentive compensation practices and the ideologies supporting them may be partly cyclical in nature (see Barley & Kunda, 1992). Longitudinal studies could extend research by Zajac and Westphal (1995) to consider the evolving "dialectic" of incentive justifications.

Although the discussion thus far has emphasized the role of symbolic management in mediating between managerial interests and external/institutional demands regarding incentive compensation, incentives can also have symbolic value to organizational participants. For instance, by accepting greater compensation risk in their pay packages, top executives signal a willingness to "share the pain" during periods of downsizing or cost cutting, thus enhancing their attractiveness and credibility as transformational leaders. In effect, managerial incentives can reinforce more traditional symbolic management (see Pfeffer, 1981b). Such an approach may be especially important where "organizational cynicism" is high (Wanous, Reichers, & Austin, 1994). In such cases, concrete evidence of top management's personal commitment to change may be necessary to secure the organizational commitment of lower-level employees.

More generally, although strategic management scholars have long recognized the importance of compensation policy to effective organizational change and strategy implementation (Galbraith & Kazanjian, 1978), the symbolic role of incentives is typically not addressed in this literature. Instead, incentives are presumed to facilitate strategy implementation simply by affecting individual employees' effort–reward expectancies, thus shifting individual motivation in the desired direction (Lawler, 1990). However, this undersocialized view may seriously understate the potential ability of incentives to facilitate organizational change. From a symbolic management perspective, incentives provide a vehicle for articulating the organization's goals and priorities to employees. Accordingly, incentives may have symbolic value independent of their effect on effort–reward expectancies. Indeed, the mere introduction of performance-contingent compensation can send a powerful signal to employees.

Similarly, conventional economic and psychological perspectives on incentive compensation cannot fully explain the motivational effects of "group incentives" (Baker, Jensen, & Murphy, 1988; Lawler, 1990). Such reward schemes provide a concrete symbol of an organization's new emphasis on teamwork, thus reinforcing a more team-oriented employee culture (see Cooke & Rousseau, 1988) even without affecting individuals' financial motivation. More generally, although incentive plans can demonstrate commitment to shareholder values, as discussed previously, they can also provide a vehicle for "importing" normative values into the organization. Thus, to the extent that group incentives symbolize both a collectivist and a meritocratic orientation, their introduction helps to foster such a hybrid culture in organizations.

Finally, given recent evidence that director network ties among corporate leaders can explain the spread of specific changes in managerial incentive arrangements (Westphal & Zajac, 1995b), as discussed previously, network analysis offers another approach to investigating the effect of macrostructural factors on organizational incentives. Network structure can help explain how and why normative values are imported into the organization (see Burt, 1987), including values about incentive compensation itself. In addition, given that network diffusion frequently rests on microlevel processes such as reciprocity and socialization, a network approach can incorporate microlevel mechanisms into a macrolevel, social structural context to provide a cross-level explanation for change in managerial incentive practices. Moreover, this causal process may have cyclical, recursive elements. The evidence discussed previously showing that director networks are "segmented" according to executive incentive practices indicates how compensation practices can have reciprocal effects on the social structural context.

In conclusion, an expanded model of managerial incentive practices encompassing macrostructural factors and microbehavioral processes could provide a richer understanding of the determinants and consequences of managerial incentives in organizations. The interdisciplinary perspective advanced in this chapter views the determination of managerial incentive practices as a dynamic and contested organizational decision-making process invested with social and personal significance as well as economic importance. In the process of developing this perspective further, researchers could offer new insights into power and political behavior, institutional processes, and the role of these factors in organizational decision making.

Notes

1 For example, we do not review the substantial body of psychological research on theories of human motivation, which itself could be the subject of a book-length analysis.

2 Our argument applies most directly to the issue of compensation levels. We recognize, of course, that the form of compensation (e.g., the portion of compensation that is contingent on performance) may affect investment decision making and hence could represent a more significant source of inefficiency. The issues of pay mix and level are often intertwined in theory and practice, however. For example, Jensen and Murphy (1990b) view higher overall levels of compensation as not necessarily undesirable if the contingent component is increased. In fact, from an agency perspective, increasing the contingent component might require an increase in compensation level, given the risk premium that must be paid to CEOs for accepting greater compensation risk (see Beatty & Zajac, 1994).

3 As noted in the next section, the normative agency literature is more discriminating on this issue, showing that managerial risk aversion creates situations in which a heavy emphasis on pay-for-performance compensation is not necessarily optimal.

4 As noted previously, political models differ from economic perspectives on managerial incentives that presume a unitary set of organizational interests with power to determine the incentive structure. Of course, political perspectives may be entirely consistent with microeconomic models of managerial behavior, wherein top managers utilize political influence tactics to promote their own welfare.

References

Alderfer, C. P. (1986). The invisible director on corporate boards. *Harvard Business Review, 64*, 38–52.

Axelrod, R. (1984). *The evolution of cooperation.* New York: Basic Books.

Baker, G. P., Jensen, M. C., & Murphy, K. J. (1988). Compensation and incentives: Practice vs. theory. *Journal of Finance, 43*, 593–616.

Barley, S. R., & Kunda, G. (1992). Design and devotion: Surges of rational and normative ideologies of control in managerial discourse. *Administrative Science Quarterly, 37*, 363–399.

Baron, J. P., Dobbin, F., & Jennings, P. D. (1986). War and peace: The evolution of modern personnel administration in U.S. industry. *American Journal of Sociology, 92*, 250–283.

Beatty, R. P., & Zajac, E. J. (1994). Top management incentives, monitoring, and risk sharing: A study of executive compensation, ownership and board structure in initial public offerings. *Administrative Science Quarterly, 39*, 313–336.

Benston, G. J. (1985). The self-serving management hypothesis: Some evidence. *Journal of Accounting and Economics, 7*, 67–84.

Burt, R. S. (1987). Social contagion and innovation: Cohesion versus structural equivalence. *American Journal of Sociology, 92*, 1287–1335.

Business Week. (1992, March 30). Executive pay.

Business Week. (1994, February 21). How to handle a CEO.

Cooke, R. A., & Rousseau, D. M. (1988). Behavioral norms and expectations. *Group and Organization Studies, 13*, 245–273.

Coughlin, A. T., & Schmidt, R. M. (1985). Executive compensation, executive turnover, and firm performance. *Journal of Accounting and Economics, 7*, 43–66.

Crystal, G. S. (1984). *Questions and answers on executive compensation.* Englewood Cliffs, NJ: Prentice-Hall.

Crystal, G. S. (1991). *In search of excess: The overcompensation of American executives.* New York: W. W. Norton.

Davis, G. F., & Thompson, T. A. (1994). A social movement perspective on corporate control. *Administrative Science Quarterly, 39*, 141–173.

Dawes, R. M. (1991). Social dilemmas, economic self-interest, and evolutionary theory. In D. Brown & J. E. Smith (Eds.), *Recent research in psychology: Frontiers of mathematical psychology: Essays in honor of Clyde Coombs,* New York: Springer-Verlag.

Dewey, J. (1922). *Human nature and conduct.* New York: Modern Library.

DiMaggio, P. J. (1988). Interest and agency in institutional theory. In L. G. Zucker (Ed.), *Institutional patterns and organizations* (pp. 3–22). Cambridge, MA: Ballinger.

DiMaggio, P. J., & Powell, W. W. (1983). The iron cage revisited: Institutional isomorphism and collective rationality in organizational fields. *American Sociological Review, 48*, 147–160.

Edelman, L. B. (1992). Legal ambiguity and symbolic structures: Organizational mediation of civil rights law. *American Journal of Sociology, 97*, 1531–1577.

Eisenhardt, K. M., & Zbaracki, M. J. (1992). Strategic decision making. *Strategic Management Journal, 13*, 17–37.

Ekeh, P. P. (1974). *Social exchange theory: The two traditions.* Cambridge, MA: Harvard University Press.

Elsbach, K. D., & Sutton, R. I. (1992). Acquiring organizational legitimacy through illegitimate actions: A marriage of institutional and impression management theories. *Academy of Management Journal, 35*, 699–738.

Fama, E. F. (1980). Agency problems and the theory of the firm. *Journal of Political Economy, 88*, 288–307.

Fama, E. F., & Jensen, M. C. (1983). The separation of ownership and control. *Journal of Law and Economics, 26*, 301–325.

Finkelstein, S. (1992). Power in top management teams: Dimensions, measurement, and validation. *Academy of Management Journal, 35*, 505–538.

Finkelstein, S., & Hambrick, D. C. (1988). Chief executive compensation: A synthesis and reconciliation. *Strategic Management Journal, 9,* 543–558.

Finkelstein, S., & Hambrick, D. C. (1989). Chief executive compensation: A study of the intersection of markets and political processes. *Strategic Management Journal, 10,* 121–134.

Fredrickson, J. W., Hambrick, D. C., & Baumrin, S. (1988). A model of CEO dismissal. *Academy of Management Review, 13,* 255–270.

French, J. R. P., Jr., & Raven, B. (1959). The bases of social power. In D. Cartwright (Ed.), *Studies in social power* (pp. 150–167). Ann Arbor: Institute for Social Research, University of Michigan.

Friedland, R., & Alford, R. R. (1991). Bringing society back in: Symbols, practices, and institutional contradictions. In W. W. Powell & P. J. DiMaggio (Eds.), *The new institutionalism in organizational analysis* (pp. 232–263). Chicago: University of Chicago Press.

Galbraith, J. R., & Kazanjian, R. K. (1978). *Strategy implementation: Structure, systems and process.* New York: West.

Gaver, J. J., Gaver, K. M., & Battistel, G. P. (1992). The stock market reaction to performance plan adoption. *The Accounting Review, 67,* 172–182.

Goffman, E. (1971). *Relations in public.* New York: Basic Books.

Gouldner, A. W. (1960). The norm of reciprocity: A preliminary statement. *American Sociological Review, 25,* 161–178.

Hambrick, D. C., & Mason, P. (1984). Upper echelons: The organization as a reflection of its top managers. *Academy of Management Review, 2,* 193–206.

Harris, M., & Raviv, A. (1979). Some results on incentive contracts with imperfect information. *Journal of Economic Theory, 20,* 231–259.

Hill, C. W., & Phan, P. (1991). CEO tenure as a determinant of CEO pay. *Academy of Management Journal, 34,* 707–717.

Hirsch, P. M. (1972). Processing fads and fashions: An organization-set analysis of cultural industry systems. *American Journal of Sociology, 77,* 639–659.

Hirsch, P. M. (1986). From ambushes to golden parachutes: Corporate takeovers as an instance of cultural framing and institutional integration. *American Journal of Sociology, 91,* 800–837.

Holmstrom, B. (1979). Moral hazard and observability. *Bell Journal of Economics, 14,* 74–91.

Holmstrom, B. (1982). Managerial incentive problems – a dynamic perspective. In *Essays in economics and management in honor of Lars Wahlbeck* (pp. 209–230). Helsinki: Swedish School of Economics.

Holmstrom, B. (1987). Incentive compensation: Practical design from a theory point of view. In H. R. Nalbantian (Ed.), *Incentives, cooperation, and risk sharing: Economic and psychological perspectives on employment contracts* (pp. 176–185). Toyota, NJ: Rowman and Littlefield.

Jarrell, G. A. (1993). An overview of the executive compensation debate. *Journal of Applied Corporate Finance, 5,* 76–82.

Jensen, M. C. (1983). Organization theory and methodology. *Accounting Review, 58,* 319–339.

Jensen, M. C., & Meckling, W. H. (1976). Theory of the firm: Managerial behavior, agency costs, and ownership structure. *Journal of Financial Economics, 3,* 305–350.

Jensen, M. C., & Murphy, K. J. (1990a). Performance pay and top-management incentives. *Journal of Political Economy, 98,* 225–263.

Jensen, M. C., & Murphy, K. J. (1990b). CEO incentives – it's not how much you pay, but how. *Harvard Business Review, 68,* 138–153.

Jensen, M. C., & Zimmerman, J. L. (1985). Management compensation and the managerial labor market. *Journal of Financial Economics, 7,* 3–9.

Kanter, R. M. (1977). *Men and women of the corporation.* New York: Basic Books.

Kerr, S. (1975). On the folly of rewarding A, while still hoping for B. *Academy of Management Journal, 18,* 769–783.

Kerr, J., & Bettis, R. A. (1987). Boards of directors, top management compensation, and shareholder returns. *Academy of Management Journal, 30,* 645–664.

Kumar, R., & Sopariwala, P. R. (1992). The effect of adoption of long-term performance plans on stock prices and accounting numbers. *Journal of Finance, 67,* 561–573.

Larcker, D. F. (1983). The association between performance plan adoption and corporate capital investment. *Journal of Accounting and Economics, 5,* 3–30.

Lawler, E. E. (1971). *Pay and organizational effectiveness: A psychological view.* New York: McGraw-Hill.

Lawler, E. E. (1990). *Strategic pay: Aligning organizational strategies and pay systems.* San Francisco: Jossey-Bass.

Lazear, E. P. (1987). Incentive contracts. In J. Eatwell, M. Milgate, & P. Newman (Eds.), *The new Palgrave: A dictionary of economics* (Vol. 2, pp. 744–748). London: Macmillan.

Levinthal, D. (1988). A survey of agency models of organizations. *Journal of Economic Behavior and Organization, 9,* 153–185.

Lévi-Strauss, C. (1969). *The elementary structures of kinship.* Boston: Beacon Press.

Lewellen, W. G., & Huntsman, B. (1970). Managerial pay and corporate performance. *American Economic Review, 6,* 710–720.

Lewellen, W., Loderer, C., & Martin, K. (1987). Executive compensation and executive incentive problems: An empirical analysis. *Journal of Accounting and Economics, 9,* 287–310.

Lorsch, J. W., & MacIver, E. (1989). *Pawns or potentates: The reality of America's corporate boards.* Boston: Harvard Business School Press.

Mace, M. L. (1971). *Directors: Myth and reality.* Boston: Harvard Business School Press.

Mahoney, T. A. (1979). *Compensation and reward practices.* Homewood, IL: Richard D. Irwin.

March, J. G. (1962). The business firm as a political coalition. *The Journal of Politics, 24,* 662–678.

March, J. G. (1984, August). Notes on ambiguity and executive compensation. *Scandinavian Journal of Management Studies,* 53–64.

Masson, R. T. (1971). Executive motivations, earnings, and consequent equity performance. *Journal of Political Economy, 79,* 1278–1292.

Meindl, J. R., Ehrlich, S. B., & Dukerich, J. J. (1985). The romance of leadership. *Administrative Science Quarterly, 30,* 78–102.

Meyer, J. W., & Rowan, B. (1977). Institutional organizations: Formal structure as myth and ceremony. *American Journal of Sociology, 83,* 340–363.

Milkovich, G. T., & Newman, J. M. (1984). *Compensation.* Plano, TX: Business Publications.

Murphy, K. J. (1985). Corporate earnings and managerial remuneration. *Journal of Accounting and Economics, 7,* 11–42.

Murphy, K. J. (1986). Top executives are worth every nickel they get. *Harvard Business Review, 64,* 125–132.

O'Reilly, C. A., III, Caldwell, D. F., & Barnett, W. P. (1989). Work group demography, social integration, and turnover. *Administrative Science Quarterly, 34,* 21–37.

O'Reilly, C. A., III, Main, B. G., & Crystal, G. S. (1988). CEO compensation as tournament and social comparison. *Administrative Science Quarterly, 33,* 257–274.

Ouchi, W. G. (1980). Markets, bureaucracies and clans. *Administrative Science Quarterly, 25,* 129–141.

Patton, A., & Baker, J. C. (1987). Why won't directors rock the boat? *Harvard Business Review, 65,* 10–18.

Perrow, C. (1972). Departmental power and perspectives in industrial firms. In M. N. Zald (Ed.), *Power in organizations* (pp. 58–89). Nashville, TN: Vanderbilt University Press.

Pettigrew, A. M. (1992). On studying managerial elites. *Strategic Management Journal, 13,* 163–182.

Pfeffer, J. (1981a). *Power in organizations.* Cambridge, MA: Harper & Row.

Pfeffer, J. (1981b). Management as symbolic action: The creation and maintenance of organizational paradigms. In L. L. Cummings & B. M. Staw (Eds.), *Research in organizational behavior* (Vol. 3, pp. 1–52). Greenwich, CT: JAI Press.

Pfeffer, J. (1983). Organizational demography. In L. L. Cummings & B. M. Staw (Eds.), *Research in organizational behavior* (Vol. 5, pp. 299–357). Greenwich, CT: JAI Press.

Pfeffer, J. (1992). *Managing with power.* Boston: Harvard Business School Press.

Pfeffer, J. (1994). *Competitive advantage through people.* Boston: Harvard Business School Press.

Porter, L. W., Allen, R. W., & Angle, H. L. (1981). The politics of upward influence in organizations. In L. L. Cummings & B. M. Staw (Eds.), *Research in organizational behavior* (Vol. 3, pp. 109–149). Greenwich, CT: JAI Press.

Ross, S. (1973). The economic theory of agency: The principal's problem. *American Economic Review, 63,* 134–139.

Scott, W. R. (1987). *Organizations: Rational, natural, and open systems.* Englewood Cliffs, NJ: Prentice-Hall.

Shavell, S. (1979). Risk sharing and incentives in the principal and agent relationship. *Bell Journal of Economics, 10,* 55–73.

Stiglitz, J. E. (1987). The design of labor contracts. In H. R. Nalbantian (Ed.), *Incentives, cooperation, and risk sharing: Economic and psychological perspectives on employment contracts* (pp. 47–68). Toyota, NJ: Rowman and Littlefield.

Tehranian, H., Travlos, N. G., & Waegelein, J. F. (1987). The effect of long-term performance plans on corporate sell-off-induced abnormal returns. *Journal of Finance, 42,* 933–942.

Time. (1993, March 1). Rolling back executive pay, pp. 49–50.

Tolbert, P. S., & Zucker, L. G. (1983). Institutional sources of change in the formal structure of organizations: The diffusion of civil service reform. *Administrative Science Quarterly, 28,* 22–39.

Tosi, H. L., & Gomez-Mejia, L. R. (1989). The decoupling of CEO pay and performance: An agency theory perspective. *Administrative Science Quarterly, 34,* 169–189.

Tosi, H. L., House, R. J., & Dunnette, M. D. (Eds.). (1972). *Managerial motivation and compensation.* East Lansing, MI: MSU Business Studies.

Useem, M. (1984). *The inner circle.* Oxford: Oxford University Press.

Useem, M. (1993). *Executive defense: Shareholder power and corporate reorganization.* Cambridge, MA: Harvard University Press.

Vance, S. C. (1983). *Corporate leadership: Boards of directors and strategy.* New York: McGraw-Hill.

Wade, J. B., O'Reilly, C. A., & Chandratat, I. (1990). Golden parachutes: CEOs and the exercise of social influence. *Administrative Science Quarterly, 35,* 587–603.

Walsh, J. P., & Seward, J. K. (1990). On the efficiency of internal and external corporate control mechanisms. *Academy of Management Review, 15,* 421–458.

Walster, E., Bersheid, E., & Walster, G. W. (1973). New directions in equity research. *Journal of Personality and Social Psychology, 25,* 151–176.

Wanous, J. P., Reichers, A. E., & Austin, J. T. (1994). Organizational cynicism: An initial study. *Academy of Management Best Papers Proceedings,* pp. 269–273.

Westphal, J. D. (1995). *Interpersonal influence behavior in the CEO/board relationship: Structural antecedents and strategic consequences.* Ph.D. dissertation, Northwestern University.

Westphal, J. D., & Zajac, E. J. (1994). Substance and symbolism in CEOs' long-term incentive plans. *Administrative Science Quarterly, 39,* 367–390.

Westphal, J. D., & Zajac, E. J. (1995a). Who shall govern? CEO/board power, demographic similarity, and new director selection. *Administrative Science Quarterly, 40,* 60–83.

Westphal, J. D., & Zajac, E. J. (1995b). Defections from the inner circle: Social exchange, reciprocity, and the diffusion of board independence in U.S. corporations. *Academy of Management Best Papers Proceedings,* pp. 281–285.

Wright, P. M., McMahan, G. C., & McWilliams, A. (1994). Human resources and sustained competitive advantage: A resource-based perspective. *International Journal of Human Resource Management, 5,* 301–326.

Zajac, E. J. (1990). CEO selection, succession, compensation and firm performance: A theoretical integration and empirical analysis. *Strategic Management Journal, 11,* 217–230.

Zajac, E. J., & Westphal, J. D. (1994). The costs and benefits of incentives and monitoring in the largest U.S. corporations: When is more not better? *Strategic Management Journal, 15,* 121–142.

Zajac, E. J., & Westphal, J. D. (1995). Accounting for the explanations for CEO compensation: Substance and symbolism. *Administrative Science Quarterly, 40,* 283–308.

Zajac, E. J., & Westphal, J. D. (1996). Who shall rule after a CEO succession? How CEO/board preferences and power affect the choice of new CEOs. *Academy of Management Journal, 39,* 64–90.

Zenger, T. R., & Lawrence, B. S. (1989). Organizational demography: The differential effects of age and tenure distributions on technical communication. *Academy of Management Journal, 32,* 353–376.

8 Coordination in organizations: A game-theoretic perspective

Colin Camerer and Marc Knez

8.1 Introduction

Classic literature on organizations recognizes that the paramount function of an organization is the coordination of physical and human assets to produce a good or service (e.g., Barnard, 1938; Chisholm, 1989; Schein, 1985). *Coordination* in this early literature was defined broadly, as for example by Mooney (1947, p. 5): "Coordination therefore, is the orderly arrangement of group effort, to provide unity of action in the pursuit of a common purpose." Mooney argues further that coordination is the first principle of organization and that any other organizational principles "are simply principles through which coordination operates and thus becomes effective" (p. 5). The landmark work of Thompson (1967) distinguished kinds of interdependence that give rise to coordination problems and ways in which coordination might occur – for example, by standardization, planning, or mutual adjustment. Coordination also plays a central role in recent thinking about the economics of internal organization (Becker & Murphy, 1992; Milgrom & Roberts, 1992), the history of business organization (Lamoreaux & Raff, 1995, esp. p. 5), *core competencies* in business strategy, *mutualism* and legitimation in organizational evolution, macroeconomics (Cooper & John, 1988), and other fields.

The need for coordination arises if the organization's success depends on the decisions made by each of a group of actors, and the decisions interact in determining success. In the traditional sense, a *coordination problem* exists if achievement of a particular organizational goal requires that each actor select the appropriate action, and the goal is not fully achieved if all members of the group do not select goal-fulfilling actions.

We thank participants in seminars at the Chicago GSB Behavioral Science workshop, the UCLA Policy and Organization workshop, the 1995 Academy of Management meetings, Don Kleinmuntz, Roy Radner, and Zur Shapira for comments and ideas.

To illustrate coordination problems, it may help to first imagine an organization that does *not* require much coordination. Picture a room full of equally skilled workers who draw similar garment pieces from a central bin and sew them together. If the sewing is simple enough, then the "organization's" total output is just the sum of each worker's output, and coordination of workers' efforts is not important. Extending the example shows how likely it is that coordination really *is* important. If the garments differ in complexity and workers differ in skill, then assigning hard work to the best workers improves output, so some coordination of workers' garment choices is required. If work on a particular garment is spread over time, so that one worker adds additional stitching to a garment previously worked on by another (as on an assembly line), then workers' output speeds are clearly interdependent and coordination is again necessary. If certain workers like each other, and being physically located near their friends helps their productivity (or hinders it!), then coordinating where workers sit improves productivity.

Our chapter presents a game-theoretic perspective on coordination problems like these. It belongs in this book because choosing which action to take in a coordination game is a social decision; it requires people to think about what others will do (and also about social values, such as whether they care to maximize their own payoffs or the group's payoffs). In addition, we make a few comments about how decisions in coordination games may reflect heuristics visible in individual decision making.

The main goal of the chapter is to describe a class of *coordination games*, argue for their relevance to the study of organizational decision making, and describe findings from several experiments on such games. A secondary goal is to whet readers' appetites for broader application of game theory to the study of organizational behavior in the spirit of Murnighan (1994) and Gibbons (in press).

8.2 Three kinds of impediments to coordination

Broadly speaking, the literature on organizations has recognized three kinds of impediments to coordination. In each case, we describe the impediment, characterize it using a slightly different coordination game, and give an organizational example.

8.2.1 Team decisions and matching games

The organizational problem. One kind of impediment to coordination arises when group members all have the same preference rankings over the set of possible group outcomes (i.e., any action that leads to a higher payoff to one group member also leads to higher payoffs to all other members) but reaching the best outcome is not easy. A group like this is called a *team* (Marschak & Radner, 1972).

Coordination failures in teams are typically attributed to the complexity of multiperson interactions and to the fact that group members have different information or control different actions. For example, a firm may want to produce a single national-brand shoe, but five regional marketing directors all have different opinions (based on their local information) about which shoe will sell best. Their problem is how to aggregate information, not what to do afterward.

Analysis of team decision-making problems focuses on the derivation of optimal decision policies under alternative information structures. Although the theory of teams is interesting and important in its own right, from a behavioral perspective it is naturally limited because it assumes that team members all have the same goal. Radner's chapter in this book describes some important recent results on how to design team organizations to aggregate information optimally when information processing takes time and information depreciates over time.

The game. A (noncooperative) game involves a set of players, strategies those players can choose, consequences that result from each combination of strategies, utilities that express how players value the possible consequences, rules for which players move when and what players know when they move, and random choices by an exogenous "nature" (which may include outside players who are uninterested in the outcome). A spate of recent books have made the basics of game theory accessible at many levels (e.g., Gibbons 1992); we will not dwell on details or definitions except when necessary.

The simplest expression of a team coordination problem is a *matching game,* shown in Figure 8.1. Two players, labeled person 1 and person 2, choose either L or H simultaneously. Each cell of the matrix shows the payoffs to the two players (in utilities) from each combination of choices; the first (second) number denotes person 1 (2) payoffs. For example, if both players choose L, denoted (L,L), they each get 5, and if both choose H, they each get 10. Figure 8.1 captures the most basic property of a team coordination problem because players agree that the outcome (H,H) is better than (L,L).

Notice that the matching game captures the basic property of coordination we mentioned in the introduction because the player's payoffs are an interactive function of their choices: If they match choices they both do well, but if they mismatch they get nothing.

An example. Consider a luxury hotel that strives to provide a high quality of customer service by encouraging its staff to be attentive to customers' needs. Suppose that the hotel slightly prefers customers to check out by 1 P.M. rather than 2 P.M., but mainly worries that customers are not told two different checkout times by different employees (because customers take the confusion to be a sign of low-quality service, for example, or resent

Person 2

Person 1	L	H
L	5, 5	0, 0
H	0, 0	10, 10

Figure 8.1. Matching game.

wasting more time finding out which time is correct). Now consider the game played by two employees who must tell a guest the checkout time. If they share the group's (hotel's) payoffs, their payoffs are like those in a matching game. The two employees would like to match the times they announce and prefer to both say 1 P.M., but their main concern is to avoid mismatching times.

Obviously, this coordination problem appears to be easily solved by instructing employees to announce a single checkout time. But problems may arise under many circumstances – for example when new employees arrive from other hotels with 2 P.M. checkout times. Now the old employees must guess whether new employees will remember to say 1 P.M. or will forgetfully say 2 P.M.; the old employees must guess what new employees will guess they will guess; and so on.

8.2.2 Mixed-motive conflict, bargaining, and battle-of-the-sexes games

The organizational problem. A second impediment to coordination arises when group members have different preferences about organizational outcomes (e.g., principal–agent conflicts). For example, many applications of negotiations to organizational behavior discuss the bargaining problem that arises between organization members (e.g., Neale & Bazerman, 1991). The typical bargaining problem has a set of mutually agreeable possible solutions and an impasse or no-agreement point that is worse than any of the candidate solutions. Bargainers all prefer *one* of the solution points to reaching an impasse, but each bargainer prefers a different point. This *mixed-motive* situation creates a coordination problem because bargainers would like to agree on *some* solution rather than none, but there are many possible solutions.

Similarly, March and Simon (1958) and many others have stressed the importance of getting organization members to identify with organizational goals. Our discussion breaks "identification" into two different parts. In mixed-motive games the outcomes two players desire are not the same (though both desire to avoid some undesirable outcomes); hence there is no clear, single organizational goal both can identify with. In the risky coordination games we describe later, there is a clear, commonly desired outcome but players are not sure that others will risk striving for it. In these

Person 2

Person 1	L	H
L	10, 5	0, 0
H	0, 0	5, 10

Figure 8.2. Battle-of-the-sexes game.

games, "identifying" the organizational goal means not knowing that a goal exists but believing that others will strive for it.

The game. A simple game known as *battle of the sexes* (*BOS*) captures this second impediment to coordination. Figure 8.2 shows payoffs in a BOS. Persons 1 and 2 both prefer matching to mismatching (and getting nothing). But person 1 would rather match on (L,L) and get 10, and person 2 would rather match on (H,H) and get 5. In a sense, persons 1 and 2 are bargaining over whether to divide a total possible gain of 15 into (10,5) or (5,10) or to mismatch and get nothing.

An example. Returning to the hotel, consider two room service waiters standing in different parts of the kitchen as an order is finished, ready for delivery, and the cook signals for a waiter. Assume that both prefer to have the order delivered promptly (otherwise the customer's wrath will lead to substantial punishment for both of them), neither one wants to deliver it (or both do[1]), and if both rush over to grab the order, an argument ensues that slows the delivery and harms them both. Then the game they play is a BOS with strategies relabeled (L corresponds to person 1 delivering, H to person 2 delivering). If they can communicate or have some shared organizational rule (see March's and Zhou's chapters in this book), like seniority or delivery rotation, the bargaining problem is probably easily solved. But if communication is difficult, no rule exists, and the stakes are high, a coordination failure could result.

8.2.3 Risky coordination, and assurance games

The organizational problem. A third impediment to coordination arises when group members have common preferences over outcomes but the best outcome requires a risky action that group members do not want to take unless others do. Organizational change is like this if it requires members to make investments in learning new techniques that they prefer to make if, and only if, others do too.

The game. Risky coordination can be captured in an *assurance game*, as in Figure 8.3 (also called *stag hunt* in game theory jargon). Suppose persons 1

Person 2

Person 1	L	H
L	5, 5	5, 0
H	0, 5	10, 10

Figure 8.3. Assurance game.

and 2 can exert high (H) or low (L) effort. Low effort yields a certain 5 for the person exerting that low effort. High effort costs more, so choosing H alone yields 0, but if both players choose H they each earn 10. (If $H_i = 1$ when player i chooses H, the payoff function for person 1 can be expressed as $5 - 5H_1 + 10H_1H_2$, so the interaction or productive synergy between the effort choices of persons 1 and 2 are clear from the product term H_1H_2.)

The players' preferences are consistent because person 1 is better off selecting action H if player 2 also selects H and better off selecting L if 2 also selects L. But the interdependence of each player's actions is fundamental because person 1 is better off choosing H *only* if person 2 chooses H as well. Note that the assurance game is a form of matching because players want to match other players' choices. The difference is that the mismatch payoffs are not all zero (as in Figure 8.1 matching). Because the mismatch payoff from choosing L is 5 and the mismatch payoff from choosing H is 0, L is less risky than H and might be chosen even though (H,H) is better.

An example. Back to the hotel. Suppose that a customer's total level of satisfaction is disproportionately affected by the minimum level of service she receives; if she has a bad experience with anyone on the hotel staff, her overall level of customer satisfaction is low. Moreover, suppose that the combination of intrinsic and extrinsic rewards implies that each employee prefers that customers receive the highest level of job satisfaction, but each employee does not want to exert extra effort toward this goal if the extra effort does not raise the customer's overall level of satisfaction. Under these assumptions, a hotel employee's decision to exert extra effort to increase a customer's level of satisfaction depends on his expectations concerning the minimum level of service that will be provided by the other hotel employees. If his expectations are low, then he does not want to risk providing high-quality service. Conversely, if his expectations are high, then he does not want to be the only one to upset the customer by providing low-quality service. High levels of customer satisfaction will be achieved only if each employee expects that a significant number of other employees will provide high-quality service.

Notice that prescribing a policy of high-quality service would work in a team theory framework (captured by the matching game), but in an assurance game it works only if employees believe others will adhere to the policy. Simply announcing the policy is not enough: It must be credible, widely believed, and so on.

8.2.4 An aside on terminology: Equilibrium

Up to now we have defined a coordination problem as a joint decision-making problem. This definition is useful for categorizing impediments to coordination, but it makes no predictions about how players will behave. The central predictive tool in simple games like these is the *Nash equilibrium*, a set of strategies that are mutual best responses to one another. Notice that *strategy* is simply a fancy word for the choices players can make. An *equilibrium* is some predicted outcome of the game or *set* of strategies chosen by players.

To illustrate the Nash equilibrium concept, consider the assurance game in Figure 8.3. This game has two (pure-strategy) Nash equilibria – the low equilibrium (L,L) and the high equilibrium (H,H). The outcome (L,L) is a Nash equilibrium because if one player expects the other player to select L, then that player should also select L. (The two L choices are mutual best responses.) The same is true for the outcome (H,H). If each player expects the other player to select H, then it is a best response to also select H. Note also that both players are better off in the H equilibrium, so we call (H,H) *efficient* and (L,L) *inefficient*.

The outcomes (H,L) and (L,H) are not Nash equilibria. For example, suppose player 1 expects player 2 to select L, and player 2 expects player 1 to select H. Then player 1 should select L (not H), and player 2 should select H (not L). The key difference is that in equilibrium, expectations are aligned with actions, whereas out of equilibrium they are not. This notion of equilibrium is not very different from the same term used by Kurt Lewin, who saw equilibria as the result of conflicting social forces pushing in various directions.

Now that we have explained what an equilibrium is, we can use the BOS in Figure 8.2 to illustrate why getting game theory right is important. In addition to the equilibria (L,L) and (H,H) in BOS, there is a third *mixed strategy* equilibrium in which both players choose random mixtures, playing L with two-thirds probability and H with one-third probability. (Those mixtures by one player make the other player indifferent between playing L and H, so the mixed strategies are *weak* best responses to each other.) The mixed strategies yield an expected payoff of $10(2/9) + 5(2/9) = 30/9$, or 3.33 to each player. Notice that two players using this strategy will have a joint payoff of (3.33,3.33), which is lower for both of them than either the (L,L) payoff of (10,5) or the (H,L) payoff of (5,10). But (3.33,3.33) is an equilibrium because players choosing it are too stubborn, put loosely, to switch unilaterally to something better. Therefore, as in Figures 8.1 and 8.3, the players could choose a pair of strategies that are best responses, and hence a (Nash) equilibrium, but that are inefficient. A critic who then concludes that players are not rational, or not obeying game theory, misunderstands the game theory.

The assurance game illustrates the two key features of a *coordination game:* The game has multiple Nash equilibria, and the set of equilibria are Pareto-rankable. *Pareto-rankable* simply means that for any two Nash equilibria in the game, one equilibrium is better for both players than the other. Notice that this game-theoretic definition is narrower than the traditional definition we gave at the start of this chapter. Most important, the traditional definition includes a situation in which a Pareto-optimal outcome is not a Nash equilibrium (hence, players have no individual incentive to work toward the group goal) as a kind of coordination problem.

8.3 The subtle relation between cooperation and coordination

The use of simple games to study organizational phenomena is not new. However, such research has focused largely on the *N*-player prisoners' dilemma (PD) games (or *social dilemmas*). Although the application of the *N*-player PD has taught us about the conditions under which cooperation may be observed in an organization, we argue next that very few true PDs exist in organizational life and that the essential property of most apparent PDs is the coordination problem embedded in them.

8.3.1 Prisoners' dilemma game

Coordination failure occurs in the assurance game (Figure 8.3) because each player's expectations are not aligned on the (H,H) outcome. If player 1 expects player 2 to select L, then her optimal action is to also select L, and likewise for player 2. This coordination problem is distinct from a problem of cooperation, where achieving optimal group outcomes requires that individual members of the group suboptimize their individual payoffs.

In Figure 8.4 we alter the assurance game in Figure 8.3 to create a version of the well-known PD. The payoffs are identical to those of the assurance game except for the payoff to a player if he or she selects D (defect) and the other player selects C (cooperate) (known as the *temptation* payoff in the PD literature). This payoff has been raised from 5 to 12. So, for example, if player 1 selects D and player 2 selects C, then player 1 receives 12, his or her highest payoff. This changes the game dramatically. Because neither player has an incentive to select the high-quality action, the low-quality outcome will occur, resulting in the lowest possible total payoffs. The only way the players will be able to coordinate their actions on the high-quality outcome is if they both forego maximizing their individual payoffs in the interest of maximizing their joint payoff.

Note that PD has a unique equilibrium, so it does not represent an impediment to coordination in the game-theoretic sense. However, it *does* characterize a situation in which players' choices will lead to inefficiency.

<u>Person 2</u>

Person 1	D	C
D	5, 5	12, 0
C	0, 12	10, 10

Figure 8.4. Prisoners' dilemma.

8.3.2 How to tell PD and coordination games apart

The central feature of a PD is that players have dominant strategies that, when played by everyone, lead to an inefficient outcome that everyone dislikes. The central feature of coordination, as we have defined it, is that players *do not* have dominant strategies because they prefer to reciprocate (or match) the strategy that produces the efficient outcome; but they also prefer to reciprocate an inefficient strategy. Hence, the crucial difference between the two kinds of games is the answer to a simple question: Do players prefer to reciprocate the high-outcome strategy? If not, the game is PD. If so, the game is coordination.

8.3.3 Are most apparent PDs really coordination games?

We argue that under three common conditions, games classified as PDs are essentially coordination games because players would like to reciprocate cooperation.

1. In many apparent PDs, players can earn more money by defecting when another player cooperates (so defection is a dominant strategy), but they reciprocate cooperation instead. For example, about half of the subjects cooperate in one-shot experimental PDs (e.g., Ledyard, 1995), and players who expect cooperation tend to cooperate more frequently than those who expect defection. These players appear to care about something besides maximizing their own monetary payoffs; they prefer to reciprocate "nice" behavior (sacrificing money to enrich another person) with niceness (Rabin, 1993; Sally 1995). The players appear to have an internal representation of the game as a problem of coordinating levels of niceness or cooperativeness.

2. In many apparent PDs, there is a superadditive synergy or complementarity if both players cooperate. (Think of members of an R&D team who hold different pieces of a scientific puzzle and whose pieces are worth much less until they are combined. *Step-level* or *threshold* public-good games have this property too; see Rapoport, 1987. Games with *participation* or *network externalities* or *bandwagon effects* are coordination games too.) Conversely, it may be easy to identify players who defect and exclude them from sharing gains from cooperation by others. For example, team mem-

bers can report whether others contributed or not, and supervisors use these self-reports to allocate rewards. If synergies from mutual cooperation are large enough or exclusion of defectors is easy enough, then players who reciprocate cooperation will earn more money than defectors. Then the game is a coordination game, not a PD.

3. Suppose PD is infinitely repeated, with no apparent end in sight, players are not too impatient (i.e., they have a low discount rate), and they can change their behavior in any one period to respond to what others did before. Then a well-known *folk theorem* in game theory implies that reciprocating cooperation is one money-maximizing strategy (if failing to do so triggers tit-for-tat punishment in later periods). The repeated PD is thus a coordination game; players need to coordinate on *when* to defect – preferably never!

These arguments show that an apparent PD is essentially a coordination game unless *all* of the following conditions are met: (1) the players don't care whether others are nice or not, (2) there are low synergies or ability to punish defectors, and (3) there is either a limited time horizon, impatient players, or forgetful players. It is easy to think of unorganized social situations, like looting during catastrophes or overusing a common resource pool like a field, river, or lake, which may satisfy all three criteria and hence are pure PDs. But because organizations usually have long time horizons and can observe members, who know each other and may be friends, it is hard to think of any organizational examples that satisfy all three of these criteria.

For example, some people have written about organizations as "common pool resource dilemmas" in which players can take resources from a common pool that reproduces or replenishes itself at a natural rate (e.g., Kramer, 1990; Mannix & White, 1992; see also Kidwell & Bennett, 1993). In most organizations, taking resources is largely constrained by organizational rules. Putting that obvious criticism aside, if the organization is long-lived, then there are equilibria in which players take patiently from the common pool and an inefficient equilibrium in which everyone takes everything immediately, if they can. Hence the core problem in such a dilemma is coordinating on the good (slow consumption) equilibrium.

An interesting exception may be organizations near bankruptcy or undergoing downsizing, in which workers may become angry at employers and time horizons shrink. Otherwise, we hope to have shifted the burden of proof to those scholars who study PDs, to show precisely why the key feature of any situation they model is PD (dominant strategies yielding Pareto-inefficiency) rather than coordination.

8.3.4 Are coordination games more common than PDs?

There are at least two mathematical ways in which we can compare how common coordination and PD games are. First, Rapoport and Guyer (1976) classified all two-strategy, two-player (2×2) games into one of 78 types. Only one is a PD and several are coordination games in one of the three categories illustrated by our hotel examples. Seen this way, PDs are actually quite rare and coordination games are much more common.

Second, Stanford (1995) extends several remarkable theorems on how many pure-strategy equilibria exist in games where players' payoffs are randomly and independently determined. He shows that as the number of strategies grows, the chance that a game has exactly k pure-strategy equilibria approaches $.37/k!$. This simple expression implies that the frequency of single-equilibrium games ($k = 1$) is about 37% as the number of strategies expand. But PDs are a special type of single-equilibrium game: They require all players to have dominated strategies that lead to a Pareto-inefficient outcome. (As the number of strategies expands, the chance that a game with random payoffs has this special PD property goes toward zero.) Hence, PDs are only a small fraction of the 37% of single-equilibrium games.

At the same time, one can show that games with two or more equilibria occur randomly 26% of the time; *all* of these games represent coordination problems. Therefore, as the number of strategies grows large, there is a strict mathematical sense in which coordination problems become more and more (relatively) frequent than PDs (assuming payoffs are randomly chosen). And because enlarging the number of strategies makes games more realistic, we can argue that with a realistic view of the world, PD is a much less likely representation of an organizational problem than coordination is.

8.3.5 Example: The employment relationship as a coordination problem

Several different literatures focus on the underlying structure of the employment relationship. An emerging literature on organizational citizenship behavior posits that organizationally beneficial behavior exists within organizations that is not driven by formal obligations dictated by the employment contract (Organ, 1988). Work on psychological contracting focuses on workers' and managers' perceptions of the unwritten terms of their employment contract (see Rousseau & Parks, 1992). The analogous question in economics is how contracting parties behave under an implicit contract, or when unspecified contingencies occur. The economists' answer is usually pessimistic: Parties try to exploit one another when something not explicitly covered in their contract occurs. An alternative answer some economists have advanced is that happy workers repay "gifts" given to them by firms in the form of higher-than-market-clearing wages (beneficial nonwage gifts work equally well) with unmeasured effort (Akerlof & Yellen, 1990).

From the perspective of game theory, all of these literatures describe the same fundamental phenomenon. In workplaces there are (at least) two sorts of equilibria: (1) Firms treat workers well and workers reciprocate by providing more effort than is required, or (2) firms and workers strike an emotionally neutral bargain to exchange money for clearly specified work; when something unforeseen occurs, neither side gives anything extra. If outcome (1) is an equilibrium, because workers acquire sympathy, affection, or loyalty, for their firm, then the game is one of coordination, not cooperation. Workers and employers are trying to coordinate on whether to behave nicely or not.

8.4 Uses (and misuses) of game theory in studying organizations

So far we have discussed kinds of coordination problems in firms, simple games that capture the features of these problems, and have argued that coordination rather than PD may be the kind of game most common in organizational life. Before proceeding, we offer a few comments about why many studies of organizational behavior have been reluctant to incorporate even simple aspects of game theory (beyond PD). An important barrier to thinking game-theoretically may be a misunderstanding of what game theory is good for and is meant to do.

8.4.1 What is game theory good for?

Game theory can be separated into two distinct parts: (1) a library of games as a system for classifying social situations and (2) a body of mathematical knowledge about how idealized players with varying degrees of rationality would actually play (equilibrium analysis).

The usefulness of games as a classification system (Aumann, 1985) is largely independent of whether the mathematics in part (2) is useful, nonsensical, empirically wrong, or whatever. For example, in the discussion so far, we have not leaned heavily on the idea of equilibrium or discussed the rationality of players (beyond simple utility maximization, which in these examples simply means picking the highest of three numbers). Our claim is that merely describing three kinds of coordination problems in game-theoretic terms provides a parsimonious, clear language that can help classify them. Furthermore, carefully distinguishing PD from coordination, in the previous section, makes it clear that very few organizational situations are pure PDs, and most have elements of coordination. Thus, even without doing any equilibrium analysis or predicting how people will play these games, simply using the games as a classification system can be of some use.

An analogy to biology may help illustrate our point. Biologists have produced careful classifications of organisms, into categories of varying depth – warm- and cold-blooded mammals, birds, plants, and so on. Each category is precisely defined by a small set of features (birds have feathers, fly, and lay eggs), and some exceptions are noted (penguins). Biologists also study the deepest workings of barely observable features of organisms, like DNA, genes, and neurons. But the scientific validity of the latter work has little to do with the usefulness of the former. Birdwatchers will find species classifications extremely useful even if their understanding of the genetic bases of diseases is incomplete or wrong.

8.4.2 What is equilibrium analysis good for?

The mathematical ideas in game theory about how rational players might play (in equilibrium) have come under reasonable attack from philosophers, psychologists, experimentalists – and many game theorists – as exaggerated descriptions of how normally intelligent people would behave (e.g., Zajac & Bazerman, 1991). Virtually all game theorists now concede this point. In response, current research generally takes equilibria derived from mathematical reasoning as possible limiting points to which players might converge in repeated play and asks whether simple (boundedly rational), adaptive decision rules or evolutionary dynamics will lead mathematically to these equilibria or to others. The criticism that equilibrium analysis is irrelevant because people aren't smart enough to figure out the equilibria misses the point of the adaptive and evolutionary analyses.

8.4.3 Games are mental models

Game theory is usually silent on "where" a game exists. Because games are written carefully in matrices (like Figures 8.1 to 8.4), and sometimes in more complicated trees, the immediate image is something like a scoreboard at which all the players look, showing a payoff matrix. This image is misleading.

Instead, consider a team of basketball players in a large arena, where the scoreboard hangs above their heads so that they can't see it as they play. "Where" is the score? It is sensible to say that the score exists both on the scoreboard above the players (where fans can see it) and also in the players' heads as they play.

Similarly, it is sensible to think of games as internal representations, or mental models, which exist entirely in the heads of players. The games we write down and discuss in this chapter are like the score on the scoreboard above the basketball players' heads. The assurance game in Figure 8.3, for example, is *our* understanding of the most basic features of how two organizational members think about the consequences of their choices.

The mental model interpretation of games raises many new questions: Do players have the same mental models? How are mental models constructed and revised? When players are given written models, how do they create mental models from them? (How oversimplified are their models? See Neale and Bazerman, 1991.) These questions are novel for game theory because generally the game-theoretic action begins after a game is posed and becomes ripe for equilibrium analysis. But addressing them could prove a very important application of psychology and organization studies to empirical game theory. Porac, Thomas, and Emme's (1987) study of perceived competition among businesses is an interesting start.

8.4.4 Why are researchers so fascinated by PD?

Echoing Murnighan (1994) and Gibbons (in press), an underlying theme of our chapter is that organizational researchers should consider a wider variety of games than PD. This raises a natural question: Why is PD so popular among so many scholars? Besides being studied by various types of organization researchers, PDs are widely studied by social psychologists, political scientists, biologists, and many others.

We think some of the popularity of PD arises from a simple combination of an error in logic and ignorance of other kinds of games. In theory, players engaging in a PD or social dilemma will choose inefficiently. (That is, individually rational players make choices that make everyone worse off.) Because PD implies inefficiency, organizational researchers looking for a game-theoretic model of how conflict between personal and group goals results in organizational inefficiency might instinctively think of PD as if it were *the* right model of individual–group conflict. This is simply wrong because many other interesting games predict possible inefficiencies and may be better models for organizational phenomena than PD.

For example, in the coordination games we describe, efficient outcomes *and* inefficient outcomes are possible. Groups or firms can get stuck in an equilibrium nobody likes because they cannot coordinate a simultaneous switch to a better equilibrium (and players will voluntarily switch only if they think others will). This simple feature seems to characterize problems of "dinosaur" firms (like Sears and GM) at least as well as PD does (see also Rumelt, 1995, esp. pp. 115–117). It can also account for path dependencies, the tyranny of the past, the extreme sensitivity of equilibrium results to initial conditions, and other features commonly associated with organizational paradox. In Knez and Camerer (1994) we draw the analogy between norms or beliefs in coordination games and intangible *expectational* assets, which are one kind of resource described in popular *resource-based* views of differential firm success in business strategy research. Notice that a history of coordination on an inefficient equilibrium is like an expectational *liability* and, like a bad reputation, it cannot be easily disposed of.

Another class of games that often exhibit inefficiencies are games with information asymmetries. Gibbons (in press) argues cogently that games of this sort may serve as sharp models of many sorts of organizational behavior that appear perverse. In these games, inefficiencies typically result because players must take inefficient actions to convey their information credibly (or "signal") to others. For example, the current game-theoretic theory of strikes is that labor or management strikes in order to signal private information credibly about their own reservation wages to the other side (Kennan & Wilson, 1990). Other papers model inefficiencies that arise from the "herd behavior" of rational corporate managers. For example, in Scharfstein and Stein (1990), managers will sometimes choose to forego unusual, high-profit projects and instead follow the herd, mimicking what other managers do, to avoid the risk of being thought of as bad managers. Kanodia, Bushman, and Dickhaut (1989) argue similarly that escalation to organizational commitment may result from managers' refusal to abandon projects to protect their reputations. Prendergast (1993) builds a theory of "yes men" around the idea that subjective evaluations of workers by superiors are necessary to help an organization decide who to promote, but this evaluation process naturally gives workers too strong an incentive to please their bosses.

We do not believe that game-theoretic models like these are definitive explanations for inefficient organizational practices. Indeed, these rationalizations usually compete directly with other behavioral explanations that are widely accepted by decision researchers. But such models create sharp competition between explanations based on incomplete information and those based on bounded rationality, and clarify what sort of data would support each explanation in an empirical competition that constitutes the logical next step.

8.5 Coordination and organizational expectations

The application of simple coordination games to organizational coordination problems focuses attention on mechanisms that transform expectations rather than mechanisms that transform preferences. We will refer to such expectations as *organizational expectations.* Coordination is achieved through organizational expectations because all members share a *common* expectation of how all the other members will behave. Building on the chapters of March and Zhou (this book), organizational expectations support organizational rules (or norms) that define the actions a member should take (or not take) in a particular situation, and result in the coordination and control of organizational activities.

Until recently, economists have had little to say about organizational expectations. Such issues had been contained in the "black box" of organizational processes that economists found convenient to ignore. However, the extensive introduction of noncooperative game theory into economics starting in the late 1970s and continuing today has provided economists with the analytic machinery to begin addressing this topic.

Game theory allows us to be precise about the structure of organizational expectations. Simplifying a bit, what is required is that each member's belief about the other member's intention to follow a particular rule is mutually understood. For example, in the assurance game, the rule "select the action associated with the most efficient outcome" (the *efficiency rule* for short) selects the Pareto-efficient outcome (H,H). In order for the efficiency rule to be followed, player 1 must believe that player 2 expects him (player 1) to follow the rule, and likewise player 2 believes that player 1 expects him (player 2) to follow the rule. In game theory this is known as the *mutual knowledge* condition and is a necessary condition for the existence of a Nash equilibrium.[2]

The mutual knowledge condition merely formalizes the notion that in order for a rule of behavior to be followed, there must exist mutually reinforcing expectations between the players that the rule will be followed. Since mutual knowledge is a necessary condition for a Nash equilibrium, we can study organizational expectations by studying the selection of Nash equilibria. Unfortunately, game theory does *not* provide us with a strong theory that predicts which equilibria will be selected in coordination games. Instead, we are left with less satisfying *focal principles* (Schelling, 1960). A focal principle posits that certain deductive properties of the game being played will create mutually consistent beliefs among its players about how others will play the game. The most well-studied focal principle is *payoff dominance* (Harsanyi & Selten, 1988). Under payoff dominance, if a unique Pareto-efficient equilibrium exists, then it will be selected in the interest of efficiency.[3] That is, players will intuit that all other players will select the Pareto-efficient strategy because they also believe that everyone else will do the same. *Pareto dominance* is simply a fancy name for the efficiency rule discussed earlier.

Selection principles such as Pareto dominance are predictions about how players intuit rules of behavior from the mere structure of payoffs in the game. Any additional information about how other players in the game will behave, through either direct or third-party communication, is treated separately. Although game theorists and experimental economists who study equilibrium selection in coordination games do not normally address the more specific issue of organizational expectations, we argue that it provides a fruitful research paradigm for studying this issue.

Up to now, most of the research on equilibrium selection in coordination games has focused on how the structure of coordination games affects equilibrium selection. Loosely put, a game's structure is described by its payoffs, the number of players, and the set of actions available to each player. Specifically, researchers ask: Does the structure of a particular coordination game provide players with enough information to intuit the mutual knowledge condition underlying a well-specified rule of behavior (such as the efficiency rule)? Normally, the following baseline conditions are created to answer this question experimentally: (1) the structure of the game (payoffs, number of players, actions) is common knowledge and (2) players are not able to communicate with each other, nor do they know the identity of the other players (no possibility of repeated interaction). The outcome in the baseline condition (e.g., the efficient equilibrium versus the inefficient equilibrium in the assurance game) tells us whether or not more formal forms of communication are required to induce mutual knowledge.

In the following section, we highlight recent experimental work in this area. As we proceed, the experimental results reported involve richer hypotheses that begin to shed light on the issue of organizational expectations.

8.6 Experimental results on coordination games

Several recent experiments study how subjects play coordination games. In this section, we describe previous findings that represent initial steps in understanding the game-theoretic structure of organizational expectations. After describing the results, we make some remarks about experimental methods and how psychological experiments might differ in style from the ones we describe.

8.6.1 Results on two-player assurance games with and without "cheaptalk"

Cooper, DeJong, Forsythe, and Ross (1992) examine behavior in a 2×2 "assurance" coordination game shown in Figure 8.5. If subjects choose L, they earn $.80 for sure. If they choose H, they earn nothing if others choose L and $1 if others also choose H. Hence, choosing L is an equilibrium. Choosing H is an equilibrium also – which yields $1 points for each player – but it is riskier because it pays nothing if the other players choose L. The authors' subjects played the one-shot assurance game 11 times with different players. Players did not know the identity of the players they were paired with, nor did they know the history of decisions other than in their own previous games.

Out of a total of 165 subject pairs, 160 (97%) played the inefficient equilibrium (L,L). The remaining five pairs played disequilibrium outcomes (L,H) or (H,L). Notice that even though (H,H) is an equilibrium, players *never* reached it. Choosing H maximizes the expected payoff only if the probability that one's partner chooses H is above 80%. This required level of assurance seems to be too high.

Cooper et al. (1992, 1994) also studied the impact of one-way and two-way communication on assurance and subsequent choices. Under one-way communication, only one player sends a message announcing the action she intends to select. Subjects are not required to choose the action they announced (in game theory this nonbinding preplay communication is called *cheap talk*). Under one-way communication, most players (87%) said they would play H. (All data we report are from the last 11 of 22 periods.) Then 88 of the 165 subject pairs (53%) played the efficient equilibrium (H,H), 51 pairs (31%) played disequilibrium outcomes, and the remaining

Person 2

Person 1	L	H
L	.8, .8	.8, 0
H	0, .8	1, 1

Figure 8.5. Assurance game payoffs (in dollars). (From Cooper et al., 1992)

16% played the inefficient outcome (L,L). The problem was that many players who received the H message (24%) weren't willing to bet that the message sender would follow through and chose the safe L instead. Indeed, many of those who sent H *did not* choose H subsequently (20%). Hence, although one-way communication raises the percentage of (H,H) play from virtually none to about half, it does not fully solve the coordination problem.

Under two-way communication both players simultaneously send messages. Then players *always* announced they would H, and 150 of the 165 subject pairs (90%) did play the efficient (H,H) equilibrium. Two-way communication almost fully resolves the coordination problem in the assurance game.

8.6.2 Basic results on the weakest-link game

The *weakest-link* (or *minimum-action*) game is a many-player version of the assurance game that captures the gist of any situation in which a group or organizational goal is disproportionately affected by the lowest quality of each individual's inputs.[4] Figure 8.6 provides a matrix-form example of the weakest-link game in which players choose numbers[5] 1–7. The figure shows the payoffs to a subject who chooses a Row action when the minimum action chosen by any subject in a group (including the row player) is shown in Column. For example, suppose there are three players, A, B, and C, and player A selects a 5, player B selects a 4, and player C selects a 3. The minimum action selected is 3; hence, player A receives $.70, player B receives $.80, and player C receives $.90. In this example, player A "loses" $.20 by selecting an action two increments above the minimum action selected. Each player wants to select exactly the minimum of the other players, and everyone wants the minimum to be as high as possible. But selecting high actions is risky because other players may select low actions. The assurance game is a two-person weakest-link game, and the payoffs in Figure 8.3 provide a way to extend the game to more players.

The customer satisfaction problem described earlier is an example of a weakest-link game. Assume that a customer's level of satisfaction with hotel service is determined by the lowest quality of service she receives. Then the weakest link in the chain of customer service is most important.

SMALLEST VALUE OF X CHOSEN

		7	6	5	4	3	2	1
	7	1.30	1.10	0.90	0.70	0.50	0.30	0.10
YOUR	6		1.20	1.00	0.80	0.60	0.40	0.20
CHOICE	5			1.10	0.90	0.70	0.50	0.30
OF X	4				1.00	0.80	0.60	0.40
	3					0.90	0.70	0.50
	2						0.80	0.60
	1							0.70

Figure 8.6. Weakest-link game.

Other organizational examples include (1) manufacturing a sensitive product, which is very likely to fail if any single part fails (some food and chemical production requires strict adherence to a "recipe" and very pure inputs; one bad ingredient ruins the whole batch); (2) production of safety in high-reliability organizations, which fail if a single failure occurs; (3) keeping a secret (or not repeating an organizational rumor), assuming that one or more leaks are equally harmful and assuming that everyone prefers to keep the secret only if everyone else will too; and (4) games of timing in which a project cannot be completed until all the parts are complete, such as assembling a report or prospectus or producing a book or special issue like this one (which can't be published until all chapters are in).

In all these cases, if poor quality of specific inputs is difficult to identify, and if participants dislike putting in high-quality inputs but share in an improved group output if everyone puts in high quality, then the weakest-link game provides a crisp description of an incentive problem that does not depend on the existence of a social dilemma. Inefficient behavior is created by the mere expectation that there is at least one weak link in the chain rather than by the incentive to free-ride if others are strong links.

Van Huyck, Battalio, and Beil (1990) (hereafter VBB) were the first to study behavior in the weakest-link game. In their experiments, roughly 15 undergraduate subjects played the game 10 times for the dollar payoffs shown in Figure 8.3. After each period of play the minimum action was publicly announced.

In all seven of their experimental replications, the number 1 was the minimum action selected after 10 periods of play, and roughly 75–90% of the subjects selected a 1 in the 10th period of play (see Fig. 8.7). Hence, not only do large numbers of players find it difficult to play the weakest-link game efficiently, they tend to play the most inefficient equilibrium.

	3-player games (KC, 1995)			14-16 player games (VBB, 1990)		
Actions	Actions period 1	Minima period 1	Minima period 5	Actions period 1	Minima period 1	Minima period 5
1	8 (.13)	5	6	2 (.02)	2	7
2	3 (.05)	1	3	5 (.05)	2	0
3	8 (.13)	7	4	5 (.05)	1	0
4	11 (.18)	3	3	18 (.17)	1	0
5	4 (.07)	1	0	34 (.32)	1	0
6	1 (.02)	0	0	10 (.09)	0	0
7	25 (.42)	3	4	33 (.31)	0	0
total	60 (1.00)	20	20	107 (1.00)	7	7

Figure 8.7. Distribution of individual actions and group minima in weakest-link game experiments.

In Knez and Camerer (1994) we study three-player weakest-link games where players play the game for five periods with the same people. We find that three-player groups also have difficulty playing the weakest-link game efficiently. The distribution of individual actions in the first period, and minimum actions across 20 groups in the first and fifth period of play, are described in Figure 8.7. In both the 3-player and 15-player games, there is significant dispersion in the minimum action selected in the first period of play. This dispersion remains in the fifth period of play in the three-player games, and four of the groups reach an efficient minimum of 7. But in the 14- to 16-player games the minimum action selected in the fifth period is a 1 in every group. (Minima of 1 were also observed by Cachon and Camerer, 1996, for nine-player groups and by Knez and Camerer, 1994, for six-player groups.)

It appears that although small groups of players do not generally play the weakest-link game efficiently (only 4 of 20 reached the efficient outcome of 7), they do a better job of maintaining the level of efficiency achieved in early periods of play than do larger groups.

8.6.3 The effect of feedback, subject pools, and group expansion

Five treatments that may be of special interest to organizational researchers have been studied.

Feedback. In most of their sessions, VBB (1990) announced only the minimum action chosen in a group to the group members. An organization could announce the entire distribution of actions, and this might improve a group's ability to coordinate on a number higher than 1. In some sessions, VBB did announce the full distribution, but this did not matter much; if anything, it speeded up the inexorable process of convergence to 1 across trials.

Subject pools. The general pattern of convergence to low-number choices is robust across small variations in subject pools. Besides undergraduates (at Texas A&M University, the University of Chicago, and the Wharton School), the weakest-link results have been replicated with strategy professors (Knez & Camerer, 1994) and psychology professors. It would be useful to know whether enhancing group affiliation or organizational identification (e.g., Kramer, 1992) improves coordination.

Group size. Several studies suggest two interesting effects of varying group size in the weakest-link game. First, it is natural to expect that the ability of a group of players to achieve the efficient outcomes increases as group size shrinks, and it does. If the probability that any one of N players will select a small number is equal to p, then the probability that a small number is selected by at least one player is $1 - (1 - p)^N$, which increases rapidly as N rises. Second, players do not seem to appreciate how quickly this effect operates because Figure 8.7 shows that the distributions of first-period actions is almost the same in 3- and in 14- to 16-person games. (If anything, the small groups choose lower actions than the larger groups do.) If subjects form vague beliefs over the choices others would make and then compute their optimal response to the distribution of *minima* in their groups, they should choose much lower numbers when their groups are large. The fact that they do not suggests a kind of "law of small numbers" or representative thinking. Subjects seem to think a low minimum is equally likely in a large group and a small group (see the small- versus large-hospital problem in Kahneman & Tversky, 1972).

Group formation. Knez and Camerer (1994) combined two three-person groups, after five periods of weakest-link play, into a single six-person group. Suppose one group reached a minimum of 4 and the other reached a lower minimum of 2. Would the combined group achieve a new minimum of 4, 2, or something else? In all 10 combined groups, the new group's minimum was the *lower* of the previous two minima (a bad norm or expectation drove out a good one). This effect occurred regardless of whether or not each three-person group knew the other group's previous history when they were combined.

Bonus announcements. Knez and Camerer also studied (but did not report) the effect of an announced bonus on performance. First, six-person groups reliably converged to low number minima over several trials (7 of 10 groups reached 1). Then the authors announced publicly that each member of a group would receive an extra bonus of 20 or 50 cents if everyone in the group chose a 7. (Notice that a group with a minimum of 1 has an implicit bonus of 60 cents available already, since choosing 7 pays $1.30, whereas choosing 1 pays $.70.) This announcement had a dramatic effect: Eight of 10 groups immediately moved to a minimum of 7. This result reminds us, as Cooper et al.'s two-way communication showed, how effective a small amount of public communication can be in improving coordination.[6]

8.6.4 Norms and precedent formation

The experimental results reported so far all concern the selection of the efficient equilibrium in various coordination games. The results provide powerful evidence that the mere risk that other players in the game will not select the efficient action results in inefficient behavior. In other words, under consistent preferences the mere existence of a Pareto-dominant outcome is not enough to induce efficient outcomes. These results serve as a foundation for the broader study of organizational rules and norms. An organizational rule is, by definition, a rule of behavior that exists prior to the selection of actions by the players in the game. This leaves open the question of how such rules develop and how robust they are to changes in the structure of the environment.

The traditional approach to norm development (Schein, 1985) assumes the dynamic process described by Homans (1951, p. 127):

Norms do not materialize out of nothing: they emerge from on-going activities. . . . Men bring their norms to a group; they work out new norms through their experience in the group; they take old norms, confirmed or weakened, and the new ones, as developed, to other groups they are members of. If the norms take hold there, a general tradition, the same in many groups, may grow up.

There are two parts to Homans's description of the norm development process. First is the development of norms within subgroups of the organization. Second is the transfer of norms across the subgroups. Hence, an organizational norm or rule arises as previously developed group rules are transferred to new groups over and over again. In order for an organizational rule to develop, this adjustment process must lead to the development in the organization of common beliefs about appropriate modes of behavior in the organization.

At the heart of this adjustment process are *precedent effects*. The rules that emerge in prior interactions serve as precedents for future interactions. In the language of coordination games, the equilibria selected in previous coordination games serve as precedents for future coordination games.

Research on experimental coordination games has documented the significant role of precedents. Among the most notable examples is the work by VBB (1991) on the median-action game. In this game each player selects a number from the set of integers 1–7. Every player's payoff is higher if the median number chosen is higher, and a player's payoff falls if her number is further above or below the median. VBB find strong precedent effects in two forms in groups of 9–27 subjects. First, across *all* of the experimental treatments, the median action selected in all periods of play was exactly the same as the median action in the first period of play. The precedent set in the first period of play *completely* determined behavior in later periods. (Cachon & Camerer, 1996, replicated these results with nine-player groups.) Second, the equilibrium played in previous average opinion games transferred to analogous average opinion games.

Bettenhausen and Murnighan (1985) studied precedent in repeated PDs, most of which had payoffs that make them coordination games. They found strong transfer of cooperative norms across changes in game parameters.

In Knez and Camerer (1995) we document strong precedent effects of two forms. In the experiments reported, subjects played both the weakest-link game in Figure 8.6 repeatedly, as well as two-player and three-player PD games. In one treatment, subjects played all two-player games; in the other treatment, subjects played all three-player games. In both games the efficient outcome has all players selecting the number 7. In the weakest-link games the efficient outcome is a Nash equilibrium; in the PD games it is not. We were interested in whether a norm of efficiency in the weakest-link game would transfer to the PD game.

In the two-player experiments, under treatment WP subjects played the weakest-link game for five periods and then played the PD game for five periods. Subjects played with the same opponents in all 10 periods of play. Under treatment WP, all five pairs of subjects played the efficient equilibrium in all five periods of play of the weakest-link game. (The fact that all the two-player groups reach efficiency is remarkable because Figure 8.7 shows that only 20% of three-player groups reach the efficient equilibrium. There appears to be an important leap from two- to three-player groups.) In the subsequent PD, 90% of the subjects who experienced the precedent of efficient play in the weakest-link game selected a 7, the cooperative choice, in the first round of the PD game.

Under treatment PW, subjects played the PD game for five periods and then played the weakest-link game for five periods. In this treatment subjects do not experience the precedent of efficiency before playing the PD (since they play it right away), and only 25% (5 out of 20) of the subjects select a 7 in their first PD game. This difference between the fractions picking efficient 7's in the WP and PW treatments (90% versus 25%) is highly significant ($X^2 = 11.32$, $p < .001$). This is a dramatic example of norm transfer.

In the three-player treatments, Knez and Camerer had to take extra steps to get subjects to experience the precedent of efficiency because subjects rarely play the efficient equilibrium in the three-player weakest-link game. In round 1, four pairs of subjects first played the weakest-link game for five periods. *All* of these four pairs played the efficient equilibrium (all choosing 7) in all five periods of play. In round 2, one subject was added to the two-player groups from round 1. All the new players observed the history of play of the two-player groups they were entering, and the round 1 players knew this. Hence, the precedent of efficient play in round 1 was common knowledge in round 2. All four three-player groups played the efficient equilibrium in all five periods of round 2. These results are in striking contrast to the behavior observed in three-player weakest-link games where subjects had not experienced the precedent of efficient play in the two-player games.

Finally, when players start out in three-player groups a precedent of *in*efficient play in the weakest-link game develops, but when they start out in two-player groups the precedent of efficiency develops. Again, we found a strong and significant precedent effect. Under the precedent of efficiency, 73% of the subjects select a 7 in the first period of the three-player PD game, whereas under the inefficient precedent only 22% select a 7 ($X^2 = 8.62$, $p < .004$).

In summary, Knez and Camerer (1995) found that the precedent of efficiency transfers from the weakest-link game to the PD game in both two-player and three-player groups. They also found that efficient behavior can be induced in three-player weakest-link games by first allowing players to develop the home-grown precedent of efficient play in the two-player weakest-link game. (We conjecture that one can develop efficient groups of any size in the weakest-link game this way by letting n-person groups play long enough to establish a firm history of efficient play of choosing 7's, letting newcomers know about this history, and adding only two or three players at a time.)

8.6.5 A digression on economic and psychological experimental methods

Most readers of this book are probably familiar with the experimental paradigm followed by organizational psychologists and relatively unfamiliar with (or even hostile to) the methods experimental economists use (e.g., Davis & Holt, 1992). For example, the experiments we just described may seem overly simple and devoid of context. We think the design differences in the two approaches spring largely, and defensibly, from basic differences in how knowledge is compiled in economics and psychology. We summarize this argument briefly (see Camerer, in press).

The purpose of most economics experiments is to clearly operationalize a setting in which a theory makes a clear prediction. As a direct result of this goal, to study assurance games it is essential to create a situation in which (L,L) and (H,H) are both equilibria and (H,H) is better for everyone but riskier. If we cannot be sure that these conditions are met, then the game-theoretic predictions are not being tested and nothing is contributed to economic knowledge. To meet these conditions, the experiment uses an abstract, a-realistic *context* (subjects choose numbers or letters). Subjects are also paid substantial *financial incentives* to help ensure that they really do prefer (H,H) to (L,L). The key design elements – abstract context and financial incentives – fit together to achieve the main purpose, which is to operationalize a setting about which game theory makes a prediction.

The purpose of psychology experiments[7] is generally to express an informal intuition or regularity in a dramatic, lifelike way or yield data with which to construct a new theory. Because subjects are often unpaid (e.g., participating for course credit), an abstract task might bore or confuse them, so a concrete one is better. Because their purpose is different from the theory-testing motive of economists, psychologists might study coordination differently.

For example, we could ask two subjects to perform a mildly aversive task, like pedaling a bicycle at either of two programmed rates, slow or fast, and pay them each a larger prize if they both pedal fast. (Tasks like this were used in early "social loafing" experiments; see Kidwell & Bennett, 1993.) Simultaneous pedaling resembles an assurance game, but we cannot be sure it is. It is *not* an assurance game if either subject is fanatic enough about exercise to simply prefer pedaling faster; then (fast) is a dominant strategy so (slow,slow) is not an equilibrium. It is also *not* an assurance game if one subject (or both) dislikes pedaling so much that he would rather forego his prize than match the other player's fast pedaling; then (slow) is a dominant strategy and (fast,fast) is not an equilibrium. So to be sure that pedaling is really an assurance game, we must be sure that both players do not like pedaling too much or like it too little (and also be sure that players know this about others) or else control these preferences and beliefs.[8] One way to control them is to use an abstract task like choosing letters or numbers and pay financial rewards, as in Figure 8.2.

The advantage of a task like pedaling is its improvement in realism, external validity, or generalizability to organizations (compared to abstract number choosing for money). But this apparent improvement can be reasonably disputed on two grounds.

First, judgments of external validity should be grounded in a statistical understanding of what organizational situations are common. Are pedaling-like tasks really more common than choosing abstract symbols that yield monetary rewards? The answer is hard to know. Consider a law firm. Attorneys on a litigation team who spend long hours in court, exerting fatiguing effort, may be like subjects pedaling bikes. But other lawyers research legal details in a library or compile abstract symbols into briefs; perhaps their work is more like choosing letters that yield financial payoffs than like bike pedaling.

Second, it is unclear that experiments *should be* like a random sample of realistic organizational situations. Scientists routinely oversample unusual situations (neglecting mundane ones). Neuroscientists study victims of unusual traumas, biologists study strange species, economists study depressions and market crashes, and astronomers study supernovas. These phenomena are all rare and hence highly unrealistic, but they provide an efficient way to learn about general processes. While hesitating to claim the same status for the simple experiments described previously, we simply want to question (1) how to determine which experiments are most realistic and (2) whether realism is desirable.

A final thought about context: Economic experiments are happily unrealistic because economics and game theory make no special predictions about behavior in more or less realistic situations. (If the purpose of the experiment is theory testing, the experiments need only be as realistic as the theory.) This *does not* mean that game theorists insist that context does not matter to outcomes. It simply means that there is no systematic theory of precisely how context matters. Obviously, one way to build up such a theory is to start with context-free baseline experiments (like the 2 × 2 results described earlier) and then experiment incrementally with contextual changes (like one- and two-way communication). Further changes of organizational interest can be added easily.

8.7 Conclusion

We began the chapter by pointing out three kinds of coordination problems in firms. Matching problems occur when players agree on what is the best outcome for the organization (and for themselves) but, for one reason or another, cannot necessarily achieve it. Mixed-motive bargaining problems occur when players would like to strike some mutually agreeable deal (rather than cause an impasse) but different players prefer different deals. Assurance problems occur when players agree on what is best but actions that lead to the best outcome are riskier, so players want to take them only if others probably will as well.

We then introduced a simple class of games from noncooperative game theory, known as *coordination games,* which precisely operationalize these three coordination problems. We contrasted these games with the PD and argued that the conditions for true PDs are rarely met in actual organizations; instead, those games are coordination games.

Next, we elaborated on the point that the application of simple coordination games to organizational coordination problems focuses attention on mechanisms that transform expectations rather than mechanisms that transform preferences. We refer to such expectations as *organizational expectations,* which are loosely defined as the mutual beliefs by all members of an organization that all members will follow a particular rule or norm. We argued that this mutual-belief condition is at the foundation of organizational rules and norms. Hence, understanding the factors that govern the structure and development of mutual beliefs will provide important insights into organizational rules and norms.

We concluded by describing experimental research on coordination games, which represents the first steps in examining the behavioral under-pinnings of organizational expectations. This experimental research documents that risky coordination does indeed lead to inefficient behavior. In other words, despite the simplicity of these games, subjects are not able to intuit (or are unwilling to bet that others have intuited) the rule of efficient play. Each subject understands that 7 in the weakest-link game is the right action, but they are not sufficiently confident that all other subjects understand this too. We are presently exploring the impact of many variants of this game. Our goal is to understand the conditions necessary for such a rule provision in order to create the mutual knowledge required to select the efficient equilibrium.

We also highlighted experimental research that documented strong precedent effects across trials of the same coordination game, as well as transfer of precedents from coordination games to PD games. We see these results as first steps in using these simple coordinations games to examine the development and transfer of organizational rules and norms.

Our most basic claim is that game theory is useful as a system for classifying organizational situations, analyzing how people might behave in them, and making clear predictions that can be tested experimentally or, with more work, in the field. Indeed, it is hard to think of a decision a person makes inside an organization that is not a strategy in a game (in the sense that the choices others make at the same time affect the payoff from a certain decision).

In future work, we hope to apply the PD–coordination distinction to highlight the difference between a coordination perspective and the Williamsonian theory of the firm, which focuses on "holdup" problems that are eliminated by integration. We also think that some anomalous features of faddish business practices (like total quality management and reengineering) can be thought of as solutions to the problem of coordinating organizational change (see Camerer & Knez, in press).

Notes

1   This example does not require aversion to effort or shirking. A BOS results if they both prefer to deliver the order, either for sheer pleasure, to impress a supervisor, or in the expectation of being tipped well.
2   Our discussion is a simplification of mutual knowledge. Aumann and Brandenburger (1995) show that the two necessary conditions for the existence of a pure strategy Nash equilibrium are mutual knowledge of beliefs and mutual knowledge of rationality. *Mutual knowledge of beliefs* means that each player knows the other player's beliefs. *Mutual knowledge of rationality* means that each player knows that the other player selects the action that maximizes her expected payoff given her beliefs. We focus on the mutual knowledge of beliefs conditions, and for simplicity we refer to it as the *mutual knowledge condition*.

3 An outcome is Pareto efficient if there is no alternative outcome for which one player is made better off without making another player worse off. The most notable example is cooperation in the PD. But note that although cooperation in the (single-play) PD is Pareto efficient, it is not a Nash equilibrium.

4 Cobb–Douglas production functions, commonly used in econometric studies of labor–capital productivity, exhibit this property for extreme parameter values. Cornes (1993) shows that if q_i are n separate inputs, the function $Q = a[(1/n)(q_1^v + q_2^v + \ldots q_n^v)]^{1/v}$ exhibits precisely the weakest-link structure as v grows large and negative, and includes other interesting structures as alternative special cases (see also Hirshleifer 1983). Jacobs (1981) presents a sociological discussion of weak-link production in organizations.

5 Restricting actions to picking numbers seems highly artificial. But the numbers are not essential; they are simply used to label equilibrium outcomes from best (for everyone) to worst. *Any* set of nonnumerical choices that yields Pareto-rankable outcomes could be used as well. For example, the actions could represent seven different methods of restructuring (or acquisition targets, strategic alliances, etc.) labeled A through G. Suppose A is more valuable than B, B than C, and so forth, if incumbent managers allocate scarce resources and energy to making restructuring A work. And suppose they prefer to do so if other managers will, but they do not want to invest in C, say, if some other manager will only invest in E. Then they play a weakest-link game that is formally equivalent to the game we study. The actions are numbered just to denote which methods are best.

6 Hypersensitivity to communication raises an important methodological concern: Because communicating with members is one thing most organizations can do well, why study a class of problems that would be so easily solved by real organizations through communication? Our answer is that we think genuine coordination problems involve some combination of other features, deliberately left out of our experiments, that make coordination difficult even with communication. For example, effective communication may have to be public, and with most members present. Also, large coordination problems with thousands of players, or high-stakes problems where the penalty from mismatch is severe, may be harder to solve with limited communication. Finally, the same criticism about hypersensitivity to communication can be leveled at many studies of PDs, because we know that some kinds of communication improve cooperation substantially (Sally, 1995).

7 Here we have in mind the kinds of experiments conducted by psychologists most likely to be interested in coordination, namely, social psychologists. Other subfields work differently. Perceptual and cognitive psychology, for example, use much simpler stimuli to get at basic cognitive processes and resemble the experimental economics style.

8 Preferences and beliefs about pedaling could be measured independently of the assurance task, but that might require inefficiently discarding many subjects before recruiting enough who are not too exercise crazy or averse. Or beliefs could be created through the use of deception or confederate subjects, but deception can be objected to on other grounds (see Camerer, in press). For example, if the beliefs being induced – say, that Californian subjects do not like pedaling too much – are unlikely to arise naturally and so must be induced through deception, then one must wonder whether subjects believe the decep-

tion. Experimental economists also worry about long-run harm to experimenter credibility from repeated deception.

References

Akerlof, G., & Yellen, J. (1990). The fair wage-effort hypothesis and unemployment. *Quarterly Journal of Economics, 105,* 255–283.

Aumann, R. (1985). What is game theory trying to accomplish? In K. J. Arrow & S. Honkapohja (Eds.), *Frontiers of economics* (pp. 28–76). Oxford: Basil Blackwell.

Aumann, R., & Bradenburger, A. (1995). Epistemic conditions for Nash equilibrium. *Econometrica, 63,* 1161–1180.

Barnard, C. (1938). *The functions of the executive.* Cambridge, MA: Harvard University Press.

Becker, G. S., & Murphy, K. J. (1992). The division of labor and coordination. *Quarterly Journal of Economics, 107,* 1137–1160.

Bettenhausen, K., & Murnighan, J. (1985). The emergence of norms in competitive decision-making groups. *Administrative Science Quarterly, 30,* 350–372.

Cachon, G., & Camerer, C. F. (1996). Loss-avoidance and forward induction in experimental coordination games. *Quarterly Journal of Economics, 110,* 165–194.

Camerer, C. F. (in press). Rules for experimenting in psychology and economics, and why they differ. In W. Güth & E. Van Damme (Eds.), *Essays in honor of Reinhard Selten,* Springer-Verlag.

Camerer, C. F., & Knez, M. (in press). Coordination, organizational boundaries, and fads in business practice. *Industrial and Corporate Change.*

Chisholm, D. (1989). *Coordination without hierarchy: Informal structures in multiorganizational systems.* Berkeley: University of California Press.

Cooper, R., DeJong, D. V., Forsythe, R., & Ross, T. W. (1989). Selection criteria in coordination games. *American Economic Review, 80,* 218–233.

Cooper, R., DeJong, D., Forsythe, R., & Ross, T. (1992). Communication in coordination games. *Quarterly Journal of Economics, 107,* 739–771.

Cooper, R., DeJong, D., Forsythe, R., & Ross, T. (1994). Alternative institutions for resolving coordination problems: Experimental evidence on forward induction and preplay communication. In J. Friedman (Ed.), *Problems of coordination in economic activity* (pp. 129–146). Norwell, MA: Kluwer.

Cooper, R., & John, A. (1988). Coordinating coordination failures in Keynesian models. *Quarterly Journal of Economics, 103,* 441–464.

Cornes, R. (1993). Dyke maintenance and other stories: Some neglected types of public goods. *Quarterly Journal of Economics, 108,* 259–272.

Davis, D., & Holt, C. (1992). *Experimental economics.* Princeton, NJ: Princeton University Press.

Gibbons, R. (1992). *Game theory for applied economists.* Princeton, NJ: Princeton University Press.

Gibbons, R. (in press). Game theory and garbage cans. In J. Halpern & R. Stern (Eds.), *Nonrational decision making in organizations.* Ithaca, NY: ILR Press, Cornell University.

Harsanyi, J., & Selten, R. (1988). *A general theory of equilibrium selection in games.* Cambridge, MA: MIT Press.

Hirshleifer, J. (1983). From weakest-link to best-shot: The voluntary provision of public goods. *Public Choice, 41*, 371–386.

Homans, G. (1951). *The human group.* New Brunswick, NJ: Transaction.

Jacobs, D. (1981). Toward a theory of mobility and behavior in organizations: An inquiry into the consequences of some relationships between individual performance and organizational success. *American Journal of Sociology, 87*, 684–707.

Kahneman, D., & Tversky, A. (1972). Subjective probability: A judgment of representativeness. *Cognitive Psychology, 3*, 430–454.

Kanodia, C., Bushman, R., & Dickhaut, J. (1989). Escalation errors and the sunk cost effect: An explanation based on reputation and information asymmetries. *Journal of Accounting Research, 27*, 59–77.

Keenan, J., & Wilson, R. (1990). Theories of bargaining delays. *Science, 249*, 1124–1128.

Kidwell, R. E., Jr., & Bennett, N. (1993). Employee propensity to withhold effort: A conceptual model to intersect three avenues of research. *Academy of Management Review, 18*, 429–456.

Knez, M., & Camerer, C. (1994). Creating expectational assets in the laboratory: Coordination in "weakest-link" games. *Strategic Management Journal, 15*, 101–119.

Knez, M., & Camerer, C. (1995). *Norm transfer in coordination and social dilemma games.* Working paper, University of Chicago Graduate School of Business.

Kramer, R. (1990). Multi-party negotiation and the "tragedy of the commons" in organizations: Social psychological aspects of strategic choice. In R. Lewicki, B. Shepard, & M. Bazerman (Eds.), *Research on negotiations in organizations* (Vol. 3). Greenwich, CT: JAI Press.

Kramer, R. (1992). Cooperation and organizational/identification. In K. Murnighan (Ed.), *Social psychology in organizations* (pp. 244–269). Englewood Cliffs, NJ: Prentice-Hall.

Lamoreaux, N., & Raff, D. (1995). *Coordination and information: Historical perspectives on the organization of enterprise.* Chicago: University of Chicago Press.

Ledyard, J. (1995). Public goods. In J. Kagel & A. Roth (Eds.), *Handbook of experimental economics* (pp. 111–194). Princeton, NJ: Princeton University Press, 111–194.

Mannix, E., & White, S. B. (1992). The impact of distributive uncertainty on coalition formation in organizations. *Organizational Behavior and Human Decision Processes, 51*, 198–219.

March, J., & Simon, H. (1958). *Organizations.* New York: Wiley.

Marschak, J., & Radner, R. (1972). *Economic theory of teams.* New Haven, CT: Yale University Press.

Milgrom, P., & Roberts, J. (1992). *Economics, organization, and management.* Englewood Cliffs, NJ: Prentice-Hall.

Miller, G. (1992). *Managerial dilemmas: The political economy of hierarchy.* New York: Cambridge University Press.

Mooney, J. (1947). *Principles of organization.* New York: Harper & Brothers.

Murnighan, J. K. (1994). Game theory in organizational behavior. In B. Staw & L. Cummings (Eds.), *Research in Organizational Behavior* (Vol. 16, pp. 83–123). Greenwich, CT: JAI Press.

Neale, M., & Bazerman, M. (1991). *Cognition and rationality in negotiations.* New York: Free Press.

Orbell, J., van de Kragt, A., & Dawes, R. (1988). Explaining discussion-induced cooperation. *Journal of Personality and Social Psychology, 54,* 811–819.

Organ, D. W. (1988). *Organizational citizenship behavior: The good soldier syndrome.* Lexington, MA: Heath.

Porac, J., Thomas, H., & Emme, B. (1987). Knowing the competition: The mental models of retailing strategists. In G. Johnson (Ed.), *Business strategy and retailing* (pp. 59–79). New York: Wiley.

Prendergast, C. (1993). A theory of "yes men." *American Economic Review, 83,* 757–770.

Rabin, M. (1993). Incorporating fairness into game theory and economics. *American Economic Review, 83,* 1281–1302.

Rapoport, Am. (1987). Research paradigms and expected utility models for the provision of step-level public goods. *Psychological Review, 94,* 74–83.

Rapoport, Am., & Guyer, M. (1976). *The 2 × 2 game.* Ann Arbor: University of Michigan Press.

Rousseau, D., & Parks, J. (1992). The contracts of individuals and organizations. In L. Cummings & B. Staw (Eds.), *Research in organizational behavior* (Vol. 15, pp. 1–43). Greenwich, CT: JAI Press.

Rumelt, R. (1995). Inertia and transformation. In C. Montgomery (Ed.), *Resource-based and evolutionary theories of the firm: Towards a synthesis* (pp. 101–132). Norwell MA: Kluwer.

Sally, D. (1995). *On sympathy.* Working paper, Cornell University Johnson Graduate School of Management.

Scharfstein, D., & Stein, J. (1990). Herd behavior and investment. *American Economic Review, 80,* 465–479.

Schein, E. (1985). *Organizational culture and leadership.* San Francisco: Jossey-Bass.

Schelling, T. (1960). *The strategy of conflict.* Cambridge, MA: Harvard University Press.

Stanford, W. (1995). A note on the probability of k pure Nash equilibria in matrix games. *Games and Economic Behavior, 9,* 238–246.

Thompson, J. D. (1967). *Organizations in action.* New York: McGraw-Hill.

Van Huyck, J. B., Battalio, R. B., & Beil, R. O. (1990). Tacit coordination games, strategic uncertainty, and coordination failure. *American Economic Review, 80,* 234–248.

Van Huyck, J. B., Battalio, R. B., & Beil, R. O. (1991). Strategic uncertainty, equilibrium selection principles, and coordination failure in average opinion games. *The Quarterly Journal of Economics, 106,* 885–910.

Zajac, E., & Bazerman, M. (1991). Blind spots in industry and competitor analysis: Implications of interfirm (mis)perceptions for strategic decisions. *Academy of Management Review, 16,* 37–56.

Part IV

Decision processes

9 The escalation of commitment: An update and appraisal

Barry M. Staw

Introduction

This chapter is about decision making in escalation situations. It is about the way people deal with predicaments in which things not only have gone wrong but in which corrective actions can actually deepen or compound the difficulty. Let me provide some examples.

When people have lost money in common stocks or mutual funds, they often face a dilemma. Should they stick with their losing investments, increase their stake (perhaps through dollar cost averaging), or move their holdings to an entirely different investment vehicle? Virtually the same dilemma confronts people who are dissatisfied with their current jobs, careers, or marriages. They must decide whether it is wise to continue in these situations or start anew with different firms, occupations, or partners.

Organizations must also cope with escalation dilemmas. Corporations can spend enormous sums developing new products, only to find that the consumer response is lukewarm. When this occurs, should the firm spend further resources to promote the lagging product as it currently exists, send it back to the laboratory for reengineering, or scrap it altogether? In the financial sector, banks face a similar predicament when they deal with problem loans. If the borrower is not making interest payments, banks must determine whether it is better to work with the troubled client (perhaps by providing additional financing), take additional collateral, or withdraw from the account altogether.

Although these personal and organizational examples come from very different areas of experience, they do contain common elements. The situations all have negative outcomes – a course of action is not working as expected or a loss has resulted from an earlier decision. The situations also involve multiple decisions. They are not the one-shot choices with which most decision-making research deals, but choices about entire courses of action. Finally, in each of the situations, withdrawal or persistence are not obvious or clear-cut solutions to the problem. Even though withdrawal can end a sequence of losses, it may also involve material and/or psychological costs. And, even though persistence may involve the further risk of capital, it can bring about eventual gain. Thus, we can define escalation situations as those where losses have been suffered, where there is an opportunity to persist or withdraw, and where the consequences of these actions are uncertain.

The escalation question

If we assume that escalation situations have certain defining characteristics, is it possible to predict any general pattern of behavior when individuals and organizations face these predicaments?

Judging by popular press accounts and the observation of everyday events, one might argue that there is a tendency to become locked into escalation situations, that is, to throw good money (or resources) after bad. This tendency was most graphically described by George Ball during the early days of the Vietnam War. As undersecretary of state, Ball wrote the following memo to President Lyndon Johnson predicting the outcome of the war:

The decision you face now is crucial. Once large numbers of U.S. troops are committed to direct combat, they will begin to take heavy casualties in a war they are ill equipped to fight in a noncooperative if not downright hostile countryside. Once we suffer large casualties, we will have started a well-nigh irreversible process. Our involvement will be so great that we cannot – without national humiliation – stop short of achieving our complete objectives. Of the two possibilities, I think humiliation would be more likely than the achievement of our objectives – even after we have paid terrible costs. (Sheehan & Kenworthy, 1971; memo dated July 1, 1965)

A recent corporate example also illustrates the escalation tendency (see Ross & Staw, 1993). The Long Island Lighting Company, a large public utility serving the New York area, wanted to diversify its energy-producing capacity by building a nuclear power facility. So in the 1970s they began construction of the Shoreham Nuclear Power Plant. Although the plant was originally slated to cost about $70 million, a long series of cost overruns, regulatory delays, and changes in public sentiment about nuclear power steadily drove the cost to more than $5 billion. Certainly the utility would never have proposed building a $5 billion plant in the first place. Yet, they stayed with the construction of Shoreham for nearly 20 years. In the end, Shoreham was sold to the State of New York for $1.00. The plant was never operated at commercial levels. It was dismantled and sold for scrap.

The Vietnam and Shoreham examples show the potential downside of escalation situations. They show how the escalation of commitment can be more damaging than even singularly bad mistakes, for escalation involves the compounding of losses over time. The examples also point to the possibility that a pathology may exist – that people and organizations may have a tendency to get stuck in losing courses of action.

The nature of escalation research

Several early studies addressed the question of whether there is a tendency toward escalation. These studies were designed to show whether decision makers do throw good money after bad or whether we are simply paying too much attention to retrospective reports of disaster.

The early studies generally found evidence for an escalation effect. Staw (1976), for example, used a simulated business case to show that those responsible for a losing course of action will invest more than decision makers not responsible for prior losses. In a series of experiments, Teger (1980) used a competitive bidding game to demonstrate that people can become so committed to a position that they will pay more for a monetary reward than it is worth. Brockner and Rubin (1985) likewise showed that people will expend substantial amounts of time and money to achieve a receding or elusive goal. Finally, Arkes and Blumer (1985) found that the more money a person has spent on a project, the more likely he or she will stick with the venture until its completion.

Of course, not all the evidence has been so supportive of the escalation effect. Some studies have shown that repeated negative feedback can lead to withdrawal rather than persistence (e.g., McCain, 1986). Other research has shown that presenting people with alternatives (i.e., opportunity costs) that are clearly superior to the present course of action will lead to change (Northcraft & Neale, 1986). These findings have reinforced some researchers' (e.g., Bowen, 1987; Northcraft & Wolf, 1984) claim that escalation effects cannot be demonstrated when clear-cut financial data are available to the decision maker – when the person can clearly see that persistence is more costly than withdrawal.

Although there are data supporting both sides of the escalation question, the crux of the debate has rested so far on definitional rather than empirical grounds. Whereas Brockner and Rubin (1985) and Staw and Ross (1987) defined escalation as the product of uncertain situations (where neither persistence nor withdrawal is an obvious solution), other authors (e.g., Bowen, 1987; Northcraft & Wolf, 1984) have insisted that tests of escalation include complete information about the probabilities and consequences of future actions. Meeting such a high hurdle has generally been resisted. Few doubt that escalation effects would disappear if the decision maker is confronted with clear-cut information that persistence will lead to disaster, while withdrawal would bring positive results. And as Simonson and Staw (1992) point out, simply showing that persistence is reduced by altering the clarity or direction of investment information does not solve the problem of escalation. If escalation occurs under conditions of uncertainty, then procedures that provide clear-cut probabilities and outcomes may eliminate the very conditions underlying escalation effects.

When we look behind calls for more economic data in testing escalation, we are likely to find a basic skepticism about findings that contradict common sense. Common sense tells us that people try to avoid losing courses of action and instead follow paths likely to bring positive outcomes. Investing over $5 billion in an inoperable nuclear power plant, getting stuck in a predictably difficult war, and bidding substantially more for an object than it is worth do not seem to be the products of good common sense. Yet, are such actions irrational? The answer to this question is complicated and the subject of much controversy.

Escalation versus rationality

The key issue in determining whether an action is irrational or not is deciding what the appropriate baseline is. One can certainly debate whether rationality *should* or *should not* include full information search, thorough processing, logical choice, and actions based on utility maximization (e.g., Kahneman & Tversky, 1982; March, 1978; Simon 1979). However, for simplicity's sake, most escalation researchers have used the traditional economic model as their baseline for rationality. They have assumed that rational decision makers should be able to calculate expected gains and losses from at least two courses of action (e.g., persistence versus withdrawal) and make decisions maximizing future economic outcomes.

Even with these rather strict assumptions of rationality, some of the early escalation studies cannot easily rule out rational economic choice. Consider Teger's (1980) studies using the dollar auction game. In this procedure (Shubik, 1971), both the first and second highest bidders had to pay in their last bids, regardless of who won the auction. Thus, it made economic sense for subjects to do everything possible to avoid getting stuck in second place, where they had to pay for a prize they would not receive. Engaging in a bidding war to win the auction, even if this meant paying more for a prize than it was worth, could therefore be interpreted as a reasonable economic strategy.

Although Teger's results can be explained by rational economic decision making, this is not the case with a number of other escalation findings. Consider, for example, Staw's (1976) comparison of decision making under conditions of high and low responsibility. Given exactly the same economic data, those who were responsible for prior losses committed more resources to a course of action than those who were not responsible for the losses. Consider also Brockner and Rubin's (1985, chapter 7) finding that information (a payoff chart) presented to people *before* embarking on a course of action had a significant influence on behavior, whereas exactly

the same information presented *after* resources had already been committed did not have an effect. Finally, consider the fact that sunk costs have
been found to affect investment choices (Arkes & Blumer, 1985), even
though economic principles dictate that resources should be allocated only
when marginal revenues exceed marginal costs. None of these findings can
be explained by traditional economic logic.

Of course, it is always possible to expand that logic. If, for example, one
broadens the idea of economic rationality beyond monetary costs and benefits to include a range of psychological and social outcomes, then much of
the escalation literature can be subsumed under the rationality umbrella.
This is essentially what a few researchers have done, using theoretical
notions such as agency theory to explain escalation effects (Baiman, 1990;
Harrison & Harrell, 1993; Kanodia, Bushman, & Dickhaut, 1989). Still, one
must ask whether broadening the notion of rationality really adds anything
beyond what is already known from relevant behavioral theories. My own
view is that rational models such as agency theory have simply translated
social and psychological concepts into cost–benefit analyses, providing
few advantages in making a priori predictions about escalation.

Escalation as a multidetermined outcome

Just because many escalation effects cannot (or should not) be subsumed
under rational economic models does not mean that costs and benefits are
unimportant in escalation decisions. Too often behavioral theories are constructed in black-white, either-or terms, especially in the early stages of a
research literature. For example, it was once popular to argue that escalation decisions are entirely determined by either economic or psychological
forces. Now the study of escalation has matured to the point where multiple causes must be considered seriously.

One way of dealing with multiple causes of escalation is to conduct
competitive tests, determining which variables are most and least important to escalation decisions. Another path is the contingency approach, in
which conflicting explanations are resolved by third variables or moderating conditions. Here there is an effort to isolate the conditions under which
each theoretical explanation will likely hold. A third perspective, and the
one I have followed, is to accept the fact that the world has multiple determinants, where behavior is caused by several often competing forces. Such
a view of reality means that escalation decisions can be determined by
behavioral and economic forces operating simultaneously.

Multidetermination also means that escalation can be influenced by
forces at more than one level of analysis. Individual decisions to escalate
are rarely exercised in isolation, as is usually assumed by decision theorists. These choices are influenced by social and organizational forces surrounding the decision maker. Likewise, when considering organizational

decisions to persist in a course of action, one must account for various structural and contextual forces influencing the organization. Just how these various forces operate is one of the key questions facing contemporary research on escalation.

Lack of theoretical direction or limits

Although multidetermination is a realistic way of looking at escalation, the approach does not come without a price. There is often a loss of conceptual discipline when researchers work outside a single theoretical perspective or paradigm (Pfeffer, 1993). By advocating a multiplicity of forces we are, in a sense, opening the doors to a literature without theoretical limits and a research agenda without agreement on its direction.

Some of the drawbacks of multidetermination have already become evident. Over the past decade, escalation determinants have been borrowed from disparate areas of behavioral research (e.g., decision making, attitude change, social influence) and applied, often cavalierly, to the escalation situation. Theories have been plucked wholesale from cognitive psychology, social psychology, and sociology to explain why decision makers may persist in a losing course of action. Such borrowing is not necessarily wrong or inappropriate in its own right. However, because this borrowing has occurred without the guidance of an overarching model or theory, it is difficult to know whether progress has really been made. Without a guiding theory, we are left with little more than a laundry list of findings showing various effects on decision making.

In the remainder of this chapter I work toward a model of escalation – one that incorporates much, although certainly not all, of the research literature. I am not so bold as to assume that whatever theory is presented is a full representation of reality. Nor do I presume that the resulting model will survive (without revision) repeated empirical tests. Still, the loosely connected literature on escalation needs some guideline, a point of departure from which research progress can be gauged.

A classification scheme

Because so many variables have been used as predictors of escalation, it is necessary to have some reduction in complexity before a general model can be formulated. Therefore, Jerry Ross and I proposed a classification scheme to place most of the previously researched determinants of escalation (Staw & Ross, 1987, 1989). We labeled four broad groupings as project, psychological, social, and organizational determinants of escalation. Later, we added a fifth category for contextual variables (Ross & Staw, 1993). I briefly summarize the kinds of research studies that have been conducted under each of these rubrics and show how they can be integrated into an overall conceptual model (for more complete reviews see Brockner, 1992; Brockner & Rubin, 1985; Staw & Ross, 1987).

Project determinants

Project determinants are the most obvious causes of persistence. They include the objective features of a project that affect the financial value or utility of a course of action. They also include the broader economics of the investment situation.

A number of objective aspects of escalation situations have been shown to lead to persistence. Some of these include whether a setback is due to permanent or temporary causes (Leatherwood & Conlon, 1985; Levi, 1982), the efficacy of further investments/actions in turning a losing situation around (Bateman, 1983; Conlon & Wolf, 1980; Staw & Fox, 1977), the size of a project's goal or eventual payoff (Rubin & Brockner, 1975) the level of future expenditures or costs necessary to complete a project goal or payoff (Brockner, Rubin, & Lang, 1981), the availability of feasible alternatives to a course of action (Bateman, 1983; Northcraft & Neale, 1986), and the salvage value or closing costs for ending a project (Northcraft & Wolf, 1984). All of these variables could be applied to any investment context. Perhaps as a result, none of these variables (by themselves) have attracted major interest or controversy.

Drawing more attention have been conditions that virtually lock decision makers into a course of action. As already noted, Teger's (1980) studies using the dollar auction game were precisely structured to yield escalation behavior. The situation was structured so that the cost of withdrawal was high, so high that bidding often proceeded well beyond $1.00 or $5.00 to win the $1.00 or $5.00 prize. Ross and Staw (1993) observed a similar set of incentives during the latter stages of the Shoreham project. Shoreham's executives were literally trapped into completing the costly facility, because withdrawal would have meant likely bankruptcy for the utility. Almost the same features were present in British Columbia's decision to continue with the world's fair, Expo 86 (see Ross & Staw, 1986). Expo was a project with the combination of huge up-front expenditures, little salvage value, and substantial closing costs if terminated before completion. Revenues would not be realized until the project was finished and ready to open. Thus, Expo was structured in such a way that almost guaranteed persistence.

The Expo and Shoreham cases point to large-scale R&D and construction projects as prime candidates for escalation. Once substantial funds are committed to such ventures, it is very difficult to walk away. The closer one gets to the project's completion, the more likely it is that marginal revenues will exceed marginal costs. Thus, ventures that do not make economic sense at their outset (and yield negative outcomes overall) may be very committing (in an economic sense) at later points in their life cycles.

Psychological determinants

Although losing projects can be highly committing in their later stages, one must ask why such ventures survived so long in the first place. Why don't people turn away from courses of action when the first real signs of trouble appear, when it starts to become evident that the promised benefits are not going to materialize? To answer this question, one must look to psychological determinants of escalation. For brevity, I will consider only four psychological determinants, even though a much longer list could easily be mustered.

Optimism and illusions of control. When facing investment decisions, people often assume that their cost–benefit projections are accurate or at least an unbiased rendering of reality. However, an established stream of research has shown that economic data are not objective facts that are neutrally processed by decision makers. Two of the biases most relevant to investment situations are optimism and control (Taylor, 1989). People tend to overestimate the likelihood that positive events will occur in their lives and to underestimate the likelihood of negative outcomes. They see themselves as performing better than others in most situations and as able to avoid future mishaps. Accidents and illness are things that happen to *other* people. Poor achievement is the fate of others, not oneself (see Taylor & Brown, 1988, for a review).

Underlying such optimism is the belief that one can control one's destiny. People think they have special skills to ensure a more positive future than what lies in store for others. These beliefs have been labeled an *illusion of control,* since they can occur even when the situation is obviously random (Langer, 1975). Gamblers blow on dice, and throw softly or hard, to "ensure" a winning turn at the gaming table (Goffman, 1967). Managers likewise believe that risk is something that can be brought under their control. As Shapira (1995, p. 127) notes, "The experience of successful managers teaches them that the probabilities of life do not apply to them. . . . Practicing (and successful) managers believe, and their experience appears to have told them, that they can change the odds, that what appears to be a probabilistic process can usually be controlled."

The implications of optimism and control biases are inflated project expectations. Like the "winner's curse" (Samuelson & Bazerman, 1985), in which the winning bid is the one containing the most unreasonably optimistic expectations, projects are likely to get funded precisely when they beat out other, lesser (and perhaps more realistically appraised) alternatives. Once an initial investment decision has been made, the potential biasing of information does not end, however. Other postdecision processes may then come into play.

Self-justification. There is a long literature in psychology showing that decision making is itself a psychologically binding act. Some have argued that making decisions creates a motivated state that must be resolved or justified through changes in attitudes and beliefs (e.g., Aronson, 1972; Festinger, 1957). Others have argued that decision making sets in motion a self-inference process by which individuals take on attitudes or beliefs that are consistent with their behavior (e.g., Bem, 1972; Kiesler, 1971). In either case, the consequence is that people's attitudes and beliefs can be shaped by the decisions they make. Following a decision, people convince themselves that it was the right thing to do; they believe in what they have done.

Staw (1976) applied the notion of self-justification to the escalation context. He argued that people may not just bias information following a decision; they may also change behaviors such as the allocation of resources. Individuals, he noted, may commit more resources to a losing project precisely because they need to justify or rationalize their decisions. To test this hypothesis, Staw asked business students to play the role of a corporate financial officer allocating R&D funds to one of two divisions of a hypothetical company. Half of the subjects were assigned to a high-responsibility condition in which they chose which corporate division should receive additional R&D funds. They received feedback on this decision and then made a second decision about whether further funds should be allocated to the same corporate division. The other half of the subjects were assigned to a low-responsibility condition in which they did not make the initial investment decision themselves but were told that it was made by another financial officer of the firm. Feedback was manipulated so that half of the subjects received positive results on their initial decisions and half received negative results.

Results of the study showed that subjects invested more resources following negative than positive consequences. This finding should not by itself be interpreted as evidence for escalation, however. The case materials used in the study specifically prompted subjects to believe that R&D expenditures were the best way of increasing sales and profits, thus making further investment the logical response to negative outcomes. The study's more important results concerned the manipulation of personal responsibility. There was a main effect showing that subjects became more committed to decisions for which *they* rather than another financial officer were responsible. There was also a significant interaction showing that subjects made the greatest commitment of resources when they were responsible for negative consequences, exactly as one would predict from the justification hypothesis.

The self-justification explanation of escalation has been supported by a number of other studies (see Brockner, 1992, for an analytical review). Being responsible for negative results has been shown to affect not only the allocation of resources but also the search for information about a course of action and the evaluation of that information (e.g., Bazerman, Beekum, & Schoorman, 1982; Bazerman, Giuliano, & Appelman, 1984; Bazerman,

Schoorman, & Goodman, 1980; Caldwell & O'Reilly, 1982; Conlon & Parks, 1987; Schoorman, 1988; Staw & Fox, 1977). Being responsible for negative outcomes has also been shown to affect escalation decisions in the field. Staw, Barsade, and Koput (1995) recently demonstrated how responsibility for prior decisions influenced the way bank officers dealt with problem loans. Using 9 years of data for a large sample of California banks, these authors examined whether executive turnover (putting new people in charge who were not responsible for prior losses) speeded withdrawal from bad loans. Their results showed that executive turnover predicted both the allocation of funds to loan loss reserves and the writeoff of bad loans.

Framing effects. Some authors (e.g., Bazerman, 1984; Whyte, 1986) have argued that motivated states such as self-justification can be replaced by more general decision errors in explaining escalation. Cognitive framing (Kahneman & Tversky, 1979) has been suggested as the prime candidate. Framing research has shown that people do not have the same risk preferences for positive and negative outcomes. In positively framed situations, individuals act in a risk-averse manner to keep clear-cut or certain gains. In negatively framed situations, people act in a risk-seeking manner to avoid possible losses. Thus, decision makers may allocate further resources to a losing course of action if they believe there is a chance to turn the situation around, to convert the losing situation into one of positive gain. Ironically, in trying to avoid certain losses, decision makers may subject themselves to the risk of even greater negative consequences.

From the framing point of view, it is not important whether the decision maker is responsible for the losses, only that the losses have occurred. Therefore, if framing can replace justification, it must also account for any observed effects of personal responsibility. So far, it cannot. In the few studies specifically designed to compare the framing and justification perspectives, support has been found for both approaches (e.g., Davis & Bobko, 1986; Schoorman, Mayer, Douglas, & Hetrick, 1995).

Sunk cost effects. Whereas framing and self-justification are both concerned with the psychological effects of negative outcomes, a separate stream of research has emerged to deal with the expenditure of resources over time. Although economists universally agree that sunk costs should be ignored in investment situations (Frank, 1991; Samuelson & Nordhaus, 1985), a number of studies have shown that sunk costs may continue to influence people's behavior over time.

In the most well-known study of sunk costs, Arkes and Blumer (1985) asked students to imagine they were the president of an aircraft company deciding whether to invest $1 million in research on an airplane not detectable by conventional radar. In one condition, the funds were to be used to start the project. In a second condition, the project was already 90% completed. The catch was that in both conditions subjects were told that the radar-blank plane was not an economically promising project because another firm already had a superior product. Thus, any difference in the amount of expenditures between the two conditions could be attributed to the influence of sunk costs. Results of Arkes and Blumer's study showed that over 85% of the subjects chose to spend the money to complete the plane that was already 90% finished, whereas only 16.7% chose to commit funds at the outset.

Follow-up studies by Garland and his colleagues have both replicated these findings and posed questions about the sunk cost effect. Using variations of Arkes and Blumer's (1985) radar-blank plane scenario, Garland (1990) demonstrated that sunk costs influenced investment decisions across several combinations of prior expenditure and project completion. However, when Conlon and Garland (1993) independently manipulated the level of prior expenditures and the degree of project completion, they found only effects for degree of completion. A similar absence of sunk cost effects was also found by Garland, Sandefur, and Rogers (1990) in an experiment using an oil drilling scenario. Prior expenditures on dry wells were not associated with continued drilling, perhaps because dry wells were so clearly seen as reducing rather than increasing the likelihood of future oil production. Thus, it appears that sunk costs may influence project decisions only when they are linked to the perception (if not the reality) of progress on a course of action.

A more robust sunk cost effect has been demonstrated for resource utilization decisions. In Arkes and Blumer's (1985) questionnaire studies, students said they would be more likely to use goods for which they had paid the most money. Support for the sunk cost effect has also come from an interesting field experiment. Arkes and Blumer (1985) arranged to have theater tickets sold at different prices, with subsequent theater attendance monitored by researchers. For at least the first half of the season, people who purchased theater tickets at full price attended plays in greater number than those who purchased equivalent tickets at a discount.

Recently, Staw and Hoang (1995) also used the notion of sunk costs to explain personnel decisions in professional basketball. They posited that National Basketball Association (NBA) teams invest in players much as corporations commit funds to promising projects or products. They argued that when teams expend substantial resources to obtain a particular player, they are likely to give that player more time on the court than would be merited by his objective performance. Likewise, teams are more likely to retain a highly selected player than would be merited by performance. These predictions were confirmed using longitudinal data from the NBA. Controlling for objective performance (e.g., scoring, assists, rebounds), players taken early in the NBA college draft were given extra playing time, traded less often, and survived longer in the league.

Many theoretical mechanisms have been offered for the sunk cost effect.

Arkes and Blumer (1985) described it as a judgment error, noting that people believe they are saving money or avoiding losses by using sunk costs in their calculations. This desire not to "waste" sunk costs might result from a perceived but erroneous covariation between expenditure and progress on a project or a misunderstanding of the relationship between cost and the value of a resource. It can also result from a primitive form of mental budgeting in which decision makers simply want to recoup past investments, regardless of their utility (Heath, 1995). Regardless of the theoretical mechanism involved, sunk cost research has provided another noneconomic reason why decision makers may persist in costly courses of action.

Social determinants

Much of the escalation literature has dealt with either project or psychological variables. Yet escalation situations are usually multiparty events rather than something that affects just a single individual. Managers must make decisions in an organizational context. Leaders of the organization must answer to various constituents both inside and outside the firm. These complications mean that escalation decisions are social events conducted in ongoing interpersonal relationships rather than the isolated choices usually studied by decision theorists.

External justification and binding. In an early test of social determinants of escalation, Fox and Staw (1979) posited that justification motives can be focused externally as well as internally. They noted that individuals are not just concerned with their own sense of accuracy and competence; people seek to demonstrate competence to others in organizational settings. Thus, administrators may fight to preserve a losing project because to withdraw from it might lead to accusations of incompetence from others. Like politicians whose actions are closely scrutinized by the opposition (Tetlock, 1985), managers have rivals waiting to take their places when weaknesses are exposed. Withdrawal and admission of error are costly actions in a highly politicized environment. A graphic example of these costs was the hostile reaction to former Secretary of Defense Robert McNamara's (1995) recent admission of error in escalating the Vietnam War, nearly 20 years after the end of U.S. involvement.

Fox and Staw (1979) conducted an experimental test of external justification by having business students play an administrative role under varying conditions of job security and policy resistance. They posited that administrators who implement unpopular policies and who are vulnerable to job loss would be most motivated to try to turn a losing situation around. The results showed exactly these effects. Under both policy resistance and job insecurity, subjects increased their commitment to the losing course of action.

Bobocel and Meyer (1994) showed a similar effect for what they called "public justification," noting that accountability to others can be at least as important as any internal need to rationalize. Somewhat parallel results have also been reported by Harrison and Harrell (1993). They showed that managers hesitate to recognize losing projects when their external reputations are at risk and when information about a project's performance is not widely known, interpreting the effects as a test of agency theory. Brockner, Rubin, and Lang (1981) also found persistence to be highest when there is a large audience and high social anxiety, interpreting these results as a face-saving effect.

The need to justify one's actions to others, to save face, or to protect one's external reputation all point to the fact that commitment is not an isolated affair. The binding of people to courses of action can be strongly influenced by social motivation. It can also be determined by audiences or constituencies surrounding the decision maker (Ginzel, Kramer, & Sutton, 1993). Just as people form beliefs based upon self-inference processes (Salancik, 1977), observers infer capabilities and motives to actors after watching their behavior (Jones & Davis, 1965). Thus, an administrator's social identity can become linked to the fate of a particular course of action. Political rivals may encourage this labeling ("that's Jim's baby") when a project looks as if it is going to fail but try to refute or cloud this labeling ("we had the same idea") when there is the likelihood of a positive outcome. The binding of administrators to policies can therefore have reciprocal and dynamic qualities. It may be a product of shared interpersonal relationships as well as the shifting tides of organizational politics.

Leadership norms. Another social determinant of escalation involves the attribution of leadership. Whereas external justification and binding imply social costs for withdrawal (e.g., loss of face or a threat to one's image in the organization), there may also be social rewards for persistence. Converting a losing project into a winner may lead to positive attributions of leadership. To test this notion, Staw and Ross (1980) asked people to read about the behavior of a state administrator trying to cope with a housing crisis. The administrator had appointed a blue ribbon commission to recommend ways of improving housing in his state. In the *experimenting* condition, the administrator chose the first recommended course of action and waited for the results. When he saw no improvement in housing data, he switched to the second recommended policy. Then when there was again no improvement, he moved to the third policy option. In the *consistent* condition, the administrator was described as persisting with the initial recommendation, regardless of the lack of progress reflected by housing statistics.

In addition to the style of decision making, Staw and Ross (1980) manipulated the ultimate fate of the chosen policy. Some administrators were described as being ultimately successful with their actions because the housing data finally improved over time. Some were described as continuing to fail, with the housing data showing no upturn at all. As predicted, there were main effects of consistency and success on subjects' ratings of leadership (see Evans & Medcof, 1984, for a replication of these effects). Interestingly, the ratings also showed a significant interaction. Subjects offered special praise for those who were both consistent *and* successful. They were the heroes who were lauded for "sticking to their guns" in the face of seemingly bleak odds, only to have their patience and "insight" rewarded in the end.

Organizational determinants

Although the consideration of social determinants broadens the escalation literature, it still treats escalation as a micro or individual decision. Missing from this analysis are determinants of *organizational* decisions to persist in a losing course of action. Because organizational decisions cannot always be tied to particular individuals and because they are the product of social interaction, it is necessary to consider macro-level variables in understanding this phenomenon.

Probably the simplest organizational determinant of escalation is institutional inertia. Just as there is less than full consistency between individual attitudes and behavior (Zanna & Fazio, 1982), there is also a very loose coupling between organizational goals and action (March & Olsen, 1976). Organizations have very imperfect sensory systems, making them relatively impervious to changes in their environments. And because of breakdowns in internal communication and difficulties in mobilizing various constituencies, organizations are often slow to respond. Thus, even when the need for change is recognized, it may not occur. If it is necessary to alter long-standing policies, rules, or procedures, change can be especially difficult to muster, even though many parties inside and outside the organization may see it as useful.

Organizations attempting to withdraw from a losing course of action can also face political problems. Those directly employed by a project are likely to resist its dismantling. Political resistance may also be expected from an array of parties aligned with the venture and its sponsors. If these supporters have enough power, the fate of the losing project can depend more on the nature of organizational politics than on the objective costs and benefits of the undertaking.

On occasion, a project, product, or policy can become so closely tied to the values and purposes of the organization that it becomes almost unthinkable to consider withdrawal. When a course of action is so institutionalized (Goodman, Bazerman, & Conlon, 1980), it can take enormous financial losses to prompt withdrawal. Consider the case of Pan American

Airlines. More than most airlines, Pan Am suffered major losses after deregulation of the industry. However, as losses accumulated, it successively
sold off most of its nonairline assets. First, the Pan Am building was sold to
meet debt obligations. Then, as losses continued to mount, the Interconti-
nental Hotel chain was sold. Finally, Pan Am was forced to sell its valuable
Pacific routes to United Airlines. Withdrawing from the real estate and
hotel businesses was probably easier than ending its long-standing presence in the airline industry. Yet, if Pan Am had withdrawn from the airline,
its most institutionalized business, and kept its other, more profitable ventures, it might have survived as an ongoing organization.

Contextual effects

Not only is it necessary to consider organization-level variables as determinants of escalation. Sometimes escalation can be determined by forces
larger than the organization itself. In the case of the Shoreham Nuclear
Power Plant, the U.S. Department of Energy and pronuclear constituencies
were very active parties in the decision to persist with the reactor (Ross &
Staw, 1993). The decision to hold Expo 86 was also determined, at least in
part, by political pressures placed upon the government of British Columbia by local business interests (Ross & Staw, 1986). Other instances of
external parties holding an organization to a losing course of action might
include the actions of the federal government in bailing out Lockheed (with
its large defense business) and Chrysler (with its large employment base).
In each of these cases, agents in the organization's environment worked to
preserve an activity, even if it meant continued losses or the possibility of a
"permanently failing organization" (Meyer & Zucker, 1989). Thus, to explain persistence in losing courses of action, it is sometimes necessary to
expand the scope of inquiry from organizational to contextual determinants.

What does the classification scheme buy us?

The Staw and Ross classification scheme does not *explain* escalation. Placing
variables into various categories does not, by itself, show how decision
makers become committed to a course of action. But having a classification
scheme does provide a couple of important benefits. First, it makes the
study of escalation more comprehensible, if only because a long list of
variables has been reduced to a less daunting set of determinants. Second,
the classification scheme highlights how prior research has been distributed. Although this review has been illustrative rather than exhaustive,
one can easily see that most prior work has concentrated on project and
psychological determinants, to the near exclusion of organizational and
contextual factors. Most typical have been laboratory experiments on various psychological theories of escalation, often using economic variables as

a competing explanation. Perhaps because it is easier to study people than organizations, the field has concentrated on escalation as a product of individual decision making rather than organizational action.

Theoretical models

A temporal model of escalation

Ross and Staw (1986) used the classification scheme to document various influences on the decision to hold the money-losing fair, Expo 86. But they had to go beyond the classification scheme to explain the sequence or causal ordering of variables. To do this, they constructed a temporal model of escalation, a variant of which is shown in Figure 9.1.

Figure 9.1 divides the escalation episode into three distinct phases. It is hypothesized that the first phase is dominated by the economics of a project. The initial reason for allocating resources to a course of action is the promise of positive returns. This is not to say that people are fully rational decision makers who make complete use of information and follow the rules of normative economic behavior. They may be overly optimistic and pursue economically unwise investments. They may also fall prey to illusions of control, thinking they can manage situations that are largely subject to outside forces. Nonetheless, managers do start most projects with an emphasis on the numbers – on projections of gain and loss, however faulty or unrealistic these projections might turn out to be.

The second stage of an escalation episode is posited to begin after questionable or negative results are received. Such results not only affect the objective prospects of a project (e.g., whether it will be finished on time or result in future losses). They also may trigger psychological and social forces for persistence. At this time decision makers may start to justify a course of action, emphasizing its prospects for gain or minimizing its likelihood of losses. Sunk costs may also start to assume importance if substantial expenditures have already been made. Social identities may likewise become linked to the fate of the project. Each of these behavioral forces can exert influence directly by binding the decision maker to a line of behavior. They may also exert influence indirectly by biasing perceptions about the merits of a particular policy or project. Information may be slanted, omitted, highlighted, and forgotten in ways that depart from objective reality.

Psychological and social processes can be strong enough to hold decision makers in place as losses accumulate over time. As a result, many escalation episodes can be expected to reach a third phase. At this point, results can become so negative that outside parties such as the press (and even researchers) start to take note. Yet, instead of moving quickly toward withdrawal, organizations can remain stuck in the losing course of action. Underlying this persistence may be the fact that, just as economic prospects worsen, organizational and contextual forces start to take hold. The

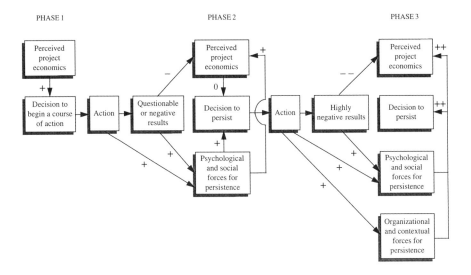

Figure 9.1. A temporal model of escalation.

organization may stake its corporate identity on the fate of a particular product or division. The sponsors of a losing project may be able to muster enough organizational power to stave off criticism and/or budget reductions. The closing of a facility may be protested by employees who will lose their jobs. Closure may also be opposed by other firms that will lose a source of supply or by communities that will lose a base of employment. For any of these reasons, it may take relatively large losses to offset the accumulation of behavioral forces in an escalation situation. The protracted war in Indochina could be the classic example of these situational dynamics. Another may be Long Island Lighting's commitment to the Shoreham Nuclear Reactor. In each of these cases, losses had to reach enormous proportions before the organization (or nation) could extricate itself from the losing course of action.

Some assumptions of the temporal model

Although the temporal model makes sense theoretically, it has several built-in assumptions. One assumption is that behavioral forces become activated as negative outcomes materialize or become salient. Without such synchronization of behavioral and economic forces, organizations would be much more likely to withdraw from losing courses of action. Thus, we would expect a quick exit when there are sharp and immediate losses because there would be little time for behavioral sources of commitment to accumulate. In contrast, slowly souring ventures would be much more likely to show escalation tendencies (see Golz, 1992, 1993; Hantula & Crowell, 1994, for a reinforcement view of these same predicted effects).

A second assumption underlying the temporal model is that behavioral forces can take either a direct or an indirect path of influence. They may comprise a set of identifiable costs of withdrawal such as loss of self-esteem or external reputation. They may also come camouflaged as part of the economic data under consideration. Because project projections are often based as much on conjecture as on hard facts, it is posited that behavioral forces can enter decision calculations in a sub rosa rather than up-front manner. This is one reason why escalation experiments that provide a complete set of projections from presumably accurate sources (i.e., the experimenter or experimental materials) are probably missing a very important aspect of the escalation phenomenon.

A third assumption concerns the sequencing of behavioral effects according to levels of analysis. Individual effects are hypothesized to come first. They are followed in order by social, organizational, and contextual influences. The rationale for such symmetrical unfolding might be as follows. Projects, at their outset, can be considered to be mainly the product of individual decisions because there is often a project champion who promotes a venture and/or a strong leader who decides to allocate resources to it. As projects develop, social binding may start to occur because careers and interpersonal relations become tied to the venture. Finally, as projects mature, they may become more fully embedded in the firm, engendering organizational and even contextual influences. Thus, the temporal model can be viewed as a progression of forces from the micro to macro levels of analysis.

An aggregate model

As logical as the temporal model now appears, there still is not much empirical evidence to support it. Even the Shoreham case study, specifically designed to test the temporal model, did not reveal a pattern of events that precisely fit the theory. Therefore, at this stage of research, it might be best to treat the temporal model as a useful conceptual tool rather than an accurate representation of reality. The model shows an idealized sequencing of events that most escalation episodes can be expected to depart from.

Figure 9.2 presents a simpler and perhaps more representative model. The model shows aggregate effects rather than the separation of behavioral forces over time. Because of its generality, the model can accommodate the changing economics of a project – from initial promise, to the likelihood of losses, to end-game situations where withdrawal might bankrupt the firm. Behavioral variables can also be seen as influencing the perception of project economics (e.g., optimism effects) as well as directly affecting the level of commitment to a course of action. The emphasis of the model is upon the continual ebb and flow of commitment to a policy, product, or project.

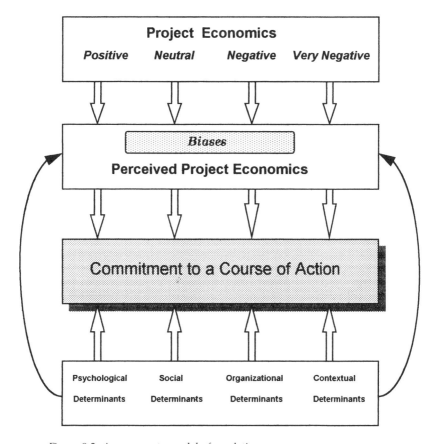

Figure 9.2. An aggregate model of escalation.

The crucial assumption is that behavioral forces must match or exceed the strength of any negative economic data in order to hold organizations (and their decision makers) in a losing course of action.

The aggregate model's emphasis is upon the accumulation and balance of forces rather than the ordering of effects over time. Because of its generality, the aggregate model can accommodate escalation episodes that develop in the proposed (or idealized) fashion, where negative effects are matched first by micro and then by macro organizational forces. The model can also fit those circumstances where macro determinants arise before psychological and social forces. The aggregate model does not rely on a particular developmental or stage theory of escalation.

Although my own research (especially with Jerry Ross) has emphasized the temporal approach to escalation, I present the aggregate model as a reasonable alternative. I do this for two reasons. First, most escalation studies are not longitudinal in nature, so they cannot possibly test a temporal model of escalation. Second, I believe the question of *which* forces combine to create escalation effects is inherently a more basic (or primary) inquiry than the question of *how* these forces interact over time. Therefore, one might logically argue that an aggregate model should be verified before getting too bogged down in arguments over any particular sequencing of effects. Although temporal models can draw attention to prototypical episodes of escalation, they are intrinsically more speculative than the aggregate approach.

Final comments

Rationality versus irrationality revisited

As I noted at the outset of this chapter, some researchers have argued that escalation decisions should be treated as purely economic actions unless it can be shown that people violate the assumptions of rationality. Thus, many escalation studies are criticized as presenting subjects with uncertain courses of action instead of alternatives with specified outcomes and known probabilities. In a sense, these researchers want escalation situations to be converted from states of uncertainty (where probabilities cannot be specified) to questions of risk and reward. They want to convert complicated but realistic situations into contexts where simple calculations and decision rules are most useful.

In my view, the study of escalation has spent far too long debating whether commitment is always determined by the rational accounting of costs and benefits. The very fact that behavioral predictions can be validated in an escalation context means that they need to be accounted for. It is not necessary to show that an economic calculus fails to influence decisions in order to argue that behavioral processes are important. Thus, although it is interesting to demonstrate that some psychological mechanisms (such as the sunk cost effect) contradict economic principles, it is not essential for the explanation of escalation. In fact, by requiring a *repeated* test of behavioral versus economic forces, one is implicitly assuming that economic explanations are somehow closer to the truth than behavioral approaches.

What both the temporal and aggregate models of escalation illustrate is that economic and behavioral processes are not necessarily at war. Each is seen operating in the organizational world. Therefore, it makes as little sense for us to leave out the behavioral determinants of commitment as it does to assume that the economics of a project are unimportant. Both are at work in the confluence of forces that make up an escalation episode.

Some directions for future research

Instead of arguing for the acceptance or rejection of any particular theoretical perspective, I would rather press for changes in the methodology of escalation research. As I see it, most laboratory studies on escalation still rely on rather arid, hypothetical examples of decision making. They use a one- or two-sentence description of an escalation situation rather than a more complete scenario as the context for decision making. They often require subjects to imagine they have made or are responsible for a previous decision without ever putting people through the event in question. Such shortcuts may be routine for behavioral decision research. These procedures may also do a good job of holding background information constant so that manipulated variables are salient. Yet, as Schoorman et al. (1994) have shown, some well-known decision biases (such as framing) may not replicate when the situation is presented in more detailed (and realistic) form. Although escalation findings survived the tests by Schoorman and his colleagues, I worry that the use of abbreviated scenarios will produce weakened rather than exaggerated escalation effects. Without some contextual richness to ground the phenomena, it may be difficult to simulate the behavioral forces operating in real escalation situations.

My recommendation is not to avoid laboratory research on escalation but to conduct it in a more realistic fashion. Cases with greater complexity can be presented to research subjects as long as escalation variables are made salient. And it is possible to capture temporal realism by extending scenarios over time (see, e.g., Golz's 1992 and 1993 longitudinal studies on reinforcement/extinction effects). Quite possibly, future developments in interactive computer technology (e.g., virtual reality) may provide the means necessary for simulations that are both situationally and temporally relevant.

In addition to making laboratory studies on escalation more realistic, further escalation research within field settings is needed. Additional field work not only will help resolve the usual questions concerning external validity, it will also help us better understand the phenomenon in question. Qualitative field studies force researchers to become intimately familiar with the settings and characters they are studying. Such familiarity leads researchers to construct theoretical models based on events as they actually occur rather than on how they should or could occur. As someone most comfortable with the laboratory method, I can attest to the difficulty *and* usefulness of having to deal with grounded, qualitative data.

Escalation studies should also come in the form of grounded, quantitative research. So far, however, there has been almost a total absence of such work in the escalation literature. In fact, I am aware of only three examples. One is Arkes and Blumer's (1985) theater study demonstrating the influence of sunk costs on attendance at plays. Another is Staw and Hoang's (1995) longitudinal study of sunk costs in professional basketball. A third is Staw, Barsade, and Koput's (1995) study showing how executive turnover influenced the writeoff of bad loans at California banks. Each of these studies operationalized an escalation-relevant variable and measured its consequences in a natural setting over time.

I believe the completion of additional field studies, both quantitative and qualitative in nature, should be given our highest priority. Not only can these forms of research help the escalation literature in its quest for understanding the forces for persistence versus withdrawal, such research might also be a vehicle for the more general inquiry on how individual behavior is transformed into organizational action (Staw & Sutton, 1993). As we all know, it is much easier to argue that organizational decision making is a product of individual, interpersonal, and structural effects than it is to specify the linkages across these levels of analysis. Because of its inherent interdisciplinary nature, escalation research could be an ideal forum for learning about cross-level effects. Thus, furthering our knowledge of escalation may help us make strides toward understanding the very essence of organizational behavior.

References

Arkes, H., & Blumer, C. (1985). The psychology of sunk costs. *Organizational Behavior and Human Decision Processes, 35,* 124–140.

Aronson, E. (1972). *The social animal.* San Francisco: W. H. Freeman.

Baiman, S. (1990). Agency theory in managerial accounting: A second look. *Accounting, Organizations, and Society, 15,* 341–371.

Bateman, T. (1983). *Resource allocation after success and failure: The roles of attributions of powerful others and probabilities of future success.* Working paper, Texas A&M University, Department of Management.

Bazerman, M. H. (1984). The relevance of Kahneman and Tversky's concept of framing to organizational behavior. *Journal of Management, 10,* 333–343.

Bazerman, M. H., Beekun, R. I., & Schoorman, F. D. (1982). Performance evaluation in dynamic context: The impact of a prior commitment to the ratee. *Journal of Applied Psychology, 67,* 873–876.

Bazerman, M. H., Giuliano, T., & Appelman, A. (1984). Escalation in individual and group decision making. *Organizational Behavior and Human Performance, 33,* 141–152.

Bazerman, M. H., Schoorman, F. D., & Goodman, P. S. (1980). *A cognitive evaluation of escalation processes in managerial decision making.* Unpublished manuscript, Boston University.

Bem, D. J. (1972). Self-perception theory. In L. Berkowitz (Ed.), *Advances in experimental social psychology* (Vol. 6, pp. 1–62). New York: Academic Press.

Bobocel, D. R., & Meyer, J. P. (1994). Escalation commitment to a failing course of action: Separating the roles of choice and justification. *Journal of Applied Psychology, 79,* 360–363.

Bowen, M. G. (1987). The escalation phenomenon reconsidered. Decision dilemmas or decision errors? *Academy of Management Review, 12,* 52–66.

Brockner, J. (1992). The escalation of commitment to a failing course of action: Toward theoretical progress. *Academy of Management Review, 17,* 39–61.

Brockner, J., & Rubin, J. Z. (1985). *Entrapment in escalating conflicts: A social psychological analysis.* New York: Springer-Verlag.

Brockner, J., Rubin, J. Z., & Lang, E. (1981). Face-saving and entrapment. *Journal of Experimental Social Psychology, 17,* 68–79.

Caldwell, D. F., & O'Reilly, C. (1982). Response to failure: The effects of choice and responsibility on impression management. *Academy of Management Journal, 25,* 121–136.

Conlon, D. E., & Garland, H. (1993). The role of project completion information in resource allocation decisions. *Academy of Management Journal, 36,* 402–413.

Conlon, E. J., & Parks, J. M. (1987). Information requests in the context of escalation. *Journal of Applied Psychology, 72,* 344–350.

Conlon, E. J., & Wolf, G. (1980). The moderating effects of strategy, visibility, and involvement on allocation behavior. *Organizational Behavior and Human Performance, 26,* 172–192.

Davis, M., & Bobko, P. (1986). Contextual effects on escalation processes in public sector decision making. *Organizational Behavior and Human Decision Processes, 37,* 121–138.

Evans, M. G., & Medcof, J. W. (1984). The paradox of precedent. *Canadian Journal of Administrative Science, 1,* 383–398.

Festinger, L. (1957). *A theory of cognitive dissonance.* Evanston, IL: Row, Peterson.

Fox, F. V., & Staw, B. M. (1979). The trapped administrator: Effects of job insecurity and policy resistance upon commitment to a course of action. *Administrative Science Quarterly, 24,* 449–471.

Frank, R. H. (1991). *Microeconomics and behavior.* New York: McGraw-Hill.

Garland, H. (1990). Throwing good money after bad: The effect of sunk costs on the decision to escalate commitment to an ongoing project. *Journal of Applied Psychology, 75,* 728–731.

Garland, H., Sandefur, C. A., & Rogers, A. C. (1990). De-escalation of commitment in oil exploration: When sunk costs and negative feedback coincide. *Journal of Applied Psychology, 75,* 921–927.

Ginzel, L. E., Kramer, R. M., & Sutton, R. I. (1993). Organizational impression management as a reciprocal influence process: The neglected role of the organizational audience. In L. L. Cummings & B. M. Staw (Eds.), *Research in organizational behavior,* (Vol. 15, pp. 227–266). Greenwich, CT: JAI Press.

Goffman, E. (1967). *Interaction ritual.* Newport Beach, CA: Westcliff.

Goltz, S. M. (1992). A sequential analysis of continued investments of organizational resources in non-performing courses of action. *Journal of Applied Behavior Analysis, 25,* 561–574.

Goltz, S. M. (1993). Examining the joint roles of responsibility and reinforcement history in recommitment. *Decision Sciences, 24,* 977–994.

Goodman, P. S., Bazerman, M., & Conlon, E. (1980). Institutionalization of planned organizational change. In B. M. Staw & L. L. Cummings (Eds.), *Research in organizational behavior* (Vol. 2, pp. 215–246). Greenwich, CT: JAI Press.

Hantula, D. A., & Crowell, C. R. (1994). Intermittent reinforcement and escalation processes in sequential decision making: A replication and theoretical analysis. *Journal of Organizational Behavior Management, 14,* 7–36.

Harrison, P. D., & Harrell, A. (1993). Impact of "adverse selection" on managers' project evaluation decisions. *Academy of Management Journal, 36,* 635–643.

Heath, C. (1995). Escalation and de-escalation of commitment in response to sunk costs: The role of budgeting in mental accounting. *Organizational Behavior and Human Decision Processes, 62,* 38–54.

Jones, E. E., & Davis, K. E. (1965. From acts to dispositions: The attribution process in person perception. In L. Berkowitz (Ed.), *Advances in Experimental Social Psychology* (Vol. 2, pp. 219–266). New York: Academic Press.

Kahneman, D., & Tversky, A. (1979). Prospect theory: An analysis of decisions under risk. *Econometrica, 47*, 263–291.

Kahneman, D., & Tversky, A. (1982). Psychology of preferences. *Scientific American, 246*, 161–173.

Kanodia, C., Bushman, R., & Dickhaut, J. (1989). Escalation errors and the sunk cost effect: An explanation based on reputation and information asymmetries. *Journal of Accounting Research, 27*, 59–77.

Kiesler, C. A. (1971). *The psychology of commitment.* New York: Academic Press.

Langer, E. J. (1975). The illusion of control. *Journal of Personality and Social Psychology, 32*, 311–328.

Leatherwood, M. L., & Conlon, E. J. (1987). Diffusibility of blame: Effects on persistence in a project. *Academy of Management Journal, 30*, 836–847.

Levi, A. (1982). *Escalating commitment and risk taking in dynamic decision behavior.* Unpublished manuscript, Yale University.

March, J. G. (1978). Bounded rationality, ambiguity, and the engineering of choice. *Bell Journal of Economics, 9*, 587–608.

March, J. G., & Olsen, J. P. (1976). *Ambiguity and choice in organizations.* Bergen, Norway: Universitetsforlager.

McCain, B. E. (1986). Continuing investment under conditions of failure: A laboratory study of the limits to escalation. *Journal of Applied Psychology, 71*, 280–284.

McNamara, R. S. (1995). *In retrospect.* New York: Times Books.

Meyer, M. W., & Zucker, L. G. (1989). *Permanently failing organizations.* Newbury Park, CA: Sage.

Northcraft, G., & Neale, M. A. (1986). Opportunity costs and the framing of resource allocation decisions. *Organizational Behavior and Human Decision Processes, 37*, 348–356.

Northcraft, G. B., & Wolf, G. (1984). Dollars, sense, and sunk costs: A life-cycle model of resource allocation decisions. *Academy of Management Review, 9*, 225–234.

Pfeffer, J. (1993). Barriers to the advance of organizational science: Paradigm development as a dependent variable. *Academy of Management Review, 18*, 599–620.

Ross, J., & Staw, B. M. (1986). Expo 86: An escalation prototype. *Administrative Science Quarterly, 32*, 274–297.

Ross, J., & Staw, B. M. (1993). Organizational escalation and exit: The case of the Shoreham nuclear power plant. *Academy of Management Journal, 36*, 701–732.

Salancik, G. R. (1977). Commitment and the control of organizational behavior and belief. In B. M. Staw & G. R. Salancik (Eds.), *New directions in organizational behavior* (pp. 1–54). Malabor, FL: Robert E. Kreiger.

Samuelson, P. A., & Nordhaus, W. D. (1985). Economics (12th ed.). New York: McGraw-Hill.

Samuelson, W. F., & Bazerman, M. H. (1985). The winners' curse in bilateral negotiations. In V. Smith (Ed.), *Research in experimental economics* (Vol. 3, pp. 105–137). Greenwich, CT: JAI Press.

Schoorman, F. D. (1988). Escalation bias in performance appraisals: An unintended consequence of supervisor participation in hiring decision. *Journal of Applied Psychology, 73*, 58–62.

Schoorman, F. D., Mayer, R. C., Douglas, C. A., & Hetrick, C. T. (1994). Escalation of commitment and the framing effect: An empirical investigation. *Journal of Applied Social Psychology, 24,* 509–528.

Shapira, Z. (1995). *Risk taking: A managerial perspective.* New York: Russell Sage Foundation.

Sheehan, N., & Kenworthy, E. W. (1971). *The Pentagon papers.* New York: Quadrangle Books.

Shubik, M. (1971). The dollar auction game: A paradox in noncooperative behavior and escalation. *Journal of Conflict Resolution, 15,* 109–111.

Simon, H. A. (1979). Rational decision making in business organizations. *American Economic Review, 69,* 493–513.

Simonson, I., & Staw, B. M. (1992). Deescalation strategies: A comparison of techniques for reducing commitment to losing courses of action. *Journal of Applied Psychology, 77,* 419–426.

Staw, B. M. (1976). Knee-deep in the big muddy: A study of escalating commitment to a chosen course of action. *Organizational Behavior and Human Performance, 16,* 27–44.

Staw, B. M., Barsade, S. G., & Koput, K. W. (1995). *Escalation and de-escalation at the credit window: A longitudinal study of bank executives' handling of problem loans.* Working paper, Haas School of Business, University of California, Berkeley.

Staw, B. M., and Fox, F. (1977). Escalation: Some determinants to a previously chosen course of action. *Human Relations, 30,* 431–450.

Staw, B. M., & Hoang, H. (1995). Sunk costs in the NBA: A behavioral determinant of playing time and survival in professional basketball. *Administrative Science Quarterly, 40,* 474–494.

Staw, B. M., & Ross, J. (1980). Commitment in an experimenting society: An experiment on the attribution of leadership from administrative scenarios. *Journal of Applied Psychology, 65,* 249–260.

Staw, B. M., & Ross, J. (1987). Understanding escalation situation: Antecedent, prototypes, and solution. In B. M. Staw & L. L. Cummings (Eds.), *Research in organization behavior* (pp. 39–78). Greenwich, CT: JAI Press.

Staw, B. M., & Ross, J. (1989). Understanding behavior in escalation situations. *Science, 246,* 216–220.

Staw, B. M., & Sutton, R. (1993). Macro-organizational psychology. In J. K. Murnighan (Ed.), *Handbook of organizational psychology in organizations* (pp. 350–384). Englewood Cliffs, NJ: Prentice-Hall.

Taylor, S. E. (1989). *Positive illusions.* New York: Basic Books.

Taylor, S. E., & Brown, J. (1988). Illusion and well-being: A social psychological perspective on mental health. *Psychological Bulletin, 103,* 193–210.

Teger, A. (1980). *Too much invested to quit.* New York: Wiley.

Tetlock, P. E. (1985). Accountability: The neglected social context of judgment and choice. In B. M. Staw & L. L. Cummings (Eds.), *Research in organizational behavior* (pp. 297–332). Greenwich, CT: JAI Press.

Whyte, G. (1986). Escalating commitment to a course of action: A reinterpretation. *Academy of Management Review, 11,* 311–321.

Zanna, M. P., & Fazio, R. H. (1982). The attitude–behavior relation: Moving toward a third generation of research. In M. P. Zanna, E. T. Higgins, & C. P. Herman (Eds.), *Consistency in social behavior* (pp. 283–301). Hillsdale, NJ: Erlbaum.

10 The possibility of distributed decision making

Baruch Fischhoff and Stephen Johnson

Increasingly in organizations, the information and authority for critical decisions are distributed over geographically separated individuals or groups. Such *distributed decision making* can be found in such diverse settings as voluntary organizations, multinational corporations, diplomatic corps, government agencies, and even married couples managing a household. This chapter analyzes how the distributed character of these systems affects their core cognitive activity: making decisions. As an organizing device, the chapter develops a general *task analysis* for distributed decision-making systems, detailing the performance issues that accrue with successive levels of complication as one goes from the simplest situation (involving a single individual possessing complete information about a static situation) to the most complex (with heterogeneous, multiperson systems facing dynamic, uncertain, and hostile environments). Drawing on experience with several such systems and on research in various disciplines, the analysis suggests both problems and possible solutions. It also derives some general conclusions regarding the design and management of distributed decision-making systems, as well as the asymptotic limits to their performance.

By starting simple, the analysis reflects a bottom-up view of organizations, focused on the properties that emerge as a result of complicating the roles assigned to the individuals in them. It also treats diverse circumstances in the same general terms. Its application to specific circumstances would obviously require more detailed analyses, perhaps beginning with classes of systems (e.g., those undergoing endogenous technological change). The analysis also focuses on a particular view of individual perfor-

Partial support for this research was provided by the Office of Naval Research and the National Science Foundation. An earlier version appeared as the Appendix to *Distributed decision making: Report of a workshop*. National Academy Press, Washington, DC (1990). We would like to thank the editor and Andreas Garcia for their comments on an earlier draft.

mance: that emerging from the cognitive studies of behavioral decision making. It could be enriched by alternative perspectives (e.g., affective, social processes) and elaborated over time as new research results appear.

A short history of individual decision-making research

It is common knowledge that decision making is often hard. One clear indication of this difficulty is the proliferation of decision aids, whether consultants, analytical tools, or computerized support systems (Stokey & Zeckhauser, 1978; von Winterfeldt & Edwards, 1986; Wheeler & Janis, 1980). Equally clear but perhaps more subtle evidence is the variety of devices that people use to avoid decision making. These include procrastination, endless pursuit of better information, reliance on habit or tradition, and deferral to aids even when there is no particular reason to think that they can do better (Corbin, 1980; Fischhoff, 1996; Langer, 1991). A common symptom of this reluctance to make decisions is the attempt to convert decision making, involving a gamble surrounded by uncertainty (regarding what one will get and how one will like it) into problem solving, involving a search for the one right solution (Montgomery, 1983; Simon, 1957).

For the past 40 years, the field of behavioral decision theory has attempted to explain why decision making is so hard, as a step toward helping to reduce those difficulties (Edwards, 1954; Einhorn & Hogarth, 1981; Rappoport & Wallsten, 1972; Yates, 1989). Its hopes are pinned on a mixture of prescriptive and descriptive research. The former asks how people should make decisions, and the latter asks how they actually make them. In combination, these research programs attempt to build from people's strengths while compensating for their weaknesses. Their premise is that one should worry about trusting significant decisions to either unaided intuition or computational procedures. Finding the optimal division of labor requires an understanding of where people are, in their intuitive decision making, and where they should be in order to make effective decisions.

Initially, behavioral decision theory took its marching orders from standard American economics, which assumes that people always know what they want and choose the optimal course of action for getting it. Taken literally, these strong assumptions leave a narrow role for descriptive research: finding out what people want by observing their decisions, then working backward to identify the objectives that were optimized. These assumptions leave no role at all for prescriptive research because people can already fend quite well for themselves. As a result, the economic perspective is not very helpful for the erstwhile decision aider – if its assumptions are true.

However, the market for decision aiding suggests that the assumptions are not true. The initial work of behavioral decision-making researchers was to document the discrepancy between ideal and actual performance. Producing demonstrations of suboptimality proved straightforward (Arkes & Hammond, 1988; Fischhoff, 1988; Kahneman, Slovic, & Tversky, 1982; Pitz & Sachs, 1984; Slovic, Lichtenstein, & Fischhoff, 1988). It can be helpful just to know the size of the problem in particular situations. It can show how much to worry, where to be ready for surprises, where to seek help, and how much to invest in that help. However, size estimates are not very informative about how to make performance better.

Realizing this limitation, researchers turned their attention from what people are not doing (making optimal decisions) to what they are doing and why it is not working (Montgomery & Svenson, 1993; Nisbett, 1993; Payne, Bettman, & Johnson, 1988). Aside from their theoretical interest, such psychological perspectives offer several points of leverage for erstwhile decision aiders. One is that they allow prediction of where the problems will be greatest by describing how people respond to particular situations. A second is that they help decision aiders talk to decision makers by showing how the latter think about their tasks. A third is that psychological research can identify the processes that must be changed if people are to perform more effectively. Although it would be nice to make people over as model decision makers, the reality is that they have to be moved in gradual steps from where they are now. A primary vehicle for applying this research has been decision analysis, a family of procedures for combining judgments according to the rules of decision theory (Grayson, 1960; Raiffa, 1968; Watson & Buede, 1990). It assumes that people are the essential source of insight regarding the substance of decisions: the options, consequences, values, and uncertainties. However, the combination of these components is best left to computational procedures. These procedures are readily mounted in computerized systems of the sort that can be used to coordinate distributed decision-making systems. For decision analysis to work, people must be able to describe their beliefs and values in the standardized terms required by the computational decision models. As might be expected, success has been mixed, partly reflecting limits to the underlying judgmental processes, partly reflecting limits to translating them into model-relevant terms (Fischhoff, 1980, 1988). As telecommunications replace direct communications, translating beliefs into standard terms may become increasingly important. As decisions come to involve increasingly diverse and distributed individuals, judgmental processes may be increasingly strained (Kiesler & Sproull, 1992). After a brief summary of research on individual decision making, we consider these complications.

Why is individual decision making so hard?

According to most prescriptive schemes, good decision making involves the following steps:

1. Identify all possible courses of action (including perhaps inaction).

2. Evaluate the attractiveness (or aversiveness) of the consequences that may arise if each course of action is adopted.
3. Assess the likelihood of each consequence actually happening (should each action be taken?).
4. Integrate all these considerations, using a defensible (i.e., rational) decision rule to select the best (i.e., optimal) action.

The empirical research has shown difficulties at each of these steps.

Option generation

When they think of action options, people may neglect seemingly obvious candidates and be relatively insensitive to the number or importance of these omitted alternatives (Fischhoff, Slovic, & Lichtenstein, 1978; Gettys, Pliske, Manning, & Casey, 1987). Options that would otherwise command attention are out of mind when they are out of sight, leaving people with the impression that they have analyzed problems more thoroughly than is actually the case.

Those options that are noted are often defined quite vaguely, making it difficult to evaluate them precisely, communicate them to others, follow them once adopted, or tell when circumstances have changed enough to justify rethinking the decision (Fischhoff, 1984, 1994). Imprecision makes it difficult to evaluate decisions in the light of subsequent experience insofar as it is hard to reconstruct exactly what one was trying to do and why. That reconstruction is further complicated by hindsight bias, the tendency to exaggerate in hindsight what one knew in foresight. The feeling that one knew all along what was going to happen can lead one to be unduly harsh in evaluating past decisions (if it was obvious what was going to happen, then failure to select the best option must mean incompetence) and to be unduly optimistic about future decisions (by encouraging the feeling that things are generally well understood, even if they are not working out so well) (Fischhoff, 1975, 1982; Hoch & Loewenstein, 1989).

Value assessment

Evaluating potential consequences might seem to be the easy part of decision making insofar as people should know what they want and like. Although this is doubtless true for familiar and simple consequences, many interesting decisions present novel outcomes in unusual juxtapositions. For example, two potential consequences that may arise when deciding whether to dye one's graying hair are reconciling oneself to aging and increasing the risk of cancer 10 to 20 years hence. Who knows what either event is *really* like, particularly with the precision needed to make trade-offs between the two? In such cases, one must go back to some set of basic values (e.g., those concerned with pain, prestige, vanity), decide which are pertinent, and determine what role to assign them. As a result, evaluation becomes an inferential problem (Fischhoff, 1991; Rokeach, 1973).

The evidence suggests that people have trouble making such inferences (Fischhoff, Slovic, & Lichtenstein, 1980; Hogarth, 1982). They may fail to identify all relevant values, to recognize the conflicts among them, or to reconcile those conflicts that are recognized. As a result, the values they express are often highly (and unwittingly) sensitive to the exact way in which evaluation questions are posed, whether by survey researchers, decision aids, politicians, merchants, or themselves. To take just three examples, (1) the relative attractiveness of two gambles may depend on whether people are asked how attractive each is or how much they would pay to play it (Slovic & Lichtenstein, 1983); (2) an insurance policy may become much less attractive when its "premium" is described as a "sure loss" (Hershey, Kunreuther, & Schoemaker, 1982); and (3) a risky venture may seem much more attractive when described in terms of the lives that it will save rather than in terms of the lives that will still be lost (Tversky & Kahneman, 1981).

People can view many trade-offs in several different lights. How richly they do view them depends on how sensitive their evaluation process is. Questions have to be asked in some way, and how they are asked may induce random error (by confusing people), systematic errors (by emphasizing some perspectives and neglecting others), or unduly extreme judgments (by failing to evoke underlying conflicts). Thus, uncertainty about values can be as serious a problem as uncertainty about facts (March, 1978).

Uncertainty assessment

Although people can recognize uncertainty about what will happen, they are not always well prepared to assess its likelihood. A rough summary of research into judgments under conditions of uncertainty would be that people are quite good at tracking repetitive aspects of their environment but not very good at combining those observations into inferences about what they have not seen (Kahneman et al., 1982; Peterson & Beach, 1967; Plous, 1993; Yates, 1989). Thus, they might be able to tell how frequently they have seen or heard about a particular cause of death but not how unrepresentative their experience has been – leading them to overestimate risks to which they have been overexposed (Tversky & Kahneman, 1973). They can tell what usually happens in a particular situation and recognize how a specific instance is special, yet not be able to integrate those two (uncertain) facts – most often focusing on the specific information and neglecting experience (Bar-Hillel, 1980). They can tell how similar a specific instance is to a prototypical case, yet not how important similarity is for making predictions – usually relying on it too much (Bar-Hillel, 1984; Kahneman & Tversky, 1972). They can tell how many times they have seen an effect follow a potential cause, yet not infer what that says about causality – often perceiving relationships when none exist (Beyth-Marom, 1982; Einhorn & Hogarth, 1978).

In addition to these difficulties in integrating information, people's intuitive predictions are afflicted by a number of systematic biases in how they gather and interpret information. These include incomplete understanding about the extent of their own knowledge (Lichtenstein, Fischhoff, & Phillips, 1982; Shlyakhter, Kammen, Broido, & Wilson, 1994; Wallsten & Budescu, 1983), underestimation of the time needed to complete projects (Kidd, 1970; Tihansky, 1976), unfair dismissal of information that threatens favored beliefs (Nisbett & Ross, 1980), exaggeration of personal immunity to various threats (Svenson, 1981; Weinstein, 1980), insensitivity to the speed with which exponential processes accelerate (Wagenaar & Sagaria, 1975), and oversimplification of others' behavior (Mischel, 1968; Ross & Nisbett, 1992).

Option choice

Decision theory is quite uncompromising regarding the rule that people should use when integrating all these judgments in the quest of a best alternative. Unless some consequences are essential, it should be an expectation rule, whereby an option is evaluated according to the attractiveness of its consequences, weighted by the likelihood of each consequence occurring (Schoemaker, 1983). Because it has become acceptable to question the descriptive validity of this rule, voluminous research has shown (1) that it often predicts behavior quite well – if one knows how people evaluate the likelihood and attractiveness of consequences; (2) that with enough ingenuity, one can usually find some set of beliefs for which the rule would dictate choosing the option that was selected – meaning that it is hard to prove that the rule was not used; and (3) that expectation rules can often predict the outcome of decision-making processes even when they do not reflect the thought processes involved – so that predicting behavior is not sufficient for understanding or aiding it (Dawes, 1988; Goldberg, 1968).

More process-oriented methods reveal a more complicated situation. People seldom acknowledge using anything as computationally demanding as an expectation rule or feel comfortable using it when asked to (Lichtenstein, Slovic, & Zink, 1969). To the extent that they do compute, they often seem to use quite different rules (Kahneman & Tversky, 1979; Tversky & Kahneman, 1981). Indeed, they even seem unimpressed by the assumptions used to justify the expectation rule (Slovic & Tversky, 1974). To the extent that they do not compute, they use a variety of simple rules whose dictates may be roughly similar to those of the expectation rule or may be very different (Beach & Mitchell, 1978; Janis & Mann, 1977; Payne, 1982; Tversky 1969). Many of these rules can be summarized as an attempt to avoid making hard choices by finding some way to view the decision as an easy choice (e.g., by ignoring consequences on which the seemingly best option rates poorly; Montgomery, 1983).

Cognitive assets and biases

This (partial) litany of the problems described by empirical researchers paints quite a dismal picture of people's ability to make novel (or analytical) decisions, so much so that the investigators have been called problem mongers (Berkeley & Humphreys, 1982; Jungermann, 1984; von Winterfeldt & Edwards, 1986). Of course, if one hopes to help people (in any arena), then the problems are what matters. In addition to meaning well, investigators in this area have also had a basically respectful attitude toward the people they study. The cognitive perspective showed how biases could emerge from honest, unemotional thought processes.

Typically, these theories show people processing information in reasonable ways that often work well but can lead to predictable trouble. A simple example would be relying on habit or tradition as a guide to decision making. That might be an efficient way of making relatively good decisions, but it would lead one astray if conditions had changed or if those past decisions reflected values that were no longer applicable.

Reliance on these simple rules seems to come from two sources. One is people's limited mental computation capacity; they have to simplify things in order to get on with life (Miller, 1956; Simon, 1957). The second is their lack of training in decision making, leading them to come up with rules that make sense but have not benefited from rigorous scrutiny. Moreover, people's day-to-day experience does not provide them with the conditions needed to learn to make judgments and decisions. Experience often does allow people to learn the solutions to specific repeated problems through trial and error. However, things get difficult when one has to get it right the first time.

What can be done about it?

Improving the judgments needed for decision making has been the topic of intensive research, with moderately consistent (although incomplete) results (Fischhoff, 1982; Plous, 1993). A number of simple solutions have proven rather ineffective. There seems to be little value to exhorting people to work harder, raising the stakes hinging on their performance, telling them about the problems that others have had with such tasks, or providing theoretical knowledge of statistics or decision theory. Similarly, it does not seem reasonable to hope that the problems will go away with time. Judgment is a skill that must be learned. Those who do not get training or who do not enjoy a naturally instructive environment (e.g., one that provides prompt, unambiguous feedback and rewards them for wisdom rather than, say, for exuding confidence) will have difficulty going beyond the hard data at their disposal.

Short of training intuitions, it may be possible to change decision-making procedures so that better use is made of people's inevitably limited intellect. Some of these procedures might be readily incorporated in online decisions aids. For example, a tendency to neglect significant options or consequences might be reduced by checklists with generic possibilities (Beach, Townes, Campbell, & Keating, 1976; Hammer, 1980; Janis, 1982. A tendency toward overconfidence might be reduced by forcing users to list reasons why they might be wrong before assessing the likelihood that they are right (Koriat, Lichtenstein, & Fischhoff, 1980). Hindsight bias might be reduced by preserving decision makers' rationale (showing how things looked when decisions were made) (Fischhoff, 1982). Incomplete value elicitation might be reduced by forcing users to consider alternative perspectives and reconcile the differences among them (Keeney, 1993). Although there is some evidence supporting each of these interventions, where and how well they work is an empirical question. For each intervention, one can think of reasons why it might not work, especially if executed clumsily (e.g., long checklists might reduce the attention paid to individual options, leading to broad but superficial analyses).

How is distributed decision making different?

If life is hard for single individuals wrestling with their fate, then what happens in multinational corporations, or worldwide merchant banks, or carrier task forces, with interdependent decision makers being responsible for incompletely overlapping portions of complex problems? Addressing these situations is a logical next step for behavioral decision theory, although not one that it can take alone. Although the essential problem is still individuals pondering the unknown, there are now machines, procedures, and doctrines in the picture, along with more fluid social relations. These require the additional skills of computer scientists, human factors specialists, substantive experts, and organizational theorists.

What follows is our attempt to pull these perspectives together into a framework for analyzing distributed decision-making systems. Such systems include high-tech examples, such as air-traffic control and multinational corporations; mid-tech examples, such as forest-fire fighting and police dispatch; and low-tech examples, such as volunteer organizations with many branches or couples rearing children.

Although geographical separation is often considered a distinguishing characteristic of distributed decision making, there can be substantial difficulties in coordinating information and initiatives among individuals in the same room or tent. From this perspective, the critical challenge to a distributed decision-making system is the creation of appropriately shared mental models of the system. Each participant must keep in mind many parts of that system – for example, how external forces are attempting to affect it, what communications links exist within it, what other participants believe about its current internal and external circumstances, and what decisions they face (in terms of options, values, constraints, and uncertainties). For the system to work, these beliefs need to be not only formulated but also communicated. That communication might be in unrestricted natural language, in the restricted vocabulary of a formal organization, or in a structured modeling language such as that of decision theory. Participants' ability to use that language sets an upper limit on the system's coordination of decision making, as does the system's capacity for information sharing.

A hierarchy of distributed decision making

At the core of distributed decision-making systems are the people who have to get the work done. As a result, this analysis begins with the reality that they face. It then proceeds to the complications arising when decision making is distributed over two individuals and, finally, those associated with multiple individuals.

What follows is a task analysis, the standard point of entry for human factors engineers, the specialists concerned with the performance of people in technical systems. Such analyses characterize systems in terms of their behaviorally significant dimensions, which must be considered when designing the system and adapting people to it (Chapanis, 1959; Perrow, 1984). Emphasizing cognitive aspects of performance means asking how people understand and manipulate their environment under reasonably unemotional conditions. Insofar as emotions degrade performance, problems unresolved at this level constitute a performance ceiling.

Single-person systems

The simplest situation faced by an individual decision maker involves a static world about which everything can be known and no formal representation of knowledge is required. The threats to performance in this basic situation are those studied most thoroughly by behavioral decision-making research. They include the difficulties that arise in identifying relevant options, reviewing available knowledge, identifying pertinent values, determining the trade-offs among them, and integrating these pieces. The most promising performance aids should be those that have been identified in the research literature, such as option checklists, multimethod value-elicitation procedures, and formal integration methods.

A first complication for individual decision making is the addition of uncertainty. With it come the difficulties of intuitive judgment under uncertainty, such as misperception of causality, inappropriate confidence in the extent of one's knowledge, and heuristic-induced prediction biases. Potential solutions include training in judgmental skills, restructuring tasks so as to overcome bad habits, and keeping a statistical record of experience so as to reduce reliance on memory. A second complication is going from a static to a dynamic external world. With it come new difficulties, such as undue adherence to currently favored hypotheses, and the accompanying potential solutions, such as reporting forms requiring reconsideration of currently unfavored hypotheses. A third complication is use of a formal modeling language for organizing knowledge and decision making. One associated problem is the users' inability to speak the modeling language; this problem might be addressed by using psycholinguistic procedures to develop the language and train people in it (e.g., Budescu & Wallsten, 1995; Fischhoff, 1994; Schwartz, 1994). Finally, the language may not be able to describe certain situations (such as those dealing with human behavior or intentions); that threat might be addressed by explicitly bounding the model's range of application.

Two-person systems

In behavioral terms, the simplest two-person system involves individuals with common goals, common experience, and a reliable communications link. Such individuals would have highly shared mental models of their circumstances and the opportunity to keep those models consistent. Having a colleague can alleviate some cognitive difficulties. For example, dividing information-processing responsibilities can reduce information overload; having someone else review one's work may catch some mistakes. These benefits will be limited if both individuals are prone to the same judgmental difficulties. Collaboration might even make matters worse if the collaborators draw unwarranted confidence from the convergence of their similarly flawed judgments.

Realizing these potential benefits means ensuring that both parties understand one another to the extent possible and recognize that extent. One threat to understanding is unwittingly using terms differently, not recognizing, say, that *risk* or *threat* or *likely* or *destructive power* have different meanings (Budescu & Wallsten, 1995; Bunn & Tsipis, 1983; Fischhoff, Watson, & Hope, 1984). For example, Samet (1975) showed that a commonly used U.S. military reporting system characterized reports in terms of their *reliability* and *validity* – even though users did not actually distinguish the two concepts. If such discrepancies go undetected, then perceptions may drift apart until some dramatic confrontation occurs. Avoiding such inopportune moments requires actively seeking and resolving such inconsistencies (e.g., National Interagency Incident Management System, 1982). Even with unrestricted communication, discrepant views can go undetected if people fail to question critical assumptions. *False consensus* refers to the erroneous belief that others share one's views (Nisbett & Ross, 1980); *pluralistic ignorance* refers to the erroneous belief that one is the odd person out (Fiske & Taylor, 1984). Such problems arise when frequent interaction creates an exaggerated perception of how completely mental models are shared.

A common complication in two-person systems is unreliable communication links. Sometimes external pressures are responsible, either directly (e.g., by deliberately disrupting communications) or indirectly (e.g., by discouraging internal communication lest secrets by exposed). Like other complications, unreliable communications can create both problems and opportunities for distributed decision making. For example, interrupting communications between individuals with deeply shared views may allow them to acquire different information and formulate independent perspectives, thereby reducing the risk of groupthink (Janis, 1972). However, it may also lead to unrecognized drift in their beliefs and unpredictable behavior when they must coordinate their actions. One possible protection is mandatory checking procedures designed to detect discrepancies in mental models. A second strategy is to study how mental models drift over time in order to determine the appropriate levels of vigilance. Even with continually open channels, communication may be restricted by institutional or technological constraints. These could include restricted vocabularies, time- or event-related reporting requirements, strict interaction protocols, or stultifying confirmation procedures (e.g., repeating each message verbatim).

At the extreme, communication might be limited to the analytical language used in the system's formal model of its world. That restriction would mean sacrificing natural contact between individuals in return for computational proficiency. As mentioned, users must then be able to speak the analytical language. Any lack of fluency represents a communication disorder, leading analytical approaches to create problems as well as solve them. For example, probabilistic risk analyses (PRA) provide a valuable tool for anticipating how various configurations of complex technical systems, such as nuclear power or chemical plants, will operate (McCormick, 1981). They do this by representing the system by the formal connections among its parts (e.g., showing how failures in one sector will affect performance in others). Both judgment and statistics are used to estimate model parameters. In this way, it is possible to pool the knowledge of many experts, expose that knowledge to external review, estimate the system's overall performance, and determine its sensitivity to variations (or uncertainties) in those parameters (Morgan & Henrion, 1990). Yet PRA often requires experts to summarize their knowledge in unfamiliar quantitative terms; it is ill suited to phenomena that are not easily decomposed (such as the behavior of the system's operators). As a result, the model can be far from reality. Moreover, it may differ in ways that the user understands poorly, just as a fluent speaker of a second language can make occasional critical gaffes. Thus, users may lose touch with the model without realizing it (Fischhoff, 1989).

Even less formal languages can suppress essential nuances of normal communication. It is unclear what substitutes people will find (or even see the need to find) when deprived of facial expression, body language, intonation, and similar cues (Kiesler & Sproull, 1992). These problems may be exacerbated when knowledge resides in a formal model without any indication of who said it, how it was said, or how far it can be trusted. Languages that cannot express confidence may not be able to instill it. It may be hard to lead through electronic mail.

A final complication in two-person distributed decision-making systems is inconsistent objectives, externalizing the value incoherence that might be found within a single individual. The two may have similar values but differ over the goals relevant to a particular case. They may have a common opponent yet stand to share differently from the spoils of victory (and the agonies of defeat). They may strive for personal power within the system, neglecting its ability to meet external challenges. Like other complications, these can be useful. For example, disagreements can uncover inconsistent values that an individual might not detect; competition can sharpen the wits of the competitors; by some accounts, conflict can bind social units together (Coser, 1954). Realizing these possibilities poses challenges to system design, such as creating reward systems that induce the correct mix of incentives.

Multiple-person systems

Most of the issues arising in the design and diagnosis of two-person systems also occur with multiple decision-maker systems, with some new wrinkles. The simplest such systems involve individuals with common goals, shared experience, and reliable communication links. As before, having more people involved means having more opportunities for views to evolve. Yet this advantage may backfire if deeply shared experience leads people to think similarly while having confidence in their degree of agreement (Lanir, 1982). As the number of parties grows, so does the volume of messages, perhaps at an accelerated pace. If everyone hears everything, then there may be too much going on for everyone to hear anything. It may be hard to keep track of who knows what and how widely expectations are shared.

Thus, as organizational size increases, the possibility of completely shared experience decreases. The maximum might be found in a hierarchical organization whose leaders have progressed through the ranks from the very bottom, so that they have a deep understanding of their subordinates' worlds. In such situations, less needs to be said and more can be predicted, making the organization more intimate than it seems. On the other hand, in a rapidly changing world, that experience may give an illusory feeling of understanding. For example, the education, equipment, and challenges of foot soldiers (or sales representatives) may be quite different now than when senior officials were in the trenches. One indicator of this threat might be the rate of technological change in the organization and its environment (Fischhoff, Lanir, & Johnson, in press). One way to ensure a common and realistic view might be periodic rotation through the ranks. Another might be providing opportunities to cut through the normal lines of communication in order to find out what is really happening. These problems might be reduced by resisting temptations to change the organization, unless the promised improvements will be so great as to compensate for the likely decrements in internal understanding.

In diverse organizations, having more people should bring more perspectives to a problem. However, the intricacies of sharing and coordinating that information may become unmanageable. It may be impossible even to discover misunderstandings such as differences in unspoken assumptions or in the usage of seemingly straightforward terms. If communications are decentralized, then local units may speak to one another, solving their problems but leaving the overall system less stable. If they are centralized, the headquarters might, in principle, create a common picture. However, doing so requires great attention to detail regarding who believes what, when, and how they express those beliefs. One aid to tracking these complex realities is to maintain formal models of the circumstances faced at different places. Comparing the models held at headquarters and in the field might provide a structured way of identifying discrepancies. Where large discrepancies persist, management by objectives might be needed to avoid micromanagement by leaders who are badly out of touch with their subordinates' reality. It can also provide an official way to resolve problems concerning conflicting goals.

Reliability problems in multiperson systems begin with those faced by two-person systems. As before, the challenge is to discern when and how communications have failed and how the system can be kept together. One potential coping mechanism is a communications protocol that emphasizes staying in touch, even when there is nothing much to say, in order to monitor reliability. Another is precluding messages that might damage future communications (e.g., ones that contain irony or discuss personalities). Another is reporting one's intentions, along with one's current status, in order to help others project what one might be doing when out of touch. Another is creating a "black box" for reconstructing what was happening before communications went down. Any of these strategies might reduce the failures of imagination that can create undue reliance on readily accessible evidence.

A final complicating factor with multiperson systems (with a relatively uninteresting two-person version) involves the heterogeneity of their parts. At one extreme lies a homogeneous organization whose parts perform roughly the same functions and whose strength depends on the sum of those parts. At the other extreme lies a heterogeneous organization with specialized parts drawing their strength from the sophistication of their interconnections. An undifferentiated infantry group or sales force might anchor one end of this continuum, an integrated carrier strike force or research lab the other.

A homogeneous system can use individuals and material interchange-ably, with relative insensitivity to the loss or failure of any particular unit. Homogeneous distributed decision-making systems should find it rela-tively easy to create a shared organizational culture, to disseminate organi-zational policies, and to act in predictable ways – reducing uncertainty about facts and values. However, the homogeneity of perspectives and skills may leave the system vulnerable to deeply shared misconceptions ("intellectual common-mode failures") and to having resources that are too inflexible to initiate significant changes (or even detect the need for them).

A heterogeneous system is designed to provide a precise response to the anticipated challenges of a complex environment. As a distributed decision-making system, it should find it relatively easy to develop task-specific procedures, policies, and communications. However, it may be hard to model or keep in mind a complex interactive system, knowing who is doing what, when, and how their actions affect one another. For exam-ple, "backlash" and "friendly fire" may be more likely across diverse units than across similar ones. It may be more difficult to formulate an organiza-tional philosophy with a common meaning for diverse contexts and units. The diversity of units may also create interoperability problems, hamper-ing their ability to communicate and cooperate. All these processes can increase uncertainty about facts and values.

Each kind of system may be most vulnerable to the threats against which the other is most strongly defended. In homogeneous systems, it is num-bers that count. A system adapted to this reality may be relatively inatten-tive to those few ways in which individual units serve vital functions, such as providing critical intelligence or testing new ideas, or create critical vulnerabilities, such as revealing organizational secrets or causing general embarrassment. For example, a merchant bank is more than the sum of its traders – if one trader can incur catastrophic losses or spot lucrative arbi-trage opportunities. In such circumstances, a higher level of coordination is needed for distributed decision making. Conversely, an organizational structure that evolved to orchestrate the pieces of a heterogeneous system may be severely challenged by situations in which mainly numbers matter. An inevitable by-product of specialization is having fewer of every spe-cialty and less ability to transcend specialty boundaries. There may there-fore be less staying power in protracted actions.

One response to these limitations is for each kind of system to incorpo-rate some properties of the other. For example, homogeneous organiza-tions might secure some heterogeneity of views by actively recruiting indi-viduals with diverse prior experience; they might develop specialist positions for confronting nonadditive issues (e.g., army intelligence offi-cers, publishers' libel watchdogs, banks' internal auditors). Heterogeneous organizations might deliberately promote generalists, with the specific aim of bridging the parts; they might transfer specialists across branches in order to encourage the sharing of perspectives (possibly with some loss of efficiency). The goal would be to share how different people think, as well as what they see.

Principles in designing distributed decision-making systems

Goals of the analysis

The preceding task analysis began with the problems faced in the simplest decision-making systems, those involving single individuals grappling with their fate under conditions of certainty, with no attempt at formal analysis. It proceeded first to look at complications in the lives of such individuals and then to consider successive levels of complication within two-person and multiperson organizations. At each level, it sketched how problems arising in simpler circumstances are exacerbated or ameliorated and what new problems arise.

A fuller version of this analysis would proceed on two levels. One involves looking at specific situations in much greater detail, such as designing a communications protocol or computer display for distributed decision making by a particular heterogeneous system. The second involves developing general design principles examining the interplay between individual and organizational behavior for use in lieu of detailed specific studies. A logical extension would consider the interplay between multiple distributed decision-making systems, characterized in the same theoretical terms. That analysis might show how the imperfections of each system can be exploited by the other or lead to mutually undesirable circumstances. For example, an analysis of rival military commands might consider the challenges that each handles least effectively. It might produce recommendations saying, in effect, "Don't test us in this way unless you really mean it. We are not equipped to respond flexibly." Or one might consider the interactions between the decision-making structures of the financial and legal branches of a corporation.

Design guidelines

Although still formative, this analysis suggests some general conclusions regarding distributed decision-making systems. One is that performance depends on the reality created for the individuals at each node in a system. For example, designers need not obsess over the intricacies of displaying vast quantities of information when the real problem is not knowing which policy to apply.

A second general conclusion is that many organizational problems can be seen as variants of individual problems. For example, a common crisis in individual decision making is determining what one wants. The organizational analog is determining how to interpret general policies in specific circumstances. Similarly, individuals' problems in dealing with uncertainty may underlie unrealistic demands for certainty in communications from others.

A third conclusion is that problems attributed to novel technologies can often be found in low-tech situations. Two people living in the same household can have difficulty communicating; restricting them to e-mail or voice mail may make matters better or worse. The speed of modern systems can induce enormous time pressures, yet many decisions are hard even with unlimited time. Telecommunications can exacerbate information overload, yet the fundamental management problem remains the simple one of determining what is relevant. The technology gives problems their precise form, creating or precluding possible solutions.

A fourth conclusion is that it may pay to accentuate the negative when designing distributed decision-making systems and to accentuate the positive when adapting people to them. That is, system design is often a top-down process, reflecting an idealization of form and function. However, it is important to realize that an aspiration is not an achievement. A bottom-up, individual-centered view might produce more realistic expectations of system performance and focus attention on places where people need help. The point of departure for that help must be people's current thought processes, so that they can be brought along from where they are toward where one would like them to be. People can change, but only under carefully structured conditions and at a moderate pace. When pushed too hard, they risk losing touch with their own reality.

Design ideologies

A fifth conclusion is that the detailed empirical work needed to design distributed decision-making systems requires resisting simplistic design philosophies. One family of simple principles concentrates on mastering mistakes, claiming either to avoid them entirely (e.g., "zero defects," "quality is free"), adapt to them immediately ("muddling through"), or correct them in hindsight ("learning from experience"). A second family of design ideologies concentrates on planning, with rigid flexibility or inflexibility, leaving all options open or planning for all contingencies. A third family emphasizes controlling the human element in systems, claiming either to select the right people or to create them (through training and incentives). A fourth family proposes avoiding the human element altogether (through automation).

Rigid subscription to such ideologies creates an impossible task for the designers and operators of a system. For example, the instruction "to avoid all errors" implies that time and price are unimportant. When this is not the case, people are left adrift, forced to make trade-offs without explicit guidance and discouraged from treating those faults that do remain. Many fail-safe systems work only because the people in them have learned, by trial and error, to diagnose and respond to problems that are not supposed to happen. If such unofficial intelligence has no official role, it may have to be hidden; it may be denied resources (e.g., for record-keeping or training exercises); or it may be destroyed by changes in the system (which invalidate operators' understanding of nuances that do not appear in official plans or training manuals). When perfection is impossible, steps toward it should be very large before they justify disrupting accustomed (and unwritten) mental models of its operation. An underlying theme in many simple philosophies is a faith in being able to engineer the human side of the operation as well as the mechanical or electronics side.

It is so easy to speculate about human behavior (and provide supporting anecdotal evidence) that systematic empirical observation may not seem needed. However, even sensitive human engineering is often misconceived. The complexity of systems makes it hard to understand the intricacies of their design. As a result, one can neither anticipate all problems nor confidently treat those that are anticipated. Complexity means that corrections made in one domain may create new problems in another. For example, when the nuclear power industry attempted to deal with the human factors problems identified at Three Mile Island, it lowered the threshold for shutting down a reactor in potentially dangerous situations. Doing so increased the frequency of transitory states in which reactors are less well controlled and in which their components are subject to greater stresses (thereby reducing their life expectancy by some poorly understood amount). Increasing the number of human factors–related regulations complicated operators' jobs and created lucrative opportunities for them to work as consultants to the industry (thereby reducing the qualified labor force at the plants).

Part of people's genius is their ability to respond to unpredictable situations in unique ways. This creativity is central to any effective distributed decision-making system (Fischhoff et al., in press). In such cases, the designers' task is to help operators understand the system rather than to manage them as part of it. A common sign of insensitivity is using "operator error" to describe problems arising from operator–system interactions. A sign of sensitivity is incorporating operators in the design process. A rule of thumb is that human problems seldom have purely technical solutions, whereas technical solutions typically create human problems, perhaps soluble ones if their existence is recognized (Perrow, 1984; Rasmussen & Rouse, 1981; Reason, 1990).

The possibility of distributed decision making

Pursuing this line of inquiry can identify problems arising in distributed decision-making systems and focus technical efforts on solving them. Those solutions might include information displays (for understanding complex realities), communication protocols (for sharing information about them), training programs (for making do with unfriendly systems), contingency plans (for coping with system failures), and standardized terminology (for coordinating diverse units). Deriving such solutions is technically difficult but part of a known craft. Investigators from various disciplines know something about how to describe such problems, devise possible remedies, subject those proposals to empirical test, and characterize their degree of success.

Nonetheless, although these solutions might make systems better, they cannot make them whole. Their pursuit may even pose a threat if it distracts attention from the broader question of how systems are conceptualized. In both design and operation, healthy systems enjoy a creative tension between various conflicting pressures. One such tension is between a top-down perspective (working toward individuals' reality from an idealization of intended operations) and a bottom-up perspective (working up toward some modest improvement in operations). Another tension is between bureaucratization and innovation (or flexibility and inflexibility). Still other tensions are between planning and reacting, between a focus on routine or crisis operations, between risk acceptance and risk aversion, and between human and technological orientation. A common threat in these tensions is the system's attitude toward uncertainty: Does it accept uncertainty as a fact of life or does it live in the future, oriented toward the day when everything is predictable or controllable?

Achieving a balance between these perspectives requires both the insight and the leadership needed to be candid about the limits. When a (dynamic) balance is reached, the system can use its personnel most effectively and develop realistic strategies. When it is lacking, the organization is in a state of crisis, vulnerable to natural events or to hostile actions that exploit its imbalances. The crisis is particularly great when the need for balance is not recognized or cannot be admitted and when an experiential gulf separates management and operators. In this light, one can tell a great deal about how a system functions by looking at its managers' philosophy. If that is oversimplified or overconfident, then the system will be too, despite any superficial complexity. The goal of a task analysis then becomes to expose the precise ways in which this vulnerability is expressed.

References

Arkes, H., & Hammond, K. R. (Eds.) (1988). *Judgment and decision making.* New York: Cambridge University Press.

Bar-Hillel, M. (1980). The base-rate fallacy in probability judgments. *Acta Psychologica, 44,* 211–233.

Bar-Hillel, M. (1984). Representativeness and fallacies of probability judgment. *Acta Psychologica, 55,* 91–107.

Beach, L. R., & Mitchell, T. R. (1978). A contingency model for the selection of decision strategies. *Academy of Management Review, 3,* 439–449.

Beach, L. R., Townes, B. D., Campbell, F. L., & Keating, G. W. (1976). Developing and testing a decision aid for birth planning decisions. *Organizational Behavior and Human Performance, 15,* 99–116.

Berkeley, D., & Humphreys, P. C. (1982). Structuring decision problems and the "bias heuristic." *Acta Psychologica, 50,* 201–252.

Beyth-Marom, R. (1982). Perception of correlation reexamined. *Memory and Cognition, 10,* 511–519.

Budescu, D. V., & Wallsten, T. S. (1995). Processing linguistic probabilities. In J. R. Busemeyer, R. Hastie, & D. Medin (Eds.), *Decision making from the perspective of cognitive psychology* (pp. 275–318). New York: Academic Press.

Bunn, M., & Tsipis, K. (1983). The uncertainties of preemptive nuclear attack. *Scientific American, 249*(5), 38–47.

Chapanis, A. (1959). *Research techniques in human engineering.* Baltimore: Johns Hopkins University Press.

Corbin, R. (1980). On decisions that might not get made. In T. Wallsten (Ed.), *Cognitive processes in choice and decision processes* (pp. 47–68). Hillsdale, NJ: Erlbaum.

Coser, L. A. (1954). *The social functions of conflict.* Glencoe, IL: Free Press.

Dawes, R. (1988). *Rational choice in an uncertain world.* San Diego, CA: Harcourt Brace Jovanovich.

Edwards, W. (1954). The theory of decision making. *Psychological Bulletin, 51,* 201–214.

Einhorn, H. J., & Hogarth, R. M. (1978). Confidence in judgment: Persistence in the illusion of validity. *Psychological Review, 85,* 395–416.

Einhorn, H. J., & Hogarth, R. M. (1981). Behavioral decision theory: Processes of judgment and choice. *Annual Review of Psychology, 32,* 53–88.

Fischhoff, B. (1975). Hindsight ≠ foresight: The effect of outcome knowledge on judgment under uncertainty. *Journal of Experimental Psychology: Human Perception and Performance, 104,* 288–299.

Fischhoff, B. (1980). Clinical decision analysis. *Operations Research 28,* 28–43.

Fischhoff, B. (1982). Debiasing. In D. Kahneman, P. Slovic, & A. Tversky (Eds.), *Judgment under uncertainty: Heuristics and biases* (pp. 422–444). New York: Cambridge University Press.

Fischhoff, B. (1984). Setting standards: a systematic approach to managing public health and safety risks. *Management Science, 30,* 823–843.

Fischhoff, B. (1988). Judgment and decision making. In R. J. Sternberg & E. E. Smith (Eds.), *The psychology of human thought* (pp. 153–187). New York: Cambridge University Press.

Fischhoff, B. (1989). Eliciting knowledge for analytical representation. *IEEE Transactions on Systems, Man and Cybernetics, 13,* 448–461.

Fischhoff, B. (1991). Value elicitation: Is there anything in there? *American Psychologist, 46,* 835–847.

Fischhoff, B. (1994). What forecasts (seem to) mean. *International Journal of Forecasting, 10,* 387–403.

Fischhoff, B. (1996). The real world: What good is it? *Organizational Behavior and Human Decision Processes, 65,* 232–248.

Fischhoff, B., Lanir, Z., & Johnson, S. (in press). Risky lessons: Conditions for organizational learning. In R. Garud, P. Nayyar, & Z. Shapira (Eds.), *Technological oversights and foresights.* New York: Cambridge University Press.

Fischhoff, B., Slovic, P., & Lichtenstein, S. (1978). Fault trees: Sensitivity of assessed failure probabilities to problem representation. *Journal of Experimental Psychology: Human Perception and Performance, 4,* 330–344.

Fischhoff, B., Slovic, P., & Lichtenstein, S. (1980). Knowing what you want: Measuring labile values. In T. Wallsten (Ed.), *Cognitive processes in choice and decision behavior* (pp. 117–141). Hillsdale, NJ: Erlbaum.

Fischhoff, B., Watson, S., & Hope, C. (1984). Defining risk. *Policy Sciences, 17,* 123–139.

Fiske, S., & Taylor, S. E. (1984). *Social cognition.* Reading, MA: Addison-Wesley.

Gettys, C. F., Pliske, R. M., Manning, C., & Casey, J. T. (1987). An evaluation of human act generation performance. *Organizational Behavior and Human Decision Processes, 39,* 23–51.

Goldberg, L. R. (1968). Simple models or simple processes? Some research on clinical judgments. *American Psychologist, 23,* 483–496.

Grayson, J. R. (1960). *Decisions under uncertainty.* Cambridge, MA: Harvard School of Business Administration.

Hammer, W. (1980). *Product safety and management engineering.* Englewood Cliffs, NJ: Prentice-Hall.

Hershey, J. C., Kunreuther, H. C., & Schoemaker, P. J. H. (1982). Sources of bias in assessment procedures for utility functions. *Management Science, 28,* 936–954.

Hoch, S., & Loewenstein, G. (1989). Outcome feedback: Hindsight and information. *Journal of Experimental Psychology: Learning, Memory and Cognition, 15,* 605–619.

Hogarth, R. M. (1982). Beyond discrete biases: functional and dysfunctional aspects of judgmental heuristics. *Psychological Bulletin, 90,* 197–217.

Janis, I. L. (1972). *Victims of groupthink.* Boston: Houghton Mifflin.

Janis, I. L. (1982). *Counseling on personal decisions.* New Haven, CT: Yale University Press.

Janis, I. L., & Mann, L. (1977). *Decision making.* New York: Free Press.

Jungermann, H. (1984). The two camps on rationality. In R. W. Scholz (Ed.), *Decision making under uncertainty.* Amsterdam: Elsevier.

Kahneman, D., Slovic, P., & Tversky, A. (Eds.). (1982). *Judgment under uncertainty: Heuristics and biases.* New York: Cambridge University Press.

Kahneman, D., & Tversky, A. (1972). Subjective probability: A judgment of representativeness. *Cognitive Psychology, 3,* 430–454.

Kahneman, D., & Tversky, A. (1979). Prospect theory: An analysis of decisions under risk. *Econometrica, 47,* 263–281.

Keeney, R. L. (1993). *Value-focused thinking.* Cambridge, MA: MIT Press.

Kidd, J. B. (1970). The utilization of subjective probabilities in production planning. *Acta Psychologica, 34,* 338–347.

Kiesler, S., & Sproull, L. (1992). Group decision making and communication technology. *Organizational Behavior and Human Decision Processes, 52,* 96–123.

Koriat, A., Lichtenstein, S., & Fischhoff, B. (1980). Reasons for confidence. *Journal of Experimental Psychology: Human Learning and Memory, 6,* 107–118.

Langer, E. (1991). *Mindlessness.* Cambridge, MA: Harvard University Press.

Lanir, Z. (1982). *Strategic surprises.* Ramat Aviv: Tel Aviv University Press.

Lichtenstein, S., Fischhoff, B., & Phillips, L. D. (1982). Calibration of probabilities: State of the art to 1980. In D. Kahneman, P. Slovic, & A. Tversky (Eds.), *Judgment under uncertainty: Heuristics and biases* (pp. 306–334). New York: Cambridge University Press.

Lichtenstein, S., Slovic, P., & Zink, D. (1969). Effect of instruction in expected value on optimality of gambling decisions. *Journal of Experimental Psychology, 79,* 236–240.

March, J. G. (1978). Bounded rationality, ambiguity, and the engineering of choice. *The Bell Journal of Economics, 9,* 587–608.

McCormick, N. J. (1981). *Reliability and risk analysis.* New York: Academic Press.

Miller, G. A. (1956). The magical number seven, plus or minus two: Some limits on our capacity for processing information. *Psychological Review, 63,* 81–97.

Mischel, W. (1968). *Personality and assessment.* New York: Wiley.

Montgomery, H. (1983). Decision rules and the search for a dominance structure: Towards a process model of decision making. In P. Humphreys, O. Svenson, & A. Vari (Eds.), *Analyzing and aiding decision processes* (pp. 343–370). Amsterdam: North Holland.

Montgomery, H., & Svenson, O. (Eds.). (1993). *Process and structure in human decision making.* Chichester: Wiley.

Morgan, M. G., & Henrion, M. (1990). *Uncertainty: A guide to dealing with uncertainty in quantitative risk and policy analysis.* New York: Cambridge University Press.

National Interagency Incident Management System. (1982). *The what, why, and how of NIIMS.* Washington, DC: U.S. Dept. of Agriculture.

Nisbett, R. (Ed.). (1993). *Rules for reasoning.* Hillsdale, NJ: Erlbaum.

Nisbett, R. E., & Ross, L. (1980). *Human inference: Strategies and shortcomings of social judgment.* Englewood Cliffs, NJ: Prentice-Hall.

Payne, J. W. (1982). Contingent decision behavior. *Psychological Bulletin, 92,* 382–401.

Payne, J. W., Bettman, J. R., & Johnson, E. J. (1988). Adaptive strategy selection in decision making. *Journal of Experimental Psychology: Learning, Memory and Cognition, 14,* 534–552.

Perrow, C. (1984). *Normal accidents.* New York: Basic Books.

Peterson, C. R., & Beach, L. R. (1967). Man as an intuitive statistician. *Psychological Bulletin, 63,* 29–46.

Pitz, G. S., & Sachs, N. J. (1984). Behavioral decision theory. *Annual Review of Psychology, 35,* 139–163.

Plous, S. (Ed.). (1993). *The psychology of judgment and decision making.* New York: McGraw-Hill.

Raiffa, H. (1968). *Decision analysis.* Reading, MA: Addison-Wesley.

Rappoport, A., & Wallsten, T. S. (1972). Individual decision behavior. *Annual Review of Psychology, 23,* 131–175.

Rasmussen, J., & Rouse, W. B. (Eds.). (1981). *Human detection and diagnosis of system failure.* New York: Plenum.

Reason, J. (1990). *Human error.* New York: Cambridge University Press.

Rokeach, M. (1973). *The nature of human values.* New York: Free Press.

Ross, L., & Nisbett, R. E. (1992). *The person and the situation: Perspectives of social psychology.* New York: McGraw-Hill.

Samet, M. G. (1975). Quantitative interpretation of two qualitative scales used to rate military intelligence. *Human Factors, 17,* 192–202.

Schoemaker, P. J. H. (1983). The expected utility model: Its variants, purposes, evidence and limitations. *Journal of Economic Literature, 20,* 528–563.

Schwartz, N. (1994). Judgment in social context. In L. Berkowitz (Ed.), *Advances in experimental social psychology* (Vol. 26). San Diego, CA: Academic Press.

Shlyakhter, A. I., Kammen, D. M., Broido, C. L., & Wilson, R. (1994). Quantifying the credibility of energy projections from trends in past data: The U.S. energy sector. *Energy Policy, 22,* 119–131.

Simon, H. (1957). *Models of man: Social and rational.* New York: Wiley.

Slovic, P., & Lichtenstein, S. (1983). Preference reversals: A broader perspective. *American Economic Review, 73,* 596–605.

Slovic, P., Lichtenstein, S., & Fischhoff, B. (1988). Decision making. In R. C. Atkinson, R. J. Herrnstein, G. Lindzey, & R. D. Luce (Eds.), *Stevens' handbook of experimental psychology* (2nd ed., pp. 673–738). New York: Wiley.

Slovic, P., & Tversky, A. (1974). Who accepts Savage's axiom? *Behavioral Science, 19,* 368–373.

Stokey, E., & Zeckhauser, R. (1978). *A primer for policy analysis.* New York: W. W. Norton.

Svenson, O. (1981). Are we all less risky and more skillful than our fellow drivers? *Acta Psychologica, 47,* 143–148.

Tihansky, D. (1976). Confidence assessment of military air frame cost predictions. *Operations Research, 24,* 26–43.

Tversky, A. (1969). Intransitivity of preferences. *Psychological Review, 76,* 31–48.

Tversky, A., & Kahneman, D. (1973). Availability: A heuristic for judging frequency and probability. *Cognitive Psychology, 4,* 207–232.

Tversky, A., & Kahneman, D. (1981). The framing of decisions and the psychology of choice. *Science, 21,* 453–458.

von Winterfeldt, D., & Edwards, W. (1986). *Decision analysis and behavioral research.* New York: Cambridge University Press.

Wagenaar, W., & Sagaria, S. (1975). Misperception of experimental growth. *Perception and Psychophysics, 18,* 416–422.

Wallsten, T., & Budescu, D. (1983). Encoding subjective probabilities: A psychological and psychometric review. *Management Science, 29,* 151–173.

Watson, S., & Buede, D. (1990). *Decision synthesis.* New York: Cambridge University Press.

Weinstein, N. D. (1980). Unrealistic optimism about future life events. *Journal of Personality and Social Psychology, 39,* 806–820.

Wheeler, D. D., & Janis, I. L. (1980). *A practical guide for making decisions.* New York: Free Press.

Wilson, R., & Crouch, E. (1982). *Risk/benefit analysis.* Cambridge, MA: Ballinger.

Yates, J. F. (1989). *Judgment and decision making.* Chichester, England: Wiley.

11 Aligning the residuals: Risk, return, responsibility, and authority

Raghu Garud and Zur Shapira

The notion of proper governance structures is strongly related to the idea of checks and balances. Such an idea is evident in the institutional structure of modern states where power is distributed among the legislative, executive, and judicial branches. In modern corporations the question of checks and balances is centered on control – that is, who has the authority to make decisions. Since business firms are operating under uncertainty, many of their decisions are risky choices that may lead to undesired outcomes.

Consider the case of Nicholas Leeson, whose risky future trading decisions led to the downfall of the 250-year-old Barings Bank. Although investigators can end up blaming other managers for the disaster, the question of governance should have been dealt with prior to the downfall. Indeed, due to the devastating consequences of Leeson's activities for the bank's shareholders, managers, and employees, this case also raises questions about the identification of the parties in whose interests modern firms are run and how they should be governed.

The Leeson case points at a major problem in corporate governance: Control was not aligned with risk. Such an alignment is a basic premise of a firm's decision-making process (Milgrom & Roberts, 1992). Those who stand to lose their investment should have control over risk-taking activities. Indeed, this was the basic premise of the entrepreneurial theory of the firm (see Coase, 1993, p. 59). Under this approach, firms were identified with an entrepreneur who risked his or her capital and thus had control over the decisions made with this capital. Control and risk were therefore aligned.

As firms grew larger, entrepreneurs were no longer able to make all decisions. Consequently, entrepreneurs hired managers to run their firms.

We have benefited from the comments of Roger Dunbar, Edward Freeman, Don Kleinmuntz, and Arun Kumaraswamy.

This *separation of ownership and control* (Berle & Means, 1932), is a major turning point in the history of the firm. A problem that entrepreneurs faced once they hired managers was to make sure that managers made decisions in line with their interests. This *agency problem* (Alchian & Demsetz, 1972; Jensen & Meckling, 1976), is at the heart of the principal (owner)–agent (manager) relationship and may lead to potential differences in risk preferences. A manager may be interested, among other things, in protecting his or her job, and that may lead the manager to make decisions that may not be in line with the principal's risk preferences. To solve this problem, managerial returns had to be aligned with owners' interests.

From this discussion it appears that three major concepts need to be aligned: control, risk, and return. More accurately, what needs to be aligned are the *residuals* of these concepts – that is, what is left by issues that are not covered by the general legal agreements, rules, and regulations that govern a firm's decision-making process. Thus, *residual control* (or the *residual right to control*) refers to the right to make a decision about an asset's use that is not explicitly assigned by law or contract to another party (Milgrom & Roberts, 1992). *Residual return* refers to income left after all fixed obligations (including payments to lenders and bond holders) are met. *Residual risk* has been defined as the "difference between stochastic inflows of resources and promised payments to agents" (Fama & Jensen, 1983, p. 302).

The classical economics approach to corporate governance suggested that contracts be written to align the residuals. However, it is clear that complete contracts, those that specify all contingencies, cannot be written. Consequently, economists have struggled with the problem of contract incompleteness. To solve problems that could not be fully stipulated in *legal* contracts, economists developed ideas about *incentive* contracts to align managerial returns with owners' interests. Yet, recent scandals such as those at the Barings and Daiwa banks suggest that even the addition of incentive contracts to legal contracts is not sufficient to solve the control problem. In both cases, managers took risks that were "out of control," so to speak. This raises the question of whether there's more to risk than can be written in incentive contracts.

A basic premise of agency theory is that there is a divergence in interests between owners and agents, and that these divergences get translated into differences in risk preferences. Thus, it is possible that the control problems stem from risk-seeking managers who may take advantage of opportunities to behave in a reckless manner, as was the case in the Barings and Daiwa banks. Does the evidence support such a conjecture? It appears that the problem is actually reversed; managers are generally described as risk-averse agents who need to be induced to take risks (Milgrom & Roberts, 1992). The pervasiveness of risk aversion is puzzling because one would expect that incentive contracts would solve such a problem, but this is not the case. To examine this issue further, one needs to go beyond the legal and incentive contracts' layers and look at behavioral aspects of risk taking, which are at the core of the alignment of the identified residuals.

In a recent article, Kahneman and Lovallo (1993) discussed a paradoxical aspect of managerial risk taking. On the one hand, managers often provide overly optimistic forecasts, yet their attitudes toward risk are overly conservative. Kahneman and Lovallo documented several studies showing that managers are indeed risk averse and offered a cognitive account as to why these opposing trends in managerial behavior coexist. According to their analysis, an inside focus on the problem leads to biased-optimistic forecasts, while failure to aggregate over alternative projects leads to excessive risk aversion. Another perspective was offered in Shapira's (1995) analysis of managerial risk taking. He noted that managerial risk aversion is primarily determined by the salience of the ramifications of the negative consequences following risk taking that ended in failure. Both of these accounts suggests that risk and return may not be aligned in the minds of managers, at least not to the degree implied by finance theory (Sharpe, 1964).

As Shapira (1995, chapter 9) noted, the problem of assuming responsibility for failure in organizational decision making is an important aspect of managerial risk taking. It may be a major determinant of the pervasiveness of risk aversion in managerial decision making. According to his analysis, neither the legal nor the incentive contracts layers can solve the problem. Rather, the salience of the potential consequences of failure should be analyzed by looking at the perception and mutual understanding of an employee and a supervisor as to what constitutes sound risk taking. Only by invoking these behavioral aspects of risk taking can we hope to approach the problem of how to align risk, return, and control effectively.

This chapter attempts to deal with the problem by looking at the intimate relations between risk taking and the nature of the firm as it is defined by alternative notions of contracting. To that end, we start with a historical perspective on the firm, moving from the entrepreneurial theory of the firm through managerial capitalism to stakeholder approaches. Next, we examine control and risk as central issues in governance. We analyze the concept of control by breaking it into elements of authority and responsibility, and examine the similarities and differences between risk and return. The fourth section looks at determinants of aligned and misaligned residuals. Finally, an overview and some implications are offered in the Conclusion.

A historical perspective on the firm

Several books provide a historical account of the nature of the firm, and our purpose is not to provide a thorough overview. Rather, the goal is to provide the basic premises of three major approaches to the theory of the firm that prevail in this century. Entrepreneurial capitalism was a central approach in the 1930s (see Coase, 1993). Managerial capitalism started with the idea of separation of ownership and control (Berle & Means, 1932). One of its manifestation is agency theory, which thrived in the 1970s. Finally, stakeholder approaches were basic premises of the behavioral theory of the firm (Cyert & March, 1963) and got more attention in the 1980s (see Freeman, 1984).

Entrepreneurial capitalism

Entrepreneurs often bore residual risks, especially in early industrial settings, where all of their wealth was directly tied to the success or failure of an enterprise. In contrast, employees who entered into fixed wage-contracts with these entrepreneurs assumed less risk, preferring to earn a steady, regular wage over time. Indeed, the premium that these employees were willing to pay for their guaranteed wage was the source of the entrepreneurial wealth (Aoki, 1984; Knight, 1921).

During this era of entrepreneurial capitalism, residual control was also vested in entrepreneurs. One reason for aligning control and risk was to create the right incentives for entrepreneurs to maintain and increase the value of the firm (Milgrom & Roberts, 1992). Concentration of residual control also served to address two other problems. First, task indivisibilities created a context where individuals could free-ride on others. Free riding became possible because of the difficulties involved in measuring individual outputs and in giving each worker title to what he or she produced. Alchian and Demsetz's (1972) solution to the problem of moral hazard was to give one member of a team responsibility to monitor the activities of other members. To ensure that the monitor would have the appropriate incentives, he or she would be the residual claimant, as well as having residual control over the activities of the group. The result is a firm – an organization in which the entrepreneur hires, fires, and directs workers who are paid a fixed wage. This entrepreneur receives the residual returns.

Problems associated with contract incompleteness are another reason for the concentration of control in the hands of the entrepreneur (Milgrom & Roberts, 1992). Given the bounds to human rationality, it is difficult and costly to specify contingent claim contracts, especially under conditions of uncertainty. This leaves a contractual association open to conflict and negotiations, a prospect that can be costly too (Williamson, 1985).[1] A way to overcome this problem is to assign residual control to a group of people. Again, such an effort gives rise to a firm where the entrepreneur has administrative authority to direct his or her employees within a "zone of indifference" (Barnard, 1938).

Separation of ownership from control

As modern corporations became large, venture capitalists and shareholders found that they did not possess the managerial skills to run the companies they wanted to fund. Consequently, separation of ownership and control occurred (Berle & Means, 1932). Shareholders and venture capitalists bore residual risks while vesting residual control in managers.

The separation of ownership and control raised a key question: How should governance structures and incentive mechanisms be designed to ensure that those in control would maximize the wealth of those who bore the risk? After all, managers were the agents appointed by shareholders, who were the principal recipients of residual returns (see, e.g., Eisenhardt, 1989; Levinthal, 1988; Williamson & Winter, 1993). And, it was possible that the interests of principals and agents might diverge.

Because of the possibility of a divergence in interests between principal and agent, many control and monitoring systems have been instituted. For instance, even though they may have delegated the day-to-day functioning of a firm to its managers, shareholders have always retained the right to decide important issues that affect the firm. To help shareholders oversee the day-to-day operations of the firm and to provide them with the information needed to make decisions about larger issues, a board of directors was put in place to oversee managers' activities.

Shareholders' gains would increase to the extent that monitoring is minimized because monitoring is costly. A way to reduce monitoring costs was to provide managers with strong incentives (such as stock options) to align their interests with those of shareholders (see Zajac and Westphal, this volume). The expectation was that managers would be more likely to exercise control to increase the value of the corporation for shareholders and for themselves to the extent that the interests of the two parties were aligned.

Managerial capitalism

These governance mechanisms and incentive structures were a response to the increasing size and complexity of modern industrial corporations. However, these changing attributes set the stage for the advent of managerial capitalism. As firms grew very large and complex, it became difficult, if not impossible, for outsiders such as board members and shareholders to gain meaningful data from insiders – managers. In any case, because of the dispersion of ownership, many shareholders were at best absentee owners, with little motivation or knowledge to control the operations of a large corporation. Moreover, members of the board of directors who were supposed to monitor and control the activities of managers were themselves coopted by the managers (Finkelstein & Hambrick, 1989; O'Reilly, Main, & Crystal, 1988).

In the meantime, the very incentives that were supposed to align the interests of agents (the managers) and principals (the shareholders) led to a situation where the agents became more important than the principals themselves. Managers' salaries, perks, and stock options became exorbitant, and in many cases bore little resemblance to the performance of the firm (Crystal, 1991). Moreover, many managers crafted "golden para-chutes" that protected them from termination and "golden handcuffs" that compensated them in case their jobs were prematurely terminated (Wade, O'Reilly, & Chandratat, 1990). In short, firms were run by managers for managers – primarily top management.

It might appear that risk and control were both aligned with managers. However, this is not entirely the case. The notion of stock options demands that we refine traditional notions of risk. By providing managers with the right but not the obligation to exercise them, stock options effectively re-duce the downside risks associated with the variability of stock prices. Moreover, managers' control over the functioning of a highly complex operation provides them with an opportunity to manipulate stock prices so that they can benefit in the short term, even though their actions may not be in the best interest of the firm in the long run.

Consequently, rather than view risk as variability of outcomes, it is im-portant to distinguish between negative and positive outcomes; the former represent risks and the latter represent returns. Indeed, as Shapira (1995) found in his study of managerial attitudes and perceptions of risk taking, the former set of outcomes are associated with risk, whereas the latter set of outcomes are associated with returns. As March and Shapira (1992) suggest, this distinction has important behavioral implications relating to the kinds of "bets" that managers might make, depending upon whether they perceive themselves to be in a zone of risk or not.

From the perspective of those embracing the ideal of entrepreneurial capitalism, managerial capitalism represents a situation where share-holders bore the residual risk (by risking their capital), whereas managers gained residual returns, often making a bundle through the exercise of stock options while being protected by golden parachutes. However, a closer look at the activities of shareholders reveals that their losses too are limited, while there are few limits to their potential gains. Specifically, limited liability limits shareholders' losses to the value of their stock. And although such losses may be large, they are still limited compared to the devastating effect that entrepreneurs may suffer if all of their money is tied up in their own firm.

Besides limited liability protection, the very nature and meaning of shareholding have changed from the days of entrepreneurial capitalism. Specifically, shareholders can diversify their risks by investing in a portfo-lio of securities. Moreover, shareholders too can exercise "options," buying or selling shares (either directly or through mutual funds), depending upon the value of the stock. Indeed, the presence of shareholdings through mutual funds facilitates the dispersion of shareholdings and in-creases the ease with which options can be exercised, thereby further dis-tancing shareholders from firms.

Thus, distinguishing between risks and returns appears to be as useful for shareholders as it is for managers. Specifically, shareholders, like managers, enjoy both limited losses and unlimited gains. Consequently, a key question, from the perspective of incentives and governance, is: If the losses (and therefore the risk, as defined as the occurrence of negative outcomes) that managers and shareholders can suffer are limited, who else is at risk?

Stakeholder theories

An answer to this question provides an opening to those articulating a *stakeholder* view of the firm (e.g., Cyert & March, 1963; Freeman, 1984). This perspective suggests that there are stakeholders besides shareholders and managers whose interests must feature in determining the purpose and functioning of the firm. These stakeholders bear some of the residual risks and therefore must have some of the residual returns and controls.

Consider one group of stakeholders – employees. From the vantage point of entrepreneurial and managerial capitalism, risk-averse employees are paid a steady, fair wage and therefore should not receive residual returns. However, from a different perspective, employees are at tremendous risk. First, they develop firm-specific skills that are not easily re-deployable to other settings. In this sense, they have fewer options than shareholders and managers. Second, even if they have transferrable skills, employees are poorly protected from the downside risk of termination. If they are terminated, employees with firm-specific skills find it difficult to obtain comparable jobs in different firms. Third, unlike shareholders, traditional employees cannot diversify away their risk by taking other jobs in different organizations.

Employees are but one example of several stakeholders who bear residual risks involved in the functioning of modern corporations. Noting how risk is distributed among many stakeholders, researchers have argued that returns and controls must also be distributed. To redress existing imbalances, proponents of this perspective have argued that employees and other stakeholders must be given representation on the board of directors. They have also argued that employees must be given stock option plans so that their returns are commensurate with the risks they bear.

According to this historical perspective, the firm evolved from a simple, homogeneous entity to a more complex, heterogeneous one. This may make the alignment of residuals a more complicated task. Similarly, the concepts of risk and control may be more complex than they appear. To get a closer look at the problems associated with the alignment of risk and control, the next section provides an analysis that breaks the notion of control into elements of authority and responsibility and analyzes the asymmetries between risk and return.

Governance issues

The brief historical review illustrated that risks, returns, and controls were perfectly aligned in the era of entrepreneurial capitalism. However, when firms grew larger and ownership and control were separated, risks and controls ceased to be aligned. For a better understanding of these misalignments, the concepts of risk and control can be broken further. Control in organizational settings can be described as the power or authority to make decisions such as hiring and firing of employees or making investment decisions. A related issue is the notion of *responsibility*. A manager makes a decision, using her authority, and the decision leads to failure. Who is responsible for the failure, and who should suffer the consequences? In modern corporations, these questions are becoming increasingly important. Noting the potentially negative consequences of decisions, one can also claim that the process of making risky decisions should be distinguished from the decisions' consequences. As will be argued, dividing control into authority and responsibility on the one hand, and risk into downside and upside components on the other, may further our understanding of the problems associated with risk taking in organizations.

Authority and responsibility

Consider a home owner who decides not to install a new roof on his house and then suffers some damage to his house from a winter's storm. Clearly, the owner bears the risks of his decision and consequently has to pay for the damage that was caused. Consider the same decision, except that this time it was made by the owner's agent. Who is to blame now for the damage – the owner or the agent? As can be seen from the preceding example, the discussion of agency is intimately related to property rights (Alchian & Demsetz, 1972). Questions of decisions and their negative consequences are preeminent in organizations dealing with a variety of risky choices, such as medical decisions or those involving low-probability, high-consequences events (see Kunreuther & Meszaros, this volume).

In discussing the premises of governance in organizations, Arrow (1974) compares several alternatives, such as authority versus consensus and rules. He claims that discretionary authority, which is needed to coordinate activities in organizations, is often more efficient than more egalitarian mechanisms based on consensus. Arrow notes, however, that authority will often go wrong due to the inappropriate information available to the decision makers who have the authority, as well as to information overload. Consequently, he suggests that under conditions of uncertainty, responsible authority should find ways of reducing error. He links responsibility and authority by saying, "The basic deficiency of irresponsible authority from the functional viewpoint is the likelihood of unnecessary error" (p. 73).

Arrow's functional treatment of responsibility is based on information processing in organizations. He emphasizes the issue of overload and the capacity of managers to process information. In discussing the role of responsibility in risk taking in organizations, Shapira (1995) pursues the issue further by focusing on the judgment of the decision maker. Using the notion of an *employment contract,* Shapira argues that although such contracts specify the legal conditions under which a manager may be dismissed, they "do not include negative performance deviations arrived at by legal actions, but by faulty judgment" (p. 122). He further argues, similarly to Arrow, that the conditions under which risky decisions are made in organizational settings are characterized by uncertainty and ambiguity; hence, the issues of error and the ensuing responsibility are of major importance.

Indeed, these issues are central for middle and upper middle management. Shapira (1995) found that managers are very concerned about the consequences of risk taking that leads to failure. Although most managers reported that their organizations had no formal procedures for dealing with risk taking, many were unambiguous about the potential ramifications of risk taking that turned into failure. A vice president for a large commercial bank commented on reward and penalty arrangements in his organization by saying, "There are no penalties, except if you take risk and you guess wrong . . . you might get fired" (p. 57). And a financial analyst said, "Being the only analyst to recommend a certain stock, if you are right it singles you out as a star. If you are wrong, it won't be forgotten" (p. 56). Thus, even if the consequence of erroneous judgment is not job termination, managers feel that their superiors harbor negative feelings that will be held against them in future decisions.

Risk versus return

Two measures are most commonly used in the theory of finance to describe risk: the variance of the outcome distribution and the beta coefficient, which measures the degree to which a certain security or portfolio varies with the market portfolio (Sharpe, 1964). Both are measures of volatility depicting price movements that are associated with both positive and negative outcomes. Managers, however, although they acknowledge these measures, tend to think of risk in a different way. For them, risk is associated with the negative outcomes alone and hence is closer to the definition of a hazard rather than that of volatility. Indeed, managers define the downside part of the outcome distribution as risk while considering the upside part as return (Shapira, 1995).

The classical theory of finance (Sharpe, 1964) also stipulates that, on average, risk and return are positively correlated. Thus, if a person wants to obtain higher returns, she should take, on average, higher risks. Executives have different perspectives on this relationship, at least as it relates to the world of managerial risk taking. Their conception of the relationship is well captured by a senior vice president who responded to the statement "If you don't take risks, there won't be returns." His comment to the interviewer was, "The person who told you that did not prepare his homework well" (Shapira, 1995, p. 59). Evidently, for executives, managerial skills allow them to obtain high returns while minimizing risks (see Brenner & Shapira, 1983; Shapira, 1995). Such views, of course, are not immune to the "illusion of control" (Langer, 1975).

These managerial ideas about the differences between downside risks and upside returns, as well as the causal interpretation of the relationship between the two, lead executives to categorically deny that managerial risk taking is similar to gambling. Even though the difference may be obscured for a statistical decision theorist, good (i.e., ultimately successful) managers are perceived as risk takers but not as gamblers (i.e., those who failed). This distinction is embedded in the societal value system that approves of risk taking if the outcome is a success and deplores failures as resulting from gambling, almost without regard to the conditions that existed at the time of choice (March & Shapira, 1987). Furthermore, the definitions of success and failure are often post hoc reconstructions; therefore, one should not wonder why many managers hesitate to make risky choices. Evidently, the issue of responsibility for risk taking that led to failure looms large in their minds.

Aligning risks and controls

The preceding discussion suggests that in the minds of managers, risks are the downside and returns are the upside parts of the outcome distribution. Although the normative theory of decision doesn't make this distinction, it is evident that managers are worried about downside risks more than they tune to upside returns. This leads to a concern with the responsibility for one's own decisions. When controls are analyzed as composed of authority and responsibility, the importance of aligning the two becomes evident.

It is important to note that although authority has a legal basis, it cannot rest only on legal sanctions to be implemented. As Arrow (1974) noted, following Simon (1951), an employment contract is different from a regular contract to purchase or sell a commodity. The former is an explicit arrangement by which the employee accepts the authority of a superior. Arrow argues that achieving authority (control) using reward/punishment sanctions cannot be fully achieved and that it may be very costly to implement. He argues that "Ultimately, authority is viable to the extent that it is the focus of convergent expectations" (p. 72). Such a view echoes Barnard's (1938) notion of the *zone of indifference* and Simon's (1947) notion of the *zone of acceptance,* which clarify the reciprocal nature of subordinate–superior relation that leads to effective authority. These notions have been the cornerstones of the treatment of authority in the organizational behavior literature.

Applying similar ideas to risk taking in organizations, Shapira (1995) suggested that there are three layers determining the relation between responsibility and sound risk taking in organizations. First, there is the *legal layer*, which stipulates the general guidelines governing risk taking but doesn't cover those situations in which negative outcomes occur due to legal actions but faulty judgment. A second layer that has been proposed to deal with such situations is the use of *incentive contracts*. However, although such contracts may align the interests of a principal and an agent, they don't cover all potential contingencies (e.g., contract incompleteness). In addition, as noted by Baker, Jensen, and Murphy (1988), the practice of linking rewards to performance in business firms is not common.

Clearly, neither legal nor incentive contracts provide an answer to the question of who should assume responsibility for the failed outcomes of decisions arrived at by a properly motivated agent who had faulty (in retrospect) judgment. If both principals and agents were rational, according to the classical approach to risk taking, the problem might not have existed. However, as the preceding discussion demonstrates, in the minds of both agents and principals, the responsibility for failed risk taking is not a peripheral issue. This is important because both would most likely acknowledge that in taking risks under conditions of uncertainty and ambiguity, outcomes can be defined only up to a probability distribution. Consequently, under conditions of uncertainty and ambiguity, there may be differences between a manager and her superior regarding who is responsible for risky decisions that led to bad outcomes. Thus, Shapira (1995) proposed the need for a third layer (beyond the legal and incentive contract layers) focusing on the *perceptions* and *mutual understanding* between a manager and her superior as to what constitutes sound risk taking.

The question of responsibility for risk taking is therefore a consequence of the inevitability of errors when decisions are made under conditions of uncertainty and ambiguity. Both legal and incentive contracts suffer from the problem of contract incompleteness and cannot solve the problem of responsibility. Contract incompleteness is acknowledged in the arena of market transactions and contracting as well (Williamson, 1981). Dealing with the issue of residual risks in market transactions goes beyond the domain of a formal contract to the domain of *trust*. The comparable element in organizational settings is the treatment of residual risks and control by invoking the concept of trust and its role in corporate culture (Gibbons, in press; Kreps, 1990). The preceding discussion deals with the basics of trust and culture because the issue of shared perceptions and understanding (Shapira, 1995) and convergent expectations (Arrow, 1974) are the building blocks of trust and corporate culture. In the language used in the first parts of this chapter, these are the building blocks that may lead to alignment of risks, returns, and controls in the modern corporation.

Building an organizational culture that consists of shared perceptions and convergent expectations, one that fosters mutual understanding, may be easier said than done. Do such elements exist in modern corporations? The answer may not be as positive as one may wish. In the next section, a couple of examples are described and some determinants of aligned and misaligned residuals are discussed.

Contrasting approaches to corporate governance

The situation in Japanese corporations

Milgrom and Roberts (1992, p. 317) reported that a typical board of directors in a Japanese firm is made up almost exclusively of full-time employees. The stock in Japanese firms is, to a large extent, in the friendly hands of affiliated companies, suppliers, customers, or banks with long-term relationships with the firm. These owners will not sell a firm's stock under normal conditions, nor are they likely to participate in a proxy contest. The executives of major Japanese corporations have typically spent their entire careers in their companies, and there is little possibility of a senior executive being lured away from one major firm to another.

In whose interests are Japanese corporations run? The results of a survey of Japanese middle managers and presidents of major Japanese firms are revealing. When asked to whom the firm should belong, middle managers ranked employees and society higher than shareholders and customers. Presidents ranked employees almost as highly as they did shareholders. Both groups ranked employees as the major beneficiaries when asked in whose interests they thought firms were actually run (Milgrom & Roberts, 1992, p. 41). Indeed, as Aoki (1984) stated, managers in Japanese corporations can be viewed as mediating between the interests of two different principals – employees and investors.

In support of Aoki's observations, Milgrom and Roberts suggest that in many ways Japanese employees are residual claimants on firms' assets and have residual decision-making power at least on par with that of the investors in the firm. They report that decision-making power is pushed down the managerial hierarchy to the shop floor. Employees receive a sizable proportion of their income in the form of bonuses that are linked to the performance of the firm. Only a small proportion of the firm's cash flow is paid out to investors as dividends; the majority is reinvested in the firm to permit its continued growth and survival (1992, pp. 349–350).

The situation in American corporations

These practices stand out in clear contrast to those of firms in many other industrialized countries, including the United States. It was noted before how in the United States, for instance, managerial and entrepreneurial capitalism resulted in the creation of externalities wherein residual control and return might reside with one group and residual risk might reside with another. In recent years, American corporations have become more aware of the interests of other stakeholders. Thus, social responsibility and environmental issues have gotten more attention. Yet, it appears that concern with control occupies the minds of shareholders and top management. The struggle for corporate control in the 1980s brought waves of mergers, leveraged buyouts, and hostile takeovers. These led to a debate about the efficiency, or rather inefficiency, of market mechanisms versus internal mechanisms for corporate control (Jensen, 1993).

It appears that the relations between top management and shareholders are not smooth, and there are many accusations that top management is not pursuing the goals of the shareholders (Crystal, 1991: Jensen, 1993). At the same time, relations between top management and employees are often described as adversarial. Consider the hostile takeovers discussed by Shleifer and Summers (1988). They provide additional arguments that suggest how employees are at much higher risk than they might imagine because of hostile takeovers. Shleifer and Summers argue that hostile takeovers create a breach of trust that effectively changes the balance between risks and returns. Specifically, there is a premium attached to the trust that employees bestow on their current employers for continued employment. The tacit understanding that emerges from this trusting relationship translates into a depressed wage initially but one that will, over the life of the contract, lead to a wage that might be considered fair. Shleifer and Summers suggest that this arrangement works only to the extent to which there is trust and understanding between managers and employees. The problem is that after a hostile takeover, the new management is under little obligation to honor the implicit contract. In many such instances, existing employees are let go, truncating their income stream at a point in their employment contract that does not adequately compensate them for their prior efforts.

Some impediments to alignment

The previous examples indicate that aligning risks, returns, and controls among different stakeholders is not easy. There are some enduring differences that work against the prospect of successful alignment. Some of these elements have to do with asymmetries in the power, perspectives, and aspirations of different stakeholders.

Asymmetries in power. Often those who wield authority (managers) have the power to structure transactions so that the risks and returns are borne asymmetrically. This power is enhanced by their access to information, allowing them to shape the information that shareholders, members of the board, and employees may receive. For instance, as Heath, Knez, and

Camerer (1993) suggest, managers may strategically withhold information from their employees in an attempt to maintain employee motivation. Withholding strategic information can lead employees to believe that they are secure under the current contract, when in fact they may not be.

This problem is further exacerbated by the impossibility of ascribing responsibility later to an event. It arises from the ways in which decisions are sometimes made in modern corporations. Specifically, managers often set the premises of decisions while not making the decisions themselves. While not constituting decisions in themselves, these premises set the stage for certain decisions to emerge. Eventually, if something goes wrong, there is always a shield of "plausible deniability" that protects managers while exposing employees to the consequences of an action.

Asymmetries in perspectives. Employees' false sense of security may be bolstered by two types of biases that employees' position can create. To understand the nature of these biases, we use the distinction between *inside* and *outside perspectives* (Kahneman & Lovallo, 1993). By implication insiders are those who are directly engaged in an activity. By contrast, outsiders may be associated with an activity, but only indirectly. Of course, any distinction between insiders and outsiders is a matter of degree. In addition, a person may be an insider on one problem and an outsider on another. However, along a spectrum, employees are more insiders than shareholders, with managers falling somewhere in between.

Insiders may be more prone to exhibit overconfidence (Kahneman & Lovallo, 1993). In particular, insiders are more likely to ignore statistics that can provide a realistic sense of how others have fared (on average) on similar jobs. Moreover, insiders are likely to ignore negative cues; instead, they attempt to enact their realities by projecting particularly rosy scenarios (Garud & Ahlstrom, 1995).

Overconfidence frequently leads to a situation where insiders who are at risk may not perceive themselves to be at risk. For instance, Heath et al. (1993) point out that for strategic and emotional reasons, people may be particularly unwilling to imagine the occurrence of negative events. Moreover, employees may have inflated expectations about their employment contracts as a reasonable response to biased information that they might receive from their employers. Insiders may assume that they are operating under the explicit directions of superiors who will supposedly be responsible for the consequences of decisions. However, as suggested earlier, responsibility is often an intractable concept when applied to large, complex corporations. Under such conditions, responsibility for an outcome often "rests" with those who are unable to create a shield of plausible deniability – often the employees.

Furthermore, perspectives can change over time. Thus, considering the preceding analysis by Shleifer and Summers (1988), it can be argued that shareholders would occasionally prefer hostile takeovers, as they, along with the new management, benefit from the wages not paid to employees under the implicit contract with them. Thus, shareholders may exhibit dynamic inconsistency over time. On the one hand, they would like to establish a trusting relationship with employees ex-ante. On the other hand, once employees develop nonfungible skills, shareholders may prefer a hostile takeover to increase their own wealth. Employees, in contrast, are often unable to appreciate the risks they may be exposed to for several reasons. First, employees are likely to systematically underestimate the probability of negative events. Second, they may not even recognize exceptional situations when they occur (Heath et al., 1993). Such perceptions may evolve from overconfidence or from emotional and strategic reasons alluded to previously. Third, employees may not appreciate that their entitlements might change when these negative events occur. For all these reasons, those who might be at risk ex-post may not realize that they are at risk ex-ante. Therefore, they may not have the incentives to structure a contract that adequately compensates them for the residual risk they might bear ex-post.

Asymmetries in aspirations. In March and Shapira's (1987, 1992) model, risk taking is affected by the decision maker's resources, as well as by the target she focuses on when making a choice. Given the same resources, a person can take different degrees of risk if she focuses on survival or on her aspiration level. In particular, the model suggests that a person who is below her aspiration target would take larger risks if she focuses on the aspiration level than if she focuses on the target of survival. Risk taking is therefore context dependent, and the same person is likely to take different risks (with the same resources) when focusing on alternative targets.

Consider a firm that encounters difficulties and is unable to pay its debts. Increases in its earnings may have to be paid to the lenders, who become the claimants of the residual returns. A post hoc externalization of risk is exacerbated by some of the dynamics that unfold as the firm deteriorates. Managers who have authority and who are partly residual claimants are motivated to take on more risks when the firm's performance deteriorates below a certain point. Protected by golden parachutes and golden handcuffs, managers have little to lose but much to gain from any efforts that enhance the value of their stock options. Moreover, the shield of plausible deniability further protects managers even when they make particularly risky choices that verge on gambling. The additional risk that managers might expose a firm to through their actions is eventually borne by those stakeholders (such as employees) who have little say in shaping the premises of a decision. Thus, the externalization of risk and the abnegation of responsibility by those in authority create a context where corporations and the communities built around them might fail.

Conclusion

In the traditions of behavioral decision theory, organizational decision making, and organization theory, we looked at the issues of aligning risk, return, and control as they affect risk taking in organizations, and as they are affected by and reflected in the changing nature of the firm. It appears that these issues are at the core of individual risk taking in organizations, as well as basic to the definition of the firm.

We started with the paradox noted by Kahneman and Lovallo (1993) regarding excessive risk aversion in organizations, followed by Shapira's (1995) observation that the paradox lies within the problem of assuming responsibility for the consequences of failed risk taking in organizations. In the development of the theory of the firm from entrepreneurial through managerial to stakeholder capitalism, it is evident that aligning risks, returns, and controls became more difficult due to growth in the size and complexity of the firm. Acknowledging that increased complexity leads to indeterminacy (Radner, this volume), on the one hand, and to increased concerns by middle management with the consequences of failed risk taking, on the other, it appears that a major concept underlying the theory of the firm should be *contract incompleteness*. As noted previously, under the naive view of entrepreneurial capitalism, residuals were aligned and legal contracts completely spelled out the alignment. Following the separation of ownership and control, it became clear that risk, return, and control may not be aligned, and incentive contracts were proposed as a remedy. However, as agency theorists concede (Baker et al., 1988; Jensen, 1993), these did not solve the problem. Shapira's (1995) analysis pointed to the need to specify a third layer (on top of the legal and incentive contracts layers) to address the question of residual responsibility. The idea is that shared perceptions, mutual understanding (Shapira, 1995), and convergent expectations (Arrow, 1974) are needed to deal with the responsibility question. These notions are intimately related to the notion of psychological contracting (Robinson & Rousseau, 1994; Rousseau, 1989) and relational contracting (MacNeil, 1983) that are aimed at closing the gap in standard notions of contracting.

Diagnosing the problem as one of contract incompleteness is common to a variety of disciplines such as economics, organizational behavior, and organization theory. Diagnosis itself does not mean that tools to deal with the problem are at hand. The concepts that emerge from the discussion of contract incompleteness have to do with trust, corporate culture, mutual understanding, and convergent expectations. Work is underway by many researchers to analyze these concepts. Based on this work, a framework for a theory of the firm will be developed.

Two main lines of thought have led the way. One has to do with the notion of *implicit* contracting and the other with *explicit* contracting. The former prevails in the Japanese culture, and as Smitka (1994) noted, their idea is that contracting itself is the major issue and that it can be done without a written, legal contract. The alternative notion had been suggested by economists (Gibbons, in press) who are trying to define trust and corporate culture based on the notion of repeated games (Kreps, 1990). These attempts will continue and may even converge (see Radner's discussion, this volume). Time will tell whether one, the other, or a combination of the two provides a more useful approach.

In the meantime, as the tradition of decision making has taught us, both approaches, implicit and explicit contracting, may be needed in different situations. Borrowing from behavioral decision theory, we can follow Kahneman and Tversky (1986), who noted that expected utility may be a good approach for analyzing individual decision making under *transparent* conditions but that alternative models such as prospect theory may do a better job in *opaque* situations. On the organizational decision-making level, March and Shapira (1982) and March (this volume) pointed to alternative perspectives that are needed to further our understanding of decision making in organizational settings. The collaborative effort of researchers in different paradigms may lead to a more comprehensive analysis of the causes and consequences of contract incompleteness, which in turn will lead to a better understanding of the nature of the firm.

Note

1   A similar analysis with respect to the difficulties in discovering prices in the market led Coase (1937) to propose a rationale for why firms exixt.

References

Alchian, A., & Demsetz, H. (1972). Production, information costs, and economic organization. *American Economic Review, 62,* 777–797.
Aoki, M. (1984). *The co-operative game theory of the firm.* New York: Oxford University Press.
Arrow, K. (1974). *The limits of organization.* New York: W. W. Norton.
Baker, G., Jensen, M., & Murphy, K. (1988). Compensation and incentives: Practice vs. theory. *Journal of Finance, 43,* 593–616.
Barnard, C. (1938). *The functions of the executive.* Cambridge, MA: Harvard University Press.
Berle, A. A., & Means, G. C. (1932). *The modern corporation and private property.* New York: Macmillan.
Brenner, M., & Shapira, Z. (1983). Environmental uncertainty as determining merger activity. In W. Goldberg (Ed.), *Mergers: Motives, modes, methods* (pp. 51–65). New Brunswick, NJ: Nichols.
Coase, R. H. (1937). The nature of the firm. *Economica, 4,* 386–405.
Coase, R. H. (1993). The nature of the firm: Meaning. In O. Williamson & S. Winter (Eds.), *The nature of the firm: Origins, evolution and development* (pp. 18–33). New York: Oxford University Press.

Crystal, G. S. (1991). *In search of excess: The overcompensation of American executives,* New York: W. W. Norton.

Cyert, R., & March, J. (1963). *A behavioral theory of the firm.* Englewood Cliffs, NJ: Prentice-Hall.

Eisehardt, K. (1989). Agency theory: An assessment and review. *Academy of Management Review, 14,* 57–74.

Fama, E. F., & Jensen, M. C. (1983). Agency problems and residual claims. *Journal of Law and Economics, 26,* 327–349.

Finkelstein, S., & Hambrick, D. C. (1989). Chief executive compensation: A study of the intersection of markets and political processes. *Strategic Management Journal, 10,* 121–134.

Freeman, R. E. (1984). *Strategic management: A stakeholder approach.* Boston: Pitman.

Garud, R., & Ahlstrom, D. (1995). *Differences in the assessment of technological fields by insider and outsider researchers.* Working paper, New York University.

Gibbons, R. (In press). Game theory and garbage cans: An introduction to the economics of internal organization. In J. Halpern & R. Stern (Eds.), *Debating rationality: Nonrational aspects of organizational decision making.* Ithaca, NY: Cornell University Press.

Heath, C., Knez, M., & Camerer, C. (1993). The strategic management of the entitlement process in the employment relationship. *Strategic Management Journal, 14,* 74–93.

Jensen, M. (1993). The modern industrial revolution, exit, and the failure of internal control mechanisms. *Journal of Finance, 48,* 831–880.

Jensen, M. C., & Meckling, W. H. (1976). Theory of the firm: Managerial, behavior, agency costs and ownership structure. *Journal of Financial Economics, 3,* 305–360.

Kahneman, D., & Lovallo, D. (1993). Timid choices and bold forecasts: A cognitive perspective on risk taking. *Management Science , 39,* 17–31.

Kahneman, D., & Tversky, A. (1986). Rational choice and the framing of decisions. *Journal of Business, 59,* S251–S278.

Knight, F. H. (1921). *Risk, uncertainty, and profit.* Boston: Houghton Mifflin.

Kreps, D. (1990). Corporate culture and economic theory. In J. Alt & K. Shepsle (Eds.), *Perspectives on positive political economy* (pp. 90–143). New York: Cambridge University Press.

Langer, E. (1975). The illusion of control. *Journal of Personality and Social Psychology, 32,* 311–328.

Levinthal, D. (1988). A survey of agency models in organizations. *Journal of Economic Behavior and Organization, 9,* 153–185.

MacNeil, I. (1983). *The new social contract: An inquiry into modern contractual relations.* New Haven, CT: Yale University Press.

March, J. G., & Shapira, Z. (1982). Behavioral decision theory and organizational decision theory. In G. Ungson & D. Braunstein (Eds.), *Decision making: An interdisciplinary inquiry* (pp. 92–115). Boston: Kent.

March, J. G., & Shapira, Z. (1987). Managerial perspectives on risk and risk taking. *Management Science, 33,* 1404–1418.

March, J. G., & Shapira, Z. (1992). Variable risk preferences and the focus of attention. *Psychological Review, 99,* 172–183.

Milgrom, P., & Roberts, J. (1992). *Economics, organization and management.* Englewood Cliffs, NJ: Prentice-Hall.

O'Reilly, C., Main, B., & Crystal, G. (1988). CEO compensation as tournament and social comparison: A tale of two theories. *Administrative Science Quarterly, 25,* 129–141.

Robinson, S., & Rousseau, D. (1994). Violating the psychological contract: Not the exception but the rule. *Journal of Organizational Behavior, 15,* 245–259.

Rousseau, D. (1989). Psychological and implied contracts in organizations. *Employees Responsibilities and Rights Journal, 2,* 121–139.

Shapira, Z. (1995). *Risk taking: A managerial perspective.* New York: Russell Sage Foundation.

Sharpe, W. (1964). Capital asset prices: A theory of market equilibrium under conditions of risk. *Journal of Finance, 19,* 425–442.

Shleifer, A., & Summers, L. H. (1988). Breach of trust in hostile takeovers. In A. J. Auerbach (Ed.), *Corporate takeovers: Causes and consequences* (pp. 33–67). Chicago: University of Chicago Press.

Simon, H. (1947). *Administrative behavior.* New York: Free Press.

Simon, H. (1951). A formal theory of the employment relation. *Econometrica, 19,* 293–305.

Smitka, M. (1994). Contracting without contracts: How Japanese manage organizational transactions. In S. Sitkin & R. Bies (Eds.), *The legalistic organization.* Thousands Oaks, CA: Sage.

Wade, J. B., O'Reilly, C. A., & Chandratat I. (1990). Golden parachutes: CEO's and the exercise of social influence. *Administrative Science Quarterly, 35,* 587–603.

Williamson, O. E. (1981). The modern corporation: Origins, evolution, attributes. *Journal of Economic Literature, 19,* 1537–1568.

Williamson, O. E. (1985). *The economic institutions of capitalism.* New York: Free Press.

Williamson, O. E., & Winter, S. G. (Eds.). (1993). *The nature of the firm: Origins, evolution and development.* New York: Oxford University Press.

12 Organizational decision making as rule following

Xueguang Zhou

Introduction

In recent years, studies of decision making have witnessed an increasing sophistication in modeling decision situations. Since the early days of simple choice-based probabilistic models, we have witnessed the evolution of complex statistical techniques incorporating uncertainty, multiple objectives, n-players, dynamic games, and Bayesian models. These models introduce additional factors in decision-making processes and in this sense move closer to real decision situations. Nonetheless, they put enormous demands on the decision makers to collect and make use of information and to adopt complex decision rules. In contrast, there is mounting evidence that individuals and organizations tend to adopt simple rules and heuristics in making decisions. Satisficing rather than optimizing has long been recognized as a basic rule regulating organizational decisions (Simon, 1957). Organizations often adopt simple rules in making decisions about R&D investment (Dosi, 1988). Predictable behaviors (i.e., simpler decisions) are induced precisely because of the complexity of the decision situation (Heiner, 1983). There is also evidence that simple rules often outperform complex models in game experiments (Axelrod, 1984). Organizational decision making is often governed by stable rules, and much of organizational decision making can be characterized as rule-following behavior. "Action is often based more on identifying the normatively appropriate behavior than on calculating the return expected from alternative choices" (March & Olsen, 1989, p. 22).

This chapter is based on an ongoing collaborative research project with James March and Martin Schulz on the evolution of organizational rules. The ideas developed here have benefited from conversations with them on many occasions. I am grateful to Frank Dobbin, Shin-Kap Han, John Meyer, Zur Shapira, and Patricia Thornton for their constructive comments that helped improve this chapter.

In this chapter, I explore the basis of rule-following behavior and its implications for understanding organizational decision making. By *rule following*, I refer to the regularity and predictability in individual and organizational behavioral patterns that are either "preprogrammed" by implicit rules, such as norms, conventions, and standards, or based on explicit rules, such as formal procedures, policies, and regulations. My purpose is to develop a broader conceptualization of the rule-following behavior that rests on social processes beyond organizational boundaries and the immediate decision situation, and to extend these ideas to the study of organizational decision making. I first explore the basis of rule-following behavior and its effects on the social construction of the decision makers and the decision-making process. My discussion is organized around two imageries of rationality, collective and contextual, in contrast to models of individual rationality. I then extend these ideas to explore the implications of rule-following behavior for organizational flexibility, change, and innovation. Empirical evidence is drawn from my research on the evolution of organizational rules at Stanford University as well as from secondary sources in the literature.

Choice versus rule following

Let me begin by contrasting two models of organizational decision making: choice versus rule following. Behaviors portrayed in these two models entail two different if not incompatible logics. Behavior in rational choice models follows the logic of optimization, albeit subject to various constraints. In a stylistic model, individuals are expected to have a well-defined utility function, face a set of alternatives, evaluate the consequences attached to these alternatives, and make decisions according to a set of decision rules such that the outcome maximizes the decision maker's (expected) utility function, subject to various constraints imposed on the decision situation.

Rule-following behavior, in contrast, follows the logic of appropriateness. March (1994, this volume) describes three issues decision makers commonly face: (1) the question of recognition, whereby the decision makers make sense of the decision situation; (2) based on such recognition, a search for self-identity located in the particular organizational context; and (3) applying appropriate rules to the specific decision context. In contrast to the decision maker in the rational choice model, the rule-following actor does not attempt to maximize the outcome; rather, he or she asks "What is the appropriate course of action that I should take?" The process of decision making is that of recognizing the social role one is to play and matching appropriate rules to the situation (March & Olsen, 1989).

Several corollaries can be drawn from these two models. First, decision making in the rational choice model is characteristically calculating. Decision makers are expected to gather information, compare alternatives, and assess their respective consequences. In contrast, rule following is based on routines, which economize on information, and eliminate alternatives. Second, consequential calculation is characteristic of anticipating behavior, focusing on the immediate decision situation, whereas rule following emphasizes interpretation, making sense of expectations that are embedded in context and history. Third, behavior in the rational choice model portrays an optimization effort specific, and hence local, to the immediate decision situation. By contrast, rule-following behavior tends to be based on general principles independent of the decision situation. Thus, rule-following behavior suggests a trade-off between global stability and local maximization.

That much of what an organization does can be characterized as rule following is not novel. The idea was presented in Weber's classic model of bureaucracy and elaborated in the early organization literature (Cyert & March, 1963; March & Simon, 1958). Organizational rules specify authority relationships, maintain everyday activities, and span the boundaries of the organization. Organizational decision making follows rules, too. As Cyert and March (1963) pointed out: "The way in which the organization searches for alternatives is substantially a function of the operating rules it has" (p. 112).

In the current literature, however, organizational rules and rule-following behavior are construed in a narrow sense. One interpretation, originated by Weber (1946), sees organizational rules as the technical requirements to ensure the efficiency of modern bureaucracy. In this light, rules are seen as part of the functional structure of the organization. Another interpretation in the decision literature sees rules and norms as emerging from the immediate interaction among the players or at least traceable to iterated games well understood by the players or the analysts. Such an interpretation treats rules and rule-following behavior as merely the derivative of individual optimizing behavior and thereby can be understood within the decision context.

I adopt a broad conceptualization of the rule-following behavior. To understand organizational decision making, we need to go beyond the immediate decision situation and appreciate the formal or informal rules that constrain decision makers, shape their judgment on risks and preferences, frame their choices and alternatives, and construct the decision rules that they are taught to follow. At the micro level, the role of the decision maker may be framed through the construction of social identities, expectations, and behavioral patterns. Activities by decision makers can be understood in part as a search for identity fulfillment and applying appropriate rules to the decision situation. At the macro level, processes of decision making are structured and constrained by the broader social context outside organizations. Thus a focus on rule-following behavior directs us to examine the institutional processes that generate and construct social identities and rational imageries that decision makers are to follow.

Organizational rules as collective rationality

It is well recognized that stability and predictability are virtues for an organization, valued both by those who engage in transactions with the organization and those affected by decisions within the organization (Hannan & Freeman, 1984; March, 1991). Organizational rules provide the structure for predictable behavior and establish identities for organizations. It is not incidental that rule-following behavior prevails especially in the organizational context. The effectiveness of rules depends on the capacity to enforce them and on the existence of devices to sanction those who violate them. Stable organizational structures provide persistent incentives, monitoring and sanction mechanisms to enforce rules and induce rule-following behavior. It is also true that decision making in an organizational setting is, to borrow an expression from game theory, a repeated game in which learning can accumulate and behavior is conditioned. Even in the model of choice, as Akerlof (1980) noted, utility-maximizing behavior by rule breaking may not be imitated if there exist social sanctions such as a loss of reputation.

In contrast to the perception of rules as technical requirements, research on organizational rules often describes them as the embodiment of a "negotiated order": Rules are used to define collective goods or to record the collective understanding of the boundaries of individual goods. As such, organizational rules reflect a form of collectively constructed rationality that deviates considerably from that of individual rationality. Three themes are especially prevalent in the literature: rules as management of conflicts, as management of uncertainty, and as retention of organizational learning.

Rules as management of conflicts

In an earlier study of organizations in the industrial setting, Gouldner (1954) found that bureaucratic rules are used as the managerial control device that substitutes for "close supervision" (see esp. chapter 4). The use of rules avoids tensions between impersonal bureaucratic authority and social norms surrounding the organization. Rules become substitutes for direct authority relationships. In the French context, Crozier (1964) studied two public agencies and found the pervasive use of organizational rules in routinization of behavior: "[N]othing seems to be left of arbitrary whim and individual initiative of an organization member. The daily behavior of everyone, as well as his chances of having to perform a different routine later, can be predicted exactly. In such a system, as we have established, hierarchical dependence relationships tend to disappear or at least to decline considerably" (p. 188).

In a different light, organizational rules are also seen as protective mechanisms for those regulated by rules. Perrow (1986) argued that "rules protect those who are subject to them. Rules are means of preserving group autonomy and freedom; to reduce the number of rules in an organization generally means to make it more impersonal, more inflexible, more standardized" (p. 24). To Perrow, the reduction of formal rules leaves employees vulnerable to the arbitrary intervention and judgment by managers. It is observed that employees in organizations often see organizational rules as protective mechanisms and resist changes in these procedures (Crozier 1964).

Rules as management of uncertainty

Conventional wisdom tells us that rule-following behavior occurs in situations where repetitive tasks are performed. Recognizing bounded rationality in information processing in organizations, Cyert and March (1963) advocated the idea that organizations use rules to manage information flow and regulate decision processes. In this light, the demand for rules occurs exactly in times of uncertainty.

Heiner's (1983) theory of the origin of predictable behavior is especially relevant in this respect. Heiner pointed out that uncertainty is generated by the inevitable gap between limited competence and the difficulty in selecting most preferred alternatives, and that the limits to maximizing and the prevalence of uncertainty are the basic sources of predictable behavior. He demonstrated that deviations from rules are at times desirable but ignored because of uncertainty in reliably interpreting potential information about when to deviate. Heiner also noted that "optimizing with no uncertainty in choosing more preferred alternatives does not tend to produce systematic and stable regularity in behavior. Rather, it tends to destroy such regularity as successively more information can be reliably interpreted in guiding more complex behavior" (p. 572). In a world of uncertainty, then, predictable behavior is rewarded and behavior aimed at optimization is often penalized. As a result, reducing variance in performance is valued more highly than increasing the mean (March 1988). A large proportion of managerial behavior can be understood in this light. For instance, Brenner and Shapira (1983) examined the merger activities among American corporations between 1948 and 1972 and found that they were largely managerial efforts to reduce environmental uncertainty. In a study of the proliferation of special rules in the U.S. House of Representatives, Bach and Smith (1988) argued that the proliferation of restrictive rules has less to do with the centralization of power than with the effort to manage the high uncertainty resulting from the complicated process of agenda setting. Consequently, the promulgation of restrictive rules was supported not only by the Democratic party leaders and Rules Committee members, but also by those standing committees whose legislation is at risk on the floor.

Although uncertainty also occupies a central place in recent models of choice, the striking difference is that in models of choice, uncertainty produces more sophisticated calculation, whereas in models of rule following uncertainty leads to a narrower range of choice and more stable rule-following behavior. Rules and rule-governed behavior are often motivated less by optimization considerations than by an effort to avoid uncertainty.

Rules as retention of learning experience

Organizations are based on routines, which embody the knowledge an organization accumulates over time with regard to the technology, process, and operation of the organization. As such they are closely related to organizational learning. In this light, organizational rules such as routines, standard operating procedures, and regulations are the storage of organizational memory (Levitt & March, 1988; Nelson & Winter, 1982). Learning plays an important role in recent studies of the emergence of norms and institutions. For instance, Axelrod (1986) proposes an evolutionary approach to the emergence of norms: Players retain those practices that worked better and discard those that failed.

The accumulation of knowledge is often an incremental learning process. An often noted aspect of this process is learning by doing, or experiential learning. This model assumes an endogenous process within the specific history path whereby the accumulation of experience induces, and is reflected in, the subsequent modification of behavior. The core idea in the learning-by-doing process is path dependency. That is, organizations are constrained by the structure and knowledge that are built up in their history. Arrow (1974) attributes the characteristic of path dependency to the cost of information. Experience and information gained in the past decrease the cost of learning in the neighborhood of the familiar area and put a higher price tag on explorations into unfamiliar territories. Path dependency may result from the stable authority relationships within the organization. It may also reflect the stability of conventions, norms, and morality within the community, which sustain the system of formal rules.

If experiential learning portrays an incremental process of change, the second process, problem solving, is characteristic of drama and discontinuity. Students of organizations have long recognized the role of rules in the problem solving process (Cyert & March, 1963). Organizational learning is often activated in response to crisis, uncertainty, and the disruption of routine processes – "putting out fires," as Radner and Rothschild (1975) put it. This is the occasion when previous experience or formal knowledge fails to accommodate unexpected problems. Successful solutions become the repertoire for organizational retention, often in the form of formal rules.

All these processes are commonly observed in organizations. In the evolution of the rule system at Stanford University over its 100-year history (Zhou, 1991), for instance, many rules on academic affairs were made based on the codification of the previous informal practice, reflecting the cumulation of knowledge through experiential learning. Often previous practice was formalized into rules to ensure standardization as the organization grew in size. In some instances, however, the making of organizational rules is often a direct consequence of conflicts within the organization. For instance, all major changes in the tenure rules at Stanford were associated with controversial organizational decisions that generated unexpected conflicts and uncertainty, such as the termination of tenured faculty, irregular downsizing due to budgetary crisis, or campus "disturbances" during particular historical periods. The conflicts and uncertainty that accompanied these decisions led to the demand for establishing new rules or clarifying existing rules (Zhou, 1991).

As a result, the process of decision making is closely related to that of organizational rule making. Obviously, rule making itself is part of organizational decision making, which involves changes in allocation of responsibilities among subunits, resource distribution, and authority relationship. Often the activation of organizational rule making is triggered by the failure of existing routines to apply to a decision situation. In a university setting, for instance, events such as the rejection of a tenure promotion, irregular budgetary practice, student misconduct, and other situations that cannot be dealt with in the course of routine decision making generate tensions and a call for organizational search. The resulting search effort often leads to new rules or a revision of existing rules to accommodate the new situation. Frequently, organizational rules are generated as an unintended consequence of the organizational response to crises.

The central theme in the imagery of rule-as-collective-rationality is that organizational rules are not necessarily derived from the technical requirement of tasks or result from rational calculation. Rather, they are a collective product based on compromise and are used to avoid conflicts and decision making. Rules and rule-following behavior, seen in this light, have important implications for organizational decision making. Decision making based on rules is history dependent and constrained by its past experience. History dependency has its advantages: It ensures the predictability and continuity of the organization and of decision processes. However, history may not be efficient, and collective memory may not be consistent (March & Olsen, 1989). Rules may reflect superstitious learning and a competency trap (Levitt & March, 1988); they often emerge in response to crisis and, as a result, may absorb external shocks (Zhou, 1993).

Organizational rules as contextual rationality

As March (1988, p. 14) pointed out: "Decision making is a highly contextual, sacred activity, surrounded by myth and ritual, and as much concerned with the interpretive order as with the specifics of particular choices." This view is widely shared by students of organizations (Brunsson, 1989; Meyer & Scott, 1983; Pfeffer, 1981). Building on this tradition, Reed (1991) adopted the notion of *contextual rationality*, which "stresses the moral and symbolic aspects of human action. It emphasizes the need for social actors to create and maintain intersubjectively binding normative structures that are constitutive of the social relationships in which they are implicated" (p. 564). I now move from the organizational setting to a broad social context and explore the linkage between contextual rationality and rule following behavior.

From a sociological point of view, the logic of appropriateness in rule-following behavior is deeply rooted in socially constructed reality. Two processes are especially salient in producing rule-following behavior. First, at the micro level, socially constructed roles and self shape the decision maker's preferences and choice sets and provide the shared beliefs on which the hierarchical order of organizations is maintained. Second, the macro-institutional processes, as embodied in legal systems, governmental regulations, and cultural rules, penetrate and construct the internal decision processes in modern organizations. Rules define collective goods, individuals' positions in the social hierarchy, and the purposes of action. Therefore, we need a broad conception of rules and rule-following behavior that is based on social processes beyond the organizational boundary and the decision situation.

The micro-construction of the decision maker

In an interview, a law professor who had served on a faculty search committee at the Stanford Law School was asked about the effect of rules on the tenure decision. He proclaimed: "We never look at the rules. We make decisions according to our judgment and the secretary fills in the procedures" (Zhou, 1991, p. 110). How do we interpret the apparent absence of rules in guiding organizational decision making in this and other similar cases?

In contrast to models of choice, I begin with the recognition that organizations and organizational decision making operate within and are influenced by preexisting social institutions. Decision making starts long before individuals begin the decision-making process. We need to understand those social processes that construct the images of leadership, managerial styles, and the situations of organizational decision making.

Sociologists have long been fascinated by the role of social norms, morality, and implicit or explicit rules in constructing social reality and the processes that come to influence individual judgments and decisions. Earlier studies identified several processes that contribute to the emergence of norms and the social construction of roles. Through the socialization process, individuals learn, or are socialized into, different roles in different contexts. Social institutions – family, school, church, and the workplace – diffuse values, expectations, and attitudes among their members. The socialization process is seen as providing the appropriate qualities and traits for individuals to play particular roles in these situations. The second process – professionalization – is more directly related to modern organizations and the decision-making process. Through processes of professional training and practice, an individual learns not only the skills and competence associated with a special area but, more important, professional values, norms, ethics, and rules of conduct that are embedded in the specific roles one is to play. The professionalization of management is a major turning point in modern industrial organizations (Chandler, 1977). These arguments emphasize a learning process, the internalization of values, expectations, and behavioral patterns for those socialized into professional as well as managerial positions.

Recent theories of social identification point to a significantly different source of rule-following behavior. Tajfel, Flament, Billig, and Bundy (1971) reported an illuminating study of the role of social categorization. In an experimental situation where the subjects were randomly classified into distinct groups, but with no interaction, social structure, or shared goals among the participants, the subjects tended to discriminate in favor of ingroup and against outgroup members (see Turner & Oakes, 1989, pp. 236–237, for a brief summary of the findings). This highly reliable and robust finding demonstrates that social identities carry shared meanings and behavioral expectations associated with roles and group memberships. However, it is less the internal learning process than one's social location in the externally constructed social hierarchy that shapes one's identification or self-categorization with a group. On this basis, social identity theory proposes that individual behavior is based on the social identification constructed by the hierarchical order of social categories with respect to power, status, and prestige (Hogg & Abrams, 1988). "The central idea of self-categorization analysis of social influence is that agreement with identical others in relevant respects in a given situation creates subjective validity" (Turner & Oakes, 1989, p. 251). In this picture, the search for self-identity becomes a crucial factor influencing individuals' judgment, orientation, and decision making. Once such social identification is constructed, individuals are subject to the influence of stereotyping that affects attitudes, beliefs, values, affective reactions, and behavioral norms.

These ideas parallel the sociological recognition that social knowledge is "structurally socialized" in the sense that there is a "reciprocity of perspectives" such that perspectives are attached to particular social locations rather than individuals (Schutz, 1967). Shifting social locations tend to produce different perceptions even for the same individual. In this light, Meyer (1977) argued that education is less a socialization process of instilling skills and qualities in individuals than an institutional process of allocating individuals to different social positions. Zucker (1977) demonstrated the institutional effects of cultural norms and paradigms on individual judgment and behavior. Similarly, March and Olsen (1989) argued for the importance of roles that shape the behavior of individuals in the political arena.

What are the implications of social categorization for organizational decision making? The social categorization process creates the link between the individual and the social structure mediated by the organizational hierarchy. It introduces the processes through which societal norms constructed by social categories, positional designations, and role designations are translated into individual identities (Stryker, 1991).

In this view, corporate leaders and decision makers are in part the cultural products of social categorization. Participation in the decision-making process involves a matching process through personnel selection (Chatman, 1991; Rothstein & Jackson, 1980). Modern managers are trained in business schools and training programs based on highly institutionalized cultural paradigms (Scott & Meyer, 1991). Barley and Kunda (1992) demonstrated that the formulation of managerial theories is embedded in cultural systems and varies with the changing social context. Similarly, Astley (1985) argued that the body of knowledge about administrative science is a socially constructed product, which shapes the ways we understand organizations. Personnel training programs that aim at increasing the "self-efficacy and outcome expectancies" of managers facilitate a process of social construction of the group boundaries and identities for the decision makers (Latham, 1988). Gib Akin examined the learning experiences of 60 managers in training programs and found that emulation and role taking play a major part in their experiential learning. As he commented: "Learning is experienced as a personal transformation. A person does not gather learning as possessions but rather becomes a new person. . . . To learn is not to have, it is to be" (quoted in Bennis, 1989, p. 56). Training produces standardization, rationalization, and a reconstruction of self-identity. The selection and promotion of managers, in this sense, can be seen as a classification process: Promotion to a certain position itself implies the establishment of one's identification with a certain group and the acceptance of rules and roles associated with that position. Appropriate behavior in the decision situation follows accordingly.

Social categorization also directly shapes the very choices and preferences of the decision makers. As Wittgenstein (1966, p. 214) pointed out: "In learning the rules you get a more and more refined judgment. Learning the rules actually changes your judgment." Recent studies have emphasized the effect of categorization in decision making (March, 1994) and social judgment (Kulik, 1989). The literature on leadership teaches character, competence, and risk taking. Training programs facilitate learning the expectations, rules, and norms associated with the managerial role: to calculate, to rationalize, and to take risk (Bennis, 1989; Kouzes & Posner, 1987). These cultural categories on the one hand define the decision situation, such as organizational goals, interpretation of uncertainty, and corporate strategies, and on the other shape the decision makers, in particular their perceptions of right, truth, and appropriate roles (Dobbin, 1994; Douglas & Wildavsky, 1982). The heuristics and biases in individual decision making and the estimation of risk are systematically affected by social institutions (see Heimer, 1988, for a review). In this sense, managerial activities may be seen as following rules constructed by higher-order cultural paradigms.

The recognition of the importance of explicit or implicit rules, responsibilities and obligations, and expectations constructed around positions and roles suggests that organizational decision making is a process of sense making in which decision makers search for their identities, make sense of the decision situation and their roles in it, and piece together existing routines, remote memories, and available solutions (March, 1988; Weick, 1993). To appreciate the choice of actions, then, we need to understand the interpretive order maintained by a system of rules and roles.

Macro-institutional processes

Macro-institutional processes provide another source of rule-following behavior within and among organizations. Meyer and Rowan (1977) argued that formal organizations embody externally constructed symbols, procedures, and policies in their internal structures for the purpose of legitimacy rather than efficiency. The importance of appropriateness and legitimation leads to institutionalization, in which internal organizational structure and decision making are increasingly constructed by the external environment, such as governmental regulations, laws, and cultural rules. DiMaggio and Powell (1983) argued that in response to normative or coercive pressures, organizations adopt institutionalized processes or structures by imitating successful models. The rise of rational bureaucratic organizations was itself the product of the rationalization of the capitalist economy (Weber, 1946). In this light, organizations are cultural systems infused with values, norms, and meanings (Dobbin, 1994; Zucker, 1983). Where these externally constructed norms and rules are available and widely accepted, incentives are high for organizations to imitate and adopt these forms. Organizations that follow such rules are rewarded and those that deviate are penalized. From the decision makers' point of view, then, rule following as embodied in imitation and compliance implies both efficiency and uncertainty avoidance.

One widely recognized consequence of institutionalization for organizational decision making is an increased emphasis on procedural rationality rather than outcome sensitiveness (Dobbin, Sutton, Meyer, & Scott, 1993; Edelman, 1990; Sutton, Dobbin, Meyer, & Scott, 1994). Lind, Kulik, Ambrose, and Park (1993) found that in making judgments about litigation decisions, corporations as well as individuals are heavily influenced by their perception of fairness and procedural rationality. Even technical decisions in business organizations are shadowed by legal consequences resulting from governmental regulations (Carroll, 1993). In a university setting, the emphasis on procedural appropriateness is especially salient, as a staff member in the Provost's Office at Stanford once remarked: "General

Electric has a slogan which says 'quality is our most important product.' At Stanford, *process* is our most important product" (Zhou, 1991 pp. 106–107).

Typically, organizational decision making is triggered by organization-specific problems or context-specific issues. However, in an environment where external pressures prevail, the search for solutions is not necessarily confined within local boundaries. Often organizational searches look for global solutions – those that are constructed beyond the organizational boundary. Senior decision makers are especially aware of competitors or those organizations in the social category that they see as models. Take the tenure rules at Stanford University as an example. The activation of tenure policies was often aimed at dealing with a specific problem the administration identified. However, a controversial decision would, in turn, trigger the rule-making process. In dealing with a financial crisis in the 1970s, the administration attempted to tighten the criteria used in the tenure decision process. This effort led to an unexpectedly high rate of tenure promotion rejection and generated pressures from the faculty for the elaboration of tenure rules. In the process of elaborating tenure criteria, the university administration consciously made social comparisons with "comparable institutions" and appealed to the social norms of protecting "academic freedom." The resulting tenure policies incorporated the widely adopted guidelines and policies developed by the American Association of University Professors. Legal experts often intervened to make sure that decisions and rules conformed to the relevant law. For instance, in a wave of tenure policy reformulation in 1974, the legal councilor of the university advised the Faculty Senate to formalize tenure rules that governed the tenure decision-making process, stating that "it is no longer acceptable to say that a decision is so personal and subjective that its rationale can't be articulated. That is just no longer acceptable in court" (*The Campus Report*, June 19, 1974). Organizational decisions regarding student conduct at Stanford showed a parallel evolution. In the earlier days, these decisions were largely made in closed-door committee meetings consisting exclusively of appointed faculty members. Since the late 1960s, the intervention of the legal system and the changing political landscape have forced the unilateral decision processes to give way to highly formalized procedures reflecting many features of the legal process. As a result, the decision-making process at Stanford has been increasingly formalized over time.

To be sure, the extent to which externally constructed processes are incorporated into the decision situation varies. What is paradoxical is the fact that the more complicated the decision, the larger the stakes, and the more uncertain the outcome, the more likely that rule-following behavior will prevail. If decision situations were as well defined as those assumed in models of choice, the external social processes would become irrelevant because alternatives would be well known and consequences for each alternative clearly specified. In the real world, decision situations are often much more complicated, goals are shifting and conflicting, and information is scarce and ambiguous. In such situations, decision makers tend to rely on stable patterns or regularities for cues and guidelines. Socially constructed rules become the basis for decisions.

An important implication of the preceding discussion is that the prevalence of rule-following behavior simplifies decision situations by enlarging the arena of nondecisions (Bachrach & Baratz, 1963). In reviewing the literature on decision making at the top of organizations, Hickson (1987) pointed out that behind the grip of top managers on organizational activities "lie the rules of the game as those are expressed in the constitution and structure of the organization itself" (p. 174). He also noted the importance of "the taken-for-granted values and managerial language that may divert or suppress the formulation by powerless interests of matters they would otherwise bring forward" (p. 175). The behavioral constraints embedded in these implicit rules and norms often frame choices to prevent certain issues on the decision-making agenda from emerging. These observations are quite consistent with the rule-following behavior discussed here. Institutional processes and the construction of self-identity create and reinforce an organizational ideology that, as Brunsson (1989, p. 17) put it, "cuts down the need for making decisions. It is often obvious what action should be taken. The ideology chooses the action, and no other choice process is needed. If a decision is nonetheless taken, its purpose is to reinforce the willingness to act rather than to reach a choice between possible alternatives. The decision is meant to reinforce people's expectations that a given organizational action really will be undertaken, to motivate the relevant actors to carry it out and to commit them to the action."

Organizational decision making, in this light, is a process of imitation and compliance with externally imposed rules. This is analogous to the scenario in economic analysis where firms increase their performance to a level of competitive equilibrium as a result of competition and natural selection. Here we observe that organizations and decision makers adapt their behavior according to those "appropriateness" criteria constructed outside organizations. However, the mechanisms are different. The incentive is to increase legitimation, to reduce uncertainty, and to conform to those norms and expectations that specify what is rational and appropriate. In this sense, organizational rules and rule-following behavior should be understood broadly, including not only those procedures and routines established within the organization, but also those cultural scripts outside organizations that shape the decision situation as well as the roles, expectations, and behavioral patterns of the decision makers.

Rule following, flexibility, and innovation

Does rule following lead to the "iron cage" of bureaucracy, as Weber predicted? Indeed, the very notion of rule following often creates an image of rigidity, conformity, and "oversocialization" that is in direct contrast to the notion of decision makers' innovation and risk taking that our individualistic culture cherishes. If we accept the narrow conception of organizational rules as functional imperative or mutual understanding in a game situation where there is a tight coupling between rules and behavior, then this is an inevitable consequence.

Our observations of organizational activities seem contradictory to this image. Individuals or organizations seem much more imaginative in exploiting, selecting, and neglecting rules. The broad conceptions of rules and rule-following behavior developed previously shed light on this issue. I now extend these ideas to explore the symbolic nature of rules, the ecology of rule-following behavior, and the existence of multiple rules and roles and their implications for rule dynamics, organizational flexibility, and innovation.

Rules and flexibility

The broad social basis of rules and rule-following behavior implies multiple processes in the making and use of organizational rules. The resulting rule dynamics introduce flexibility in organizational structure and change. I now discuss some noticeable mechanisms underlying the rule dynamics and their implications for organizational flexibility.

Interpretation. Rules are symbols and require interpretation. In fact, several types of interpretation are involved. For instance, the activation of a rule requires an interpretation of its contents before it can be applied to a specific setting. Given the symbolic nature of rules, each occasion provides the opportunity for a reinterpretation, and hence a new interpretation. Rules are also interpreted by different participants in the decision process, thereby providing the basis for differential but stable behaviors. Moreover, like the legal processes in the common law tradition, rules are formally reformulated from time to time to instill new meanings to fit new circumstances, which is the main sources of rule flexibility.

Interpretation also goes beyond the contents of the rules. It often involves an interpretation of the situation in which the rules were made. More often than not, rules are selectively used or ignored to fit particular situations. A case at Stanford University illustrates this point. The "Policy on Campus Disruption" was established in the early 1970s in response to student protests on campus. It specifies the circumstances of "disruption" and the corresponding penalties. In one instance in 1985, student demonstrators lay down behind the trustees' parked cars to express their conviction on the "divestment" issue. "The conduct was clearly not protected by First Amendment principles and was a provable violation of the Policy on Campus Disruption." But "the University has refrained from legitimate disciplinary action in the interest of permitting peaceful expression" (*The Campus Report*, Feb. 8, 1989).

Finally, rules may also indicate "mine fields" that individuals and organizations should try to avoid. In the late 1980s, several racial incidents at Stanford generated pressures for the making of a new rule to regulate "discriminatory harassment." The resulting rule took the form of the "Interpretation" to the Fundamental Standard that regulates student conduct. However, the 18 months of controversy, debate, and compromise during the rule-making process led many to view the rule itself as creating a chilling effect on campus. In an interview, a university judicial affairs officer observed that because of the high controversy associated with the rule, she would be reluctant to invoke it. In such situations, rules lead to the avoidance of action in organizations.

Attention allocation. As Douglas (1986, pp. 69–70) noted: "Institutions create shadowed places in which nothing can be seen and no questions asked. They make other areas show finely discriminated detail, which is closely scrutinized and ordered." Rules play such a role by partitioning and regulating organizational attention, thus imposing order and rhythm in decision making. Attention allocation is the key to the process of decision making (March, 1988). The existence of monitoring agencies in specific areas, such as affirmative action office, safety inspection office, or environmental protection agency, facilitates attention management and produces a tight coupling between rules and behavior. The shift of attention to a problem area often produces a tightly coupled system, leading to activation of the decision-making process. By regulating attention allocation, then, formal rules can effectively accelerate or delay organizational action.

An interesting phenomenon at Stanford is that organizational decisions, especially in the academic areas, came in waves (Zhou, 1993). That is, decisions were clustered in certain time periods. A closer examination of the decision-making process revealed that this pattern could be attributed largely to the management of attention by the university rule system. The Faculty Senate, which is the main decision-making body in the academic areas, has explicit rules on the timing of the annual reports of its various committees and subcommittees. These rules allow the Faculty Senate to direct its attention to specific areas and set deadlines for the decision-making agents in these areas to produce decisions. Similarly, the rules regulating the timing of annual reports on student conduct by various offices periodically attract organizational attention to these issues, accelerating new organizational decisions.

However, rules may also suppress information, hence avoiding pressures for organizational decisions. Faculty disciplinary procedures and university grievance procedures at Stanford provide an example. The secrecy afforded by these procedures has avoided attracting much attention to these problem areas. Cases are processed and resolved with little knowledge outside of the immediate parties involved. As a result, these activities seldom surface on organizational agendas, except on those rare occasions when the procedures fail to solve the conflicts they are intended to address. In such cases, organizational actors break from the predesignated channels and activate other decision-making processes, often involving higher authorities in the university.

Structural inconsistencies. Brunsson (1989) noted the practice of incorporating different organizational structures, processes, and ideologies to provide flexibility for organizational responses to complex environments. Similar observations can be made about organizational rules. Rules arise in an organization in different ways and are located in different parts of the organization due to specific historical contingencies. A decision maker may have multiple identities as well. The implications of these multiple rules and roles for judgment and decision making have been elaborated by Elster (1985) and March (1994). It is useful to recognize that multiple rules and identities may be inconsistent with each other or may address different aspects of the same issue. The resulting structural inconsistencies allow members of organizations to exploit the opportunities or gaps between rules and provide the basis for flexible behavior that is protected by rules.

From a dynamic point of view, we may see the role or organizational rules as varying with occasions. Like any other products of social engineering, rules decay. This may be due to the loss of fit between the rules and the situation, or result from the weakening of enforcement, or may simply be forgotten by members of the organization. For instance, certain rules governing faculty conduct at Stanford quietly disappeared from the *Faculty Handbook* because, according to the assistant provost who manages the *Handbook,* "they have never been used in the past." Rules are often based on temporary coalitions or enacted in response to crises. As the coupling between rules and behavior changes, the role of rules also evolves. Rules may be initially adopted as symbols but later become routinized as a consequence of persistent institutional pressures. Conversely, rules may be adopted as bureaucratic procedures but later decoupled from behavior due to the lack of enforcement. Rules may be conveniently "forgotten" on some occasions but stubbornly "remembered" on others. In short, a rule may play different roles over its life course. Rules as interpretive orders (and their multiplicity) provide the symbolic basis for such dynamics.

Consequently, the effects of organizational rules on decision making should also be seen as a dynamic process. Rigidity and flexibility may both be characteristics of the same rule, contingent on the specific organizational and social contexts. The recognition of rule dynamics also suggests clues to surprises in organizational decisions that cannot be captured from the point of view of individual optimization behavior. An interesting characteristic of decision making at Stanford is that crises resulting from controversial decisions – rejection of tenure promotion, redistribution of resources in budget setting, or penalties for student misconduct resulting from racial prejudice – are often diffused or amplified through the strategic use of the rule system, leading to decision outcomes that cannot be fully explained by the players involved (Zhou, 1991).

Rule following and innovation

Innovation, according to Schumpeter, is the "carrying out of new combinations." Here I wish to treat innovation in a broader sense: It includes organizational decisions that are substantially different from their previous practice, such as the introduction of new products, the setting of higher or lower prices, or the adoption of new policies or programs. These decisions are innovative in the sense that the consequences of their outcomes are not tested in the marketplace, and any cost–benefit evaluation is ambiguous and uncertain. Innovative behaviors, as defined here, are crucial for maintaining an organization's competitive advantage, resource acquisition capacity, and economic status.

Routines and rules are pervasive in the process of innovation. Organizational rules and procedures are used to ensure the allocation of resources to R&D investment and organizational search. Rules are also used to stabilize innovation activities. Schumpeter's (1942) thesis of the "routinization of innovation" first recognized the importance of innovation in the advancement of the capitalist economy. He originally proposed that larger firms are in a better position to absorb the uncertainty inherent in innovation and thus to devote more resources to R&D. In this sense, Nelson and Winter (1982) argued that recombination of existing routines is the main basis for organizational innovation. March and Olsen (1989) saw it similarly: "A repertoire of routines is also the basis for an institutional approach to novel situations. For in the end, novelty is not a property of a situation so much as it is of our reaction to it; and the most standard organizational response to novelty is to find a set of routines that can be used" (p. 34). Recent studies have noted that under uncertainty, organizations tend to internalize and routinize innovative processes (Heiner, 1983). Dosi's (1988) review of the innovation literature observed that "companies tend to adopt steady policies [rules], because they face complex and unpredictable environments where they cannot forecast future states of the world" (p. 134). Organizations may also design stable strategies and behavior patterns to reduce potential errors in technical systems and technological innovation (Fischhoff, this volume; Garud, Nayyar, & Shapira, in press).

How is innovation related to rule-following behavior? A closer examination suggests that it may be attributable in part to conditions that lead to rule-following behavior. As noted before, rules create occasions for organizational action. Moreover, implicit rules (social identity) and explicit rules (formal procedures and policies) may provide incentives and a favorable environment for innovative behavior.

Innovation involves risk taking. But the very perception of risk and opportunity is socially constructed. Our previous discussion on the social construction of the decision makers shed light on the link between social identity and innovative behavior. As Douglas and Wildavsky (1982, p. 6) pointed out: "The perception of risk is a social process. . . . The differential social principles that guide behavior affect the judgment of what dangers should be most feared, what risks are worth taking, and who should be allowed to take them." In a study of innovative entrepreneurs, Drucker (1985) argued that the perception of opportunities is as important as the availability of opportunities in the initiation of an innovation. He used a series of examples to illustrate how innovative entrepreneurs perceive opportunities that most others do not. A central theme of the social identification argument is that individuals (and organizations) are institutionalized into different social roles and positions. This implies that their differential behavioral patterns are justified and legitimized. As a result, social categorization affects aspiration levels, motivation, and judgment (Kulik, 1989; March, 1988). Top-level managers are legitimized to play the role of innovator and risk taker. In this sense, innovative behavior may be induced by the duties and obligations of their designated roles or by their response to normative pressures, as well as by the more rational explanations of competitive pressures.

In my view, innovative behavior may be more relevant to the expectations, encouragement, and tolerance surrounding certain positions or roles that individuals or organizations occupy than the current studies have acknowledged. If rule following results from the hierarchical order embedded in the social structure, then it is likely that under certain conditions, rule following encourages innovation and entrepreneurship by certain individuals or organizations at the ecological level. Firms that see themselves, and are seen by others, as leaders tend to devote more resources to innovative explorations, are more prone to make bold decisions (like being a price leader or a product leader), and are more likely to affect their environment and be followed by others. Consider those firms that invest enormous resources in R&D activities. Given the ambiguity about alternatives, information, and outcomes, it seems that such decisions are less a result of a choice-based evaluation of alternatives and information than a *belief* that such investment will eventually benefit the firms. Such a belief may be maintained by the perception of their leading position and an effort to maintain such a position. Therefore, the differential R&D investment decisions across firms may be partly explained by the appropriate roles they see themselves playing in the industry. Such a normative identification mediates the decision processes, shapes the mentality of the decision makers, and affects the outcome of the decision. Decision making is based on evaluation of information and assessment of alternatives, but the alternatives are themselves constructed by the very role an actor plays. Social identification may thus provide incentives for certain organizations to innovate in order to maintain or ensure social or market positions consistent with their self-categorization.

This view may help explain some intriguing organizational behavior in innovation. Studies of innovation have consistently found that firms of medium size or market share are more active in innovation than either large or small firms (Dosi, 1988). This may be due partly to social identification processes. In social categorization theory, consensual position is not defined by the mean position in a group. Rather, it is the most *prototypical* position, the one that best represents, and is recognized as such by, the group as a whole (Turner & Oakes, 1989, p. 258). These middle-level firms tend to identify with the larger (and more successful) firms in their industry. To catch up with these larger firms, they invest heavily in R&D in order to gain advantage in products and technology. In an interesting study of the structure of the auditing market, Han (1994) found that middle-level firms in an industry tend to imitate larger firms in selecting accounting firms of high reputation, despite the higher cost associated with their services. This decision cannot be explained by a typical cost–benefit analysis. Han attributed such a behavioral pattern to the efforts by those middle-level firms to acquire legitimacy. Clearly, the self-categorization of these firms with the large firms in their industry plays a role that cannot be simply reduced to a rational economic calculation.

Now consider the ecology of interorganizational relationships in an industry. Ecologically, innovative behavior may also be sustained by another process of rule-following behavior characteristic of imitating and copying across organizations. Such imitation and copying lead to a redistribution of risks and consequences among organizations. In particular, they may induce innovative behavior by reducing the potentially negative consequences for the innovative organization. Innovative organizations take more risks than noninnovators, given the uncertainty about alternatives and the nature of the technology being explored (Garud et al., in press). Ecologically, however, these risks may be substantially reduced because of the rule-following behavior of other imitating firms. Imagine the price leader in an industry. In making decisions about price setting, it anticipates imitative behavior by followers, which will subsequently decrease the potential cost of the exit response from consumers. If an innovative decision is successful, it reinforces the shared belief about the innovative leader's position in the social hierarchy. If the decision is a miscalculation, however, imitative behavior by others tends to cause them to stumble as well, helping the risk taker to maintain its relative advantage in the social hierarchy. That is, the potential cost of the risk-taking leader's behavior may be shared due to rapid imitation by other social actors, leading to what Akerlof (1984) has called "a lower level equilibrium trap" (p. 32). The resulting inefficiency at the collective level conceals the initial misstep by the leader. The recent history of IBM in the computer industry serves as an illuminating example. In the early 1980s, the shared belief in the computer industry that IBM was the innovative leader led other firms to imitate, and follow the standard set by, IBM products. Such imitating behavior provided leverage for IBM's mistakes in innovative behavior. When IBM's new technology, the PC Jr. product, was poorly received in the market, the failed innovation and consequent market vacuum were not capitalized by other competing firms. Rather, these firms waited for IBM to develop new technology for them to imitate. Such imitative behavior reduced the potential cost of the failed innovation and gave IBM precious time to recover from its mistakes (Carroll, 1993). Consequently, we often observe more durable leadership positions for some reputable firms in an industry than a purely competitive selection process might sustain. This is especially so in an environment of uncertainty, ambiguity, and weak selection mechanisms. In such a context, reputation and social position play an especially important role in corrupting judgment.

Thus far, I have discussed the ubiquitous phenomenon of rule following and the flexibility of rules. How can we reconcile the apparent tensions and inconsistencies between these two views? Flexibility is inherent in organizational rules due to their symbolic, interpretive nature and relative inconsistencies. Organizational decision making, in this light, is used to apply the rules in specific situations. But this does not mean that rules are merely decorating decision making. As Atiyah and Summers' (1987) discussion of Anglo-American law pointed out: "[A] legal system as we know it requires that many of its rules be treated as generating formal reasons for decisions, and not simply as additional factors to be weighed or balanced against reasons of substance, or treated as merely a summing up of the normal balance of such reasons, liable to be displaced whenever a decision-maker has to probe more deeply into the grounds of decision" (p. 70). For a decision analytist, the broad basis of rules and rule-following behavior provides important clues to understanding the stable patterns of organizational decision making.

Concluding remarks

What is the place of rules in a world of judgment? In the organization literature, decision making and rule following are typically treated as two distinct processes applying to two qualitatively different worlds. Rules are seen as applying to repetitive tasks performed by lower-level workers, whose behavior is regulated or protected by the rules. Managers, by contrast, appear to inhabit a world of adventure, and decision making is seen as a creative process that requires innovation, calculation, and risk taking. In this chapter, I have shown that the logic of rule following fits the analysis of managerial behavior and organizational decision making as well.

My main argument developed here is that much of what the decision makers do can be understood as, in a broad sense, rule-following behavior, and that these rules and behaviors are constructed by social processes that are independent of the specific decision process under scrutiny. As a result, the effort to model actors and choices as circumscribed by the immediate

decision situation, and to treat them as derivations of individual optimizing behavior, may have focused on a spurious relationship between individual rationality and decision outcomes. The very understanding of the
costs, benefits, and decision rules, and what the desired decision outcomes
are, may be the products of a logic that is embedded in culture rather than
in naked self-interest.

The recognition of the broad basis of rule-following behavior beyond
organizational boundaries and decision processes has important implications for understanding organizational phenomena. In particular, the interaction between macroinstitutional processes and micro–self-categorization
provides important insights into both the isomorphism and divergence in
organizational behavior and styles of decision making. Fundamental in
these ideas is the recognition of the normative sources for *differential* patterns of imitation and diffusion among organizations and decision participants. The logic of appropriateness invites subjective validation among
organizations and individuals through social comparison and group identification, leading to the construction of different social categories. On the
one hand, macrosocial processes make available highly institutionalized
structures or procedures; on the other, individuals and organizations tend
to adopt those elements perceived as fitting their own social categories.
Given the existence of different social categories, decision makers and
organizations in different structural positions thus have different views of
the world and of their self-identities in this world. This, in turn, leads to
differential trajectories of change among organizations and individuals
based on different reference frameworks, different assessments of risks
and preferences, and different models for imitation. Seen in this light,
culturally based rules and rule following provide not only the basis for
isomorphic behavioral patterns among organizations and decision makers
within their respective social categories, but also the basis for distinctive
behavior patterns across these categories.

These ideas help us trace the flow of ideas across organizations. As
organizations make decisions on which direction they will move, they
borrow ideas and models from those with whom they identify. A research
university is likely to look for models from similar institutions that are seen
as leaders, whereas a teaching college may look for ideas from a leading
teaching college. This pattern may also help explain the flow of personnel
across organizations and sectors. The likelihood of managers from large
corporations moving to other large corporations may be less a result of
experience or compensation than of social identification with the comparable social categories across these organizations.

To return to the contrast between models of choice and models of rule
following, it seems that choice-based decision making interacts closely with
rule-based decision making. My observation of the decision-making processes in a university setting suggest that decision making based on consequential calculation appears only as infrequent episodes interrupting the

routine activities of the organization. They are often subsumed by the pervasive rules or the subsequent demands for rules. When organizational decision making is not based on routines, as sometimes occurs in times of crisis, it often triggers controversies and uncertainty, which provide the impetus for activation of the rule-making process to restructure and stabilize the decision-making process based on new routines. It is conceivable that in a competitive environment where organizational performance is evaluated more promptly, such as corporations in the business environment, we may expect to find a different dynamic between routine-based and choice-based behaviors. But once we take into consideration the pervasive rule-following behavior discussed in this chapter, the role of the decision makers in the choice-based decisions is likely to be much more modest.

The emphasis on rule-following behavior shifts the focus of analysis to the broader social processes that shape the actors, as well as their decision environment. Such a shift does not necessarily increase our precision in predicting the specific outcome from an organizational decision process. It does, however, redirect our attention from the immediate decision situation to those parameters that are embedded in a broader context and history, and to processes beyond the particular organizational decision. Thus, a focus on the role of rules and rule-following behavior provides a richer, and at times deeper, understanding of organizational decision making. In this light, studies of organizational decision making may benefit more from interpretive and contextual analyses than from analyses of particular interactions among decision makers. Consequently, our attention should be less on complicated models of decision making and more on subtle models of rule following that explain the behavioral regularities underlining organizational decision making.

References

Akerlof, G. A. (1980). A theory of social custom, of which unemployment may be one consequence. *Quarterly Journal of Economics, 94,* 749–775.

Akerlof, G. A. (1984). *An economic theorist's book of tales.* Cambridge: Cambridge University Press.

Arrow, K. (1974). *The limits of organization.* New York: W. W. Norton.

Astley, W. G. (1985). Administrative science as socially constructed truth. *Administrative Science Quarterly, 30,* 497–513.

Atiyah, P. S., & Summers, R. S. (1987). *Form and substance in Anglo-American law.* Oxford: Clarendon Press.

Axelrod, R. (1984). *The evolution of cooperation.* New York: Basic Books.

Axelrod, R. (1986). An evolutionary approach to norms. *American Political Science Review, 80,* 1096–1111.

Bach, S., & Smith, S. S. (1988). *Managing uncertainty in the house of representatives: Adaptation and innovation in special rules.* Washington, DC: Brookings Institution.

Bachrach, P., & Baratz, M. S. (1963). Decisions and nondecisions: An analytical framework. *American Political Science Review, 57*, 632–642.

Barley, S. R., & Kunda, G. (1992). Design and devotion: surges of rational and normative ideologies of control in managerial discourse. *Administrative Science Quarterly, 37*, 363–399.

Bennis, W. (1989). *On becoming a leader.* New York: Addison-Wesley.

Brenner, M., & Shapira, Z. (1983). Environmental uncertainty as determining merger activity. In W. Golderg (Ed.), *Mergers: Motives, modes, methods* (pp. 51–65). London: Gower.

Brunsson, N. (1989). *The organization of hypocrisy.* New York: Wiley.

Carroll, P. (1993). *Big blues: The unmaking of IBM.* New York: Crown.

Chandler, A. (1977). *The visible hand.* Cambridge, MA: Belknap Press.

Chatman, J. (1991). Matching people and organizations: Selection and socialization in public accounting firms. *Administrative Science Quarterly, 36*, 459–484.

Crozier, M. (1964). *The bureaucratic phenomenon.* Chicago: University of Chicago Press.

Cyert, R. M., & March, J. G. (1963). *A behavioral theory of the firm.* Englewood Cliffs, NJ: Prentice-Hall.

DiMaggio, P. J., & Powell, W. W. (1983). The iron cage revisited: Institutional isomorphism and collective rationality in organizational fields. *American Sociological Review, 48*, 47–60.

Dobbin, F. R. (1994). Cultural models of organization: The social construction of rational organizing principles. In Crane, A. (Ed.), *The sociology of culture* (pp. 117–163). Cambridge: Blackwell.

Dobbin, F. R., Sutton, J. R., Meyer, J. W., & Scott, W. (1993). Equal opportunity law and the construction of internal labor markets. *American Journal of Sociology, 99*, 396–427.

Dosi, G. (1988). Sources, procedures, and microeconomic effects of innovation. *Journal of Economic Literature, 26*, 1120–1171.

Douglas, M. (1986). *How institutions think.* Syracuse, NY: Syracuse University Press.

Douglas, M., & Wildavsky, A. (1982). *Risk and culture.* Berkeley: University of California Press.

Drucker, P. F. (1985). *Innovation and entrepreneurship.* New York: HarperBusiness.

Edelman, L. B. (1990). Legal environments and organizational governance: the expansion of due process in the American workplace. *American Journal of Sociology, 95*, 1401–1440.

Elster, J. (Ed.). (1985). *The multiple self.* London: Cambridge University Press.

Garud, R., Nayyar, P. R., & Shapira, Z. (In press). Technological choices and the inevitability of errors. R. Garud, P. R. Nayyar, & Z. Shapira (Eds.), *Technological Foresights and Oversights.* New York: Cambridge University Press.

Gouldner, A. W. (1954). *Patterns of industrial bureaucracy.* Glencoe, IL: Free Press.

Han, S.-K. (1994). Mimetic Isomorphism and its effect on the audit services market. *Social Forces, 73*, 637–663.

Hannan, M. T., & Freeman, J. H. (1984). Structural inertia and organizational change. *American Sociological Review, 49*, 149–164.

Heimer, C. (1988). Social structure, psychology, and the estimation of risk. *Annual Review of Sociology, 14*, 491–519.

Heiner, R. A. (1983). The origin of predictable behavior. *American Economic Review, 73*, 560–595.

Hickson, D. J. (1987). Decision-making at the top of the organization. *Annual Review of Sociology, 13,* 165–192.

Hogg, M. A., & Abrams, D. (1988). *Social identifications: A social psychology of intergroup relations and group processes.* New York: Routledge.

Kouzes, J. M., & Posner, B. Z. (1987). *The leadership challenge: How to get extraordinary things done in organizations.* San Francisco: Jossey-Bass.

Kulik, C. T. (1989). The effects of job categorization on judgments of motivating potential of jobs. *Administrative Science Quarterly, 34,* 68–90.

Latham, G. P. (1988). Human resource training and development. *Annual Review of Psychology, 39,* 545–582.

Levitt, B., & March, J. G. (1988). Organizational learning. *Annual Review of Sociology, 14,* 319–340.

Lind, E. A., Kulik, C. T., Ambrose, M., & de Vera Park, M. V. (1993). Individual and corporate dispute resolution: Using procedural fairness as a decision heuristic. *Administrative Science Quarterly, 38,* 224–251.

March, J. (1988). *Decisions and organizations.* Oxford: Basil Blackwell.

March, J. G. (1991). Exploration and exploitation in organizational learning. *Organization Science, 2,* 71–87.

March, J. G. (1994). *A primer on decision making.* New York: Free Press.

March, J. G., & Olsen, J. P. (1989). *Rediscovering institutions: The organizational basis of politics.* New York: Free Press.

March, J. G., & Simon, H. A. (1958). *Organizations.* New York: Wiley.

Meyer, J. W. (1977). The effect of education as an institution. *American Journal of Sociology, 83,* 55–77.

Meyer, J. W., & Rowan, B. (1977). Institutionalized organizations: Formal structure as myth and ceremony. *American Journal of Sociology, 83,* 340–363.

Meyer, J. W., & Scott, W. R. (1983). *Organizational environments: ritual and rationality.* Beverly Hills, CA: Sage.

Nelson, R., & Winter, S. (1982). *An evolutionary theory of economic change.* Cambridge, MA: Harvard University Press.

Perrow, C. (1986). *Complex organizations* (3rd ed.). New York: Random House.

Pfeffer, J. (1981). Management as symbolic action. *Research in Organizational Behavior, 3,* 1–52.

Radner, R., & Rothschild, M. (1975). On the allocation of effort. *Journal of Economic Theory, 10,* 358–376.

Reed, M. (1991). Organizations and rationality: The odd couple?" *Journal of Management Studies, 28,* 559–567.

Rothstein, M., & Jackson, D. N. (1980). Decision making in the employment interview: An experimental approach. *Journal of Applied Psychology, 65,* 271–283.

Schumpeter, J. A. (1976 [1942]). *Capitalism, socialism, and democracy.* New York: Harper Colophon Books.

Schutz, A. (1967). *Collected papers I: The problem of social reality.* The Hague: Nijhoff. Reprinted in M. Douglas (Ed.), *Rules and meanings* (pp. 227–231). Baltimore: Penguin Books.

Scott, W. R., & Meyer, J. W. (1991). The rise of training programs in firms and agencies: An institutional perspective. *Research in Organizational Behavior, 13,* 297–326.

Simon, H. A. (1957). *Administrative behavior.* New York: Macmillan.

Stryker, S. (1991). Exploring the relevance of social cognition for the relationship of self and society: Linking the cognitive perspective and identity theory. In J. A. Howard & P. L. Callero (Eds.), *The self-society dynamic: Cognition, emotion, and action* (pp. 19–41). Cambridge: Cambridge University Press.

Sutton, J. R., Dobbin, F., Meyer, J. W., & Scott, W. R. (1994). The legalization of the workplace. *American Journal of Sociology, 99,* 944–971.

Tajfel, H., Flament, C., Billig, M. G., & Bundy, R. F. (1971). Social categorization and intergroup behavior. *European Journal of Social Psychology, 1,* 149–177.

Turner, J. C., & Oakes, P. J. (1989). Self-categorization theory and social influence. In P. B. Paulus (Ed.), *In Psychology of group influence* (2nd ed., pp. 233–275). Hillsdale, NJ: Erlbaum.

Weber, M. (1946). *From Max Weber: Essays in sociology.* Translated, edited and with an introduction by H. H. Gerth & C. Wright Mills. New York: Oxford University Press.

Weick, K. E. (1993). The collapse of sensemaking in organizations: The Mann Gulch disaster. *Administrative Science Quarterly, 38,* 628–652.

Wittgenstein, L. (1966). *Lectures and conversations on aesthetics, psychology and religious belief.* Edited by Cyril Barett. Oxford: Basil Blackwell. Reprinted in M. Douglas (Ed.), *Rules and meanings* (pp. 213–215). Baltimore: Penguin Books.

Zhou, X. (1991). *The dynamics of organizational rules: Stanford University 1891–1987.* Unpublished Ph.D. dissertation, Stanford University.

Zhou, X. (1993). The dynamics of organizational rules. *American Journal of Sociology, 98,* 1134–1166.

Zucker, L. G. (1977). The role of institutionalization in cultural persistence. *American Sociological Review, 42,* 726–743.

Zucker, L. G. (1983). Organizations as institutions. In S. B. Bacharach (Ed.), *Research in the sociology of organizations* (pp. 1–47). Greenwich, CT: JAI Press.

Part V

Alternative approaches

13 Naturalistic decision making and the new organizational context

Terry Connolly and Ken Koput

Introduction

Naturalistic decision making (NDM) is gaining some currency as a label for a loose grouping of nonstandard models of individual decision making. These models, although very different from one another, all address the descriptive inadequacies of the classical, subjective expected utility (SEU) view of economic rationality and its closer descendants, such as prospect theory (Kahneman & Tversky, 1979) and generalized utility theory (Camerer, 1992). Continuing work within the SEU tradition is essentially conservative, aiming to preserve the important achievements of the theory while adding modifications to accommodate the most embarrassing empirical violations. NDM theories, in contrast, are generally more radical. They conceive of decision making in ways quite different from SEU theory.

The source of this radicalism is simple: SEU theory appears to offer little descriptive purchase on a broad range of everyday decision phenomena. Decisions are frequently made under time pressure, precluding the sorts of careful balancing and computation SEU implies. Decisions are made in dynamic, uncertain, or ambiguous environments, making the notion of an "expectation" problematic. Goals and preferences may be unclear, making notions of stable, known utilities hard to apply. There may be multiple participants, with shifting roles as collaborators, advisors, or opponents. (See Orasanu and Connolly, 1993, for a sample of this critical literature.) Because observations of organizational contexts suggest that these complicating factors are often present, NDM takes organizational decision making as a primary domain of application.

A somewhat parallel but essentially independent cluster of radical theorizing is emerging in organization theory: We shall refer to it here as *new organization theory (NOT)*. As with NDM, the theories under this umbrella are quite varied but share as a starting point a rejection of classical economic models. Whereas NDM claims relevance to organizational processes from below, by modeling the individual, NOT claims relevance from above by examining the organization in relationship to its environment.

These two bodies of theorizing have had essentially no contact with one another. To the extent that they acknowledge one another, it has been to use the other as an oversimplified background for its own efforts. Thus NOT notes the bounded rationality or cognitive limits of organizational members as a fixed assumption of its models, whereas NDM takes for granted the organizational context as a fixed set of "difficulty factors" such as those noted previously. The primary purpose of this chapter is to develop, if only in a preliminary way, a basis for fuller contact between the two. The hope is that the study of organizational decision processes will ultimately be informed by NOT as to the substance, framing, and form of decision problems and by NDM as to the skills, limitations, and strategies of the individual participants.

Given the state of development of the two bodies of theorizing, we have no hope of making a coherent, integrated statement of either, let alone of synthesizing the two into a single overarching theory. We will proceed, instead, by example. In the following section we survey several of the main bodies of work that fall under the NDM label and trace a few of the common themes. The subsequent section presents a similar survey of some of the main themes in NOT. The final part of the chapter makes a number of connections between the two, taking the stance of an organizational decision theorist seeking guidance from both NDM and NOT. We identify a number of specific questions such a theorist might reasonably pose, and sketch the interplay of NDM and NOT in two illustrative projects: a study of the cross-situational transferability of decision skills and an application of decision cycles theory (an NDM development) to analysis of organizational networks (a hot topic in NOT). Some promising research leads emerge – the precursors, we hope, of many more.

Naturalistic decision making: Some illustrative examples

As an introduction to NDM we summarize, at a thumbnail sketch level, six theories that together reflect the diversity of content and approach that goes under this label. Later, we will comment briefly on some of the commonalities we see.

Image theory. Image theory (Beach, 1993; Beach & Mitchell, 1990) has as its core a richly interconnected network embedding the decision maker's actions, plans, projections of future outcomes and their impact on his or her purposes, objectives, principles, and values. For expository purposes, this network is described in terms of three somewhat distinct clusterings or "images": a *value image*, comprising principles, purposes, and preferences (and thus generalizing traditional utility functions); a *strategic image*, comprising the actor's action choices and their interrelationships (a more general view of the traditional "option space"); and a *trajectory image*, the individual's understanding of how possible actions will intersect with elements of the Value Image (generalizing the idea of "payoffs"). The general equilibrium position to which the decision maker strives is an acceptable degree of consistency among these three images: the choice or maintenance of a course of action whose imagined future consequences are acceptable to his or her values and preferences.

Image theory envisions several restrictions on the comprehensiveness of this equilibrium. First, only a subset of the individual's values, strategies, and projections are evoked in any specific situation, a process referred to as *framing*. Second, consideration of action possibilities is generally limited to one alternative to the status quo, with a strong presumption in favor of the latter if it remains available. Third, considerable use is made of a *compatibility test* in which potential new elements (actions, plans, values) are assessed in terms of their fit with existing components of the various images. Potential actions, for example, are screened for their potential fit with existing activities, plans, and values, and are thus evaluated as much as complements to existing commitments as alternatives to them. Finally, the theory emphasizes sequential, satisficing search rather than optimization. Rarely will evaluation continue beyond the discovery of an acceptable option to an attempt to select the best of several acceptable options using a *profitability test*. The various mechanisms proposed by the theory (screening, compatibility tests, situation-specific framing) have a strong flavor of local, incremental, conservative adjustments to reduce tension in specific parts of the values/actions/plans network rather than broad, comprehensive, radical optimization.

Decision cycles. Traditional decision theory is consequentialist in that the choice of an action is guided by its anticipated consequences. This implies that thought (about alternatives, consequences, and preferences) will generally precede action. Decision cycles theory (Connolly, 1988; Connolly & Wagner, 1988) posits an alternative rationality in which action largely precedes reflection, and is taken incrementally with a view to exploring both the external world (what will happen?) and the internal world (what preferences are engaged?). The notion of a *decision path* is offered to describe alternative interweavings of action, reflection, and feedback addressing the same choice. A continuum of such decision paths is proposed. At one pole is the traditional, reflection-first model wherein a single, decision action is taken only after (intendedly) complete consideration of all relevant factors. At the other pole is an action-first model wherein incremental action is taken after virtually no reflection, and the process is then actively managed as consequences and evoked preferences emerge. The theory specifies some of the contingencies linking alternative decision paths to situational and cognitive variables and emphasizes the generic virtues of action-first strategies. Related arguments have been advanced by Hogarth (1981), March (1978), and Weick (1983), and there is a clear connection to earlier thinking about incrementalism and experimentation in social policy (Campbell, 1969; Lindblom, 1965).

Experimental evidence (e.g., Kleinmuntz, 1985; Sterman, 1987) suggests that humans find dynamic, highly coupled task environments difficult to master even when few variables operate. In more complex worlds (such as a simulated forest fire [Brehmer, 1990] or a simulated city [Dorner, 1987]), performance is often very poor. These demonstrations present subjects with environments in which hidden variables are strongly coupled, important patterns build slowly, responses are delayed, and feedback loops are perverse – probably realistic representations of real-world complexity but cognitively overwhelming. Dorner, for example, reports such dysfunctional behaviors as excessive focus on a single problem and/or sequential problem hopping; failure to cope with slow systems response or long-term trends ("last-period focus"); and response rigidity in the face of deteriorating system performance. It is unclear whether such findings are better read as evidence of human cognitive limitation or of the ease with which intractable problems can be constructed. Highly dynamic, complexly looped environments are certainly difficult to understand and operate.

Explanation-based decision making. Pennington and Hastie (1988) examined the processes by which humans organize the potentially overwhelming mass of information associated with such decision problems as that of a juror reaching a verdict in a criminal trial. They found only indirect connections between the items of evidence presented and such elements of decision models as "probability of guilt" or "utility of false acquittal." Instead they found subjects actively assembling the disparate items into more or less coherent sequential narratives and then probing these stories for completeness, consistency, and overall believability. After they had settled on a preferred story, they compared it to the elements of alternative verdicts presented by the judge and rendered the verdict that best matched their story. Similar processes of constructing causal accounts of observed data are found in medical diagnosis: Symptoms are considered not in the spirit of conditional probabilities of a particular disease, given the symptoms, but as clues to an underlying causal (physiological) process that led to the observed symptoms, and from which prognoses with and without different interventions generated. Comparable processes are postulated by Jungermann (1985), who treats prediction of future events not as event probabilities but as *scenarios,* relatively rich sequences of events (stories about the future), including reactions of others, compensatory actions taken, and so on. Again, the connecting logic is causal or narrative rather than probabilistic. Somewhat similar themes are echoed by Lipshitz (1989) in his treatment of decision making as the assemblage of arguments for particular actions. The rationale is rhetorical rather than formal.

Situation assessment and recognition. Several authors, including Noble (1989) and Klein (1989) have emphasized the importance of the decision maker's initial reading of what is going on. Klein, for example, traces the cognitions of an experienced commander of fire fighters as he directs troops through-out the course of a rapidly escalating building fire. He finds little that corresponds to conventional decision making. Instead, Klein argues, the commander draws on a rich repertoire of memories of situations previously encountered, each of which has associated with it such elements as special threats presented, appropriate action implications, and so on. Decision making, in this model, is centrally concerned with recognizing what is happening, from a rich array of stored templates, and taking the appropri-ate action when a fit is found. (Very similar processes were postulated by de Groot, 1965, to account for the skilled performance of expert chess players.) Noble (1989) puts similar emphasis on these "front-end" diagnos-tic processes, although proposing active situation-assessment schemas rather than direct recognition as the key processes. In both cases, what looks like complex, rapid decision making to an observer is essentially a nondecision to the individual concerned.

Cognitive continuum theory. Hammond (1980; Hammond, Hamm, Grassia, & Pearson, 1987), drawing on Brunswikian social judgment theory (see Brehmer & Joyce, 1988), has argued for a spectrum of decision-making processes ranging from the purely intuitive to the purely analytic. Further, he postulates adaptive decision makers who respond to environmental and task characteristics to move flexibly along this continuum to match their decision processes to the demands of the task. Both argument and evi-dence are intricate and defy easy summary here. Although Hammond has been critical of much NDM theorizing (see Hammond, 1993), he clearly fits with other theorists who argue against the hegemony of the conventional model and who postulate richer, more flexible cognitive responses to vary-ing task demands.

Dominance search model. Montgomery (1989) focuses primarily on the eval-uation process in choice. In his model, decision makers are reluctant to face explicitly the trade-offs and ambiguities present in most real choices. In-stead, after a series of prescreening activities that eliminate clearly unac-ceptable options, the decision maker picks one promising alternative and examines it in the hope of finding it to dominate its rivals. If such domi-nance is not found, a variety of cognitive adjustments or distortions are used to create an illusion of dominance convincing to both the decision maker and spectators. Clearly, such distortions are not without limit, and it is possible that a second promising alternative may be selected and developed to dominance status. However, Montgomery sees the effort for bolstering the first candidate as often quite extensive, possibly leading to the selection of options that might, if encountered in a different order, have been clearly seen as suboptimal.

Montgomery sees decision makers as deferential to the classic model: Dominance is accepted as the simplest, most compelling argument for choice, and decision makers try to convince themselves and others that the initially preferred alternative does, in fact, enjoy this status. An incidental benefit (see decision cycles) is that the process facilitates action in various ways: A candidate is available early if speedy action is needed; arguments in support of the promising candidate are marshaled one-sidedly, allowing adversaries to be overcome (an echo of the rhetorical processes noted by Hastie and Pennington and by Lipschitz); and no explicit weighing of possible drawbacks is presented to sap the energy and commitment needed for effective implementation. The model thus provides a convincing account of commitment to action but a less convincing one of the wisdom of the action chosen.

Even this brief sampling of NDM ideas (see Klein, Orasanu, Calderwood, & Zsambok, 1993, for a broader review) suggests some of the central concerns. One theme, clearly, is adaptability (see Payne, Bettman, & Johnson, 1993), the notion that decision makers may command a range of decision-making processes and may be able to select from their repertoire to match the demands of the task. A second theme is that of situated expertise: The image is less of an individual in command of an abstract decision engine into which may be loaded content appropriate for any problem. NDM typically sees decision skill as tightly bound to knowing something (often a great deal) about the specifics of the domain. A final common theme is that decision makers may well be aware of their fallibility as brute-force information processors and tend to avoid such processing if at all possible: by telling stories, by using memories of previous encounters with similar situations, by constructing arguments for their preferred actions, or even by simply taking action. This is not to suggest that NDM is a finished or even coherent body of theorizing, but some shared lines of development are starting to emerge.

New organization theory: Some illustrative examples

In this section we review five major streams in NOT, focusing on the content and form of the decisions each places in the hands of organizational decisions makers. NOT points to the environment as both a constraint on and a venue for organizational decisions. This environment comprises other organizations, institutions, networks, and the like that contain or are themselves strategic actors. The actors both respond to the decisions made by a focal organization and change exogenously according to their own trajectories of evolutionary, life cycle, or other factors. To NOT, then, the environment is not simply a background against which decisions are made. It is the totality of interacting entities that form both substance and arena, stimulus for and response to the choices made in the focal organization.

NOT is rooted in historical observations (e.g., Merton, 1936; Parsons, 1956; Stinchcombe, 1965) that organizations are embedded in (social) environments and that these environments influence their effectiveness and functioning. Thompson (1967) added the important extension that an organization's environment consists of other organizations and that these other organizations develop norms and expectations for how each should behave. From these roots NOT has developed several active paradigms, differentiated by their perspectives on the environment, its composition, and its character.

Resource dependence. The presumption of resource dependence (RD) (Pfeffer & Salancik, 1978) is that every organization is dependent on others for resources ranging from financing to raw materials to personnel. Resource-providing organizations may thus make demands on the focal organization, and organizational decision makers must decide how to respond to these demands. They must also decide when to act proactively to avoid or minimize unresolved dependencies. It is assumed that decision makers desire discretion and, whenever possible, will act to increase the organization's autonomy. The theory gives some details about the factors that affect both when an organization must comply with given demands and how it can shape its environment to lessen the demands. The extent of compliance with a given demand is affected by the criticality of the resource, as well as by visibility, capability, priority, and the desire to survive (Pfeffer, 1982). Because "most organizations are confronted with numerous demands from a variety of social actors, and many of these demands are incompatible" (Pfeffer, 1982, p. 194), a given demand may be met with compliance or negotiation or may be simply ignored.

Resource providers are themselves strategically motivated to strengthen their own power positions by finding ways to influence the key factors. Further, a resource, once obtained, may become less critical while stocks last, so sequential attention to resource providers is possible. The relative power of each provider thus changes over time because of strategic moves and temporary resource satiation. Finally, an organization may reduce the overall interdependence and uncertainty of its industry environment by mergers, joint ventures, and officer and director interlocks. Such linkages reduce dependency by providing explicit, long-term coordination between an organization and its resource providers.

Transaction-cost economics. Transaction-cost economics (TCE) is also concerned with how an organization structures its resource exchanges. Williamson (1975), building on the work of Coase (1937), posited that structural arrangements cannot be completely explained by an internal logic of efficient production because organizations must depend on others for the tools of their production. He posits decision makers both boundedly rational and prone to "opportunism" (guileful self-seeking). Market failures are predicted, under specified conditions, if even a small minority act opportunistically and cannot be reliably distinguished from nonopportunists.

The organization, again, seeks to reduce its vulnerability to resource providers, some of whom may be opportunistic predators. Bounded rationality implies limits on decision makers' ability to identify these predators or to write contracts that would completely preclude predation. The primary decision, according to Williamson (1975, 1981), is whether to use market or hierarchical means. (Other possibilities have been proposed, such as Ouchi's [1981] clans or Powell's [1990] networks. Williamson [1991] sees these merely as hybrids, intermediate solutions to the markets-versus-hierarchies problem.)

Williamson characterizes transactions on the basis of uncertainty, frequency, and asset specificity, dimensions that have proved difficult to operationalize uniquely. These variables drive transaction costs, and decision makers aim to economize on these costs. His decision rule is simple: Choose market controls if possible because they are almost costless; choose hierarchical controls, which are costly to operate, only if market controls are likely to fail. Given the difficulties of operationalizing such notions as *asset specificity* and *degree of hierarchical control*, as well as the obvious influence of the organization's industry and regulatory environment, the empirical support for Williamson's view is currently unclear (see, e.g., Walker & Weber, 1985; Walker & Poppo, 1991).

Organizational ecology. Ecological theories of organization (Hannan & Freeman, 1977, 1989) group organizations by their common dependence on material and social resources. Attention focuses the effects of complex, dynamic environments on the aggregate properties of the group. Ecologists focus on the selection of organizations by environments to explain which kinds of firms live and die (Carroll, 1984).

Ecologists argue that under normal conditions, core adaptations are illusory. That is, attempts to change core structural arrangements will put the organization at risk of failure because they will almost surely be obsolete before they are put in place. Four factors limit the capacities of managers to reshape existing organizations: (1) internal controls, norms, and incentives; (2) scarcity of resources; (3) competitive pressures; and (4) "all the limitations on rationality described by contemporary decision theorists" (Hannan & Freeman, 1989, p. 41).

Only modest scope is left for managerial decision making. The environment places a premium on reliability and accountability in its selection, and managers can influence perceptions of these qualities through adaptable peripheral arrangements and "cosmetic" changes (Delacroix & Swaminathan, 1991). Managers can also play the active role of protecting core arrangements to ensure consistency.

Core elements of structure include stated goals, forms of authority, core technology, and marketing strategy. Organization charts and structures for specific exchanges with actors in the environment are seen as "more plastic" (Hannan & Freeman, 1989, p. 79), which leaves managerial discretion over such internal matters as departmentation, spans of control, and channels of communication and such external matters as interlocking directorates and strategic alliances. Recently, second-generation ecologists have argued that adaptations in core structures are appropriate under conditions of "fundamental environmental transformation" (Haveman, 1992, 1993), that is, when the environment undergoes sudden, discrete changes, as in regulatory change or technological breakthrough. Research suggests that both occur with some regularity (e.g., Tushman & Anderson, 1986). More specifically, a manager's role may be to control the mobilization of resources into and out of niches, markets, or industries in adaptive response to environmental conditions (Haveman, 1993). Finally, efforts have been made to link ecological models to institutional and network approaches (see the following two sections), where development of legitimacy or connectedness is a discretionary managerial role (see, e.g., Haveman, 1993; Miner, Amburgey, & Stearns 1990; Singh, Tucker, & House, 1986). Thus, whereas early statements of the ecological argument left essentially no significant role for managerial decision making, more recent formulations have found a considerable role for such activity, although still narrower than the broad strategy choices envisioned by the conventional model.

Institutional theory. Institutional theory (IT) in organizational analysis (see, e.g., Powell & Dimaggio, 1991) argues that a few special organizations in an organization's environment are "institutions" (Zucker, 1983), infused with value for their own sake, promoting stability, and reducing the destructive effects of unchecked competition. Examples include government agencies, trade associations, independent "watchdog" groups, and "lead" organizations in the focal industry or that of a resource provider.

Institutions, as distinguished from other productive organizations, control a very special resource: legitimacy. Legitimacy is unique in two ways: (1) often only one source exists and (2) it often comes in an all-or-nothing way. Legitimacy is often a prerequisite to acquiring other resources, that is, resource providers may deal only with organizations they deem legitimate. Legitimacy is granted only to organizations that conform to the "norms of rationality," the industry's standards or beliefs as to what a rational, modern organization ought to be like (Meyer & Rowan, 1977; Thompson, 1967).

Over time, the activities of institutions can become detached from their original rationale. For example, institutionally held beliefs about what facilitates productive efficiency may become obsolete as production technology changes. An organization then must balance the need for technical efficiency against the need for legitimacy in the eyes of that institution. Decision makers in such organizations must then decide when to comply, when to alter or avoid dependence, and how.

Sometimes, when operating within an institutional context, norms of rationality are clear-cut and there is little or no choice: Government regulations, for example, may impose compliance. But other institutional demands are mimetic or normative rather than coercive (Dimaggio & Powell, 1983). Institutions may authorize specific features and allow organizations to adopt them voluntarily in order to gain either a favored status or special inducements (e.g., funding). Similarly, organizations may take on arrangements that satisfy institutions through the deliberate acquisition or strategic choice of a formal structural model. Other processes include imprinting and incorporation, "a broad array of adaptive processes occurring over a period of time and ranging from cooptation . . . to evolution" (Scott, 1991, p. 179). Finally, institutional demands may focus on shared beliefs, selecting among symbols, rituals, myths, and so on in response to institutional demands to know where the organization stands. Mimetic and normative forces differ across organizations, depending on their reputation, industry ranking, and political activities.

Managerial discretion also arises in strategic choice among institutional environments within which to operate (Powell, 1991) – for example, by manipulating symbols, language, and the like. Such choices among environments are clearly not independent of the choices within environments discussed previously. Powell (1991) has argued that institutional processes are path dependent: An activity "placed" in one environment develops in accordance with the pressures of that environment.

Of the several NOT theories we have considered, IT is the clearest in emphasizing the symbolic as well as the instrumental role of "proper" decision processes. Whether or not formal, apparently rational processes select effective courses of action, they may convince important audiences that an organization is soundly run, and thus ensure continuing supplies of needed resources.

Network approaches. Network approaches argue that the organizations in a focal organization's environment are not independent entities, to be dealt with dyadically. Instead, many operate as interconnected sets to mobilize resources such as financing, support, and technical know-how. These networks are often based on social relations rather than developing as "adaptive responses to sets of [economic] incentives" (Davis & Powell, 1992, p. 335).

Network thinking largely follows the logic of resource dependency while placing greater weight on "the means by which an organization's position in a wider network of relations shapes its actions" (Davis & Powell, 1992, p. 335). For example, a firm's centrality or prestige may influence both the extent to which it need comply with demands and the extent to which others make demands.

The main focus of empirical work in this area has been on understanding the nature and shape of networks, with relatively little attention to how they are actually used. An exception is the finding that networks are used to buffer organizations from external forces, potentially offsetting fundamental liabilities (Baum & Oliver, 1992; McPherson, Popielarz, & Drobnic, 1992). In recent work (Powell, Koput, & Smith-Doerr, in press), networks have been viewed as instruments of organizational learning, especially when the core knowledge of an industry is rapidly changing, ambiguous, or widely dispersed. (We shall discuss this study further in the next section.)

As a relatively new area of inquiry, network theory remains both fragmented and underdeveloped. Still, at the very least, network considerations present decision makers with two further complexities beyond those noted already: the need to consider explicitly relations between other organizations in the environment and the choice of whether, when, and how to join networks oneself.

Steps toward an integration

In attempting to draw together insights from NOT and NDM to formulate research issues for organizational decision making, we should reiterate that neither NDM nor NOT is best thought of as a body of competing, complete theories, one of which will finally emerge as the established view of its domain. Rhetorical excesses aside, it seems unlikely that the authors of, say, recognition-primed decision theory expect to vanquish proponents of the decision cycles view or that resource dependence theorists hope to overcome network thinkers. Each would, we assume, make much more modest claims: perhaps that part of the relevant world is sometimes usefully thought of this way. The familiar parable of the blind men and the elephant seems more relevant than ever. In both NOT and NDM partial views abound, and no one can claim a comprehensive view of their own animal, let alone of how it might interact with the animal being described so variously by the neighboring discipline.

We claim no comprehensive overview of either cluster, let alone of a synthesis between them. However, it is possible to see areas where progress toward synthesis might be made. What theoretical and empirical progress would be necessary before students of organizational decision processes could look to NDM and NOT for guidance? As a stimulus to such progress, we sketch here three research projects, one quite broad, the other two more focused.

Project 1: Research issues for a study of central organizational decisions. This study concerns decision making at the top of the organization – the CEO and his or her immediate team. We suppose a well-funded research team that is proposing an ambitious mixture of cross-sectional, observational, and time-series studies of the activities of many such senior decision-making teams. What questions might the team address to NOT, and what to NDM, in formulating a research plan? We suggest the following as worthy of consideration:

Some questions for NOT

1. To what substantive issues will these senior decision makers direct their attention? Different models included in NOT clearly specify the organization's central issues: under resource dependence, the management of interdependence; under transaction cost economics, the control of opportunism; under institutional theory, the maintenance of legitimacy; and so on. Is it possible, ex ante, to predict, from knowledge of the organization's markets, history, life cycle, technology, or whatever, the content of the decisions the senior managers will face?

2. In what time frame will these issues be treated? If, for example, supplier contracting is a critical issue, can the theory predict when long rather than short contracts should be sought? If stable operation of core technologies is the issue, is stability sought at the level of weeks or decades? In short, although several models within NOT are framed as dynamic and feedback driven, the actual time available for reflection within a given pass through the loop is specified only loosely or not at all.

3. Will the critical issues be formulated as amenable to rational analysis (or some reasonable approximation thereto) or as inherently intractable uncertainties? For example, do the senior managers discuss network interconnections in the spirit of forming workable coalitions, interlocks, alliances, and so on, or do they, if touching on the issue at all, despair of finding sensible moves in a world where the ripples from any move may appear, benignly or disastrously, as an nth-order interaction? Is product pricing treated as a matter for long-run strategizing or tactical response? Is dealing with the environment treated as a game against nature or against one or more active opponents?

4. Will the senior decision makers explicitly discuss or acknowledge the need to appear, to either external or internal audiences, to act reasonably and reliably? A failure to do so would not, of course, vitiate IT's claim that legitimacy-generating activities such as rational-seeming procedures of choice are important; but a clear theoretical prediction as to when legitimacy is most important would at least allow comparison with what explicit evidence was found.

Some questions for NDM

1. How flexible are decision makers across domains? Are they best thought of as having a relatively fixed decision style with which they ap-

proach all important decisions, or are they relatively flexible? For example, are some individuals disposed to an analytical approach regardless of the setting, whereas others are more intuitive, or are most senior managers capable of using both approaches? Are some given to extensive deliberation and others to rapid incremental action in all circumstances, or is a strategy flexibly selected to match the problem?

2. At what level is expertise found? Such NDM models as recognition-primed decision making turn heavily on specific content expertise and experience: The fire fighter needs to be able to recognize and respond to the details of many specific fires, the chess expert to the details of many specific chess positions. Much NDM theorizing seems relatively unsympathetic to general-purpose analytical and decision-making skills beyond an elementary level.

3. What feedback arrangements are maximally conducive to learning of decision-related skills? A considerable body of laboratory evidence exists concerning individuals' ability to learn from feedback in judgment and decision-making tasks. However, little of this work has been developed into a specification of what constitutes good feedback in terms of level of aggregation, timing, evaluative tone, and so on. Such a specification would go a long way toward connecting the individual decision makers into the organizational learning loops postulated by several of the NOT models.

4. To what extent do the various models postulate different initial background, experience, and knowledge? Some (e.g., recognition-primed decisions, image theory) have the flavor of equilibrium models, explaining a decision maker's ongoing activity within a decision domain. Others (e.g., decision cycles) address either transitions, in which a decision maker develops experience, or attempts purposive acts in novel domains that may not be experienced again. The two may converge over time, of course, but the distinction between acquiring and demonstrating decision-making skill is worth retaining.

Project 2: A study of transferability of decision skill. We do not need a complete model of the situated decision maker before we can proceed. Consider, for example, the question of whether, and to what extent, decisional skills are transferable to new tasks. The question is of obvious interest in organizational decision making when personnel transfers within and across organizations are routine. Several lines of work in NDM suggest that decisional skills are quite local, whether tied to detailed knowledge of local substantive areas, as in recognition-primed decision making, or tied to generic classes of environment, like image theory (see Connolly & Beach, 1995, for a more detailed discussion). Empirical demonstration of the domains across which transfer is and is not effective could thus be framed as a fruitful research topic purely within NDT.

Note, however, how much richness is added if NOT perspectives are included. For example, RD theory sees firms (and thus their senior executives) as managing interdependence primarily through vertical integration, mergers, growth, interlocks, or joint ventures. The firm's ability to enact these choices is influenced by external factors such as the antitrust environment and the growth ideology. A decision maker may not transfer effectively from a highly competitive environment to one in which mergers are tolerated or encouraged. Similarly, a CEO transferring from a company using growth to manage uncertainty may flounder in a firm committed to low or no growth.

Similar shifts in decision substance and style are predicted by other NOT theories. TCE, for example, stresses opportunism as the manager's central concern and distrustful surveillance as the norm. Such an approach would be inappropriate for an environment in which strong social embedding eliminates predatory concerns. Organizational ecology sensitizes the researcher to such issues as environmental stability (required before successful core adaptation is possible) and industry age (legitimating activities being called for in emerging industries, competing ones in established industries). IT would predict poor decision maker transfer between highly institutional environments (where performance is hard to specify and measure) and highly technical environments (where standards and performance measures are less problematic). Finally, network perspectives remind us that different skill demands will face the manager in highly networked environments from those facing colleagues in less embedded, more dyadic worlds. Both interpersonally and intellectually, the two worlds are vastly different from one another and require different skills for decision-making effectiveness.

Project 3: Networks and decision cycles theory. As a final example of the potentially enriching interplay of NDM and NOT ideas, consider the following example. In a study of the biotechnology industry, Powell et al. (1996) found that the ability to manage network ties is a skill that, once developed, drives an organization's future network behavior. The biotechnology industry is characterized by all manner of interorganizational collaborations, and firms tend to have multiple ties of various types. However, any given firm's portfolio of ties does not spring into being fully developed. Rather, feedback from initial collaborations produces incremental, path-dependent "cycles of learning."

Using a learning framework, Powell et al. predicted firms' network position and growth from longitudinal relationships, using as independent variables firms' R&D activity, competence at managing R&D alliances, and overall experience with ties. Although generally supportive of their predictions, the results suggested that the learning process is even more dynamic than anticipated. Network position had reciprocal influences on R&D ties, competence, and experience. NOT led to an argument that R&D ties, competence, and experience produce central connectedness. But things do not stop there. Central connectedness feeds back to intensify a firm's commitment to learning through its networks. Viewed from the perspective of decisions cycles theory, this is quite sensible. Applying the perspective, we can speculate about the details that NOT theorists might otherwise overlook.

Firms can enter the network via R&D ties or by some other types of ties. If they begin with R&D ties, they hope to learn about the project at hand. But this is not the only learning that occurs. Unforeseen perhaps and uncertain to be sure in the initial decision to collaborate is the development of competence at managing R&D and experience with ties more generally. Because the knowledge base of the industry is complex and incomplete, firms also accumulate "absorptive capacity" (Cohen & Levinthal, 1990) and learn of new project opportunities. Further, early ties begin to establish a firm's reputation as a valuable partner. All of these consequences of alliance behavior shape subsequent decisions to maintain existing network ties and to undertake new ones. The R&D ties, then, drive a firm to become more central and produce membership in overlapping cliques. Centrality, meanwhile, as a proxy for the awareness of new projects, skill at managing ties, absorptive capacity, and reputation, intensifies a firm's use of collaborations of all kinds. If a firm begins with some other type of tie (e.g., marketing), it will still gain experience with ties and awareness of R&D projects that could be undertaken. These may then elicit decisions to begin R&D or other, additional alliances. The path to centrality is quite different but nonetheless discoverable through action.

That is part of the power of NDM here: to allow action first, with deliberation occurring over time as firms develop experience and learn to network. A firm trying to achieve some position in a network of other actors, while dynamically pursuing positional goals and acquiring competencies as it does so, creates a decision problem of almost unimaginable complexity. The problem becomes much more tractable if it is conceptualized as a series of relatively local actions, gaining competencies and alliances, learning over time, and adapting to an ever-changing environment. Decision cycles theory thus offers a plausible, process-level account of how firms achieve over time the network positions they do. It forces attention to the heterogeneous feedback mechanisms underlying the cycles of learning, and thus to the heterogeneity of learning trajectories and attendant behavior of firms.

Conclusions

As we noted at the start of this chapter, NDM and NOT share a common ancestry in the rejection of classical, utility-maximizing, economic rationality as the central assumption. Both have surrendered the power and elegance of that model for the messier, more partial road of descriptive realism. The result has been the development of two loose bodies of rich, partially inconsistent theorizing, one addressing the individual decision maker, the other the world in which he or she must operate. There has been essentially no contact between the two bodies.

This chapter has been a first attempt to establish such contact. We presented, at a thumb-nail sketch level, brief introductions to major exemplars of both NOT and NDM to start to strengthen reciprocal understanding between the two. We then outlined some initial steps toward integration in the form of research project outlines. The first, and most ambitious, project focused on a set of questions a researcher interested in high-level organizational decision making might pose to NOT, followed by a similar set he or she might pose to NDM. The second project took up a more specific topic: the transferability of decision skills across situations. NOT clearly envisions such changing situational challenges, whereas NDM generally predicts that much expertise will be rather local. Finally, we outlined some research issues that have arisen in the course of an in-progress study of network location over time and how these issues are illuminated by decision cycles theory.

These initial efforts clearly fall far short of a comprehensive theory of organizational decision making synthesizing both NOT and NDM insights. Even at this preliminary stage, however, we are impressed at the ease with which the two bodies of theory stimulate one another. Perhaps we should not be surprised. After all, NDM claims to offer rich description of (at least some of) the activities undertaken by humans when they try to make decisions in realistic contexts. NOT claims to describe (at least some of) the key issues and difficulties they face in attempting to act purposively in organizational contexts. The two bodies should then have something to say not just to others within their own theory group, but to those in the other camp too. Our hope is that this chapter will start some of these conversations.

References

Baum, J. A. C., & Oliver, C. (1992). Institutional embeddedness and the dynamics of organizational populations. *American Sociological Review, 57*, 540–559.

Beach, L. R. (1993). *Image theory: Decision making in personal and organizational contexts.* Chichester, UK: Wiley.

Beach, L. R., & Mitchell, T. R. (1990). Image theory: A behavioral theory of decisions in organizations. In B. M. Staw & L. L. Cummings (Eds.), *Research in organizational behavior* (Vol. 12, pp. 1–41). Greenwich, CT: JAI Press.

Brehmer, B. (1990). Strategies in real-time dynamic decision making. In R. M. Hogarth (Ed.), *Insights in decision making: A tribute to Hillel J. Einhorn* (pp. 262–279). Chicago: University of Chicago Press.

Brehmer, B., & Joyce, C. R. B. (Eds.). (1988). *Human judgment: The SJT view.* Amsterdam: Elsevier.

Camerer, C. F. (1992). Recent tests of generalizations of expected utility theory. In W. Edwards (Ed.), *Utility theory: Measurements and applications* (pp. 207–251). Boston: Kluwer.

Campbell, D. T. (1969). Reforms as experiments. *American Psychologist, 24,* 409–429.

Carroll, G. (1984). Organizational ecology. *Annual Review of Sociology, 10,* 71–93.

Coase, R. (1937). The nature of the firm. *Economica, 16,* 386–405.

Cohen, W., & Levinthal, D. (1990). Absorptive capacity: A new perspective on learning and innovation. *Administrative Science Quarterly, 35,* 128–152.

Connolly, T. (1988). Hedge-clipping, tree-felling, and the management of ambiguity. In M. B. McCaskey, L. R. Pondy, & H. Thomas (Eds.), *Managing the challenge of ambiguity and change* (pp. 37–50). New York: Wiley.

Connolly, T., & Beach, L. R. (1995). The theory of image theory: An examination of the central conceptual structure. In J.-P. Caverni, M. Bar-Hillel, F. H. Barron, & H. Jungermann (Eds.), *Contributions to decision making* (pp. 83–96). Amsterdam: Elsevier.

Connolly, T., & Wagner, W. G. (1988). Decision cycles. In R. L. Cardy, S. M. Puffer, & M. M. Newman (Eds.), *Advances in information processing in organizations* (Vol. 3, pp. 183–205). Greenwich, CT: JAI Press.

Davis, G. F., & Powell, W. W. (1992). Organization–environment relations. In M. Dunnette (Ed.), *Handbook of industrial and organizational psychology* (Vol. 3, 2nd ed., pp. 798–1033). Palo Alto, Ca: Consulting Psychologists Press.

de Groot, A. D. (1965). *Thought and choice in chess.* New York: Mouton.

Delacroix, J., & Swaminathan, A. (1991). Cosmetic, speculative and adaptive change in the wine industry: A longitudinal study. *Administrative Science Quarterly, 36,* 631–661.

Dimaggio, P.-J., & Powell, W. W. (1983). The iron age revisited: Institutional isomorphism and collective rationality in organizational fields. *American Sociological Review, 48,* 147–60.

Dorner, D. (1987). *On the logic of failure: Thinking, planning and decision making in uncertainty and complexity.* Working paper 54, Lehrstuhl Psychologie II, University of Bamberg, Bamberg, Germany.

Hammond, K. R. (1980). Introduction to Brunswikian theory and methods. In K. R. Hammond, & N. E. Wascoe (Eds.), *Realizations of Brunswik's experimental design*). San Francisco: Jossey-Bass.

Hammond, K. R. (1993). Naturalistic decision making from a Brunswikian viewpoint: Its past, present, future. In G. A. Klein, J. Orasanu, R. Calderwood, & C. E. Zsambok (Eds.), *Decision making in action: Models and methods* (pp. 205–227). Norwood, NJ: Ablex.

Hammond, K. R., Hamm, R. M., Grassia, J., & Pearson, T. (1987). Direct comparison of the efficacy of intuitive and analytical cognition in expert judgment. *IEEE Transactions on Systems, Man, and Cybernetics,* SMC-17, 753–770.

Hannan, M., & Freeman, J. (1977). The population ecology of organizations. *American Journal of Sociology, 82,* 929–966.

Hannan, M., & Freeman, J. (1989). *Organizational ecology.* Cambridge, MA: Harvard University Press.

Haveman, H. (1992). Between a rock and a hard place: Organizational change and performance under conditions of fundamental environmental transformation. *Administrative Science Quarterly, 37,* 48–75.

Haveman, H. (1993). Follow the leader: Mimetic isomorphism and entry into new markets. *Administrative Science Quarterly, 38,* 593–627.

Hogarth, R. M. (1981). Beyond discrete biases: Functional and dysfunctional aspects of judgmental heuristics. *Psychological Bulletin, 90,* 197–217.

Jungermann, H. (1985). Inferential processes in the construction of scenarios. *Journal of Forecasting, 4*, 321–327.

Kahneman, D., & Tversky, A. (1979). Prospect theory: An analysis of decision under risk. *Econometrica, 47*, 263–291.

Klein, G. A. (1989). Recognition-primed decisions. In W. B. Rouse (Ed.), *Advances in man–machine system research* (Vol. 5, pp. 47–92). Greenwich, CT: JAI Press.

Klein, G. A., Orasanu, R., Calderwood, R., & Zsambok, C. E. (Eds.). (1993). *Decision making in action: Models and methods*. Norwood, NJ: Ablex.

Kleinmuntz, D. N. (1985). Cognitive heuristics and feedback in a dynamic decision environment. *Management Science, 31*, 680–702.

Lindblom, C. (1965). *The intelligence of democracy,* New York: Macmillan.

Lipschitz, R. (1989). *Decision making as argument driven action.* Working paper, Boston University Center for Applied Social Science.

March, J. G. (1978). Bounded rationality, ambiguity, and the engineering of choice. *Bell Journal of Economics, 9*, 587–608.

McPherson, M., Popielarz, P., & Drobnic, S. (1992). Social networks and organizational dynamics. *American Journal of Sociology, 82*, 1212–1241.

Merton, R. K. (1936). The unanticipated consequences of purposive social action. *American Journal of Sociology, 1*, 894–904.

Meyer, J., & Rowan, B. (1977). Institutionalized organizations: Formal structure and mythandceremony.28AmericanJournalofSociology,83,340–363.

Miner, A., Amburgey, T., & Stearns, T. (1990). Institutional linkages and population dynamics: Buffering and transformational shields. *Administrative Science Quarterly, 35*, 689–713.

Montgomery, H. (1989). From cognition to action: The search for dominance in decision making. In H. Montgomery & O. Svenson (Eds.), *Process and structure in human decision making* (pp. 471–483). Chichester, U.K.: Wiley.

Noble, D. (1989). *Application of a theory of cognition to situation assessment.* Vienna, VA: Engineering Research Associates.

Orasanu, J., & Connolly, T. (1993). The reinvention of decision making. In G. A. Klein, J. Orasanu, R. Calderwood, & C. E. Zsambok (Eds.), *Decision making in action: Models and methods* (pp. 3–20). Norwood, NJ: Ablex.

Ouchi, W. (1981). Markets, bureaucracies and clans. *Administrative Science Quarterly, 25*, 129–141.

Parsons, T. (1956). Suggestions for a sociological approach to the theory of organizations: I. *Administrative Science Quarterly, 1*, 63–85.

Payne, J. W., Bettman, J. R., & Johnson, E. J. (1993). *The adaptive decision maker.* New York: Cambridge University Press.

Pennington, N., & Hastie, R. (1988). Explanation-based decision making: Effects of memory structure on judgment. *Journal of Experimental Psychology: Learning, Memory and Cognition, 14*, 521–533.

Pfeffer, J. (1982). *Organizations and organization theory.* New York: Ballinger.

Pfeffer, P., & Salancik, G. (1978). *The external control of organizations: A resource dependence perspective.* New York: Harper & Row.

Powell, W. (1990). Neither market nor hierarchy: Network forms of organization. In B. Staw (Ed.), *Research in organizational behavior* (Vol. 12, pp. 295–336). Greenwich, CT: JAI Press.

Powell, W. (1991). Expanding the scope of institutional theory. In W. Powell &

P. Dimaggio (Eds.), *The new institutionalism in organizational analysis* (pp. 183–203). Chicago: University of Chicago Press.

Powell, W., & Dimaggio, P. (Eds.). (1991). *The new institutionalism in organizational analysis.* Chicago: University of Chicago Press.

Powell, W., Koput, K., & Smith-Doerr, L. (in press). (1996). Interorganizational collaboration and the locus of innovation: Networks of learning in biotechnology. *Administration Science Quarterly.*

Scott, W. R. (1991). Unpacking institutional arguments. In W. Powell & P. Dimaggio (Eds.), *The new institutionalism in organizational analysis* (pp. 164–182). Chicago: University of Chicago Press.

Singh, J., Tucker, D., & House, R. (1986). Organizational legitimacy and the liability of newness. *Administrative Science Quarterly, 31,* 171–193.

Sterman, J. D. (1987). Testing behavioral simulation models by direct experiment. *Management Science, 33,* 1572–1592.

Stinchcombe, A. (1965). Social structure and organizations. In J. G. March (Ed.), *Handbook of Organizations* (pp. 142–193). Chicago: Rand-McNally.

Thompson, J. D. (1967). *Organizations in action.* New York: McGraw-Hill.

Tushman, M., & Anderson, P. (1986). Technological discontinuities and organizational environments. *Administrative Science Quarterly, 31,* 439–465.

Walker, G., & Poppo, L. (1991). Profit centers, single-source suppliers and transaction costs. *Administrative Science Quarterly, 36,* 66–87.

Walker, G., & Weber, D. (1985). A transaction cost approach to make or buy decisions. *Administrative Science Quarterly, 29,* 373–391.

Weick, K. E. (1983). Managerial thought in the context of action. In S. Srivastava (Ed.), *The executive mind* (pp. 137–156). San Francisco: Jossey-Bass.

Williamson, O. (1975). *Markets and hierarchies.* New York: Free Press.

Williamson, O. (1981). The economics of organizations: The transaction cost approach. *American Journal of Sociology, 87,* 548–577.

Williamson, O. (1991). Comparative economic organization: The analysis of discrete structural alternatives. *Administrative Science Quarterly, 36,* 269–296.

Zucker, L. (1983). Organizations as institutions. In S. Bacharach (Ed.), *Research in the Sociology of Organizations* (Vol. 2, pp. 1–42). Greenwich, CT: JAI Press.

14 Telling decisions: The role of narrative in organizational decision making

Ellen S. O'Connor

> When we made the decision, we had already made the decision.
>
> Corporate decision (?) maker

Organizational decision theory and the research that supports it depend largely on narrative: the selective, ordered representation of events as told, the telling of this representation to others, and the successive retellings of this telling. To discover how anything happens in an organization, we ask people to tell us stories. To convince others that we know something about how things happen in organizations, we construct and tell stories about those stories. As others react to our stories, they tell stories about the stories we have told – and so on.

Philosophers (Johnson, 1993; MacIntyre, 1981) argue that narrative is a meaning-making form and process that is central to human experience and conduct. "I can only answer the question 'What am I to do?' if I can answer the prior question, 'Of what story or stories do I find myself a part?'" (MacIntyre, 1981, p. 216). Human conduct is by nature "storied" (Sarbin, 1986): We think, imagine, and choose according to narrative structures. We connect information – random or otherwise – to form patterns and plots. These patterns and plots produce *meaning*, defined here, according to the literary theory of narrative, as the excess of the "straightforward copy of events recounted" (Barthes, 1982, p. 289). In this chapter, I argue that

I appreciate the advice and assistance of Pierre Louart, Emery Roe, Zur Shapira, and Dvora Yanow. The host organization, which shall remain anonymous, generously provided the cases I discuss, access to the decision makers involved, and, above all, valuable time and extraordinary patience. Jim March's incisive comments turned a book into a chapter. Finally, my special thanks to Richard and Alex O'Connor.

narrative is a form of human understanding comparable to heuristics in decision theory (Kahneman, Slovic, & Tversky, 1982). However, the narrative form's own complexity provides a theoretical construct that allows us to go a step further toward accommodating the complexity of life itself.

This chapter explores how an appreciation of narrative helps us understand how decisions happen in organizations and in organization theory. It builds on March's (1994) discussion of "mov[ing] meaning to the center of the analysis" (p. 218) and "treat[ing] interpretation . . . as central" (p. 208). Following narrative theory, organizational decision making and decision theorizing can be understood as the interweaving of multiple, ongoing, and unending narratives. The implications of this view for organizational decision theory involve increased attention to the imaginative nature, the social force, and the symbolic aspects of our activities as decision makers and decision theorists. March (1981) describes decision making as "a cross-section of lives" and as an intermingling with "the complexities of ordinary lives." He suggests the possibility of a contextual perspective that involves "fit[ting] the decision into the life of each participant" (pp. 229–230). Narrative theory permits exactly such an analysis.

The chapter presents a brief theoretical background on narrative theory and a case study that applies the theory to organizational decision making. The device of placement in relationship serves as the central organizing principle. This concept is fundamental to the investigation of meaning-making processes (Polkinghorne, 1988, p. 6): Semiotics addresses this relationship at the level of the text (Greimas, 1987); structural anthropology, at the level of culture (Lévi-Strauss, 1963); autopoesis, at the level of the biological organism (Maturana & Varela, 1987) and the organization (Mingers, 1995). I relate narrative theory to sociology, decision theory to narrative theory, and narrative theory to decision practices to show how attention to narrative allows us to study meaning and meaning-making processes in decision making. In larger terms, I place science and artistry, management and imagination, and fact finding and fiction making in relation to one another. "Whoever says what is . . . always tells a story" (Arendt, 1968, p. 261); in this way, the "transformation of the given raw material of sheer happenings" (p. 261) is an activity shared by organizational theorists, decision makers, and fiction writers alike.

More specifically, I relate narrative to organizational action and decision making about such action. I argue that in this case, the narratives about organizational change work to influence organizational decisions about change over the long run. They develop a "common sense" (Geertz, 1973, pp. 84–85) as to what change means, who performs it, and how and in what circumstances it is performed – so that future decisions may be "already made," in the spirit of my opening epigraph. In short, stories constitute a force in themselves, regardless of "the facts" (Roe, 1994, p. 2).

Theoretical background

Interpretive sociology and the world as construction

Interpretive sociology has a tradition that attends to meaning and meaning-making processes in ways very similar to those of narrative theory.[1] For example, interpretive sociologists use dramatistic metaphors such as framing (Goffman, 1974), self-presentation (Goffman, 1959), and imaginative construction (Mead, 1934, 1964; Schutz, 1962, 1964). In particular, Schutz, Mead, and their followers are concerned with subjectivity (in the tradition of phenomenology, how individuals make sense of the world) and with the mutual interplay and production of subjectivity and the world (following pragmatism, how individuals construct the world).[2] These two philosophical traditions work together to dissolve the distinction between objective and subjective worlds.[3] Narrative theory makes a similar move through its attention to the shaping of accounts.

William James defines *pragmatism* as the doctrine that mental activity (specifically, the "conceiving or theorizing faculty") is largely affected by emotional and practical factors (James, 1975, p. xii). In this view, he approximates phenomenology's credo that "consciousness" is always "consciousness of" something (Farber, 1943), which later becomes Schutz's notion of *relevance* (1962, p. 1970, p. 5; 283). However, pragmatism goes a step further with regard to the role of human agency in this process. Specifically, "the knower is an actor and in certain ways plays a role in creating truth" (James, 1975, p. xii). "The mind works on the data it receives very much as a sculptor works on a block of stone," he says (quoted in Diggins, 1994, p. 128). Dewey similarly considers how thought (which he calls *inquiry*) increases "the meaning of the present experience" and produces "novel solutions" (Allport, 1989, p. 276). Narrative approaches continue this metaphor of individuals shaping their experience of life as artists shape raw material.

Mead (1934) equates thought with language and language with social action. Via communication, "the individual may become an object to himself" (p. 138); this "other" is an invention and a process by which the self articulates with and even produces society. Mead emphasizes this interactive, mutually produced nature of self and society through and in language: "The changes that we make in the social order in which we are implicated necessarily involve our also making changes in our selves" (1934, p. 309). Blumer, the symbolic interactionist, acknowledges his debt to Mead in an essay (1969, pp. 61–77), noting Mead's attention to "social action . . . as a formation made by human actors" (p. 74). In the same tradition, Cicourel and Kitsuse (1963) examine how the formal organization of a school produces college-bound versus non-college-bound students. They consider "types" such as "college bound" and "underachiever" as products of socially organized activities.

In literary terms, we could say that Mead's "self" that "becomes an object to itself" is a character in a narrative – the narrative being the conversation to the self about the self in interaction with other selves. For Mead, we produce the phenomenon called *self* in relation to social contexts: "There are all sorts of different selves answering to all sorts of different relations" (1934, p. 142). We can readily relate this idea to the way an author has a character in a novel or play speak and act differently in different circumstances.

Language, cognition and the construction of reality

Sociology aside, disciplines such as cognitive psychology, rhetoric, linguistics, and literary theory have long shown a profound interest in meaning-making and interpretive processes. In particular, cognitive approaches provide a smooth transition from interpretive social science to narrative theory. These two domains are concerned, in part, with ways in which human beings organize information. However, although they agree that knowledge involves "constructs, i.e., abstractions, generalizations, formalizations, and idealizations" (Schutz, 1962, p. 5), they disagree on the extent of real-world complexity accommodated by such constructs. Specifically, whereas cognitive science views the organizing faculty as reducing complexity, narrative theory views this faculty as fully matching the complexity of experience through imaginative processes and products.

Cognitive theory invokes a number of metaphors, including the notion of metaphor itself, to describe this organizing activity (Gibbs, 1994; Lakoff & Johnson, 1980; Lakoff & Turner, 1989). Other common metaphors for cognitive processes include frames (Tversky & Kahneman, 1981), structures (Mandler, 1984), maps (Fiol & Huff, 1992), and scripts (Gioia 1986, 1992). Perhaps the most famous metaphor for cognition (and cognitive science) is the computer (Simon, 1957, 1979, 1994). This metaphor also characterizes cognitive operations in general as simplifying or reducing complexity, an idea that parallels bounded rationality in decision theory. The human being, posited as an information receiver, processor, and storer, faces stiff limits on the ability to do so. Frames, metaphors, maps, scripts, and, of course, instructions are posited as coping mechanisms.

In a move similar to pragmatist thought, cognitive studies examine the role of human invention in organizing experience. According to Bruner, Goodnow, and Austin (1977), "human beings have an exquisite capacity for making distinctions" (p. 1). But full use of this capacity would overwhelm us. Our capacity to "categorize" resolves the paradox of "discrimination capacities which, if fully used, would make us slaves to the particular" (p. 1). And "categorizing involves, if you will, an act of invention" (p. 2). Bruner et al. thus oppose Newtonian science, the objective of which "was to discover the islands of truth," such as natural phenomena. To Bacon's notion of verification against nature, they propose the pragmatic criterion of use: "The test of the invention [way of grouping] is the predictive benefits that result from the use of the invented categories" (p. 7) – consistent with James (1975, pp. 36, 44).

Bruner et al. address "certain systematic errors" in categorization, which they qualify (also pragmatically) as follows: "But these may be conceived of not so much as 'errors' as systematic behavior related to the strategy being followed" (p. 238). Thus, even when they use the term *error*, they give the benefit of the doubt to a contextual perspective with explanatory power but one they do not happen to possess. Literary and narrative theories posit the concept of *imaginative truth* that develops this idea further.

Because, in social science, the category of the literary suffers from its association with the world of imagination (interpreted as delusion), I briefly address the relationship of discovery and invention, fact and fiction. The language-based disciplines (rhetoric, linguistics, semiotics, literary theory, philosophy of language) have a long tradition in this regard, going back to debates that predate Plato and Aristotle. Similar to the manner in which interpretive sociology, through pragmatism, dissolves the distinction between objective and subjective reality, certain streams of literary and linguistic theory dissolve the distinction between fact and fiction. The dissolution of the distinction is pivotal to the incorporation of narrative theory into social science.

In the Platonian tradition, the literary pretends to be the real, which it always fails to replicate (Plato, 1968, p. 281). Augustine holds such a view of language, which Wittgenstein critiques (1958, pp. 2–5). In *The Republic*, this principle holds for all logical procedures – for example, the forming of hypotheses in geometry and calculus (Plato, 1968, p. 190). Such logic "must be grasped by argument and thought, not sight" (p. 209). However, another classical tradition, that of Aristotle, views language in a positive way – as a creative response to social contexts rather than as a dysfunctional tool to represent reality.

Aristotle (1954) says that rhetoric "exists to affect the giving of decisions," that is, precisely to influence future action (p. 8). His treatise resembles a cookbook, but instead of giving directions on how to mix objects together to make other objects, it gives directions on how to make concepts: points of view (arguments) that produce other points of view (agreements). Essentially, rhetorical theory deals with the construction of abstractions, the invention of what has not yet happened – and what may never happen. Aristotle's orator works to invent the future – specifically, a decision.

The Latin term for *fact*, which is *factum*, simply means "made," and some modern languages preserve this coincidence (the French word *fait* means both "fact" and "made"). White (1978, 1980, 1981, 1987) explores how histories, which take the form of an account of events, also take on literary forms (e.g., narrative, metaphor, allegory, irony, and other "figures" of language). White identifies one of his sources as Giambattista

Vico's *New Science,* published in 1744. Vico (1988) reconciles these distinct meanings of the term *factum,* the single Latin root. These two distinct meanings have a function: They distinguish scientific from imaginative knowledge. Although in social science the former is valued as superior to the latter, a long tradition in interpretive theory works to dissolve this distinction precisely by attending to the cognitive process identical to both types of knowledge; Vico (1988) is perhaps the first to do so (Tagliacozzo, Mooney, & Verene, 1976). Vico contributes to a discussion of narrative's place in social science, for he identifies the role of the imagination in virtually all pursuits of knowledge. He argues for two worlds: one made by man, one by God. Man can only know what man makes, not what God makes. Man proceeds from the known to the unknown strictly by way of his imagination – faculties such as association, analogy, and ultimately invention.

Narrative takes linguistic form – and language is not a "transparent vehicle of representation"; rather, it brings "cognitive baggage" (White, 1978, p. 127). This observation applies to organizational and sociological representations of reality just as it does to any other domain, including artistic ones. As interpretive sociology considers the mutual production of world and subjectivity, theories of rhetoric and literature invite social science to entertain the intermingling of fact and fiction – the factual nature of the man-made and the man-made nature of the factual.

Narrative as form, action, and symbol

The theoretical traditions presented here suggest that meaning is located, produced, and reproduced in linguistic form. Narrative is the most complex such form (Mink, 1978) in that it operates according to a "double logic" (Prince, 1994): "It simultaneously renders events ("the straightforward copy of events recounted"; Barthes, 1982, p. 289) and meaning, or the shaping of the account, which invokes the imagination.

Theorists from many traditions, including literature, psychology, and linguistics, study narrative.[4] Definitions of narrative are thus highly contextual (Polkinghorne, 1988). Smith (1981) perhaps offers the simplest: Narratives are "verbal acts consisting of someone telling someone else that something happened" (p. 182). Narrative has a verbal structure, and we can analyze the form of that structure. Furthermore, narratives constitute a *genre,* that is, a distinct category of artistic composition. Narrative theorists generally agree that this genre includes at least the following: temporal order; a beginning, a middle, and an end; characters; plot(s); narrator(s); and settings.[5] Narratives must also fulfill criteria such as coherence and plausibility. These criteria shift according to the social context of the telling: who tells what, to whom, and in what circumstances. In turn, narratives are interpreted, which means that they are placed in context with, and generate, still more narratives. For example, organizational decision theory provides narratives (theories) for making sense of other narratives (stories about decision making told by informants). Specifically, the *garbage can* narrative or theory serves to explain stories about organizational decision making. Researchers place data in relationship to these theories, that is, the theory represents or symbolizes the data. The *bounded rationality* narrative places the human mind in relationship to a computer. Narrative is thus both fixed (as a verbal form and genre) and multiplex (as subject to interpretation and generative of more narratives). The narrative form is uniquely suited to "render complexity with complexity" (Mink, 1978, p. 131). This complexity derives from its capacity to accommodate a multiplicity of meaning precisely through its interweaving of fact and fiction. Narrative produces meaning by imposing "a certain formal coherence on a virtual chaos of events" (White, 1981, p. 251). What the world produces in the way of events becomes for human beings the raw material of narrative. This interweaving of fact and fiction, event and meaning, observation and imagination parallels the pragmatists' view of the mutual production of subjectivity and reality.

Perhaps the simplest example of this interweaving occurs through processes of selection and ordering. Citing Sullivan's (1954) list of events in a life history, Linde (1993) shows how selection and ordering processes of life history data form "a particular theory of human development."

Disorders in learning toilet habits, disorders in learning speech habits, attitudes toward games and partners in them, attitudes toward competition and compromise, ambition, initial schooling, experience in college, interest in boys' or girls' clubs, preadolescent chum, puberty, unfortunate relationships in early adolescence, attitude toward risque talk, attitude toward the body, sex preference, attitude toward solitude, use of alcohol and narcotics, eating habits, sleep and sleep functions, sex life, courtships and marriage, parenthood, vocational history, avocational interests. (p. 44)

Although Sullivan presents a list, Linde argues that for all intents and purposes he presents a narrative about how human beings develop. If someone were to tell such a narrative in response to a question about her life story, "we would be surprised if the speaker began by describing experiences of toilet training" (pp. 44–45). However, if prompted by an analyst of a certain school to speak about such experiences, the narrative would not surprise us. Thus narrative reflects the conditions of its production: "the particular motives that elicited it and the particular interests and functions it . . . serve[s]" (Smith, 1981, p. 172).

One can verify the truth about "matters of fact," but one cannot verify the truth "about the possible combinations of kinds of relations" (Mink, 1978, pp. 144–145). This latter operation of narrative thus demands a basis of assessment other than verification. In this regard, narrative theory posits a number of criteria, including coherence and causality (Bruner, 1986; Burke, 1973; Linde, 1993; Mitchell, 1981; Ricoeur, 1984); morality (Johnson,

1993; White, 1981), closure (Spence, 1982, p. 170), and utility (Spence, 1982, pp. 275–277). However, some narrative theorists propose that these criteria themselves are contextually dependent. For example, Linde (1993) says that if we ask someone to explain why he chose a particular profession, he may reply, "Well, I have a precise mind and I enjoy getting all the details right." This response "relies on common-sense beliefs about character and ability as a good basis for career choice" (p. 18). Linde invokes the concept of a *coherence system*, "a system of assumptions and beliefs that are assumed to be shared by all competent members of a culture" (p. 18). Thus, to judge narrative in particular contexts requires an appreciation of the coherence systems invoked by these contexts. Using narrative theory in organizational analysis, for example, violates certain coherence systems of social science (O'Connor, 1995; O'Connor, Hatch, White, & Zald, 1995), one being the clash between the *validity* criterion and interpretive methods that inevitably involve meaning making and imagination.

I have suggested the complexity of narrative as a verbal and social form. Narrative is an object in the sense that it can be a text or a transcript and may be analyzed as such. But narrative is always situated in a particular context or ensemble of interrelationships in space and time. The rendering into narrative form both results from and produces contextualization. In this way, narrative theory may be considered as having both literary and sociological demands. Literary scholarship has an extensive tradition of *explication de texte* and close reading (O'Connor, 1995, in press). But the text is also a function of the social conditions of its production; thus narrative analysis also calls for sociological methods. Bourdieu (1993) perhaps comes closest to this parallel "micro-" and "macroscopic" scholarship in his analysis of Flaubert. His study recalls March's (1981, p. 230) reservations about the extraordinary scholarly demands of such work. The scope of this chapter, and the limits of my own scholarship, dictate that my case study provide only a suggestion of the possibilities of narrative theory and analysis for organizational decision theory.

Narrative analysis

In this section, I draw from the following theoretical streams: (1) the rhetorical tradition, in which narratives constitute a form of persuasion; (2) theories of narrative as a process of selection and definition; and (3) linguistic theory, particularly the view of language as social action.[6] My choice of these streams relates to the nature of the narratives in question – specifically, as texts produced by organizational actors to affect organizational action. Because texts in organizations inevitably relate to organizational action, narrative analysis in organizational settings proceeds from theoretical traditions that connect narrative and social action. In this context, narratives invariably strive to portray the narrators as credible and competent and their ideas as worthy and good. They work to create the future – in the same way that Aristotle describes the function of rhetoric. Even Plato, who finds language a persistently disappointing vehicle compared to reality, reminds us that we judge one's knowledge of something by his "ability to give an account of [the] thing to himself and to others" (1968, p. 213).

This section applies narrative theory to organizational decision making by studying a case of organizational change. Specifically, I aim to show a relationship between narrative and organizational action, as outlined in the introduction. My own narrative weaves together five other narratives (four given in interviews, one rendered in written form). It is shaped, of course, by my own rhetorical interest in persuading readers of this chapter to accept it as plausible and insightful – and by a narrative process very similar to the one theorized and described in this chapter.

In 1991, I happened to learn of a large (80,000-employee, Fortune 100) high-tech manufacturing company whose Organizational Development (OD) group had formed an internal network of individuals involved in large-scale organizational change. The OD group convened an annual meeting of this network. In order to participate, individuals had to present case studies documenting their change efforts. The case studies ran 20 to 30 pages long. I received permission to read a number of these studies. Then, in preparing this chapter, I selected one case for narrative analysis based on its extensive length (30 pages) and the importance of the site in question (referred to here as "Bluevale," it was the largest revenue-generating plant in the company). I also interviewed three individuals singled out in the case study for their degree of involvement in the change effort: the production manager at the plant in question, a human resources manager at the plant, and the corporate-based director of organization change. To get a top-management perspective, I interviewed the senior vice president of human resources, who reports directly to the president and chief executive officer.

Narrative 1: The case study

This section presents a highly condensed version of a recently published textual analysis (O'Connor, 1995). As mentioned earlier, the organization provided me with a copy of a case study about a specific site's change process. The text describes organizational decisions and decision-making processes, among other topics. In this section, I study how the narrative represents and generates decisions about change. These decisions relate to (1) when and why change occurs, (2) by what agency it occurs, and (3) in what way it occurs. The case writer states the narrative's usefulness as a "blueprint" for further and future change efforts, and a stated motive for writing is to "inspire readers" at other sites to decide to undertake organizational change. Even without this stated motive, one can reasonably infer a practical intent to influence organizational choices about change.

The narratives set a particular scene for organizational change: the United States during 1991 and 1992. The country is in an economic recession. Attention centers on issues such as competitiveness, global marketplaces, and the rapid pace of technological change. For the first time, according to some observers, layoffs affect white-collar as well as blue-collar workers. The narratives thus position change as a response to a narrative about present and future crises to U.S. business. This narrative is widely held and frequently circulated in the popular management literature. It occurs in its perhaps most pessimistic form in Kennedy's *Rise and Fall of the Great Powers* (1987).

The narrative identifies a *change agent,* generally a production or manufacturing manager, who experiences doubts about his organization's economic competitiveness and general morale.

Competition was increasing, distribution in certain areas of the world was particularly difficult, and areas of the organization were expressing dissatisfaction about the quality of work life in the area. This, coupled with increasing evidence of the decline of U.S. productivity versus the rest of the world began to create what became affectionately known as "sleepless nights."

This person has a conscience, simply observes what is going on, tells the truth to himself, and makes a personal decision. Anyone can do these things, and they are generally held in our society as virtues. That is, the portrayal generates a positive, if not sympathetic, view of the agent. It also portrays the decision as one that may be made autonomously, expeditiously, and obviously. The only complication, or prerequisite, is a local leadership position: That is, decision makers of organizational change should already be decision makers.

The narratives identify a process for initiating change: contact with the corporate OD function, which initiates the sociotechnical systems change program (Pasmore, 1988, cited as a source in the case studies). Thus the concept of *agent,* in this case, combines the production or manufacturing manager, the OD representative, and Pasmore (the least exposed agent but nonetheless a formative one, as the cases make some references to the paradox of using a book to produce "custom-designed" change). The case does not describe the process of selecting representatives to the design team. (The design team serves as the "brains" of the change effort.) Rather, the text refers to a selection of "key" or "influential" members and "opinion leaders" without describing this as a complication. The text describes no procedure for the selection of such individuals or consideration of the complexities involved in such a determination. This rendering has practical implications: The decision to proceed with organizational change per se, and the particular change strategy decided upon, perpetuate the existing commonsense understanding (and narrative) of "influential" members of the organization. Another representation of the change process involves the role of psychological aspects of change such as "support" and "resistance."

Resistance is to be expected to a significant change effort in an established organization. In retrospect, more time should probably have been spent educating and enlisting the support of these [managers who "lacked whole-hearted support"] and other managers.

Schafer (1981, pp. 40–44) discusses representations of resistance in psychoanalytic theory. As he says, "resistance . . . can be retold in more than one way" (p. 40). In the case study, resistance stands in relationship to ignorance and then to "education and training."

[S]ome members of the larger organization lacked an understanding of the redesign effort. This highlights the need for massive communication and education. Further, resistance to change by ignoring information can be expected until people are personally impacted.

Resistance also refers to another psychological issue: morale. At one site, orders declined while productivity rose. The number of teams went from 30 to 13. These events "resulted in a dampening of morale and a great need for retraining."

The narratives give shape to a particular definition of, stance toward, and resolution of resistance. Although conventional organizational theory may not posit this as a decision, in interpretive approaches, this narrative about resistance cuts off other definitions, stances, and resolutions. In this way, it makes a decision. Similarly, it identifies certain individuals and contexts as typical of change decision makers and contexts. It also delineates certain processes and workings of change; for example, it equates change with sociotechnical systems redesign in particular. For readers of these case studies, *change* means working with OD and doing so consistent with the change methods it employs. Thus the narratives bound change in particular ways. These bounds, being taken for granted, develop a commonsense notion of change that helps define the standards for change and for further narratives (new case studies – but, more important, new change efforts to be enacted and narrated) about change.

The following four narratives are based on conversations I had with individuals whom the case identifies as central to the change effort. Although they deal with the same theme as the case study – change at the largest site – these narratives take place in a different context: that of the research interview. Rhetorical theory suggests a slightly different shaping process, which is largely influenced by the speaker's need to come across as credible, competent, and professional.

Narrative 2: The senior vice president (SVP) of human resources

In a telephone conversation, the SVP said that around mid-1985, the executive team recognized that "the future competitive environment would be much more intense, dynamic and rapidly changing." The team began to communicate this interpretation to employees in various ways. It also communicated "a need to change." According to the SVP, "We were not sure what this meant. But the need was communicated." When I asked this executive, "What were the major decisions you made having to do with organizational change," he responded, "We decided that there was a need for it and that we needed room to experiment." In 1991, the executive team hired the director of organization change.

Narrative 3: Director of organization change (DOC)

According to the DOC, he left a full-time consulting practice to join the organization. In this practice, none of his change programs had taken place in a high-technology company. He could tell "success stories" about change, but he did not perceive them as relevant to his new employer and to his potential clients (the OD function is not corporate overhead; it is self-funded). After he was hired, he received several calls a day, including requests to speak at various sites. "I wasn't doing anything," he said, "only talking about change. I needed a project." At about that time, he received a call from an important site: a production facility, Bluevale (fictitious name), which generated 40% of the company's revenue. He made Bluevale his first client. In the meantime, anyone who called the DOC's office was placed on a mailing list for the OD change network (ODCN).

The DOC expressed a concern for diffusion and referenced the management literature on this subject. "Innovation diffuses poorly, and this is a decentralized company." In an organization with over 50,000 employees, the DOC had a change team of 3 people. "The issue was leverage." Thus he adopted the "action research" model, along with the idea of preparing "research papers" to disseminate knowledge, in order to keep his own team small but to replicate the role of change agent throughout the organization. To "heighten interest" in change activities, he said, the ODCN operated strictly through word of mouth (a "pull strategy," as he termed it).

During this time, he attended an offsite retreat with the top management team. At this meeting, he encountered limits, such as corporate compensation policies, that "did not work." After this meeting, he prepared a report and proposal recommending greater flexibility. The executives then gave him a mandate for "controlled experimentation."

Narrative 4: The production manager (PM) at Bluevale

According to the PM, he and his upper management decided upon a new business strategy that would give them greater control and profits in relation to a foreign partner. This change in strategy "changed the definition of work," meaning that it called for "a higher degree of involvement." Without some other accompanying change, he said, "I thought to myself, 'This won't be a fun place to work or to manage. We have to do something different.'" When I asked him about "major decisions" in the change process, he responded, "The decision to go outside to get help, and to go with a formal change process." He added, "We knew only enough to be dangerous." Although he made the decision to "go outside for help" unilaterally, he considered the advice of others. The other examples he gave of major decisions were the elimination of a middle layer of management and plant-wide, 3-day closure as part of the redesign process. "It sent a message to employees: 'This is different.' To those who were thinking 'We've heard this before,' it [the action] said, 'This is really happening.'"

Narrative 5: The human resources manager (HRM) at Bluevale

According to the HRM, the new business strategy had "led to a lot of down time." He described a period of several weeks in which various people advocated various courses of action. "Engineering had their own ideas; HR lobbied for team building." At some point in this lobbying process, the PM invited the DOC to Bluevale. When asked about a "major decision" with regard to organizational change, the HR manager made the comment quoted at the beginning of this chapter. He described a 6-month-long "investigation" involving tours of plants utilizing self-managing teams and extensive interviews with consultants, professors, and managers. Thus, when they finally sat down for the formal decision, "Nobody could've said 'No.'" He described the previous 6 months as "a process of enrollment, not decision."

Thus began not only the DOC's first success story but also the founding narrative of the ODCN. The Bluevale site case study became the first of what number over 100 such narratives today. As of June 1995, the ODCN had 1,200 members and met four times a year. Among all cases and all change sites, the DOC says, Bluevale remains "the trophy. . . . It is a world-class facility." The DOC showed me data on the extraordinary profit and quality statistics coming from Bluevale. He also commented that another part of the facility, whose management rejected the change effort, has since been moved to China. "They thought we were the communists when we came in to change things. Now they know what real communism is."

General observations about the narratives

The five narratives legitimize (Berger & Luckmann, 1966, pp. 85–118) a certain version of change. They also legitimize the narrators as mouth-pieces of this legitimized version. In Herrnstein Smith's (1981) terms, the narratives accomplish a social transaction. They diffuse knowledge about organizational change in general, about organization change as the OD group so names it, and about organizational development as a service entity. They also provoke interest in change within a community, for a number of readers within the organization may identify with the change agent, who struggles to manage production amid the strategic stresses of competition, recession, and hypergrowth, and the personal stress of layoffs. The case states that the ODCN and the narratives that form it "[provide] a common language of redesign . . . and [take] the mystery out of work redesign." They eliminate the need for certain decisions by making them a "natural" part of the change process. As Weick (1969, p. 101) states:

For decision-making to occur, there must first be accurate registering of the equivocality present in the information that is to be decided about. Little attention has been given to how this information is registered. The present analysis states that the way in which registration occurs will influence the way in which the decision is made . . . the decision-making which occurs in the selection process is not the most important decision-making in the system. The critical decisions . . . pertain to information stored in the retention process.

Similarly, "the person who makes decisions about [company] goals is less important to continued functioning than is the person(s) who decides what is known by the company" (p. 107). "[I]nformation strategies are as much strategies for managing interpretations" as they are for decision making (March, 1988, p. 397). The case studies "name" change: They give it a specific identity by directing attention to certain aspects of the change program, as managed by certain people, in certain ways. The study of narrative, then, is an investigation of "interpretive procedures . . . in everyday social practices" (Cicourel & Kitsuse, 1963, p. 51). Moreover, it combines the made and the discovered, the invented and the fictive, the social and the subjective (Berger & Luckmann, 1966, p. 38):

Language is capable not only of constructing symbols that are highly abstracted from everyday experience, but also of "bringing back" these symbols and representing them as objectively real elements in everyday life. In this manner, symbolism and symbolic language become essential constituents of the reality of everyday life and of the commonsense apprehension of this reality.

Narrative, then, has a pivotal function in the social construction of organizational life; narrative analysis permits reconstructions of this process.

Moreover, as artifacts, the narratives have symbolic value (Feldman & March, 1981). Specifically, any organization interested in working with the ODCN had to write a case study of its efforts. In Mauss's terms (1990), the case study functions as a symbolic offering to the OD group, which commences the ongoing network of professional relations and mutual assistance. As an extensive collection, the case studies provide symbolic testimony of the effectiveness of the OD leadership, allies, methods – and narratives.

Conclusion

Following interpretive traditions of literary theory and social science, if we wish to pursue the complexity of organizational decision making, then narrative theory and analysis have much to offer. With this approach, we may view organizational decision making as a convergence of narratives that are, in Heidegger's (1962) distinctive phrase, "always already" going on. For example, long before a decision was made to undertake large-scale organizational change at Bluevale, executives produced narratives about themselves and their organization in relation to economic and managerial narratives about global and technological change. A director produced a narrative about the need to establish credibility in a new organization – specifically, to tell compelling stories that prove how he, his organization, and his narrative about change (produced in relation to, among others, academic narratives about organizational change) could help them. A production manager produced a narrative about survivability and success in relation to a narrative that he and his management told about present and future business change – in the face of threats to his own and his organization's performance. The decision to proceed with change at Bluevale blended these narratives together. *Complexity* literally means "interwoven" or "plaited together." Narrative analysis of organization change, or organization change rendered (or reconstructed, if we accept that narrative is fundamental to human understanding) in narrative form, allows us to represent decision making in considerable complexity. It takes seriously March's suggestion to study decision making in the context of human life (1981, p. 230).

Decisions are a human construct. They are not natural phenomena in the world that we discover. They are "made" (and so designated) by theorists, observers, and participants. As the etymology of the word *decision* indicates, when we mark something as a decision, we set if off from its background in a particular way – we "cut it out" of a larger narrative or of other narratives. The narrative form and process direct attention in a particular way to particular events. March (1994, pp. 198–199) describes garbage can decision processes as a result of "a shifting intermeshing of the lives of an array of actors." I propose that we view this "shifting intermeshing" as taking narrative form and that we use narrative analysis to study it. Thus, when March says that choice opportunities collect decision makers, problems, and solutions, I say that, more precisely, the narratives that define choice opportunities, problems, and solutions as such converge with the always already occurring narratives of decision makers. And decision theory (i.e., narrative about these narratives) converges with the always already occurring narratives of decision theorists.

Interdisciplinary interpretive perspectives say that processes of invention and imagination produce meaning. Narrative and narrative analysis allow us to locate and follow these processes at work in decision theory, research, and practice. These activities involve constructing and reconstructing the narrative forms and processes that are constantly at play in organizational life. To understand a decision, we take decision narratives as a point of departure in new meaning-making activity, as I have aimed to do in this chapter. We place these narratives in relation to still other narratives, other tellings, and other fictions – to produce still more stories, storytelling, and (ever-storied) life itself.

Notes

1 For background on interpretive sociology, see Burrell and Morgan (1985), Giddens (1976), and Putnam (1983). In this chapter, I identify Mead (1934, 1959, 1964) and Schutz (1962, 1964, 1970) as transversals in interpretive sociology. That is, their work develops from philosophy (phenomenology and pragmatism, in particular) into more recent forms of interpretive work, such as symbolic interactionism and ethnomethodology.

2 Numerous references interconnect phenomenology, pragmatism, and sociology. Symbolic interactionists (e.g., Turner, 1974), ethnomethodologists (Garfinkel, 1967), and social constructionists (Berger & Luckmann, 1966), as well as historians of sociology (Burrell & Morgan, 1985; Giddens, 1976) acknowledge this relationship. Schutz is closely connected with the tradition of German idealism (Schutz, 1973, pp. xxv–xlvii); some consider him one of its pivotal exponents in sociology (Burrell & Morgan, 1985, pp. 235, 240, 302). Schutz's close colleague and "disciple" (1973, p. xi), Maurice Natanson, studied Mead extensively (Natanson, 1973). Mead is also closely associated with pragmatism (Burrell & Morgan, 1985, pp. 73–81) and is cited as influential in symbolic interactionism and ethnomethodology (Blumer, 1969, pp. 61–77; Meltzer, Petras, & Reynolds, 1975, p. 54). William James, considered a founder of pragmatism, is influenced by phenomenology (Edie, 1987; Linschoten, 1968; Wilshire, 1968).

3 For background on pragmatism, see Bernstein (1971), Diggins (1994), and Durkheim (1983).

4 Narrative theory is a highly interdisciplinary and long-standing body of work. For a brief introduction to narrative, see Prince (1994), Martin (1988), and Polkinghorne (1988).

5 A specific branch of literary theory is known as *narratology*, or the analysis of narrative literary form. This body of literature is too vast to summarize here. See, for example, Bakhtin (1981), Barthes (1984), Burke (1966, 1969, 1973), Genette (1980), Propp (1968), Ricoeur (1984–1988), and White (1978, 1981, 1987).

6 For more background on the rhetorical traditions from which I draw, see Aristotle (1954), Booth (1961), and Smith (1981); for the narrative traditions, see Burke (1966, 1969, 1973) and White (1981, 1987); for the linguistic traditions, see Austin (1962), Pratt (1977), and Searle (1979).

References

Allport, G. (1989). Dewey's individual and social psychology. In P. A. Schilpp and L. E. Hahn (Eds.), *The philosophy of John Dewey* (pp. 263–290). Carbondale: Southern Illinois University.

Arendt, H. (1968). *Between past and future.* New York: Viking.

Aristotle. (1954). *Rhetoric.* New York: Modern Library.

Austin, J. L. (1962). *How to do things with words.* Cambridge, MA: Harvard University Press.

Bakhtin, M. (1981). *The dialogic imagination: Four essays.* Trans. by C. Emerson & M. Holquist. Austin: University of Texas Press.

Barthes, R. (1982). Introduction to the structural analysis of narratives. In S. Sontag (Ed.), *A Barthes reader* (pp. 251–295). New York: Hill & Wang.

Barthes, R. (1984). *S/Z.* Trans. by R. Miller. New York: Hill & Wang.

Berger, P., & Luckmann, T. (1966). *The social construction of reality.* New York: Doubleday.

Bernstein, R. (1971). *Praxis and action: Contemporary philosophies of human activity.* Philadelphia: University of Pennsylvania Press.

Blumer, H. (1969). *Symbolic interactionism: Perspective and method.* Englewood Cliffs, NJ: Prentice-Hall.

Booth, W. (1961). *The rhetoric of fiction.* Chicago: University of Chicago Press.

Bourdieu, P. (1993). *The field of cultural production.* Trans. by R. Johnson. New York: Columbia University Press.

Bruner, J. (1986). *Acts of meaning.* Cambridge, MA: Harvard University Press.

Bruner, J. S., Goodnow, J. J., & Austin, G. A. (1977). *A study of thinking.* Huntington, NY: Krieger.

Burke, K. (1966). *Language as symbolic action.* Berkeley: University of California Press.

Burke, K. (1969). *A grammar of motives.* Berkeley: University of California Press.

Burke, K. (1973). *The philosophy of literary form: Studies in symbolic action.* Berkeley: University of California Press.

Burrell, G., & Morgan, G. (1985). *Sociological paradigms and organisational analysis.* Hants, U.K.: Gower.

Cicourel, A. V., & Kitsuse, J. I. (1963). *The educational decision-makers.* Indianapolis: Bobbs-Merrill.

Diggins, J. P. (1994). *The promise of pragmatism: Modernism and the crisis of knowledge and authority.* Chicago: University of Chicago Press.

Durkheim, E. (1983). *Pragmatism and sociology.* Trans. by J. C. Whitehouse. Cambridge: Cambridge University Press.

Edie, J. M. (1987). *William James and phenomenology.* Bloomington: Indiana University Press.

Farber, M. (1943). *The foundation of phenomenology: Edmund Husserl and the quest for a rigorous science of philosophy.* Albany: SUNY.

Feldman, M., & March, J. (1981). Information in organizations as signal and symbol. *Administrative Science Quarterly, 26,* 171–186.

Fiol, C. M., & Huff, A. S. (1992). Maps for managers: Where are we? Where do we go from here? *Journal of Management Studies, 29,* 267–285.

Garfinkel, H. (1967). *Studies in ethnomethodology.* Englewood Cliffs, NJ: Prentice-Hall.

Geertz, C. (1973). *The interpretation of cultures.* New York: Basic Books.

Genette, G. (1980). *Narrative discourse: An essay in method.* Trans. by J. Lewin. New York: Cornell University Press.

Gibbs, R. (1994). *The poetics of mind.* Cambridge: Cambridge University Press.

Giddens, A. (1976). *New rules of sociological method: A positive critique of interpretive sociologies.* New York: Basic Books.

Gioia, D. A. (1986). Symbols, scripts, and sensemaking. In H. P. Sims (Ed.), *The thinking organization* (pp. 49–74). San Francisco: Jossey-Bass.

Gioia, D. A. (1992). Pinto fires and personal ethics: A script analysis of missed opportunities. *Journal of Business Ethics, 11,* 43–53.

Goffman, E. (1959). *The presentation of self in everyday life.* New York: Doubleday.

Goffman, E. (1974). *Frame analysis: An essay on the organization of experience.* New York: Harper & Row.

Greimas, A. J. (1987). *On meaning: Selected writings in semiotic theory.* Minneapolis: University of Minnesota Press.

Heidegger, M. (1962). *Being and time.* New York: Harper.

James, W. (1975). *Pragmatism: A new name for some old ways of thinking.* Cambridge, MA: Harvard University Press.

Johnson, M. (1993). *The moral imagination.* Chicago: University of Chicago Press.

Kahneman, D., Slovic, P., & Tversky, A. (1982). *Judgment under uncertainty: Heuristics and biases.* Cambridge, U.K., and New York: Cambridge University Press.

Kennedy, P. (1987). *The rise and fall of the great powers.* New York: Random House.

Lakoff, G., & Johnson, M. (1980). *Metaphors we live by.* Chicago: University of Chicago Press.

Lakoff, G., & Turner, M. (1989). *More than cool reason: A field guide to poetic metaphor.* Chicago: University of Chicago Press.

Lévi-Strauss, C. (1963). *Structural anthropology.* Trans. by C. Jacobson & B. G. Schoepf. New York: Basic Books.

Linde, C. (1993). *Life stories: The creation of coherence.* New York: Oxford University Press.

Linschoten, H. (1968). *On the way toward a phenomenological psychology: The psychology of William James.* Pittsburgh: Duquesne University Press.

MacIntyre, A. (1981). *After virtue.* Notre Dame, IN: University of Notre Dame Press.

Mandler, J. M. (1984). *Stories, scripts and scenes: Aspects of a schema theory.* Hillsdale, NJ: Erlbaum.

March, J. G. (1981). Decisions in organizations and theories of choice. In A. H. Van de Ven & W. F. Joyce (Eds.), *Perspectives on organization design and behavior* (pp. 205–244). New York: Wiley.

March, J. G. (1988). *Decisions and organizations.* Oxford: Basil Blackwell.

March, J. G. (1994). *A primer on decision making: How decisions happen.* New York: Free Press.

Martin, W. (1986). *Recent theories of narrative.* Ithaca, NY: Cornell University Press.

Maturana, H. R., & Varela, F. J. (1987). *The tree of knowledge: The biological roots of human understanding.* Boston: New Science Library.

Mauss, M. (1990). *The gift.* New York: W. W. Norton.

Mead, G. H. (1934). *Mind, self and society.* Chicago: University of Chicago Press.

Mead, G. H. (1959). *Philosophy of the present.* La Salle, IL: Open Court Publishing.

Mead, G. H. (1964). *Philosophy of the act.* Chicago: University of Chicago Press.

Meltzer, B. N., Petras, J. W., & Reynolds, L. T. (1975). *Symbolic interactionism: Genesis, varieties and criticism.* London: Routledge & Kegan Paul.

Mingers, J. (1995). *Self-producing systems: Implications and applications of autopoesis.* New York: Plenum.

Mink, L. O. (1978). Narrative form as a cognitive instrument. In R. H. Canary & H. Kozicki (Eds.), *The writing of history: Literary form and historical understanding* (pp. 129–149). Madison: University of Wisconsin Press.

Mitchell, W. J. T. (1981). *On narrative.* Chicago: University of Chicago Press.

Natanson, M. (1973). *The social dynamics of George H. Mead*. The Hague: Martinus Nijhoff.

O'Connor, E. S. (1995). Paradoxes of participation: Textual analysis and organizational change. *Organization Studies, 16*(5), 769–803.

O'Connor, E. S. (In press). Lines of authority: Readings of foundational texts on the profession of management. *Journal of Management History.*

O'Connor, E. S., Hatch, M. J., White, H., & Zald, M. (1995). Undisciplining organizational studies: A conversation across domains, methods and beliefs. *Journal of Management Inquiry, 4*, 119–136.

Pasmore, W. A. (1988). *Designing effective organizations: The sociotechnical systems perspective*. New York: Wiley.

Plato. (1968). *The republic*. Trans. by A. Bloom. New York: Basic Books.

Polkinghorne, D. E. (1988). *Narrative knowing and the human sciences*. Albany: SUNY Press.

Pratt, M. (1977). *Toward a speech act theory of literary discourse*. Bloomington: Indiana University Press.

Prince, G. (1994). Narratology. In M. Groden & M. Kreiswirth (Eds.), *The Johns Hopkins guide to literary theory and criticism* (pp. 524–527). Baltimore: Johns Hopkins University Press.

Propp, V. (1968). *Morphology of the folktale*. Austin: University of Texas Press.

Putnam, L. L. (1983). The interpretive perspective: An alternative to functionalism. In L. L. Putnam & M. E. Pacanowsky (Eds.), *Communication and organizations: An interpretive approach* (pp. 31–54). Beverly Hills, CA: Sage.

Ricoeur, P. (1984–1988). *Time and narrative*. Chicago: University of Chicago Press.

Roe, E. (1994). *Narrative policy analysis: Theory and practice*. Durham, NC: Duke University Press.

Sarbin, T. R. (1986). *Narrative psychology: The storied nature of human conduct*. New York: Praeger.

Schafer, R. (1981). Narration in the psychoanalytic dialogue. In W. J. T. Mitchell (Ed.), *On narrative* (pp. 25–50). Chicago: University of Chicago Press.

Schutz, A. (1962). *Collected papers I: The problem of social reality*. The Hague: Martinus Nijhoff.

Schutz, A. (1964). *Collected papers II: Studies in social theory*. The Hague: Martinus Nijhoff.

Schutz, A. (1970). *On phenomenology and social relations: Selected writings*. Chicago: University of Chicago Press.

Searle, J. (1979). *Expression and meaning in the theory of speech acts*. Cambridge: Cambridge University Press.

Simon, H. (1957). Rational choice and the structure of the environment. In H. Simon (Ed.), *Models of man* (pp. 261–273). New York: Wiley.

Simon, H. (1961). *Administrative behavior: A study of decision-making processes in administrative organization*. New York: Macmillan.

Simon, H. (1979). Rational decision making in business organizations. *The American Economic Review, 69*, 493–513.

Simon, H. (1994). Literary criticism: A cognitive approach. *Stanford Humanities Review, 1*, 1–26.

Smith, B. (1981). Narrative versions, narrative theories. In I. Konigsberg (Ed.), *American criticism in the poststructuralist age* (pp. 162–186). Ann Arbor: University of Michigan Press.

Spence, D. P. (1982). *Narrative truth and historical truth: Meaning and interpretation in psychoanalysis*. New York: W. W. Norton.

Sullivan, H. S. (1954). *The psychiatric interview*. New York: W. W. Norton.

Tagliacozzo, G., Mooney, M., & Verene, D. P. (1976). *Vico and contemporary thought*. Atlantic Highlands, NJ: Humanities Press.

Turner, R. (Ed.). (1974). *Ethnomethodology*. Harmondsworth, U.K.: Penguin.

Tversky, A., & Kahneman, D. (1981). The framing of decisions and the rationality of choice. *Science, 221,* 453–458.

Vico, G. (1988). *On the most ancient wisdom of the Italians*. Trans. by L. M. Palmer. Ithaca, NY: Cornell University Press.

Weick, K. (1969). *The social psychology of organizing*. Reading, MA: Addison-Wesley.

White, H. (1978). *Tropics of discourse*. Baltimore: Johns Hopkins University Press.

White, H. (1980). *Metahistory*. Middletown, CT: Wesleyan University Press.

White, H. (1981). The narrativization of real events. In W. J. T. Mitchell (Ed.), *On narrative* (pp. 249–254). Chicago: University of Chicago Press.

White, H. (1987). *The content of the form: Narrative discourse and historical representation*. Baltimore: Johns Hopkins University Press.

Wilshire, B. (1968). *William James and phenomenology*. Bloomington: Indiana University Press.

Wittgenstein, L. (1958). *Philosophical investigations*. New York: Macmillan.

15 Bounded rationality, indeterminacy, and the managerial theory of the firm

Roy Radner

15.1 Introduction

This chapter is my response to a request for an account of "an economist's perspective on the organization of the firm." When faced with this request, I had three initial reactions. First, Oliver Hart had already written an interesting article (1989) with the same title, which, while presenting his own original point of view, also presented an excellent overview of the current ideas of economists on the subject. Second, my own perspective is probably more idiosyncratic than representative of the "generic economist," even though it is derived from such respectable authors as Arrow, Simon, Cyert, and March. Third, the subject is too vast for the confines of a short essay.

With these thoughts in mind, I decided to focus on two issues that have become increasingly apparent in attempts to apply the prevailing notions of "economic rationality" to the theory of the organization of business firms. The first goes under the rubric of *bounded rationality*. This is hardly a new idea, and has been forcefully brought to our attention in the work of Simon and others, although awareness of the problem (in economics) goes back at least to J. M. Clark (1918). I shall try to provide a more detailed taxonomy of bounded rationality than is usually done. In particular, it is important to distinguish between (1) costly rationality, like the costs of observation, communication, and even computation, that require only an extension of the standard Savage Paradigm and (2) truly bounded rationality, like not knowing the implications of everything that one knows, which – as far as I know – goes far beyond the Savage paradigm.

I thank Hsueh-Ling Huynh, Peter B. Linhart, and Zur Shapira for comments on earlier drafts. Some sections of this chapter, especially Section 15.3, rely heavily on Radner (1992). The first draft of this chapter was completed while the author was at AT&T Bell Laboratories. The views expressed here are those of the author and are not necessarily those of AT&T Bell Laboratories.

The second issue, which I shall call *indeterminacy,* arises in attempts to apply the theory of strategic games to models of organizations: That is, one often faces a very large multiplicity of solutions, which significantly weakens or even destroys the predictive power of the theory. By *solution* I mean here the so-called noncooperative equilibrium, usually associated with the names of Auguste Cournot and John Nash (and extended and refined by John Harsanyi, Reinhard Selten, and others to cover games in which the players have incomplete information). Although indeterminacy can arise even in static games with complete information, it seems to be especially prevalent in dynamic games and/or games with incomplete information.

Both of these issues have profound implications for the organization of the firm. In this chapter, and given the current state of research on the subject, I can only sketch some of these implications. In particular, I argue that they provide added credibility to the managerial theory of the firm.

In discussions of the economic organization of the firm, it has become commonplace to set up the straw figure of the firm as a black box, mysteriously choosing production and investment plans to maximize profits. It is true that there are still undergraduate price theory textbooks that present this picture, but economists have long been familiar with the phenomenon of the separation of ownership and management, at least since the publication of the book by Berle and Means (1932), if not before; in fact, Adam Smith had some trenchant comments on it (1776, pp. 264–265). This phenomenon is also referred to as the *separation of ownership and control* (see Fama & Jensen, 1983). Today one is likely to see this analyzed in terms of the *principal–agent model,* with the owner(s) cast as the principal and the manager(s) as the agent.

Going beyond this model, it is also recognized that there are many owners, managers, and workers. One approach has been to visualize the firm as a "nexus of contracts" (Jensen & Meckling, 1976). However, it is clear that many, if not most, of the relationships and activities within the firm, or even between the owners and the managers, are not closely determined by contracts in the usual sense of the word, but rather by expectations about the roles of the various actors. This leads to the idea of *incomplete contracts,* in which many contingencies are not explicitly covered by the terms of the contract, and yet the parties to it have expectations about the probable outcomes in those contingencies. If these expectations are mutually consistent and self-fulfilling, then we might model an incomplete contract as a two-part strategic game: (1) The parties first bargain about the explicit terms in the contract, to which they are committed, and then (2) the parties' postcontract actions are determined by strategies that form an "equilibrium" of the postcontract strategic game (I am being deliberately vague about the theories of bargaining and of equilibrium that underlie this description).

(Of course, all contracts are to some extent incomplete [see, e.g., Kornhauser, 1983], but intrafirm contracts may be even more incomplete than those between firms. For more on incomplete contracts and related material, see Hart, 1989, 1991; Williamson & Winter, 1991.)

It is recognized that the cognitive requirements placed upon the individual decision makers in such a model far exceed the capacities of present-day humans and computers. The question is whether this is a useful abstraction, and whether significant features of the organization of firms tend to be missed in the application of the paradigm. That is the issue that I address in this chapter, albeit rather tentatively. My reactions to the paradigm lead me in the direction of what has been called the *managerial theory of the firm*, which I discuss in the last section. The reader will see that it is as much a point of view as it is a full-fledged theory. I hope that the reader will also agree that it has the virtue of having a strong foundation of common sense. (As far as I know, the term "managerial theory of the firm" is associated with the writing of Robin Marris; see Marris, 1964; Marris & Wood, 1971; and Waldsmith, 1973.)

In Section 15.2, I consider various aspects of bounded rationality, moving from the *Savage Paradigm* of complete rationality in the face of uncertainty, through *costly rationality*, to *truly bounded rationality*. I argue that costly and bounded rationality imply the inevitability of the decentralization of information processing and decision making, together with the concomitant *Iron Law of Delay and Iron Law of Size*. In Section 15.3, I explore the implications of costly and bounded rationality for the architecture of decision in the firm, and illustrate by an example the problems that game-theoretic indeterminacy pose for the theory of mechanism design (the design of incentives). Finally, in Section 15.4, I set forth a brief defense of the managerial theory of the firm.

15.2 Decentralization and its inevitability

15.2.1 Costly and bounded rationality: Decentralization of information and decision

The Savage Paradigm of decision making under uncertainty. Although the themes of this section are bounded rationality and multiperson decision making, I start with a brief account of the paradigm of individual rational decision making under uncertainty that is dominant in economics and game theory today. This paradigm is primarily associated with the name of L. J. Savage, although Savage himself traced it to Bernoulli, Laplace, de Finetti, von Neumann, and Morgenstern, and others. In any case, Savage's book, *The Foundations of Statistics* (1954), remains the deepest and most coherent account of what I shall call here the *Savage Paradigm*.

Savage developed his theory primarily to illuminate and rationalize statistical practice, and to resolve some of the controversies that arose about statistical methodology following the appearance of the revolutionary ideas introduced by R. A. Fisher and J. Neyman. Ironically, his theory had little effect on statistical practice, but it was embraced by economists and game theorists as a powerful model of how decision makers should respond rationally to uncertainty and information.

The theory had three central themes. First, it laid down – as axioms – certain minimal principles of consistency of decision making in the face of uncertainty that, in Savage's view, embodied all of the notions of rationality that could reasonably be imposed.

Second, it showed that these principles of rationality implied that a decision maker's choices among alternative actions could be calculated as a function of two "psychological" scales: (1) a numerical scale of probabilities of events and (2) a numerical scale of the utilities of outcomes. More precisely, the rational decision maker would prefer an action that yielded the highest mathematical expectation of the utility of outcome, the expectation being defined relative to the decision maker's scale of probabilities. An important aspect of the theory is that the probability and utility scales are *personal* to the decision maker in the sense that different decision makers can reasonably differ in their scales. It should be emphasized that Savage did not assume that the rational decision maker was actually aware of these scales, or made the necessary calculations, but only that these scales could be inferred by an observer from a sufficiently rich set of decisions. Nevertheless, the theory provides guidance on how choices among complex actions can rationally be reduced by mathematical calculations to choices among simpler actions. This aspect of the theory will turn out to be important in the discussion of bounded rationality.

Third, the theory implied how a decision maker should rationally modify his or her decisions in the light of new information or, more generally, how the choice of actions should evolve in a sequential decision problem as new information is accumulated. Thus, although at the beginning of their lives as rational decision makers persons might reasonably differ in their beliefs about the likelihood of various events, they must all follow the same *rules* (formulas) for updating those beliefs in the light of new information. (Essentially, these are the rules of the calculus of conditional probability, as exemplified by Bayes's rule.) Because most realistic models of economic decision making involve sequential decisions, this is a crucial part of the theory in terms of its implications for rational behavior. It will also figure prominently in the discussion of bounded rationality.

As just sketched, the Savage Paradigm appears not to take account of the resources used in the process of decision making itself. Savage was, of course, aware of the fact that decision making requires resources, and provided a lengthy discussion of this matter. Nevertheless, he chose not to incorporate the costs of decision making explicitly into his model. It is convenient to classify the costly (resource-using) activities of decision making into three groups:

1. *observation,* or the gathering of information;
2. *memory,* or the storage of information;
3. *computation,* or the manipulation of information.

In addition, when we consider groups of decision makers, we shall have to take account of the costs of

4. *communication,* or the transmission of information.

Of these activities and their related costs, the first, second, and fourth can be accommodated by the Savage Paradigm with relatively little strain, although they do have interesting implications. However, as we shall see, a serious consideration of the costs of computation leads to serious doubt about the realism – or even approximate realism – of the paradigm as a theory of human decision making.

Costly observation and the Wald Paradigm. In his book *Statistical Decision Functions* (1950), Abraham Wald codified the idea, already implicit in the Neyman–Pearson theory of hypothesis testing, that statistical procedures could – or even should – be regarded as methods for making decisions in the face of uncertainty. Perhaps stimulated by his own pioneering studies of sequential statistical procedures, he also explicitly introduced the cost of observations into his general model of statistical decision making. The classic example that is said to have led Wald to develop his theory of sequential analysis is that of destructive testing in acceptance sampling. Typically, in order to fully test an artillery shell, one must fire it and thus destroy it (unless, of course, it fails to fire, in which case it is a dud and also useless). Before deciding to accept a lot of, say, 1,000 shells from the manufacturer, the U.S. Army typically tested some fixed number of shells from the lot and accepted the lot only if the number of defectives in the sample were less than some specified level. Because each observation (test of one shell) was costly, it was important to minimize the number of shells needed to achieve a given standard of reliability of the acceptance procedure. Wald showed how this could be done by a *sequential* procedure. Instead of fixing the sample size in advance, the decision maker should decide after each successive test whether to (1) continue testing, (2) stop testing and accept the remaining shells in the lot, or (3) stop testing and reject the lot. In fact, under certain conditions, the optimal sequential testing procedure produced significant savings compared with any fixed-sample-size procedure. (Wald was the first to develop a systematic theory of sequential statistical procedures, which appeared in Wald, 1947); see the Introduction to this last reference for a history of previous research on the topic.)

Other interesting cases of costly observation arose in the study of clinical trials. Suppose that several new drugs to treat disease X have been developed to the point where they can be tested on human patients. The responses of patients to both the old and new drugs are stochastic, so one can only measure the effectiveness of a drug by its probability of success.

The success probability of the old drug is known, but not that of the new one. The latter can only be estimated from clinical trials on real patients. In addition to the out-of-pocket costs of administering the drugs (which may be different), there is the *opportunity cost* of administering an inferior drug to a patient who might otherwise have had a greater probability of a successful treatment. Again, the optimal procedure is a sequential one in which a decision about whether to continue testing a new drug (and whether or not to adopt it) is made after observing the results for successive patients or groups of patients (see Basu, Bose, & Gosh, 1990).

In both of the preceding examples, there is no difficulty, in principle, in fitting the decision problem into the Savage Paradigm, although taking account of the costs of observation will typically complicate the analysis. In fact, it is interesting to note that problems of clinical trials are notoriously difficult to solve analytically, and the numerical computations needed to approximate an optimal policy fairly well are typically very demanding.

In these examples, it is also necessary for the decision maker to remember the results of previous observations. If the observations are complicated, the memory required to do this might be costly or even infeasible in very large problems. The costs of memory are in some sense analogous to the costs of observation, but they are not identical.

I shall not be able to discuss here the interesting problems associated with costly or limited memory (for a discussion of some implications of limited memory in strategic games, see chapter 9 of Osborne & Rubinstein, 1994).

Computation, communication, and decentralization. The decision maker who follows the Savage Paradigm will typically have to perform some computations in order to determine what actions should follow from his or her particular observations. In what follows, it will be useful to distinguish decisions that are relatively routine, or periodic, from those that are relatively rare, or one time only, and start our discussion with the former. For example, manufacturers periodically update their production plans on the basis of observed sales, market research, and observations of the economy. Firms periodically process new financial data to determine dividends, short-run borrowing, and so on. In a large firm, such decision cycles involve the collection and processing of vast amounts of data and the calculation of hundreds or thousands of individual decisions. This computational activity is far beyond the capability of any single human decision maker, even when armed with the most powerful computer. The computational task involved in corporate decision making is therefore divided among many humans and machines. *Inevitably, the activities of information processing for decision making are decentralized.* (In this sense, the activities of decision making in a firm are no different from the activities of physical production.)

The activities of information processing clearly use resources – humans, machines, materials – and are thus costly. In U.S. firms, more than a third, or even half, of all employees are engaged in information-processing activities or in jobs that support such activities (Radner, 1992).

But there is an additional, more subtle, cost of information processing, namely, the *cost of delay*. This is not an out-of-pocket cost, like salaries or machine maintenance, but a loss of profit due to the degradation of the resulting decision. For example, if it takes a year to process the statistics on recent sales, the resulting production plan will probably be obsolete long before it is completed. Up to a point, such delays can be reduced by the use of more information processors – human and machine. This is analogous to replacing a single *serial* computer with a *parallel machine* made up of many serial ones. However, it is a striking "law" of computer science that, *even with an unlimited degree of parallelization, the computational delay must increase unboundedly with the size of the problem,* given the technological capabilities of the component processors. (It would be more accurate to characterize this statement as a "folk theorem" rather than a general mathematical result; see Radner, 1993; Schwartz, 1980.)

For example, suppose that every T units of time a cohort of N numbers arrives, whose sum must be calculated. Suppose further that one has available P identical *addition processors*, and that the units of time are chosen (e.g., 1 microsecond) so that each processor takes one unit of time to do an addition. It can be shown that, no matter how large P is, and how the task of addition is divided up among the individual processors, it will take at least

$1 + \log_2 N$

units of time to add the N numbers. Furthermore, the number of processors needed to attain this minimum delay will be at least

$(1 + \log_2 N)(N/2T)$;

a smaller number of processors will result in an even longer delay. (Of course, to obtain this precise result, one needs a precise model of computation; see Radner, 1993, and Radner & Van Zandt, 1992, for details. In fact, this result holds for any associative operation, not just addition.) The delay can be further reduced only by using faster (and hence more costly) individual processors, which also has its limits, given the state of computing technology.

The preceding formulas were derived by taking account of the delay due to computation alone. Information processing also typically requires that incoming data and intermediate results be stored in memory. This adds further to the cost of information processing, and to the delays, as well, because it takes time to read data into a memory and to access the data stored there. Armchair empiricism suggests that machine memory is in some sense relatively cheap compared to computation, at least in the current state of technology.

Finally, the decentralization of information processing (parallel processing) requires that the individual processors communicate with each other.

Such communication requires additional resources and causes additional delays. Again, in the present state of technology, it seems that information *transmission* is relatively cheap compared to computation in the narrow sense; witness the flood of junk mail, telephone calls, and e-mail. It appears that today it is much easier and cheaper to send and receive memos and papers than it is to process them.

However, there is a gray area between pure transmission and pure computation, which one might call *coding* or *understanding* and which still creates significant bottlenecks in communication. In the field of artificial intelligence this area is known as *pattern recognition*. For example, progress in devising computer programs for machines to read script, understand speech, or interpret pictures has been frustratingly slow. We still rely on large numbers of humans to enter data from handwritten order sheets into computers, take down telephone instructions, or scan radar screens, not to mention driving automobiles, flying airplanes, and diagnosing diseases ("expert systems" notwithstanding). Furthermore, although humans remain better than machines in doing many of these activities, their productivity growth (through education and training) has probably been much slower than the productivity growth of machines for the transmission and storage of information and for computation in the narrow sense.

The costs and delays attributable to information processing have an obvious but important implication for organizations: It is not efficient (except in the tiniest organizations) for every decision to use all of the information available to the organization as a whole. In fact, in a large organization, only a small fraction of the available information will be brought to bear on any single decision; the efficient choice of information will be influenced by its cost and its relevance to the decision in question. Combining this observation with the fact that individual decision makers (processors) are limited in their capacity for information processing, one is led to the *inevitability of decentralized decision making*, in which different decisions – or groups of decisions – are made by different decision makers on the basis of different information.

(Bibliographic note: In the economics literature, the idea of representing human bounded rationality with a model of a computer – more precisely, a finite state automaton – is, I believe, due to T. A. Marschak and C. B. McGuire, 1971. K. R. Mount and S. Reiter have analyzed models of human organization as networks of processors in somewhat the same spirit as the preceding discussion; see Mount and Reiter, in press, and the references cited there. I should also mention the work of T. Van Zandt, in press, and the references cited there. I have already alluded to the work of Rubinstein and others, as described in Osborne and Rubinstein, 1994.)

Deciding how to decide: Truly bounded rationality. The considerations sketched in the last two sections make the typical problem of rational decision making under uncertainty appear much more complicated than the simple examples one encounters in textbooks on microeconomic theory and management science. Nevertheless, one can, *in principle*, stretch the Savage Paradigm to accommodate the various costs, individual capacities, and delays associated with observation, memory, computation, and communication in routine decision making. I shall call this suitably "stretched" theory the *Extended Savage Paradigm*.

In fact, I chose to talk about routine decision making only to fix the ideas. Nothing about the theoretical framework necessarily prevents it from being applied to one-of-a-kind decisions. In particular, one example of a one-of-a-kind decision is the problem of devising decision rules for a given set of routine decisions. In other words, it would appear that the Extended Savage Paradigm can be applied to the study of rational decision making in the firm at all levels. This, in fact, was the research program set forth in *The Economic Theory of Teams* (Marschak & Radner, 1972).

It may be instructive to inquire why progress on that research program has been so slow in the past two decades. In the theory of teams, it seemed convenient to distinguish between (1) the organization proper, including the members of the team, their tasks, their statistical decision rules, and the structure of observation and communication in the team and (2) the organizer or designer who determines everything described in (1). It soon became evident that even some simple problems in team theory could quickly become analytically – and even computationally – intractable *from the point of view of the organizer*. If this were true of the simplified theoretical models of the theory, how much truer would it be of the decision problems of real firms! (For references to literature on team theory, see Kim & Roush, 1987; Van Zandt, in press).

Here we come face to face with the hard core of bounded rationality. It is not that, in themselves, the costs of observation, communication, memory storage, and routine computation necessarily prevent a team of decision makers from conforming to the Savage Paradigm of rationality. The problem is that the task of designing decision rules that satisfy Savage's consistency requirements is beyond the intellectual capabilities of any organizer or team of organizers.

Savage understood this problem, although he did not have a satisfactory formal solution to it. He contrasted the two proverbs "Look before you leap" and "You can cross that bridge when you come to it."

Carried to its logical extreme, the "Look before you leap" principle demands that one envisage every conceivable policy for the government of his whole life (at least from now on) in its most minute details, in the light of the vast number of unknown states of the world, and decide here and now on one policy. This is utterly ridiculous, not – as some might think – because there might later be cause for regret, if things did not turn out as had been anticipated, but because the task implied in making such a decision is not even remotely resembled by human possibility. It is even beyond our power to plan a picnic or play a game of chess in accordance with the principle, even when the world of states and the set of available acts to be envisaged are artificially reduced to the narrowest reasonable limits. (Savage, 1954, p. 16)

To put it another way, decision makers are not merely uncertain about empirical events such as "It will rain tomorrow in New York City" or "General Motors has developed an efficient electric automobile." They are also uncertain about logical inferences such as "Fermat's Last Theorem follows from the axioms of arithmetic" or "The 123rd digit in the decimal expansion of pi is 3." Or, if this seem far removed from the business world, try (1) "Given all I know about the old and new drugs for treating a particular disease, what is the optimal policy for conducting clinical trials on the new ones?" or (2) "Given all that AT&T's management knows about the telecommunications industry and about AT&T's capabilities, what should be its business strategy for the next five years?" or even (3) "Given all that is known, theoretically and empirically, about business organizations in general, and about telecommunications and AT&T in particular, should AT&T reorganize itself internally, and if so, how?"

Essentially, what we are dealing with here is the decision maker's *uncertainty about the logical implications of what he or she knows.* Although I cannot justify it scientifically, I have a feeling that this kind of uncertainty is at least as important in business (and other) decision making as uncertainty about empirical events – and perhaps even more so. In any case, I am not aware of any generally acceptable theory of what it means to be rational in the face of such uncertainty. (See, however, Lipman, 1995, for a start in this direction.)

This confronts the economist with a dilemma. On the one hand, he or she can continue to investigate models of rational decision making that are simple enough to be tractable for the economist but are hopelessly unrealistic (this is the current mainstream approach). On the other hand, at the risk of being branded a "behavioral economist," he or she can abandon the attempt to explain observed behavior as rational and simply record various empirical regularities such as rules of thumb. As a compromise, the economist can try to show that competition will weed out "irrational" or "nonoptimal" behavior in the long run, although individual decision makers and organizations are not capable of deliberately determining what is optimal; in some sense, this is the best of all possible worlds. (See, e.g., Winter, 1987, and the references cited there. I should mention, however, that Winter is generally critical of the *competitive selection* hypothesis, at least in its starkest forms.) These three themes will recur in the rest of this chapter.

15.2.2 Conflict and the decentralization of authority

Conflicting goals and the power of decentralized information. Thus far I have discussed decision making in the firm as if it were simply an extension of a one-person decision problem to a group of persons and machines, this extension being made necessary by the limited capacity of individuals to perform the various activities required in the process of making decisions. However – as economists and other social scientists are fond of emphasizing – different persons in an organization are likely to have conflicting goals, or at least partly so, and these conflicts are likely to impose further costs on the organization.

Of course, if the firm has a sole owner, and if the persons hired by the owner are told exactly what to do in all circumstances, and are perfectly monitored and disciplined, then the fact that they have conflicting underlying goals will be harmless (to the owner). But if the persons are hired to make decisions, and the information processing and decision making are decentralized in the sense described in the preceding sections, then the individual decision makers will in general have some freedom to take certain actions that are more in their own interests – and less in the interest of the owner – than they would if the owner were in complete control. Thus *the decentralization of information processing and decision making confers power on the individual decision makers* (subordinates?), which they may be able to use to further their own interests at the owner's expense. The situation is even more complex if there is more than one owner, and especially if some or all of the owners are also decision makers in the firm.

For example, the owner of a firm may delegate day-to-day manufacturing decisions to a factory manager, who is supposed to adjust the detailed scheduling of work to transient variations in absenteeism, the availability and quality of materials, and so on. But such detailed supervision requires effort, so the factory manager is tempted to pay less than full attention to these fluctuations in the manufacturing environment, with a consequent lowering of average productivity compared to what might have been attained. However, because the owner is not well informed about these fluctuations in the environment, he is not able to determine what level of productivity is actually possible in any given time period. (Some readers will recognize this as the classic *principal–agent* situation.) Of course, if the owner knows enough about the business, and is a good enough statistician and game theorist, he can partially control the shirking of the manager by compensating him on the basis of his long-run average performance and various statistics about the environment, but typically the inefficiency cannot fully be eliminated.

This example illustrates two different phenomena that may be present in a principal–agent relationship, which K. J. Arrow (1974) has called *hidden action* and *hidden information;* these are also referred to as *moral hazard* and *misrepresentation*, respectively. (For a review of the theoretical literature on moral hazard, see Dutta & Radner, 1995. For game-theoretic treatments of misrepresentation see, e.g., Fudenberg & Tirole, 1991.)

As a second example, consider the case of a research and development (R&D) facility, and suppose that the issue is not one of shirking but rather one of disagreement about what R&D projects are likely to result in profitable innovations. These disagreements stem from both differences in technical information and differences in "a priori" beliefs about what kinds of innovations are likely to be profitable. Because the relevant technical information is highly specialized, decision making about R&D will be decentralized, and this leads to new problems. On the one hand, the owner would like to impose her own prior beliefs on the individual developers or development teams. On the other hand, the owner would like the decisions of her R&D subordinates to be informed by their specialized information. This confounding of prior beliefs and information results in a loss of efficiency from the owner's point of view. This loss of efficiency will be exacerbated, of course, to the extent that the R&D subordinates are influenced by the inherent scientific interest of various projects, or by other preferences, and to the extent that these interests and preferences are not perfectly correlated with potential profitability.

Incentives and mechanism design. To study the effects of conflicting goals in the presence of decentralized information and decision making, economic theorists – and experimentalists, too – have primarily utilized the general model of *games of strategy*. In any particular instance, the model specifies (1) who are the *players* in the game, that is, the decision makers; (2) what *strategies* are available to each player; and (3) the *payoff function*, which specifies the expected utility for each player corresponding to each profile of strategies chosen by the players. Thus the Games Paradigm extends the Savage Paradigm by making a decision maker's utility depend both on his or her actions *and* on the actions of other decision makers, as well as on the *state of nature* or natural environment, which is beyond any decision maker's control. Consequently, any one decision maker is uncertain not only about natural events, such as the weather, but also about the actions of the other players in the game. The most widely used predictive concepts are some variation on the idea of a *Nash equilibrium,* namely, a profile of strategies such that no player can increase his or her expected utility by *unilaterally* changing his or her own strategy.

In the application of game theory to the design of organizations, it is imagined that the organizer (owner?) can choose the rules of the game – and hence the number of players, their strategy sets, and so on – subject only to some constraints that reflect the available technology (including the technology of information processing), the availability of employees, the outside opportunities of potential employees, and other factors. It is understood that the organizer will be one of the players in the game. It is also imagined that the organizer will make this (constrained) choice to maximize his or her own expected utility; this is called the problem of *mechanism design*. Here the "mechanism" refers to the particular rules of the game chosen by the organizer.

In order to predict what expected utilities for the organizer and other players will result from a particular mechanism, theorists typically predict that the players will adopt a Nash profile of strategies. According to this theory, if the organizer chooses a mechanism so as to maximize his or her own utility, then the organizer will predict that for any choice of mechanism he or she will receive the utility corresponding to a Nash profile for that mechanism. There may, in fact, be many mechanisms that give the organizer the same (Nash) utility. In this case, competition among organizations for employees may force the organizer to adopt a mechanism that is efficient relative to what can be achieved for the players by Nash profiles of some other mechanism. Such a mechanism is called *second best.* In other words, a mechanism M is *second best* (given the technology and preferences of the players) if there is no Nash profile of any mechanism that makes every player (including the organizer) as well off as, and some player better off than, M does.

(In an alternative formulation of the problem, the organizer is some outside agency, such as a government regulator, that imposes the mechanism on the firm. In that case, the organizer's objective may be to maximize some measure of social welfare, which could include the welfare of the decision makers in the firm.)

Without going into the details of the theory, we can see immediately that the problem of mechanism design, as formulated here, is open to the same critique of truly bounded rationality that was directed against the Savage Paradigm (see the preceding section titled "Deciding How to Decide: Truly Bounded Rationality). The critique is even more severe in the present case, because even if the organizer were able to solve the mechanism design problem, could we rely on each player to deduce his or her own component of a Nash profile of strategies?

We also can see that a new problem arises if there is more than one Nash profile of strategies for the proposed mechanism. This is what I referred to in Section 15.1 as the issue of *indeterminacy.* Without some further mechanism of coordination, which is not specified in the model, how do we know which Nash profile will be adopted by the players? Indeed, how are the players going to agree on which Nash profile to adopt? Lest it be thought that these are imaginary difficulties, I should point out that experience with such models suggests that in many – if not most – cases of realistic interest, there is typically a multiplicity of Nash profiles, often infinitely many. I illustrate this phenomenon with an extended example in Section 15.3.4.

Authority and leadership. Although the previous section was quite critical of the theory of mechanism design, and game theory more generally, as a paradigm for understanding the organization of firms, the definition of a Nash profile can provide some useful insight into the elusive concept of *authority.*

One way to think about a Nash profile is as a profile of both expectations and strategies. My strategy is an expectation of what I shall do, and I also have expectations about what Nature and the other players will do, and in particular about how the other players will respond to the various actions that I might possibly take, including actions that do not conform to my expected strategy.

The phenomenon of mutiny provides an interesting illustration. Obedience to the captain and the rules of the ship ordinarily forms a Nash profile for all of the ship's crew. Normally, no single sailor can expect anything but swift punishment for unilateral disobedience. It is in this sense that the captain has authority over the ship's crew. In order for a mutiny to be successful, a significant number of sailors (and usually officers, too) must coordinate their deviations from their expected (Nash profile) behaviors. The mutiny itself can form a new Nash profile, with its own expectations and even notions of "obedience to a new authority."

How does the old Nash profile of obedience to the captain and to the ship's rules give way to the new, mutinous Nash profile? Several factors may be at work. First, the environment may change in such a way that conditions for some of the crew become so bad that a crew member may prefer disobedience and the prospect of punishment to the continuation of the status quo. Second, communication with other crew members may lead to the impression that they are also on the verge of disobedience, increasing the expectation that disobedience may be successful.

Third, some leader may actively foster the expectation that disobedience can be sufficiently coordinated to be successful. Here the phenomenon of bounded rationality may come into play. Crew members will be uncertain about what their optimal strategies are, given their expectations (which in any case are not very precise), and may be open to persuasion. I admit that the word *persuasion* is rather vague in this context, which is a reflection of our ignorance of how otherwise rational decision makers behave under the constraint of truly bounded rationality. Nevertheless, successful leaders do seem to be able to forge a new and persuasive vision of a Nash profile that is different from the current one. From this point of view, the phenomena of *leadership* and bounded rationality are inextricably linked.

The decentralization of information and decision making is related to the distinction between de facto and de jure authority. As noted previously, the decentralization of information is an inevitable consequence of bounded rationality – in both its wide and narrow senses – and this decentralization provides decision makers with opportunities to act without being perfectly monitored by supervisors and/or colleagues. Thus *bounded rationality inevitably leads, through the decentralization of information, to the de facto decentralization of authority.* Nevertheless, decision makers will remain accountable – if only imperfectly – to the individuals or groups who hold formal authority. Again, because of bounded rationality, it will not be possible to predict with certainty the circumstances under which formal authority will be invoked or be effective. In a normally functioning organization, this will be more or less regulated as part of a Nash profile of strategies. These strategies and the corresponding expectations of the members might be thought of as expressions of a particular "corporate culture" (see Kreps, 1990). However, these strategies will never completely spell out all eventualities and the players' responses to them. To these uncertainties we must add those associated with the defects in the notion of the Nash profile described earlier.

15.3 The architecture of decision making in the firm

15.3.1 Architecture and mechanism design

In the preceding section I argued that the decentralization of decision making in a large firm is inevitable. The way the tasks of information processing and decision making are defined and distributed among the members of the firm will be called here the *architecture of decision* in the firm. The presence of conflicts of interests and beliefs will also require a specification of the structures of incentives – the compensation, rewards, and punishments – for the firm's members. I include the description of the structure of incentives in the architecture of the firm. The choice of the incentive structure is sometimes called the *mechanism design problem.*

In this section I take up in turn the description of architectures for the decentralization of (1) information processing, (2) decision making, and (3) incentives. We shall see that economists have not gone very far in producing comparative economic analyses of alternative architectures. Therefore, at the end of this section, my remarks on hierarchy and bureaucracy will have to be based as much on speculation as on thorough theoretical analysis.

15.3.2 Efficient structures for information-processing

It is useful to distinguish between the architecture of information processing and the architecture of decision making, although they are obviously related. Thus, even if a particular decision (or group of decisions) is assigned to a particular manager, the task of processing the information on which that decision is based may well be distributed among several persons and machines (and typically is for a decision of any significance). The theory of the decentralization of information processing is closely related to the theory of parallel processing in computer science (see Radner, 1993; Van Zandt, in press). The topic is technically complex, and here I can only illustrate some of the ideas.

In this subsection, I ignore the complications induced by conflicts of interest and belief. In this case, a useful metaphor for a member of the firm who is engaged in information processing is that of a computer of (relatively) limited capacities. These person/computers are linked in a network, together with machine/computers, to form a system that is analogous to modern parallel-processing computing machines. Following the computer science terminology, I call the individual components (persons or machines) *processors* and the entire structure a *network*.

For example, suppose that the decision problem is to select the best (most promising) project from a given large set of candidates. A number of processors are available to perform this task, but each processor has only limited capacity, and no single processor can perform the entire task in an efficient manner.

To make the example more precise, suppose that the available processors are identical, that each processor can compare projects pairwise, and that each processor takes a certain amount of time to compare a pair of projects and pick the best one. (To simplify the presentation, I measure time so that one comparison takes one unit of time.) More specifically, suppose that a processor operates as follows. Each processor has (1) an "in-box," which can hold any number of unread project descriptions, (2) a "register," which can hold a single project description that has already been read, and (3) a "central processing unit (CPU)" that can, in one unit of time, read a project description from the in-box, compare it to the one in the register, and put the better one back in the register. (For simplicity, I assume that it also takes one unit of time for a processor to read a project description and put it in an empty register.) At any time, a processor can also send the project description in its register to the in-box of some other processor. Assume that this communication takes no additional time. However, to compare the communicated project with another, the second processor will have to reread the project description that has been put in its in-box. Finally, a processor can deliver the contents of its register to the outside as the answer. The description of the *project-selection network* includes (1) a specification of the number of individual processors (recall that they have identical capacities), (2) an initial assignment of projects to the in-boxes of processors, and (3) an algorithm that determines which processors send projects to other processors and when, and which processor delivers the final answer.

Two properties of a network will be considered to be costly: (1) the number of processors and (2) the number of units of time it takes to deliver the answer. The latter will be called the *delay*. (For simplicity, I assume that communication is costless.) Processors are costly because they have to be paid, bought, or rented. Delay is costly because a longer delay may make the decision out-of-date or obsolete. Therefore, I shall call a network *efficient* if it cannot be modified without increasing the delay, the number of processors, or both.

One can completely characterize efficient networks for the class of simple problems that I have just described. They have the form of a *tree* as illustrated in Figure 15.1, where the individual processors are represented by small circles. Except for the processors at the bottom, each processor has one or more other processors that report to it (the direction of reporting is upward in the figure). The processor at the top is called the *root* (the tree is

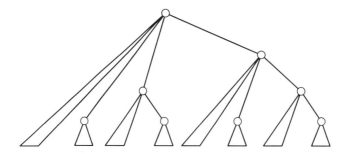

Figure 15.1. An efficient network.

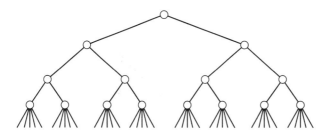

Figure 15.2. A hierarchical network with 15 processors, 40 items, and delay 10.

upside down). At the beginning of the process, the projects to be compared are distributed as equally as possible among all the processors. (These projects are represented in the figure by the triangles or "fans," one under each processor.) Each processor deals with the projects assigned to it, one by one, until it has no more projects in its in-box, at which time it sends the project in its register up to the in-box of its "superior," if it has one (along the corresponding line in the figure). When the root has no more projects in its in-box, it delivers the project in its register as the answer.

Of course, not all networks are trees, and not all trees are efficient. For example, Figure 15.2 shows a tree network with 15 processors and 40 projects. At the beginning, each of the eight processors at the bottom of the tree is assigned five projects. I leave it as an exercise for the reader to show that (1) the delay is $5 + 2 + 2 + 2 = 11$; (2) this network is not efficient; and (3) an efficient network will process the 40 items in only 8 units of time instead of 11 and use only 8 processors instead of 15 (see Radner, 1993, pp. 1395–1396).

One can also give a simple formula for the time it takes (delay) for an efficient network to process N items with P processors. In order to present this formula, I need to introduce some notation. First, recall that for integers N and P, N mod P denotes the remainder after dividing N by P. For any number x, let $D[x]$ denote the result of rounding x down to the nearest integer, and let $U[x]$ denote the result of rounding up. Finally, let log x

denote the logarithm of x to the base 2. Then the minimum delay for an efficient network to process N items with P processors is

$$C = D[N/P] + U[\log (P + N \bmod P)]. \tag{15.1}$$

In the special case in which P is a power of 2 and N is a multiple of P, this formula simplifies to

$$C = (N/P) + \log(P). \tag{15.2}$$

Equation (15.1) characterizes the trade-off (for an *efficient* network) between delay and the number of processors for a fixed number of projects. On the one hand, the delay is at a maximum when there is only one processor; in this case, the (single-processor) network processes the projects *serially*, and the resulting delay is N. On the other hand, the minimum possible delay with an unlimited number of processors is

$$\min C = 1 + U[\log N], \tag{15.3}$$

which can be obtained with a number of processors somewhat less than N; such a network uses the maximum degree of *parallelism*. Figure 15.3 illustrates this trade-off for the case of 10,000 projects ($N = 10,000$). (In the figure, both P and C are shown on logarithmic scales.)

Although this example is very special, there are several important conclusions we can draw from it that are applicable to a much broader class of cases. In the remainder of this section, I sketch these conclusions and extensions.

First, the precise results about efficient architecture and the processor-delay trade-off are true for a much broader class of operations, namely, any *associative* (binary) operation. Examples of such operations are addition, multiplication, and taking the minimum and the maximum. (Project selection exemplifies the last operation.) Familiar operations of accounting and pattern recognition can be formulated so as to fit in this category.

Second, I want to emphasize an important implication of (15.3), namely, that *as the number of projects to be processed increases, the minimum delay must also increase unboundedly, even for efficient networks and even if the number of available processors is unlimited*. I refer to this as the *Iron Law of Delay*. In light of the previous paragraph, the Iron Law of Delay will be valid for all associative information-processing operations. Indeed, it is a "folk theorem" of computer science that associative operations are the most amenable to parallelization, in which case (15.3) represents a lower bound on the delay for a much broader class of operations (not just associative ones). Of course, delay can be reduced by using more powerful (faster) processors, but the Iron Law of Delay will remain valid at any particular time if (as is realistic) the power of the processors available at any time is bounded. Furthermore, the power of human processors is increasing slowly over time, if at all, compared to that of machine processors, so as long as hu-

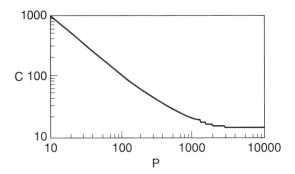

Figure 15.3. Min C versus P for 10,000 items ($N = 10,000$).

mans do a significant amount of information processing in firms, the Iron Law of Delay will be a significant factor in the performance of large firms.

Third, our example of project selection has some curious architectural implications. Although the network in Figure 15.1 is a tree, there is something odd about it as a picture of an organizational hierarchy: Every processor has subordinates at all levels below it. Reporting through skipped levels is not unheard of in corporate hierarchies, but the practice does not seem to be as widespread as the picture suggests. The reader, of course, may object to the use of the word "hierarchy" and to the particular way in which the picture in Figure 15.1 was drawn. In common usage, the word *hierarchy* has (at least) two somewhat different connotations. First, the members of the hierarchy are arranged in a tree (I shall not give a formal definition here); second, each member is assigned to a level or rank, with the constraint that if a member reports to another member, the second member must have a higher rank. For any given tree, there is typically more than one way to assign ranks to form a hierarchy consistent with the given tree structure. For example, I might have drawn the tree in Figure 15.1 as in Figure 15.4. Now skip-level reporting has apparently been eliminated, but the hierarchy looks unbalanced in terms of span of control compared to, say, Figure 15.2. In fact, in the next subsection I question whether the analysis of efficient networks for information processing tells us much at all about the hierarchies represented in traditional organization charts.

Fourth, I must point out a feature of real firms that our example ignores: Typically, new information about the environment arrives periodically and new decisions are made periodically. For example, project selection may occur quarterly, with a separate cohort of projects being compared each time. In this case, the delay criterion might be the long-run average delay over all cohorts. One might also require that the cohort delays be bounded. The problem of characterizing the efficient networks for such a sequence of information-processing tasks is more complex than the problem I have just

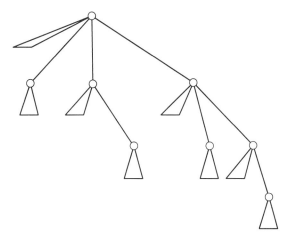

Figure 15.4. Another hierarchy for the tree of Figure 15.1.

described for the one-shot case, and the solution is correspondingly more complex as well (for more details, the reader is referred to Radner & Van Zandt, 1992).

To be more specific, consider the model of project selection described earlier, but now suppose that a new cohort of N projects arrives every T periods, and that the task is to pick the best project out of each cohort. I shall call this the *periodic case*, in contrast to the *one-shot* case described earlier. Again, there will be a trade-off in which the average delay for processing a cohort can be reduced only by increasing the amount of parallelization, and hence the total number of processors. The minimum delay now depends on both the number of projects in a cohort (N) and the time between cohorts (T). It is not possible to give a simple formula for this trade-off corresponding to equation (1), but one can derive a lower bound, which approximates the actual trade-off curve when the number of projects and processors is large. (I omit the formula; see Radner, 1993.) One can show that, just as in the one-shot case, the lower bound on the delay varies from N to $(1 + \log N)$. However, the lower bound on the number of processors varies between N/T and $(2N - 1)/T$. This contrasts with the one-shot case, in which the minimum number of processors is one (corresponding to the maximum delay of N on the trade-off curve). The reason for this contrast is that we require that the delays for successive cohorts not increase unboundedly as time goes on. Thus, in the periodic case, the Iron Law of Delay can be extended to the number of processors as well: Call a network *feasible* if the delay for successive cohorts remains bounded as time goes on; then, *in the periodic case, the number of processors in a feasible network must increase at least proportionately with the number of items per cohort*. I shall call this the *Iron Law of Size*.

To summarize the preceding discussion on the architecture of efficient information processing, we have seen that for associative operations, efficient networks are treelike but do not exhibit the regularities of hierarchies characteristic of standard organization charts, especially in the periodic case, where typically several trees are operating simultaneously and individual processors routinely rotate among different positions in the component trees. We have also seen that information processing is subject to the Iron Law of Delay and, in the periodic case, to the Iron Law of Size as well. To the extent that associative operations are, in fact, the most amenable to parallelization, these iron laws will be applicable to other kinds of information-processing operations, too.

As a coda to this subsection, I should point out that although *regular* hierarchies are not fully efficient for information processing, they may be approximately efficient under some circumstances (see Radner, 1993). Thus, if there are reasons other than efficiency for using a hierarchical network, then it may be possible to do so without sacrificing too much efficiency. In other words, although regular hierarchies are not fully efficient, our considerations of efficient information processing have not yet been sufficient to completely rule out hierarchical architectures in decision making. However, further doubts about the primacy of hierarchies will be discussed in the next subsection.

15.3.3 Efficient structures for decentralized decision making

In the typical firm, thousands of decisions are made every day. It is inconceivable that they would all be made by the same person. The same limitations that prevent any one person from deciding everything also make it uneconomical for all decisions to be based on the same data. We observe that firms take in enormous amounts of data every day, but most decisions are based on a very small part of it. As we saw in the previous subsection, the more information one brings to bear on a decision, the longer will be the delay in implementing it and the greater will be the number of required processors (the Iron Laws of Delay and Size). By contrast, for most decision problems, a small amount of information (relative to the amount available to the entire firm) enables one to make a fairly good decision if the information is chosen wisely. Of course, the information required for a "good" decision is typically different for different decision problems. The resulting situation, in which many decisions are made by different decision makers on the basis of different information, will be called here the *decentralization of information.*

The decentralization of information has important consequences for the architecture of decision making in the firm. Different decisions, or different groups of decisions, will utilize different networks for information processing. Although different decisions will be based on different information, those information sets are likely to overlap in many cases. Correspondingly, we cannot expect the different information-processing networks to be arranged in a hierarchical pattern; rather, we can expect to find networks arranged in various patterns according to (1) the pattern of interactions among the decisions and (2) the pattern of correlation among the information variables. Indeed, we would expect to find that many individual processors belong to more than one network or even move about in their assignments.

These theoretical predictions are borne out by empirical observations. First, there is now a large literature on so-called informal organization, documenting the many informal networks of information flow that coexist in organizations and that, in particular, do not coincide with the formal organization chart. Second, multiple networks are sometimes formalized, as in the case of *matrix management*.

The theoretical study of efficient architectures for the decentralization of information is the subject of the theory of teams and is still in its infancy, even though research on the topic began more than 40 years ago (see Radner, 1992, and Van Zandt, in press, for references). Nevertheless, it is clear that – from considerations of the efficiency of the processing and utilization of information alone – we would expect the architecture of decentralized information to be varied and complex, and rarely hierarchical in nature.

15.3.4 The design of incentive mechanisms

Thus far in this section, I have proceeded as if all the persons (processors) in the firm had the same goal. I have already discussed (in Section 15.2.2) how the decentralization of information confers on the individual decision makers the power to pursue – at least in part – their private interests and beliefs. I also suggested there that the methods of game theory – and especially the concept of a Nash profile – might be used to design organizational mechanisms to control the inefficiencies arising from conflicts of goals, but also that difficulties in this program might arise due to indeterminacy and bounded rationality. In this subsection I want to go into a little more detail on this topic. (For an introduction to the ideas of mechanism design and the comparison of institutions, see Hurwicz, 1995; specific models relevant to the firm are discussed in Radner, 1991.) For a somewhat critical discussion of progress in this area with respect to the organization of firms, see Radner, 1992; a more upbeat appraisal emerges from Milgrom & Roberts, 1992.)

It is interesting that the general theory of mechanism design has thus far made little headway in illuminating the choice among *alternative* architectures of incentives and decision making in the firm. The examination of a specific design problem for the firm may shed some light on the difficulties. I take as my example the problem of transfer pricing, specifically the design of bargaining mechanisms.

Divisions of large firms often "buy" goods and services from other divisions of the same firm, and there has been much discussion on how to organize such interdivisional transfers and the corresponding transfer prices. Although various formal accounting procedures have been used for this (e.g., cost-plus pricing), it is also common to allow the divisions to bargain about whether the transfer should be accomplished and at what price. In order to bring analysis to bear on the relative merits of different mechanisms (e.g., whether cost-plus pricing is better than bargaining), we need models of how the participants would behave under these different mechanisms. I shall illustrate this with a standard game-theoretic model of bargaining in an extremely simple situation.

Suppose there are two divisions, S and B, and division B (the buyer) is interested in obtaining a lot of 50,000 custom parts from division S (the supplier). The lot will have a value of V to B if B obtains it; that is, V is the maximum that B would pay to obtain the lot from S. (This is sometimes called B's *reservation price*; it may reflect the price at which B could obtain a comparable lot from an outside source.) Correspondingly, it will cost S an amount C to provide the lot to B. (This reservation price may reflect S's opportunity to use its productive capacities in some other way.) From the point of view of the firm, the transfer should take place if V is at least as large as C, in which case the transfer price should divide the "surplus" ($V - C$) in some equitable way between the two divisions. The problem is that B does not know S's cost, C, and S does not know B's value, V; furthermore, the firm's management knows neither. The firm wants to design a mechanism that will result – in situations like this – in a decision about whether S will supply the lot to B, and if so at what price; call this the *outcome*. We shall postulate that (1) a mechanism specifies the rules of a game to be played by B and S; (2) the strategies of the two players determine the outcome; and (3) the two players will choose a *Nash profile* of strategies for the game (see Section 15.2.2).

A familiar example of a mechanism is the *sealed-bid mechanism*. The rules of the game are as follows: (1) simultaneously, the buyer, B, picks an offer bid, v, and the seller, S, picks an asking bid, c (we may think of each bid as being placed in a sealed envelope); (2) the sealed bids are opened, and if v is at least as large as c, then S provides the lot to B; otherwise, no transfer takes place; (3) if the transfer takes place, the transfer price, p, is the arithmetic mean of the two bids, that is, $p = (v + c)/2$. If a transfer takes place, the buyer's profit (on this transaction) is ($V - p$) and the seller's profit is ($p - C$); if no transfer takes place, each player's profit is zero. (I assume that if no transfer takes place, then the seller incurs no cost.)

Recall, however, that B does not know C and S does not know V. Following the theory of Harsanyi, the game theorist will typically model the situation as follows. V and C are random variables with a given joint probability distribution, which is known to both players, B and S. At the beginning of the game, Nature draws particular values, V and C, from this distribution, and reveals V to B and C to S. A *strategy* for B is a rule or function, f, that determines his bid, v, as $f(V)$. Likewise, a strategy for S is a function, g, that determines his bid, c, as $g(C)$. Notice that there is no obligation for B to bid his true value or for S to bid his true cost. In fact, armchair experience would suggest that $f(V)$ would typically be less than V and $g(C)$ would be greater than C. Finally, we postulate that each player is interested in maximizing his *expected profit*, given the other player's strategy. A *Nash profile* is a pair of bidding strategies, (f^*, g^*), such that neither player can increase his expected profit by *unilaterally* changing his own strategy to some other one.

The reader may be surprised by one feature of this formulation, namely, that the buyer must decide what he would bid for every possible realization of his actual value, V, even though the transfer-price story begins with the buyer knowing V (and likewise for the seller). However, a little reflection should convince the reader that in order for the buyer to predict the consequences of any particular bid, he must have some opinion about what the seller is likely to ask. One way for the buyer to formulate this opinion is (1) to predict what the seller will ask, given alternative realizations of his cost, that is, predict the seller's strategy, and (2) to impute a probability distribution to the cost, as in the Savage Paradigm. Similar reasoning is applicable to the seller.

I shall not try to give a general definition of a *mechanism* in this situation, but here is an alternative to the sealed-bid mechanism, sometimes called the *take-it-or-leave-it mechanism*. In this mechanism, the seller makes an asking bid, and the buyer must either accept it or reject it; in the latter case, there is no trade. (A corresponding mechanism would be obtained by interchanging the roles of buyer and seller.)

What would it mean to say that a mechanism is efficient? First, we must deal with the problem that there might be more than one Nash profile for the mechanism in question. Thus we shall have to apply the adjective *efficient* to a pair consisting of a mechanism and a Nash profile for that mechanism. Accordingly, if N^* is a Nash profile for the mechanism M^*, then (M^*, N^*) is (second-best) *efficient* if there is no other mechanism and corresponding Nash profile that yields a higher expected profit to one of the players without yielding a lower expected profit to the other.

I illustrate this idea in the context of the sealed-bid mechanism. Suppose that the probability distribution of V and C is such that they are independent and identically distributed, each with a uniform distribution between 0 and 1 (we could have chosen any other interval). It can be shown that the following bidding strategies form a Nash profile:

$$f^*(V) = \begin{cases} V, & \text{if } V \le 1/4, \\ 1/4 + (2/3)(V - 1/4) & \text{if } V > 1/4, \end{cases} \tag{15.4}$$

$$g^*(C) = 1 - f^*(1 - C).$$

Thus the buyer bids his true value, V, when V is sufficiently small but "shaves" his bid for larger values of V, and the seller behaves symmetrically. Although this qualitative feature of the players' strategies may be intuitively plausible, the particular form and coefficients of the (piecewise linear) functions f^* and g^* are surely not. It can also be shown that *the sealed-bid mechanism, in combination with the Nash profile (equation 15.4), is in fact efficient in the class of all mechanisms that are relevant for this problem.* This makes the sealed-bid mechanism seem attractive in this situation until one learns that, under the same assumptions, *the sealed-bid mechanism has an uncountable infinity of Nash profiles, which range from efficient to worthless.* (By "worthless" I mean yielding each player an expected profit of zero.) (For this and other facts about the sealed-bid mechanism described here, see Leininger, Linhart, & Radner, 1989. For a survey of game-theoretic treatments of bargaining under incomplete information, see Linhart, Radner, & Satterthwaite, 1992.)

In this situation, the organizer of the firm (the mechanism designer) faces some difficult problems:

1. How can we reliably say that the sealed-bid mechanism is efficient if we don't know which Nash profile the players will choose?

2. How can the players coordinate their choice of strategies to obtain a Nash profile? One answer to this question might be that the mechanism designer should tell the players which strategies to choose, and explain why. This will work, and also solve the preceding problem, if both players take the designer's advice. However, this does not solve the next problem.

3. The efficient combination of mechanism and Nash profile depends (probably sensitively) on the particular prior probability distribution of V and C. In fact, even for the sealed-bid mechanism, Nash profiles are known for only a small class of distributions, and even then not all the Nash profiles are known.

4. In the preceding formulation, the two players agree on the distribution of V and C. What if they don't agree?

5. How can we expect the players to calculate the Nash profiles of a particular mechanism if the mechanism designer can't do so? In fact, the calculation of a Nash profile, even in this simple problem, typically requires the solution of a difficult pair of differential equations. It is interesting to note that in the experiments that have been done with the two-person sealed-bid mechanism, with the experimental conditions devised to replicate the preceding assumptions, the experimental subjects rarely appear to use Nash profile strategies. However, on average, they do about as well as they would if they used the efficient Nash profile (equation 15.4), but with different strategies. Furthermore, subject pairs use a variety of strategy profiles, which nevertheless achieve comparable average profits. (See Radner & Schotter, 1989.)

Although I have discussed here only one mechanism in detail, it should not be surprising that, given all of these problems, it is difficult to come to definite conclusions about the best mechanism to use for transfer pricing. This discouraging situation raises serious questions about the ultimate prospects for the game-theoretic approach to mechanism design, at least as we now know it.

(For a stimulating account of the managerial dilemmas inherent in mechanism design, see Miller, 1991.)

15.4 The managerial theory of the firm

Before I describe my understanding of the managerial theory of the firm, let me summarize some of the main points made in the preceding two sections.

The limitations on information-processing capacities of humans and machines force large organizations to decentralize the activities of information processing and decision making. The result is the striking growth of the managerial labor force, which today accounts for one-third to one-half (or more) of the employees of large firms. This decentralization, with its corresponding costs and capacities, does not in itself take us outside the Extended Savage Paradigm and the theory of games. The boundaries of these paradigms are crossed when we try to face the consequences of (1) truly bounded rationality in individual decision making and (2) the rampant indeterminacy of Nash profiles, especially in games of incomplete information. These twin curses prevent economic analysis from making incisive predictions of organizational behavior – at least thus far – with the mainstream tools at its disposal.

Given these problems, is it plausible that the relations between the owners of firms and the managerial labor force are primarily governed by the logic of individual rationality and game theory? More precisely, is it plausible to expect that these relations will be governed by a "nexus of explicit contracts," supplemented by another nexus of "incomplete contracts," where the behavior that is not explicitly governed by the contracts is determined by Nash profiles of strategies in the associated game?

On the contrary, we should expect that stockholders are relatively ignorant of the details of how to manage the firms in which they have shares. If a firm does badly, the stockholders are more likely to sell their shares than to inquire closely into the details of how the firm might be better managed. "Doing badly" is a relative criterion by which firms are compared with each other. Thus, the management of a firm can normally expect to stay out of trouble with its stockholders if it earns at least the market rate of return. The management faces a similar discipline from its customers and from its nonmanagerial workers. Thus the management faces a significant discipline in the various markets in which the firm operates (investment, product, labor), but *if firms differ in their potential profitabilities, the management of the better firms will retain some freedom of action within the constraints imposed by the markets.* This picture of management, either enjoying some freedom of action in the interior of its constraint set under favorable circumstance, or otherwise facing a crisis if its constraint set becomes empty, is the essence of the managerial theory of the firm. (There is, of course, the knife-edge case in which the management barely manages to satisfy all of its constraints, with no room to spare, but in a world of uncertain change this situation cannot persist long.)

This picture of the firm contrasts with the view put forward by Milton Friedman (1953, pp. 21–22):

[U]nder a wide range of circumstances individual firms behave *as if* they were seeking rationally to maximize their expected returns and had full knowledge of the data required to succeed in this attempt . . . unless the behavior of businessmen in some way or other approximated the behavior consistent with the maximization of returns, it seems unlikely that they would remain in business for long.

However, in a simple model of heterogeneous firms subject to uncertainty and bankruptcy, it can be shown that if firms have sufficiently diverse behaviors and are not identical in profitability, then *after a long time, practically all of the surviving firms will not have been maximizing profits* (Dutta & Radner, 1993). Thus, according to this model, the managerial theory of the firm is consistent with the force of market selection. (For another critique of the Friedman market selection hypothesis, see Winter, 1987, and Nelson & Winter, 1982.)

Of course, the managerial theory of the firm is not a complete theory. It describes the constraints that management faces, but it does not predict managerial behavior within that set. To complete the theory, we shall need a more complete theory of truly bounded rationality of groups, as well as of individuals. In particular, our theory will have to explain a number of things that managers (and their helpers) do that do not fit comfortably into the Savage/game theory paradigm. These activities include

1. improving solutions to problems,
2. planning future activities,
3. coordinating,
4. exercising authority,
5. providing leadership, and
6. exhorting, persuading, and setting goals and values.

Some of these activities appear to deal with bounded rationality, others with indeterminacy, and still others with both. I believe that the managerial theory of the firm will gain greater credibility as we gain a deeper understanding of how humans deal with the twin problems of (truly) bounded rationality and indeterminacy. In the meantime, as a pragmatic approach to understanding the organization and behavior of firms, the managerial theory of the firm seems to have common sense on its side.

References

Arrow, K. J. (1974). *The limits of organization.* New York: W. W. Norton.

Basu, A., Bose, A., & Gosh, J. K. (1990). *An expository review of sequential design and allocation rules.* Tech. Report 90-08, Dept. of Statistics, Purdue University (second revision, August 1990, unpublished).

Berle, A. A., & Means, G. C. (1932). *The modern corporation and private property.* New York: Harcourt, Brace and World.

Clark, J. M. (1918). Economics and modern psychology. *Journal of Political Economy, 26,* 1–30.

Dutta, P. K., & Radner, R. (1993). *Profit maximization and the market selection hypothesis.* Unpublished paper, AT&T Bell Laboratories, Murray Hill, NJ.

Dutta, P. K., & Radner, R. (1995). Moral hazard. In R. A. Aumann & S. Hart (Eds.), *Handbook of game theory* (Vol. 2, pp. 869–903). Amsterdam: North-Holland.

Fama, E. F., & Jensen, M. C. (1983). Separation of ownership and control. *Journal of Law and Economics, 26,* 301–325.

Friedman, M. (1953). *Essays in positive economics.* Chicago: University of Chicago Press.

Fudenberg, D., & Tirole, J. (1991). *Game theory.* Cambridge, MA: MIT Press.

Hart, O. (1989). An economist's perspective on the theory of the firm. *Columbia Law Review, 89,* 1757–1774.

Hart, O. (1991). Incomplete contracts and the theory of the firm. In O. E. Williamson & S. G. Winter (Eds.), *The nature of the firm* (pp. 138–158). New York: Oxford University Press.

Hurwicz, L. (1995). Economic design, adjustment processes, mechanisms, and institutions. *Economic Design, 1,* 1–14.

Jensen, M., & Meckling, W. (1976). Theory of the firm: Managerial behavior, agency costs, and ownership structure. *Journal of Financial Economics, 3,* 305–360.

Kim, K. H., & Roush, F. W. (1987). *Team theory.* New York: Halsted Press.

Kornhauser, L. A. (1983). Reliance, repetition, and breach of contract. *Journal of Law and Economics, 26,* 691–706.

Kreps, D. M. (1990). Corporate culture and economic theory. In J. Alt & K. Shepsle (Eds.), *Perspectives in positive political economy.* Cambridge: Cambridge University Press.

Leininger, W., Linhart, P. B., & Radner, R. (1989). Equilibria of the sealed-bid mechanism for bargaining with incomplete information. *Journal of Economic Theory, 48,* 63–106.

Linhart, P. B., Radner, R., & Satterthwaite, M. A. (1992). *Bargaining with incomplete information.* San Diego, CA: Academic Press.

Lipman, B. L. (1995). *Decision theory without logical omniscience: Toward an axiomatic framework for bounded rationality.* Unpublished paper, Queens University, Canada.

Marris, R. L. (1964). *The economic theory of "managerial" capitalism.* London: Macmillan.

Marris, R. L., & Wood, A. J. B. (Eds.). (1971). *The corporate economy.* London: Macmillan.

Marschak, T. A., & McGuire, C. B. (1971). *Lecture notes on economic models for organization design.* Unpublished manuscript. Berkeley: University of California.

Marschak, J., & Radner, R. (1972). *Economic theory of teams.* New Haven, CT: Cowles Foundation and Yale University Press.

Milgrom, P. R., & Roberts, J. (1992). *Economics, organization, and management.* Englewood Cliffs, NJ: Prentice-Hall.

Miller, G. J. (1991). *Managerial dilemmas.* Cambridge: Cambridge University Press.

Mount, K. R., & Reiter, S. (In press). A modular network model of bounded rationality. In M. K. Majumdar (Ed.), *Organizations with incomplete information.* Cambridge: Cambridge University Press.

Nelson, R. R., & Winter, S. G. (1982). *An evolutionary theory of economic change.* Cambridge, MA: Harvard University Press.

Osborne, M., & Rubinstein, A. (1994). *A course in game theory.* Cambridge, MA: MIT Press.

Radner, R. (1991). Dynamic games in organization theory. *Journal of Economic Behavior and Organization, 16,* 217–260.

Radner, R. (1992). Hierarchy: The economics of managing. *Journal of Economic Literature, 30,* 1382–1415.

Radner, R. (1993). The organization of decentralized information processing. *Econometrica, 61,* 1109–1146.

Radner, R., & Schotter, A. R. (1989). The sealed-bid mechanism: An experimental study. *Journal of Economic Theory, 48,* 179–220.

Radner, R., & Van Zandt, T. (1992). Information processing in firms and returns to scale. *Annales d'Economie et de Statitique,* No. 25/26, 265–298.

Savage, L. J. (1954). *The foundations of statistics.* New York: Wiley.

Schwartz, J. T. (1980). Ultracomputers. *ACM Transactions on Programming Languages and Computers, 2,* 484–521.

Smith, A. (1776). *The wealth of nations.* Reprinted 1976 by the University of Chicago Press (Cannan Edition).

Van Zandt, T. (In press). The structure and returns to scale of organizations that process information. In M. K. Majumdar (Ed.), *Organizations with incomplete information).* Cambridge: Cambridge University Press.

Wald, A. (1947). *Sequential analysis.* New York: Wiley.

Wald, A. (1950). *Statistical decision functions.* New York: Wiley.

Wildsmith, J. R. (1973). *Managerial theories of the firm.* New York: Dunellen.

Williamson, O. E., & Winter, S. G. (Eds.). (1991). *The nature of the firm.* New York: Oxford University Press.

Winter, S. G. (1987). Competition and selection. In J. Eatwell, J. Milgate, & P. Newman (Eds.), *The new Palgrave* (pp. 545–548). New York: Stockton Press.

16 The scarecrow's search: A cognitive psychologist's perspective on organizational decision making

John W. Payne

One of my favorite books is *The Wizard of Oz* (Baum, 1903). In this classic tale, the Tin Man seeks a heart, the Lion courage, and the Scarecrow a brain. Similarly, organizational behavior research can be viewed as a search for the heart, courage, and brains of an organization and its individuals. For example, Milgrom and Roberts's (1992) excellent book on organizations and management focuses on motivation and incentives (the heart) and risk sharing (courage). Milgrom and Roberts also examine the brains of organizations and managers – the methods they use to process information and make decisions. However, to examine the functioning of the brain, Milgrom and Roberts generally assume perfect rationality in the pursuit of goals.[1] Yet, the "brain" of the organization, manifested in its employees, sometimes reflects less than perfect rationality. This is the focus of the cognitive perspective on organizational research.[2]

Individual and organizational decision making

Decision making is a theme of much organizational research. For instance, Herbert A. Simon's classic work on organizations, *Administrative Behavior* (Simon, 1976) was written "on the assumption that decision making processes hold the key to the understanding of organizational phenomena" (p. xl). Further, Simon proposed similar ideas for both individual and organizational decision making. This approach is reasonable insofar as descriptions of organizational decision making are really descriptions of individual decision making within an organizational context (see Cummings, 1982).[3] Many organizational researchers who have followed Simon also have seen decision making as the paradigm for most executive activity.

Support for the preparation of this chapter was provided by the National Science Foundation. The comments of James R. Bettman, Mary Frances Luce, and Sim B. Sitkin are much appreciated.

In the 50 years or so since Simon's book was originally written, the study of decision-making processes at the levels of the organization, the group, and the individual has been extensive. Recently, there has been a growing emphasis on interorganizational decision making as well – for example, strategic alliances or networks of organizations. Today thousands of articles, chapters, and books are written each year on topics dealing with decision making. As indicated by the chapters in this volume, the study of organizational decision making is intensely interdisciplinary, employing concepts, models, and methods from anthropology, economics, political science, psychology, sociology, statistics, and other fields.

This chapter does not aim to address decision making from a wide range of perspectives. Instead, it focuses on the single perspective of cognitive psychology and individual decision research as it relates to the understanding of organizational decision making. I share Simon's belief that many of the same concepts can be used to understand phenomena at both the individual and organizational levels of analysis. However, I also appreciate the point made by Kleindorfer, Kunreuther, and Schoemaker (1993) and many others that individual decision behavior is *not* a sufficient basis for describing how organizations arrive at decisions. For instance, Pondy (1982) has argued that organizational decision theory differs from behavioral decision research because it deals with "the problem of how *collections* of individuals make complex choices in the face of *ambiguity not only in information but even in objectives*" (p. 309; emphases added). The chapters by Connolly, O'Connor, and Radner in this book provide alternative perspectives on organizational decision making, emphasizing how decision making by organizations involves factors beyond those needed to describe individual decision behavior. Nonetheless, this chapter concentrates on the links between cognitive approaches to the study of individual judgment and choice behavior and the topic of organizational decision making.

Unfortunately, given space constraints, this chapter focuses only on a few of the links between cognitive psychology, individual decision research, and organizational studies. Four topics that will be emphasized are (1) the concept of bounded rationality, (2) risk taking, (3) the theme of constructive preferences, and (4) the process tracing of decisions. See the chapter in this book by Fischhoff and Johnson for a discussion of the links between individual decision behavior and multiperson-distributed decision-making systems.

Cognitive capabilities and decision making

The concept that has played the biggest role in studies of both individual and organizational decision making is *bounded rationality* (Simon, 1955). Bounded rationality is really a simple idea. Limits on the computational (cognitive) capabilities of an individual place constraints on that individual's ability to approximate the behavior of the normative "economic man" model of decision making. Thus, perfect rationality in the pursuit of goals is not assumed. In fact, Simon has suggested that the information-processing or cognitive bounds of individuals means that, in some cases, actual decision behavior might not even be close to the behavior predicted by classic rational models of decision making. To the extent that the decisions of senior managers are impacted by these same cognitive limits, one would expect organizational actions to reflect bounded rationality.

One of the most important theoretical postulates in cognitive psychology is to describe behavior and the human information-processing system in terms of a small number of memories and processes (strategies) involving the acquisition, storage, retrieval, and utilization of information (for reviews, see Bettman, 1979; Cowan, 1988; Newell & Simon, 1972). Over the past 40 years, psychologists have expanded our knowledge of the human information-processing system's memories and processes. In this section, I briefly describe some of the key elements of the cognitive system in relation to the manager as a limited information processor.

In discussing the cognitive system, most researchers have found it useful to distinguish between two types of memories: working memory and long-term memory. Working memory contains the information under current consideration. Long-term memory holds (i.e., stores) the individual's mass of available knowledge, including facts and procedures (processes) for doing things. It should be noted that this distinction does not necessarily imply that there are two physically distinct memories. Working memory may simply be the currently activated portion of long-term memory. The different functioning of these two types of memories is the crucial distinction.

Working memory and limited capacity

Working memory can combine information from both the environment, as produced by the perceptual system, and information drawn (i.e., retrieved) from long-term memory. For example, in solving an arithmetic problem, one uses both the given information (e.g., the numbers) and the procedural information (e.g., the rules of addition) retrieved from long-term memory. Working memory, sometimes called *short-term memory*, also contains the intermediate products of thinking. The term *short-term memory* captures the important fact that items of information in working memory are lost quickly if not rehearsed actively.

The central constraint on working memory is its limited capacity. Only a few items of information can be considered at once. How few? The standard answer is: seven items of information, plus or minus two (Miller, 1956), although some researchers have suggested that roughly four or five items is a more accurate estimate (Simon, 1974). This limitation on mental capacity is easily illustrated with a memory span task. The task requires a person to recall a sequence of items in their correct order. For example, imagine that the following letters were read to you, one per second, and you were then asked to recall them in the correct order:

B-W-A-M-I-C-S-I-A-C-B-T.

Most of us would find this a very difficult task. A shorter list, such as M-C-A-S, would be easier. Seven to nine letters is the limit for most of us. The number of items of information recalled, however, can be increased by recording the information to form *chunks*. What constitutes a chunk of information is somewhat ill defined, but it might be best characterized as any piece of information represented as a single, meaningful item or that has some unitary representation in long-term memory. To illustrate, consider reordering the previous letter sequence this way:

T-W-A-I-B-M-C-I-A-C-B-S.

For most people in our culture, the 12 letters now can be formed into four chunks – TWA, IBM, CIA, CBS – that are easy to recall. This increase in recall due to chunking can be dramatic. In one instance, a student was trained to recall 81 digits (Chase & Ericsson, 1981). The student, an avid runner, was able to chunk the numbers into a much smaller set of items by relating the sequence of numbers to running times.

One implication of chunking is that one source of expertise in decision making is the ability to process larger amounts of information in the form of patterns of information.[4] Thus, in understanding organizational decision making, one may find apparently different bounds of working memory in areas of the organization that differentiate the abilities of managers to develop meaningful patterns of information. For example, to the extent that the managers at lower levels of the organization have an opportunity to experience recurrent decision problems, the learning of patterns (chunks) of information may be facilitated and processing capabilities may be enhanced. A manager at the Union Bank of Switzerland expressed it this way: "I have been working for ten years and felt that my decision making instincts were good, but I realized that they were just a trained response to similar past situations." Isenberg (1984) also sees executive intuition as including the ability to recognize familiar patterns and apply lessons learned from experience. For a more general discussion of routine organizational decision making, see Inbar (1979). For a discussion of the related concept of decision making as rule following, where the rules capture past learning, see the chapter by March in this volume and the references therein.

Another example of the limitations of working memory is provided by mental multiplication: Try multiplying two 4-digit numbers. Even if the numbers themselves are easily remembered (e.g., 1776 and 1492), the need to remember intermediate products will overwhelm most people's working memory.

An important consequence of a limited working memory, including the need to remember intermediate products, is the use of heuristics to process information (Card, Moran, & Newell, 1983). Heuristics are procedures for systematically simplifying the search through the available information about a problem. In other words, heuristics function by disregarding some of the available information. Thus, heuristics improve a person's chances of making a reasonably good decision, given the limitations in processing capacity, while also leaving some possibility of a mistake. The use of heuristic strategies to solve problems and make decisions is one of the general principles of human information processing. Newell and Simon (1981) have argued that the use of heuristic search is at the heart of intelligence. The use of particular heuristics can be premeditated, or strategies simply may be constructed or realized on the spot, given a set of resources and task contingencies.

Over the past several decades, behavioral decision researchers have identified a number of heuristics used by individuals in making judgments and developing processes (Payne, Bettman, & Johnson, 1993). For example, people often form forecasts by insufficiently adjusting a known or suggested anchor value. As a result, the final forecast is biased toward the anchor. An example is forecasting next year's sales starting with the anchor point of this year's sales. The anchoring and adjustment heuristic suggests that managers may not give enough weight to how next year might differ from this year. Instead, they might be overly anchored on this year's sales. Another example of anchoring is the use of a "base case" set of numbers in doing sensitivity analysis. The anchoring and adjustment heuristic suggests that high and low estimates from the base case might not be different enough. Thus, people may underestimate uncertainties or be overconfident. For a nice example of how overconfidence can affect planning, see Buehler, Griffin, and Ross (1994).

Other examples of judgment heuristics include the representativeness heuristic, in which the likelihood of an event's occurrence is judged by the similarity of that occurrence to stereotypes of similar occurrences, and the availability heuristic, in which the likelihood of an event is judged by the degree to which instances or occurrences of that event are readily retrievable from memory. See Bazerman (1994) for a summary of many of the heuristics used in judgment.

In the spirit of organizational decision theory as the study of individual decision making within an organization, there have been many investigations on whether the heuristics used in the laboratory exist in organizational contexts. For example, Mahajan (1992) examined overconfidence in marketing predictions. In addition, Ashton and Ashton (1995) provided numerous examples of the study of heuristic reasoning in the contexts of accounting and auditing.

Long-term memory

Unlike working memory, long-term memory's capacity is generally considered infinite. In other words, for all practical purposes there is no limit to the amount of information that can be stored in long-term memory. Again, the information stored in long-term memory can be both facts and procedures. Procedural information includes rules for making decisions.

It has been suggested that once information is transferred from working memory to long-term memory, it is never lost. Obviously, however, we do forget information. What is suggested is that "forgetting" is really just the person's inability to retrieve the information from long-term memory at a particular time. At a different time, new retrieval cues or strategies may allow the person to remember the "forgotten" information. Thus, a group process can improve decisions both by (1) increasing the pool of available information and by (2) helping any given individual in the group remember information.

Because of its capacity, long-term memory is sometimes viewed as external memory, like a library, encyclopedia, or management information system (see Simon, 1981, for an elaboration of this view). From this vantage point, problem solving and decision making involve a search for information in both the external perceptual environment and the internal memory environment, with information from one environment often guiding the search in the other.

An implication of this guided search is that the acquisition of new information by different members of an organization may be limited by the differences among those persons in terms of existing knowledge. The different ways in which individuals see or frame problems built on prior knowledge will limit the search for new knowledge options. An example of this effect is provided by the classic study of selective attention across executives by Dearborn and Simon (1958).

More recently, Melone (1994), using the method of verbal protocol analysis, has shown how two types of executives, vice-presidents of corporate development and chief financial officers, differ in their reasoning process. Melone also demonstrates how an executive's representation of knowledge in memory allows for the generation of default values for missing case information, as well as the recall of analogies when problem solving. Thus, there is clear evidence that differences among executives in prior knowledge can frame, and perhaps limit, the search for new knowledge. By contrast, Hamel and Prahalad (1994) have argued that even though "each individual in an organization may see the world somewhat differently, managerial frames within an organization are typically more alike than different" (p. 50). As a consequence, Hamel and Prahalad argue that established organizations will find it very difficult to compete successfully for future, difficult-to-imagine, markets.

The brief summary of information-processing capabilities just presented

indicates that the typical assumption that managers are extensive information processors (perfect rationality) is not always helpful. Instead, a better
assumption is that mental capacity is a scarce resource (Simon, 1978). Thus,
information processing will often be limited. People, including executives,
are only boundedly rational.

Even when information-processing capacity is not constrained completely, the fact that cognitive capacity is a scarce resource may help explain
why people often behave according to Zipf's (1949) principle of least effort.
According to this principle, a strategy is selected to ensure that the minimum effort will be involved in reaching the specific desired result. This
suggests that when making a decision, people often trade decreased accuracy for savings in effort (Payne, Bettman, & Johnson, 1993).

Uncertainty and risk taking

Some recent applications of the idea of bounded rationality to individuals
and organizations concerns the topic of risk taking. See, for example, the
chapter by March in this volume. In this section, I discuss a few of those
applications. For more on the literature dealing with the effect of risk on
decision making in organizations, see Sitkin and Pablo (1992).

Bold forecasts and timid choices

Kahneman and Lovallo (1993) offer a cognitive analysis of risk taking at the
level of the individual and discuss the implications of that analysis for
decision making in organizations. They separate the processes of judging
the potential future of an action (forecasts) from the processes of selecting
(choice) among alternative risky actions. In terms of forecasts, they argue
that most individual and organizational judgments are highly optimistic,
what they call "bold forecasts." Why "bold" forecasts? March and Shapira
(1987) offer one possible explanation when they report that most managers
believe that they can control risk. The tendency to exaggerate one's control
over even apparently random events is referred to as the *illusion of control*
(Langer, 1975). Although acknowledging the illusion of control as one possible explanation for bold forecasts, Kahneman and Lovallo (1993) argue
for a more cognitive explanation based on the adoption of an *inside view* of
problems focusing on the specifics of the case at hand rather than a class of
cases chosen as similar to the present one in relevant respects. A focus on a
class of cases is labeled an *outside view* and is seen as essentially statistical
and comparative. Although people can and do take both inside and outside
views of problems, much research suggests that an inside view is perhaps
more natural. This may be due, in part, to the relative ease of assessment
using each approach and/or to the way in which information is commonly
stored and processed by individuals (Tversky & Kahneman, 1983). Thus,
there is a link between the cognitive structure of memory and the way
managers make important business forecasts.

Kahneman and Lovallo (1993) present evidence that executives are not immune to the optimistic bias (i.e., the making of bold forecasts). Further, they argue that several features of organizations reinforce this optimistic bias. For instance, they state that the competition for organizational resources will foster the presentation of optimistic forecasts. That is, organizational systems that are adversarial will produce powerful incentives for optimistic numbers. As an example, Michael Kusnic (1994), head of corporate strategic planning at General Motors, recently argued that the classic multidivisional structure of American firms encourages optimistic numbers to be presented in a business case. This is because the corporate headquarters in such a structure often plays the role of a "critical" banker, and the operating division plays the role of an applicant for scarce resources.

Another organizational factor noted by Kahneman and Lovallo that might cause an optimistic bias in judgments is that pessimism about what the organization can do is readily interpreted as disloyal and demoralizing. Thus, groups often suppress the expression of statements of how one could be wrong. At the group level, this behavior can contribute to *groupthink* (Janis, 1982). Collections of individuals and organizations can, at times, reinforce the results of heuristic reasoning in judgments (see also Argote, Seabright, and Dyer, 1986). March (this volume), too, notes that the estimates of the risks facing an executive at present may be lower than they should be due to the experience executives have in organizations. The promotions of executives based upon past successes may lead to a feeling of confidence, perhaps overconfidence, in one's wisdom and insight. See the chapter by March in this volume for further discussions of this point.

In addition to bold forecasts, Kahneman and Lovallo (1993) discuss attitudes toward risk. A traditional assumption of economics is that people are risk averse. Cyert and March (1963) concluded that business managers avoid risk. In terms of organizations, Shapira (1995) reports that managers generally feel that organizational practices inhibit risk taking. Some forms of risk avoidance in organizations include delaying decisions ("It needs more study"), delegating decisions to others, and making decisions in terms of a shorter and shorter time horizon.

One cognitive factor that can contribute to timid choices (risk aversion) is what Kahneman and Lovallo call *narrow decision frames*. Narrow decision framing occurs when decision problems are evaluated one at a time, isolating the current problem from other choices that may be pending, as well as from future opportunities to make similar decisions. To illustrate the potential costs of narrow framing, Kahneman and Lovallo offer the following organizational example, originally suggested by Amos Tversky. The example involves two divisions of a company facing separate decision problems. "One is in a bad posture and faces a choice between a sure loss and a high probability of a larger loss; the other division faces a favorable choice. The natural bent of intuition will favor a risk-seeking solution for one and a risk-averse choice for the other, but the conjunction could be poor policy. The overall interests of the company are better served by aggregating the problems than by segregating them, and by a policy that is generally more risk-neutral than intuitive preferences" (p. 19).

Another example of narrow framing is the fact that people often express different willingness to bet when considering a "single play" or "multiple plays" of the same gamble (Keren & Wagenaar, 1987). As an example, a person might be indifferent between accepting or rejecting a gamble that offers a $250 win with $p = .5$ and a $100 loss with $p = .5$. However, if you could play the same gamble twice, your probability of a loss would drop from .5 to .25. With multiple plays, gambles that may be too risky as single plays become relatively more attractive. Thaler (1993) provides an interesting real-world discussion of how the framing of risks as multiple plays over a longer period can impact the distribution of investments between stocks and bonds.

One possible explanation for narrow framing is that it embodies an expression of bounded rationality. That is, for most people most of the time, the tendency will be to adopt a narrow frame or "minimal neutral account" (Thaler, 1993), because that reduces the cognitive load. Thaler also suggests that the use of narrower mental accounts can serve as a device for self-control. Narrow framing also relates to an inside view of forecasting insofar as both represent the treatment of a decision or a forecast as a unique instance rather than as one of an ensemble of similar decisions or judgments.

As with the case for bold forecasts, Kahneman and Lovallo (1993) speculate that organizational factors may enhance narrow framing. For example, they speculate that the more frequently a manager's performance is evaluated, the narrower his or her framing. That is, the more frequent the evaluation, the more the manager's focus will be on the values and probabilities of each decision option, without consideration of the portfolio of options available to the manager and to the organization.

Target values and attention

In seeking to understand risk-taking behavior at both the individual and the organizational level, researchers are increasingly emphasizing the importance of target, or reference, values. These values are directly related to the old idea of aspiration levels discussed by Simon (1955) in the context of bounded rationality.

One critical reference value is the point at which outcomes are coded as either gains or losses (Kahneman & Tversky, 1979). Although the evidence is somewhat mixed, there is substantial research showing that risk seeking, not risk aversion, becomes the most common response when people see themselves as faced with choices among losses. Again, there is also evidence that groups sometimes enhance this effect of risk aversion for gains and risk seeking for losses (Paese, Biester, & Tubbs, 1993).

Another critical reference value is the point at which either individual or organizational viability is threatened. This value is sometimes called the *survival target*. People seem very risk averse if an option has a possibility of leading to a ruinous loss.

A theme that both psychologists and organizational theorists use in examining risk taking is attention – specifically, the amount of attention given to a survival target compared to an aspiration level. Theories that emphasize shifts of attention as determinants of risky decision making are offered by Lopes (1987, in press) and by March and Shapira (1992).

SP/A theory

Lopes (1995) has developed what she calls the *security-potential/aspiration* (SP/A) theory of risk choice behavior. According to Lopes, risky decision making represents a conflict between the desire to avoid loss or "security mindedness," and a focus on what one might gain, or "potential minded-ness."

To illustrate SP/A theory, consider the following two multioutcome gambles or options:

Option A		Option B	
Payoff	Probability	Payoff	Probability
$130	.31	$200	.05
$115	.22	$189	.05
$101	.15	$178	.05
$ 86	.10	$168	.05
$ 71	.07	$158	.05
$ 57	.05	$147	.05
$ 43	.04	$136	.05
$ 28	.03	$126	.05
$ 13	.02	$116	.05
$ 0	.01	$105	.05
		$ 94	.05
		$ 84	.05
		$ 74	.05
		$ 63	.05
		$ 52	.05
		$ 42	.05
		$ 32	.05
		$ 21	.05
		$ 10	.05
		$ 0	.05

Source: Lopes (1995).

Note that both options have the outcomes ordered from best to worst. This representation of options in terms of a rank ordering of outcomes is a feature shared by SP/A theory and many other current theories of risky decision making (e.g., Tversky & Kahneman, 1992). An interesting empirical question concerns the conditions under which people would be expected to adopt such a representation of risk options.

According to SP/A theory, people differ in the extent to which they focus attention primarily on the worst possible outcomes (people concerned with maintaining security) or focus attention primarily on the best possible outcomes (people concerned with the potential of the gamble). Lopes (1987) discusses a farmer who follows a "safety-first" principle, taking care of subsistence needs first before planting any cash crops, as an example of someone who emphasizes security. Lopes sees entrepreneurship as the flip side of safety-first thinking, in which opportunity is more the focus of attention.[5]

Lopes (1995), however, hypothesizes that a common pattern of attention is what she calls "cautiously-hopeful." This pattern of attention gives proportionally more attention to the worst outcomes than to moderate outcomes yet directs some extra attention to the very best outcomes. Such a pattern of attention would explain both the purchase of insurance and the purchase of lottery tickets by the same individual.

Importantly, SP/A theory includes the idea of a target level that can be somewhere between the worst and best outcomes. For example, a person might have a win of $50 or more as an aspiration. According to SP/A theory, another factor impacting a risky choice between options A and B is the likelihood that an option provides for exceeding this aspiration level or target value. Thus, SP/A theory argues that attention is generally focused on the extreme outcomes of a gamble, with the exception of outcomes that correspond to aspiration target values.

To illustrate, consider options A and B in the preceding table. Given that both options involve gains, one might focus primarily on the potential offered by both gambles (Payne & Braunstein, 1971). In that case, option B would seem to be more attractive. However, if your aspiration level is to win at least $50, then option A becomes more attractive because your probability of achieving that goal is 90% with A and only 75% with option B. Whether the likelihood that the payoffs of an option will exceed an aspiration level or the desire to maximize potential will be given greater weight in your decision is, according to Lopes, dependent upon the particular situation you are in. However, note that an implication of SP/A theory is that if the target return is a gain of at least $120, then the choice should be relatively easy for the decision maker; she would choose B.

SP/A theory leads to some interesting questions that can be related to organizational environments. For instance, how do the performance appraisal and reward systems of most organizations direct attention to either the best or worst outcomes of a risky prospect? How might the performance of others in the organization direct attention to certain outcomes as aspiration levels or targets for risky decision making? Lastly, how does the situation of the manager and/or the organization impact the relative attention paid to reaching a target value versus either maximizing potential or security?

Variable risk theory

March and Shapira (1992; March, 1988; Shapira, 1995), like Lopes (1995), have emphasized variations in risk taking in terms of shifts in attention. In particular, March and Shapira have focused on how attention can shift between a survival value and an aspiration level, also called the *performance target*. They argue that much of the shift in attention is due to changes in a decision maker's resource levels. More specifically, they argue that if a person is just above the performance target in terms of resources, the primary focus of attention will be on avoiding courses of action that might result in falling below the target. Thus, one would see relatively risk-averse behavior. However, as the person's resources increase, the chances that any given uncertain action will result in an outcome that would place the decision maker below the target become less. Thus, the person is more willing to take that action (risk). By contrast, if the person has or anticipates a resource level that places him or her below the target value, the person will take greater risks in order to have a chance of reaching the target. The further away from the performance target, the greater the risk taking. When resources fall to a level near the survival point, however, a person will become very risk averse, avoiding any chance of falling below the survival level of resources. Thus, variation in one's resource level can lead to apparent variable risk preferences (attitudes).

March and Shapira also consider how risk taking can vary as a function of past successes (or failures) and shifts in aspiration level. For example, Shapira (1995) explains that when a decision maker's risk results in a successful outcome and total cumulative resources above his or her prior aspiration level, the decision maker subsequently may raise that aspiration level. Consequently, that decision maker may be even more risk averse than would be expected given the prior aspiration level. Shapira also suggests that in an organizational context, a person's aspiration level may shift as a function of the performance of others, as well as of one's own performance. For a more complete discussion of how managerial aspiration levels may change, see Shapira (1995). The key point of the March–Shapira theory of risk taking is that the rate of change of adaption to past outcomes (successes or failures), as reflected in changes in aspiration levels, will impact the degree of risk taking observed.

The dependence of risk taking upon outcomes of the gambles faced (primarily gains or losses), as defined by an aspiration level, has been the subject of extensive empirical investigation by Payne, Laughhunn, and Crum (1980, 1981, 1984). In a series of experiments involving both students and business managers as subjects, the relationship of a pair of gambles to an assumed or manipulated target or aspiration level was varied by adding to or subtracting a constant amount from all outcomes. It was shown that a translation of outcomes resulted in a reversal of preference between gambles in a pair. The key determinant of the effect of the translation of outcomes was whether the size of the translation was sufficient to result in one gamble having outcome values either all above or all below an aspiration level, while the other gamble had outcome values that were both above and below the aspiration level.[6]

A model of the effects of aspiration levels on risky choice is presented in Payne et al. (1980). In its emphasis on multiple aspiration levels, the authors' model is similar to those of Lopes (1995) and March and Shapira (1992). In support of the ideas presented in Shapira (1995), Payne et al. (1981) shows that variations in targets and, consequently, in risk taking can be influenced by reporting the performance levels of other managers to decision makers. Thus, individual risk taking can be a function of the context of an organizational environment.

Finally, Shapira (1995) argues that managers generally may be risk averse because most organizational reward systems punish failure much more than they reward success.[7] Thus, although many organizations claim that they want risk taking, they actually reward risk aversion (Kerr, 1975). Again, individual risk taking can be a function of the context provided by an organization's environment.

In the spirit of Pondy (1982), one can also view organizational risk taking in terms of how collections of individuals make decisions. For instance, Whyte (1989; Whyte & Levi, 1994) has examined some of the determinants of excessive risk taking by groups. Building upon the ideas of an aspiration level and differential attitudes toward risk by individuals when faced with gains versus losses, Whyte argues that group processes such as uniformity pressures and information sharing can lead to group polarization of opinion that results in excessive risk taking when groups see themselves as having to choose among bad options.

Constructive preferences

In their work on behavioral decision theory and organizational decision theory, March and Shapira (1982) argue that "organizations fail to achieve well-behaved coherent preference functions" (p. 103). In other words, there is ambiguity or uncertainty about preferences. In the introduction to this book (see Chapter 1), the ambiguous and unclear preferences of organizations distinguish organizational decision making from individual decision making, at least as reflected in standard theories of choice. March, in this volume, provides a summary of the properties of standard theories of choice.

March and Shapira (1982; see also March, this volume) argue that ambiguity in preferences is not necessarily bad from the perspective of organizations. Essentially, they argue that ambiguity in preferences can improve the learning of new organizational purposes (values), may enhance a commitment to morality by recognizing human weaknesses (such as inconsistent preferences), and may decrease the vulnerability of action within the organization to manipulation through rational argument, where some can be predicted to be better at such argument. In addition, the difficulty in guessing future desires is explicitly acknowledged.

I do not argue the point that organizations often have unclear preferences. I also do not argue with the position that ambiguity in preferences is *not necessarily* a bad thing from the perspective of the organization. See, for instance, the comment referenced earlier by Hamel and Prahalad (1994) regarding the danger that managers may too often see the world in like fashion. However, I *do* argue that the presence of ambiguous preferences is a distinctive feature of individual as well as organizational decision behavior. That is, individuals often have ambiguous and unclear preferences.

A viewpoint that has recently emerged in individual decision research is that preferences for objects of any complexity are often constructed – not merely revealed – in generating a response to a judgment or choice task (Payne, 1993; Slovic, Griffin, & Tversky, 1990). March (1978) attributed the constructiveness of preferences to the interaction between the limited memory and computational capabilities of decision-makers and the complexity of task environments. That is, Simon's (1955) concept of bounded rationality is seen as the basis of the constructed preferences that we observe. In March's words, "Human beings have unstable, inconsistent, incompletely evoked, and imprecise goals at least in part because human abilities limit preference orderliness" (March, 1978, p. 598). March's argument applies to belief judgments (forecasts) as well. More generally, people often construct their memories and attitudes, as well as their judgments.

The notion of constructive preferences implies more than simply stating that observed preferences are not determined by reference to a master list of values in memory. A constructive view of preferences also suggests that preferences do not necessarily result from the use of some consistent and invariant algorithm such as expected value calculation (Tversky, Sattah, & Slovic, 1988). Instead, a fundamental component of the constructive view is that decision makers have a repertoire of methods or strategies (rules) that are used to identify their preferences.[8]

The idea that in many cases people construct their preferences at the time they are asked, rather than retrieve a previously formed value, is consistent with what Fischhoff (1991) has called the *philosophy of basic values*. In contrast, there is a *philosophy of articulated values*, which assumes that people have well-formed preferences about any relevant topic and can directly retrieve an appropriate response to a judgment question. Economists often seem to assume articulated values. There clearly are times when people do have well-articulated preferences or have a consistent algorithm for generating a response (e.g., calculating the net present value of a cash flow in an investment decision). However, the evidence from more than 20 years of behavioral decision research suggests that a constructive preference assumption may more often be accurate (Payne et al., 1993).

A key implication of a more constructive view of preferences is severe context dependence of judgment and choices. This idea is consistent with the overwhelming verdict of research in cognitive psychology that decision behavior is sensitive to a wide variety of task and context factors (Payne, Bettman, & Johnson, 1993). *Task factors* are general characteristics of a decision problem (such as the number of alternatives available, the response mode, or single-play gambles) and do not depend upon the particular values of the alternatives; *context factors,* such as the similarity of alternatives, are associated with the particular values characterizing the alternatives. Task and context factors make different aspects of the problem salient and evoke different processes for combining information. Different factors can also interact to produce differing strategies (e.g., the two task factors of response mode and single play versus repeated play of gambles) (Wedell & Bockenholt, 1990). Characteristics of the decision problem therefore can lead to the use of different strategies, which at least partially determine the expressed preferences. Of course, how a solution to a decision problem is constructed will also be a function of individual difference factors, such as processing capacities (Bettman, Johnson, & Payne, 1990), prior knowledge or expertise (Shanteau, 1988), and the goals adopted for the decision episode, such as maximizing accuracy or justifiability, or minimizing effort, regret, or conflict (Einhorn & Hogarth, 1981; Tetlock, 1985).

One task variable of great interest for both individual and organizational decision making is time pressure (e.g., Eisenhardt, 1989; Svenson & Maule, 1993). At the individual level, people respond in many ways when faced with decision problems varying in time pressure. These coping mechanisms include the acceleration of processing, selectivity in processing, and shifts in decision strategies. At the organizational level, Eisenhardt (1989) has shown that organizations that respond to fast-paced environments by using evaluation strategies related to those identified as effective for individuals (Payne, Bettman, & Johnson, 1988) also seem to be more effective.

More generally, the implications of constructive preferences are many. First, the failure of organizations to achieve well-behaved, coherent preference functions (March & Shapira, 1982) should not be considered a distinguishing characteristic of organizations. Constructive preferences at the level of the individual decision maker seem to imply a degree of preference ambiguity at the organizational level. Organizations are collections of individuals. Any effect of this fact on uncertainty in preferences would seem only to magnify this feature of individual decision making. Second, the severe task and context dependence of decisions implied by constructive preferences has implications for organizations. Organizational structures, reward systems, and styles of operation may influence how individuals think about problems, and, therefore, what preferences will be expressed. For example, some organizations tend to consider options one at a time. That is, decisions are more like judgments about single alternatives. Other organizations seem to consider two or more options simultaneously when making decisions (Eisenhardt, 1989). Thus, decisions are more like classic choice problems. Given the research showing differences between judgment and choice response modes at the individual level, one would expect similar effects for organizations.

On a more positive note, the fact that individual decisions are highly contingent upon tasks can also be used in efforts to improve organizational decisions (Payne et al., 1993). Individual decision making within organizations, for example, is likely to be improved through better information display, procedures like decision analysis, and tools like computer-based decision support systems. See Payne et al. (1993) for a discussion of the implications of constructive decision behavior for the improvement of decisions and other practical matters.

Bounded rationality, risk attitudes, and the notion of constructive preferences represent theoretical linkages between individual and organizational decision making. In addition to theoretical links, however, there are possible links between cognitive psychology and organizational studies.

Process tracing

One feature of cognitive approaches to psychology is a concern not only with the product of thought but with the processes or mechanisms of thought as well. For example, in the area of decision research, cognitive psychologists are concerned with the information processing that leads to a decision in addition to the nature of the expressed judgment or choice.

In the context of the particular approach to cognitive research pioneered by Newell and Simon (1972), this emphasis on understanding process has led to a methodology with two features: (1) the use of computer simulation to model cognition and derive specific process-level predictions and (2) the collection of process-tracing data from individuals as a way of generating and testing theories about human cognition. To borrow a phrase from Simon (1991), the idea behind process tracing is a "close, almost microscopic, study of how people actually behave" (p. 364).

A number of different techniques for generating data on the processes of thought have been developed. Two examples are verbal protocol analysis and the monitoring of information-acquisition behavior. The essential part of verbal protocol analysis is to ask a subject to give continuous verbal reports, "to think aloud," while performing some task of interest to the researcher. The verbal protocol is then treated as a record of the ongoing behavior of the subject, and what is said is interpreted as an indication of the subject's state of knowledge or use of an operation. Importantly, verbal protocol techniques are designed to provide information on the sequential (time-ordered) behavior of subjects. Ericsson and Simon (1993) provide a model of how people respond to instructions to think aloud. They also address criticisms of the verbal protocol method, and they provide numerous examples of the successful use of verbal protocols in the study of cognitive processes.

The monitoring of information-acquisition behavior has become a popular form of process tracing in decision research. Essentially, the technique of information acquisition involves setting up the task so that the subject must view or select information in a way that can be measured easily. Like the method of verbal protocols, the monitoring of information-acquisition behavior provides data on the temporal properties of behavior (e.g., the order in which information is processed while making a decision). The monitoring of information-acquisition behavior would seem to have great value in the context of managerial or organizational decision making. For example, Shapira (1995) suggests that "managers are quite insensitive to estimates of probabilities of possible outcomes . . . outcome values appear to have a more central role than probabilities" (p. 16). Tversky and Fox (1995), however, suggest that sensitivity to various levels of uncertainty is an attribute that varies among decision makers. It would be interesting to see if managers consistently differ in the degree to which they search for information that deals with the likelihood of events.

Whatever the process-tracing technique(s) used, the idea is to increase the amount of time-ordered behavior that can be observed when a subject is performing a task. Carroll and Johnson (1990) provide an introduction to some of the process-tracing methods used in decision research.

At a general level, the cognitive psychology focus on the processes as well as the product of thought can be and has been extended to organizational decision making. As noted in this chapter, Eisenhardt (1989) provides an excellent example of a study on the processes of firm decision making in time-pressured environments. More specifically in terms of techniques, Cohen, March, and Olson (1972) provide an example of the use of computer simulation in studying organizational decisions, and Melone (1994) provides an example of the use of verbal protocol analysis to investigate the judgments of corporate executives. As noted previously, organizational researchers have studied the processes of organizational decisions as well as outcomes. Nonetheless, much more work looking inside the "black box" of organizational decisions seems warranted.

Conclusion

How are decisions made? This question can be asked at various levels of analysis: that of the individual decision maker, the small group, or the organization as a whole. Research on these questions can also proceed from a variety of perspectives: economics, sociology, psychology, and so on. This chapter has stressed the links between individual and organizational decision making from the perspective of cognitive psychology.

One key link among the levels of analysis is the role that the nature of the human information-processing system, particularly cognitive limits, plays in determining how managers process information and make judgments. Thus, the concept of bounded rationality applies to both individual and organizational decision making. A cognitive psychological approach to organizational decisions, however, goes beyond the concept of bounded rationality. It includes the important issues of attention in decision making, risk attitudes, targets and reference values, constructive preferences, and task effects, among many others.

Some might argue that biases in individual decisions due to cognitive constraints are less important for the organization. After all, organizations benefit from having multiple individuals involved in decisions, as well as from emphasizing the importance of decisions. In the latter case, the individual will be motivated to avoid cognitive bias; in the former case, collections of individuals will be able to overcome the limited information-processing capabilities of any individual. If only that were so. As argued in this chapter and in other chapters in this book, group processes and organizational systems, structures, and procedures may amplify rather than mitigate cognitive limits and biases in decision making. Thus, although a cognitive approach may not be a sufficient basis for describing organizational decisions, it is quite likely a necessary component of any description of how organizations arrive at decisions. We must continue on the road with the scarecrow in our search for the nature of the brains determining organizational decisions.

Notes

1 To be fair, Milgrom and Roberts clearly acknowledge that the assumption of perfect rationality prevents understanding of many important elements of organizations.

2 A recent sampling of such research is provided in a special issue of *Organizational Science* (August 1994) devoted to the relationships among "mind, management, and organization."

3 For a more general discussion of how psychological models can be used to explain organizational action, see Staw (1991). In particular, Staw argues that "if top managers are responsible for organizational decisions, then any universalistic tendency or psychological bias is likely to affect the decisions that are produced by organizations" (p. 814).

4 Ericsson and Charnes (1994) discuss how it is memory for the aspects of a situation critical to the selection of a response that distinguishes expert performance. They also emphasize that experts acquire memory skills in a given domain. Therefore, such memory still does not transfer from one domain to another.

5 The reader should consider how his or her attention to the outcomes would change if the amounts for options A and B were losses rather than gains.

6 Interestingly, Keren (1991) has recently suggested that one potential explanation for the different patterns of risk taking observed for unique (single) versus repeated gambles, discussed earlier, is that repeating a gamble n times can result in that gamble's being viewed as having a negligible probability of either not winning or not losing. Thus, a particular gamble might be viewed as having either mainly positive or mainly negative outcomes for repeated plays.

7 A recent story in the *Wall Street Journal* dealing with losses from investing in derivatives provides the following quote from an unnamed executive fired after incurring losses that illustrates this point: "The employer absorbs the upside, and the employee absorbs the downside" (After the fall: Fingers point and heads roll, *Wall Street Journal*, December 22, 1994).

8 A strategy can be viewed as a set of cognitive operations used to transform an initial state of knowledge into a final goal state of knowledge in which the decision maker feels that the decision problem is solved.

References

Argote, L., Seabright, M. A., & Dyer, L. (1986). Individual versus group use of base-rate and individuating information. *Organization Behavior and Human Decision Processes, 38,* 65–75.

Ashton, R. H., & Ashton, A. H. (1995). *Judgment and decision making research in accounting and auditing.* New York: Cambridge University Press.

Baum, L. F. (1903 [1984]). *The wizard of Oz.* New York: Grosset and Dunlop.

Bazerman, M. H. (1994). *Judgment in managerial decision making* (3rd ed.). New York: Wiley.

Bettman, J. R. (1979). *An information processing theory of consumer choice.* Reading, MA: Addison-Wesley.

Bettman, J. R., Johnson, E. J., & Payne, J. W. (1990). A componential analysis of cognitive effort in choice. *Organizational Behavior and Human Decision Processes, 45,* 111–139.

Buehler, R., Griffin, D., & Ross, M. (1994). Exploring the "planning fallacy": Why people underestimate their task completion times. *Journal of Personality and Social Psychology, 67,* 366–381.

Card, S. K., Moran, T. P., & Newell, A. (1983). *The psychology of human–computer interaction.* Hillsdale, NJ: Erlbaum.

Carroll, J. S., & Johnson, E. J. (1990). *Decision research: A field guide.* Newbury Park, CA: Sage.

Chase, W. G., & Ericsson, K. A. (1981). Skilled memory. In J. R. Anderson (Ed.), *Cognitive skills and their acquisitions.* Hillsdale, NJ: Erlbaum.

Cohen, M. D., March, J. G., & Olsen, J. P. (1972). A garbage can model of organizational choice. *Administrative Science Quarterly, 17,* 1–25.

Cowan, N. (1988). Evolving conceptions of memory storage, selective attention, and their mutual constraints within the human information-processing system. *Psychological Bulletin, 104,* 163–191.

Cummings, L. L. (1982). A framework for decision analysis and critique. In G. R. Ungson & D. N. Braunstein (Eds.), *Decision making: An interdisciplinary inquiry* (pp. 298–308). Boston: Kent.

Cyert, R., & March, J. G. (1963). *A behavioral theory of the firm.* Englewood Cliffs, NJ: Prentice-Hall.

Dearborn, D. C., & Simon, H. A. (1958). Selective perception: The identifications of executives. *Sociometry, 21,* 140–144.

Einhorn, H. J., & Hogarth, R. M. (1981). Behavioral decision theory: Processes of judgment and choice. *Annual Review of Psychology, 32,* 53–88.

Eisenhardt, K. M. (1989). Making fast strategic decisions in high velocity environments. *Academy of Management Journal, 32,* 543–576.

Ericsson, K. A., & Charness, N. (1994). Expert performance: Its structure and acquisition. *American Psychologist, 49,* 725–747.

Ericsson, K. A., & Simon, H. A. (1993). *Protocol analysis: Verbal reports as data.* Cambridge, MA: MIT Press.

Fischhoff, B. (1991). Value elicitation: Is there anything there? *American Psychologist, 46,* 835–847.

Hamel, G., & Prahalad, C. K. (1994). *Competing for the future.* Boston: Harvard Business School Press.

Inbar, M. (1979). *Routine decision making: The future of bureaucracy.* Beverly Hills, CA: Sage.

Isenberg, D. J. (1984, November–December). How senior managers think. *Harvard Business Review,* 81–90.

Janis, I. L. (1982). *Groupthink.* Boston: Houghton Mifflin.

Kahneman, D., & Tversky, A. (1979). Prospect theory: An analysis of decision making under risk. *Econometrica, 47,* 263–291.

Kahneman, D., & Lovallo, D. (1993). Timid choices and bold forecasts: A cognitive perspective on risk taking. *Management Science, 39,* 17–31.

Keren, G. (1991). Additional tests of utility theory under unique and repeated conditions. *Journal of Behavioral Decision Making, 4,* 297–304.

Keren, G., & Wagenaar, W. A. (1987). Violation of utility theory in unique and repeated gambles. *Journal of Experimental Psychology: Learning Memory and Cognition, 13,* 387–391.

Kerr, S. (1975). On the folly of rewarding A, while hoping for B. *Academy of Management Journal, 18,* 69–83.

Kleindorfer, P. R., Kunreuther, H. C., & Schoemarker, P. J. H. (1993). *Decision sciences: An integrative perspective.* New York: Cambridge University Press.

Kusnic, M. (1994). *Decision analysis at General Motors.* Presentation. Fuqua School of Business, Duke University.

Langer, E. J. (1975). The illusion of control. *Journal of Personality and Social Psychology, 32,* 311–328.

Lopes, L. L. (1987). Between hope and fear: The psychology of risk. *Advances in Experimental Social Psychology, 20,* 255–295.

Lopes, L. L. (1995). Algebra and process in the modeling of risky choices. In J. R. Busemeyer, R. Hastie, & D. L. Medlin (Eds.), *Decision making from the perspective of cognitive psychology* (pp. 177–220). Academic Press.

Mahajan, J. (1992). The overconfidence effect in marketing management predictions. *Journal of Marketing Research, 29,* 329–342.

March, J. G. (1978). Bounded rationality, ambiguity, and the engineering of choice. *Bell Journal of Economics, 9,* 587–608.

March, J. G. (1988). Variable risk preferences and adaptive aspirations. *Journal of Economic Behavior and Organization, 9,* 5–24.

March, J. G., & Shapira, Z. (1982). Behavioral decision theory. In G. R. Ungson &

D. N. Braunstein (Eds.), *Decision making: An interdisciplinary inquiry* (pp. 92–115). Boston: Kent.

March, J. G., & Shapira, Z. (1987). Managerial perspectives on risk and risk-taking. *Management Science, 33*, 1404–1418.

March, J. G., & Shapira, Z. (1992). Variable risk preferences and the focus of attention. *Psychological Review, 99*, 172–183.

Melone, W. P. (1994). Reasoning in the executive suite. The influence of role/experience-based expertise on decision processes of corporate executives. *Organizational Science, 5*, 438–455.

Milgrom, P., & Roberts, J. (1992). *Economics, organizations and management*. Englewood Cliffs, NJ: Prentice-Hall.

Miller, G. A. (1956). The magical number seven, plus or minus two: Some limits on our capacity for processing information. *Psychological Review, 63*, 81–97.

Newell, A., & Simon, H. A. (1972). *Human problem solving*. Englewood Cliffs, NJ: Prentice-Hall.

Newell, A., & Simon, H. A. (1981). Computer science as empirical inquiry: Symbols and search. In J. Haugeland (Ed.), *Mind design*. Cambridge, MA: MIT Press.

Paese, P. W., Bieser, M., & Tubbs, M. E. (1993). Framing effects and choice shifts in group decision making. *Organizational Behavior and Human Decision Processes, 56*, 149–165.

Payne, J. W., Bettman, J. R., & Johnson, E. J. (1988). Adaptive strategy selection in decision making. *Journal of Experimental Psychology: Learning, Memory, and Cognition, 14*, 534–552.

Payne, J. W., Bettman, J. R., & Johnson, E. J. (1993). *The adaptive decision maker*. New York: Cambridge University Press.

Payne, J. W., & Braunstein, M. L. (1971). Preferences among gambles with equal underlying distributions. *Journal of Experimental Psychology, 87*, 13–18.

Payne, J. W., Laughhunn, D. J., & Crum, R. (1980). Translation of gambles and aspiration level effects in risky choice behavior. *Management Science, 26*, 1039–1060.

Payne, J. W., Laughhunn, D. J., & Crum, R. (1981). Further tests of aspiration level effects in choice behavior. *Management Science, 27*, 953–958.

Payne, J. W., Laughhunn, D. J., & Crum, R. (1984). Multiattribute risky choice behavior: The editing of complex prospects. *Management Science, 30*, 1350–1361.

Pondy, L. (1982). On real decisions. In G. R. Ungson & D. N. Braunstein (Eds.), *Decision making: An interdisciplinary inquiry* (pp. 309–311). Boston: Kent.

Shanteau, J. (1988). Psychological characteristics and strategies of expert decision makers. *Acta Psychologica, 68*, 203–215.

Shapira, Z. (1995). *Risk taking: A managerial perspective*. New York: Russell Sage Foundation.

Simon, H. A. (1955). A behavioral model of rational choice. *Quarterly Journal of Economics, 69*, 99–118.

Simon, H. A. (1974). How big is a chunk? *Science, 183*, 482–488.

Simon, H. A. (1976). *Administrative Behavior* (3rd ed.). New York: Free Press.

Simon, H. A. (1978). Rationality as process and product of thought. *American Economic Review, 68*, 1–16.

Simon, H. A. (1981). *The sciences of the artificial.* (2nd ed.). Cambridge, MA: MIT Press.

Simon, H. A. (1991). *Models of my life.* New York: HarperCollins.

Sitkin, S. B., & Pablo, A. L. (1992). Reconceptualizing the determinants of risk behavior. *Academy of Management Review, 17,* 9–38.

Slovic, P., Griffin, D., & Tversky, A. (1990). Compatibility effects in judgment and choice. In R. Hogarth (Ed.), *Insights in decision making: A tribute to Hillel J. Einhorn* (pp. 5–27). Chicago: University of Chicago Press.

Staw, B. M. (1991). Dressing up like an organization: When psychological theories can explain organizational action. *Journal of Management, 17,* 805–819.

Svenson, O., & Maule, J. A. (Eds.). (1993). *Time pressure and stress in human judgment and decision making.* New York: Plenum.

Tetlock, P. (1985). Accountability: The neglected social context of judgment and choice. *Research in Organizational Behavior, 7,* 297–332.

Thaler, R. H. (1993). *Mental accounting matters.* Unpublished manuscript, Cornell University.

Tversky, A., & Fox, C. R. (1995). Weighting risk and uncertainty. *Psychological Review, 102,* 269–283.

Tversky, A., & Kahneman, D. (1983). Extensional vs. intuitive reasoning: The conjunction fallacy in probability judgment. *Psychological Review, 90,* 293–315.

Tversky, A., & Kahneman, D. (1992). Advances in prospect theory: Cumulative representation of uncertainty. *Journal of Risk and Uncertainty, 5,* 297–323.

Tversky, A., Sattath, S., & Slovic, P. (1988). Contingent weighting in judgment and choice. *Psychological Review, 95,* 371–384.

Wedell, D. H., & Bockenholt, U. (1990). Moderation of preference reversals in the long run. *Journal of Experimental Psychology: Human Perception and Performance, 16,* 429–438.

Whyte, G. (1989). Groupthink reconsidered. *Academy of Management Reviews, 14,* 40–56.

Whyte, G., & Levi, A. S. (1994). The origins and function of the reference point in risky choice decision making: The case of the Cuban missile crisis. *Journal of Behavioral Decision Making, 7,* 243–260.

Zipf, G. K. (1949). *Human behavior and the principle of least effort.* Cambridge, MA: Addison-Wesley.

Author index

Subject index